D0466061

FOREIGN LEGIONARIES
IN THE LIBERATION OF SPANISH
SOUTH AMERICA

BY

ALFRED HASBROUCK

1969

OCTAGON BOOKS

New York

Reprinted 1969
by special arrangement with Columbia University Press

OCTAGON BOOKS
A DIVISION OF FARRAR, STRAUS & GIROUX, INC.
19 Union Square West
New York, N. Y. 10003

LIBRARY OF CONGRESS CATALOG CARD NUMBER: 73-75995

Printed in U.S.A. by
NOBLE OFFSET PRINTERS, INC.
NEW YORK 3, N. Y.

To

THE HISTORIANS OF VENEZUELA AND COLOMBIA

WHO HAVE EVER BEEN GENEROUS IN THEIR PRAISE OF
THE FOREIGN LEGION AND WHO HAVE FREELY
AND COURTEOUSLY GIVEN INVALUABLE AID
TO THE AUTHOR, THIS VOLUME IS
GRATEFULLY DEDICATED

PREFACE

Soldiers of fortune, whether in fiction or in history, appeal to our latent love of romance. Tales of their adventures stir up even in the old man reading drowsily at the fireside a few unextinguished sparks of his boyhood hero-worship. There is an especial glamor about men who have gone abroad to risk their lives in a cause which was not their own, either because they were impelled by an ideal or perhaps merely because they loved fighting for its own sake. Even the ne'er-do-well who at home is regarded as a worthless drone gains a certain halo when he betakes himself to a foreign land to fight its battles. To satisfy this craving many romances have been written glorifying commonplace men into soldiers of fortune. Of late years the French Foreign Legion has in this way become familiar to readers of novels and patrons of motion-picture theatres.

South and Central America have been exploited *ad nauseam* to find background for the extraordinary deeds of impossibly superior young Americans who have only to put themselves at the head of an army to gain the presidential chair from which they may rule with the omniscience of a benignant despot, reward all their friends and marry the daughter of a wealthy planter. In the history of South America, however, there is a field for true stories of foreign military adventure which has not yet been adequately searched. Even among historians only a vague idea exists that thousands of British and Irish soldiers of fortune went thither during the early years of the nineteenth century to help fight for the independence of the Spanish colonies. Most of the histories of South America mention them in a casual way, and some books written to extol the exploits of Englishmen and Irishmen there contain chapters devoted to their prowess; but no history which tells at length the story of the men of their nationalities and others who served under Bolívar, the Liberator, has as yet appeared. The present writer therefore has assigned to himself the task of finding out and setting down the history of this first group of foreign legionaries composed of many nationalities and serving in a continent other than their own.

In doing so the author has made every effort to test the accounts of their experiences written by these men themselves, and to ascertain whether their descriptions of the conditions and hardships which they encountered on their arrival in South America were correct. He therefore made diligent search of the original materials to learn the extent to which their complaints were justified. Although in Chapters IV and V of this volume he has depicted the conditions of campaigning as seen through the eyes of the foreigners, it should be evident from his remarks there and elsewhere that he does not stand sponsor for the justice of their complaints.

To secure dramatic unity and to keep the book within reasonable limits, certain restrictions as to its scope have been determined upon. No attempt has been made to tell how the southern nations, Argentina, Chile, Uruguay and Paraguay gained their independence. No allusion appears to the foreigners who joined in that work under Gen. José de San Martín and the other heroes of those states, except in the case of a few who, like Gen. Miller, later came north to fight under Bolívar. Brazil, of course, is not included, because it was a Portuguese and not a Spanish colony. Those citizens of the United States who joined the "Leander" expedition of Miranda in 1806 or who threw in their lot with other early revolutionary leaders are given only slight mention, unless they continued their service down to the time when Bolívar took them under his command.

Bolívar was the Liberator of five nations, Venezuela, Colombia, Ecuador (then Quito), Peru and Bolivia. For sixteen years, from 1810 to 1826 he continued planning, organizing and fighting, until he had won independence for these states, at first employing only the meagre resources which the colonies themselves could furnish, but after 1817 utilizing also the aid in munitions and men which came from England, Scotland, Ireland, Germany, France, Italy, Holland, Russia, Poland, Canada, the United States, and the islands of the West Indies. There is a vast deal of romance, of adventure and of glory in the military record of the foreigners who fought under Bolívar in northern and northwestern South America during the period from 1817 to 1826.

The writing of history involves much hard and painstaking work, yet it carries with it many compensations besides those resulting from the pleasure in the work itself and from the joy of accomplishment. Chief among these are the acquaintanceships which it opens and the associations with the international brotherhood of historians which it affords. There appears to be no greater bond of comity and good will between citizens of alien nations than that which is engendered by a common interest in the study of the history of the native land of any one of them. The stranger who arrives to make this study is welcomed with open arms and is afforded every facility for his work which the native historian is able to extend. From his own experience the writer of this book is inclined to believe that there is no body of men more internationally minded than those who are engaged in the study and writing of the history of their own nations. That this is not a paradox will be realized when it is remembered that the history of no country can be understood as a detached incident, but must be studied as a link in the chain of the world's progress.

In the course of his preparation of this work the writer has visited the libraries of Harvard, Yale, Brown, and Columbia Universities, the New York Public Library, the Library of Congress, the British Museum and the national libraries of Venezuela and Colombia. He has conducted his researches in the manuscript materials stored in the Public Record Office, London, and in the national and private archives at Caracas and Bogotá. He has met the most courteous and kindly assistance from the officials of all these institutions, and from historians and bibliographers everywhere. To give credit for all the aid he has received would be impossible; but it is a pleasure to mention a few of those in each country noted, whose assistance has been such that without it this book might not have been completed.

Professor William R. Shepherd, of Columbia University, has watched this work from its inception and has throughout its progress aided the writer with kindly advice and constructive criticism. Likewise in this country the Hon. Hiram Bingham, U. S. Senator from Connecticut, has given the writer permission to use freely his collection of manuscripts stored in the Yale University Library; Mr. Edward W. Ames, an expert on Latin-American matters, has lent books and pamphlets otherwise unobtainable, and Mr. William T. Morrey, of New York, who has devoted many years to a study of the life of Bolívar, has furnished important bibliographical help. In England, Mr. F. D. Sladen, superintendent of the reading room of the British Museum, has been especially helpful in locating books, and Mr. F. A. Kirkpatrick, Reader in Spanish at Trinity College, Cambridge, has furnished kindly criticism and encouragement.

In Venezuela, Dr. Manuel Segundo Sánchez, the eminent bibliographer, and Dr. Vicente Lecuna, the noted historian, have freely devoted many hours of their valuable time to facilitating the writer's studies, lending him books and manuscripts from their private collections. Dr. Vicente Dávila, director of the national archives, has opened the wealth of documents under his charge to a foreigner with a freedom and liberality far exceeding the expectations of the latter; Dr. Luís Correa, librarian of the National Academy of History, and Dr. José E. Machado, director of the national library at Caracas, have patiently accepted frequent interruptions of their own work to assist the writer in his; Mr. Rudolf Dolge, owner of perhaps the finest private historical library in Venezuela, has allowed the writer the free run of this library, placing the keys of the more valuable cases at his disposal; Gen. E. López Contreras and his adjutant, Captain J. Moncada López, offered the use of books and battlefield maps; the Misses Ustáriz Montilla kindly permitted the use of the archives of their distinguished ancestor, Gen. Montilla; and Col. Santos Jurado y López Méndez freely displayed the treasures of his family archives.

In Colombia, the writer owes thanks to Mr. José María Carreño and to Drs. Alfonso López and Pomponio Guzmán for friendly assistance; to Dr. Eduardo Posada, the historian, for introduction to the collections in the National Academy of History; to Dr. José Miguel Rosales, director of the national library, for advice and assistance; to Mr. Francisco Pérez Jimeno, curator of the national archives, for help in finding documents, and to Dr. Julio Portocarrero for valuable information concerning his grandfather, Gen. O'Leary. The author indeed feels especial indebtedness to the keen and enthusiastic group of military historians now or formerly connected with the general staff of the army of Colombia, among whom may be mentioned for their many acts of kindness Gen. Negret and Col. Frohard. Major General J. D. Monsalve, retired, gave the writer much of the benefit of his life-long study of the history of his country, and Col Carlos Cortés Vargas facilitated, from his own wide experience, the author's researches in the national archives, and was at all times a true friend ready to help and encourage.

As a slight return for all these kindnesses, the writer hopes that the present work may inspire among readers in the United States an interest in looking further into the history of the Latin-American nations, especially Venezuela and Colombia, so that our knowledge of our neighbors to the south may be increased and we, the republics of America, may grow in mutual sympathy, understanding and esteem.

A. H.

New York, January, 1928.

TABLE OF CONTENTS

14   *CONTENTS*

CHAPTER I

THE wars for independence in South America were not merely the effort of oppressed peoples to break the chains which shackled them to their European masters. Surely they cannot be recorded so simply as that, for they contained a complex mingling of antagonistic motives and struggling personalities. By no means all the people within a colony felt the same resentment toward the mother country or the same yearning to be free. Many of them still bore for her love and loyalty so intense, or perhaps so self-interested, that they were willing to fight to preserve the adherence of their colony to Spain. Thus the wars for independence soon developed from revolts against the motherland into conflicts also among the colonists themselves. They were in reality civil wars. Large and influential classes bitterly opposed the formation of revolutionary governments, either by inveighing against them or actually by taking up arms in aid of the royalist commanders. The clergy with some notable exceptions taught their parishioners that disloyalty to the king was almost as bad as infidelity to the church. The abandonment of the first republic after the destruction of Caracas in the earthquake of 1812 may be attributed primarily to the influence of their preachings. In Pasto the inhabitants kept up the fight against independence and remained staunch royalists under the guidance of their bishop until the new republic of Great Colombia had been well established. Even to this day, it is said, the citizens of Pasto are so proud of the loyalism of their ancestors that they are accustomed still to drink the health of the King of

Spain. Another important class of royalists was of course the long list of public officials sent from Spain, who owed their livelihood to the purse of the monarch. Then, too, as in the Thirteen Colonies of Great Britain, there were many wealthy families of substantial business men or landholders who preferred anything rather than a change which might disturb commercial tranquillity and present profits. Even the poets sang in favor of the Spanish dynasty.[1]

On the patriot side was the large class of white creoles. In spite of their Spanish parentage the fact that they had been born in America was sufficient to limit their opportunities for holding high office, if not actually to prohibit their doing so. This position of inferiority rankled in their bosoms and made them the leaders in the efforts to secure independence and an equal chance for office. This group included many of the richest and most illustrious citizens, the lawyers, doctors, teachers, professional men, and merchants, as well as the restless and enthusiastic following of university students. Besides there were the foreigners resident in the country, comparatively few in number, but active in spreading the principles of national independence as gained by the revolutionists in the Thirteen Colonies, the blessing of liberty, equality, fraternity, and the rights of man, and the advantages of free trade with England.[2] The patriotic society in Caracas in 1811 contained the names of many Frenchmen who moulded the society in imitation of the Jacobin Clubs. Miranda was the president of this society. Its yellow was adopted into the new national ensign designed by him. The club paraded the streets crying " Down with

[1] José E. Machado, *Centón Lírico*, ix; George Laval Chesterton, *Peace, War and Adventure: A narrative of proceedings in Venezuela in South America in the year 1819 and 1820*, 241.

[2] Manuel Palacio Fajardo, *Outline of the revolution in Spanish America by a South American in London*, 207; *Bell's Weekly Messenger*, Dec. 28, 1817.

the tyrant ", " Down with the Spaniards ". Its student members displayed their patriotism by burning portraits of Ferdinand VII.[1] English speculators both on the mainland and in the neighboring colonies of Trinidad and the West Indies were busy trying to force an opening for English trade. North American shipmasters were studying the coasts, and filibusters were sailing from New York.

In general the conservative elements were loyalists and the radicals were patriots, but there were large sections of the population who held no firm convictions and took part with either side according to its prospects of success. Included in these were numbers of artisans discontented at their lot and anxious for any kind of change, yet distrustful and resentful of the creole merchants, professional men and landholders immediately above them in the social scale. A very important element among those who took sides according to convenience were the " llaneros ", or cowboys of the plains of the Orinoco. These lawless half-breeds, accustomed to no restraint from man, and caring only for excitement and a chance for plunder, lent their formidable aid to either side, following the leader in whom they felt the greatest confidence. At first they fought under the renegade Spaniard Boves, who devastated the Orinoco valley in the name of loyalty, but when José Antonio Páez put himself forward as a leader on the patriot side, who would give them better opportunities for fighting and glorious adventure, they switched over with equal ardor to his leadership in campaigns against the royalist troops along the Apure.

To hold these discordant elements together; to make them fight their friends and neighbors; to check the insidious influence of the loyalists in their midst; to build up a new loyalty to patriotism; to check the intrigues of ambitious

[1] Lino Duarte Level, *Cuadros de la historia militar y civil de Venezuela,* 254-257.

chieftains; to enforce the obedience of jealous generals; to compel ignorant boys and young men to leave their homes to fight for a cause which they did not understand; to collect money and cattle and supplies for an army which did not retain the adhesion of the people from whom the collections were made; to sacrifice wealth and ease and position for an ideal; to endure the hardships of campaigns, now in the humid plains of the tropics, and now in the keen winds of chill mountain heights; to keep on fighting against daily discouragements; to fall down again and again exhausted in defeat, and then to get up and begin the fight anew—that was the work of a great and noble leader. Simón Bolívar did all this and more besides. Thrice the revolution seemed crushed, but Bolívar each time came back again with renewed vigor. His superb and unquenchable spirit, refusing to be discouraged, kept him planning and preparing, struggling and fighting, marching, and winning victories until the whole of the present republics of Venezuela, Colombia, Ecuador, Peru, and Bolivia had gained their independence. That is the reason why Bolívar is called " the father of five nations " and why to-day the name of " The Liberator " is spoken almost with the reverence due a god, especially in Venezuela, land of his birth.

Without attempting to enumerate all the causes which contributed to the independence of the Spanish colonies in South America, it will be a safe generalization to say that the movements for the separation of these colonies began in 1808, when Napoleon attempted to gain control of Spain, placing his brother, Joseph, on the throne of that country, after having forced the weak king, Charles IV, to abdicate and his son, later Ferdinand VII, to renounce his right of succession. Outraged by this high-handed usurpation, the people of Spain refused to recognize Joseph and set up councils of government, called "juntas", in the name of Ferdinand VII, as the rightful king.

Following this example of the mother country, the colonies established " juntas " of their own, refusing to recognize the officials commissioned by Napoleon. At first these juntas had no idea of independence, and deluded themselves with the notion that they were maintaining his realm intact for their " well-beloved " Ferdinand. When, however, that ruler was restored to the throne of Spain after the overthrow of Napoleon, and as a stupid and stubborn Bourbon showed himself an enemy of all liberal reforms, further pretense of loyalty was cast aside. Vigorous resistance in the name of real independence was offered by the colonies to his efforts to crush them by armed force.

Venezuela was the first to recognize the unreality of the situation as it had developed since 1808. It declared independence on July 5, 1811, even before Ferdinand had had a chance to show what his intentions were.[1] Francisco de Miranda, who for years had been vainly seeking aid from England and the United States, put himself at the head of the movement and founded the federal republic of Venezuela.[2] The action was short-lived, for the people of the country were not yet ready for independence. When in 1812 an earthquake destroyed Caracas and other republican strongholds, they allowed themselves to be persuaded by their priests that this catastrophe was sent by God as an indication of his divine wrath at their disloyalty. Miranda then, despairing of further success, consented to sign a capitulation with Monteverde, the Spanish commander, whereby hostilities were to cease and the Spanish constitution of that year

[1] Mariano Torrente, *Historia de la revolución hispano-americana*, I, 223; William Spence Robertson, " The Recognition of the Hispanic American Nations in the United States " in *Hispanic-American Historical Review*, I, 240, 241.

[2] Daniel Florencio O'Leary, *Memorias del general O'Leary, Narración*, I, 35; George Dawson Flinter, *A History of the Revolution of Caracas*, 21.

was to be accepted, in return for the guarantee of the lives and property of the insurgents.[1]

This action was bitterly opposed by the other revolutionary leaders, especially Simón Bolívar, who, in the heat of their resentment, betrayed Miranda as the latter was about to flee from the country. Miranda was arrested in violation of the terms of the armistice, and sent in chains to Spain, where he died in prison at Cadiz. Many of the other revolutionists were put to death. Some were allowed to pine away in the dungeons of La Guaira and Puerto Cabello, but others, among whom was Bolívar, made good their escape.[2]

Bolívar landed at Curaçao, where he learned that revolutions had also taken place in Quito and New Granada. That in Quito had been suppressed, but New Granada had broken up into separate provinces.[3] Though the Spanish viceroy still retained command of Santa Marta, Rio Hacha and Panamá, Antioquía and Cartagena had declared themselves independent republics. Cartagena, threatened between Panamá and Santa Marta, had sent a fleet and land force to attack the latter. Bolívar thereupon offered his services to the republican government of Cartagena, accepting a post under the orders of Labatut, a French adventurer then in command.[4]

Bolívar had other plans than that of serving in a subordinate capacity in the army of another province. He had hopes of keeping alive the revolution in his own Venezuela, and of using the resources of Cartagena in aiding his compatriots to regain their independence. Therefore, in direct

[1] Torrente, *op. cit.*, I, 306; *Niles Weekly Register*, II, 427.

[2] Torrente, *op. cit.*, I, 308.

[3] José Manuel Restrepo, *Historia de la revolución de la República de Colombia en la América Meridional*, I, 155-157.

[4] Angel Maria Galán, *Las legiones británica é irlandesa*, 29; *La Nación* (Caracas), Nov. 23, 1910.

violation of orders from Labatut, he led a force of two hundred men which had been placed under his command in a rapid march up the valley of the Magdalena, gathering recruits and driving back the royalist garrisons as he advanced. After having thus opened three hundred miles of the lower Magdalena, he turned eastward at Ocaña and struck across the cordilleras, in spite of Labatut's orders for him to return. The Cartagenian authorities, however, delighted at such unexpected success, overruled Labatut and upheld Bolívar, who now felt free to carry out his cherished plan of invading Venezuela from the west.[1] In pursuance of this plan, Bolívar led his scanty troops across the Andes.[2] As he marched down the fertile foothills of Maracaibo, the population flocked to his standards, and when he entered Mérida on May 23rd, he reinstated the republican government in the midst of rejoicings. At Truxillo he made one of the most serious mistakes of his life, for it was there that, in retaliation for the practices of the royalists, he issued, on June 15, 1813, his proclamation denying quarter to all Spaniards and Canary Islanders who did not actively support the revolution.[3] This was the beginning of the terrible " war to the death ", which devastated Venezuela for seven years.

While Bolívar had been spending his time in exile and in leading the armies of Cartagena, others of the exiled republican leaders had not been idle. Among those who escaped to the British colony of Trinidad were Santiago Mariño, José Francisco Bermúdez, and Manuel Piar, who organized an expedition to keep alive the revolution in the eastern provinces of Venezuela.[4] With fifty followers and only five

[1] Restrepo, *op. cit.*, I, 182.

[2] *Ibid.*, 200.

[3] O'Leary, *op. cit., Narración*, I, 127-130; *Documentos*, XIII, 251-252; Pablo Morillo y Morillo, *Manifiesto que hace a la nación española*, 5; *View of South America and Mexico by a citizen of the United States*, 8.

[4] Restrepo, *op. cit.*, II, 174-175.

muskets they crossed the Gulf of Paria and landed at Guiria, where they replenished their stock of arms by surprising and capturing the small royalist garrison. Piar and Bermúdez then marched southward and captured the town of Maturín, while Mariño seized Cumaná.[1] By the simultaneous advance of these leaders from the eastward and of Bolívar from the westward, Monteverde was caught between two fires, and was forced to divide his command and to operate on both flanks at once. The royalist forces, thus weakened, were repeatedly overcome in detail by Bolívar in a series of engagements, until Monteverde himself was disastrously defeated at Valencia and barely escaped to Puerto Cabello. Bolívar then, on August 6, 1813, entered Caracas in triumph,[2] where he was hailed by the joyous populace with the title of " Liberator ", a title which he bore for the rest of his life.

On July 1, 1814, the Liberator summoned a popular assembly at Caracas and proposed to resign his power into its hands. Realizing the need of a strong hand at the helm, the assembly, instead of accepting this resignation, confirmed and increased his power, so that the new republican government became in reality a dictatorship under Bolívar. Jealous of this aggrandizement of the Liberator, the other republican leaders failed to support him loyally.[3] Mariño and Piar were dilatory in executing his orders and did not effect their concentrations in time to accomplish the desired results.[4] The royalist forces were likewise divided, but cooperated more effectively.

[1] Torrente, op. cit., I, 410; The Morning Chronicle (London), Dec. 25, 1818.

[2] Restrepo, op. cit., II, 163-164; Torrente, op. cit., I, 413-414.

[3] Restrepo, op. cit., II, 173; Torrente, op. cit., II, 72.

[4] Laureano Vallenilla Lanz, Críticas de sinceridad y exactitud, 143; Centenario de Boyacá, 17, 122-123; vide also Cultura Venezolana, III, 137-157.

The new viceroy, Cajigal, who had arrived to replace Monteverde, was blockaded in Puerto Cabello, but was in command of a threatening force which might break out at any time. Boves, at the head of two thousand llaneros, was terrorizing the whole valley of the Orinoco, appearing suddenly now here, now there, and wiping out any small patriot garrisons found in his way. Having temporarily rendered impotent the republican division which opposed him, he left the plains and marched into the hills to threaten Caracas.[1] Bolívar, after having tried in vain to recall his scattered divisions for the defense, himself sallied out to meet Boves, and was disastrously defeated at La Puerta on June 14. When all hope of defending Caracas was lost, Bolívar decided to evacuate the capital and to retreat to Barcelona and Cumaná. Fearing massacre by the bloodthirsty Boves, the entire population of Caracas, men, women and children, fled from the city in the wake of the Liberator. This retreat, known as the " emigration of 1814 ", lasted twenty days.[2] When Bolívar arrived at Cumaná, he found that Mariño, upon whose support he had relied, had been deserted by his troops. Under the circumstances, further resistance seemed hopeless, so Bolívar and Mariño boarded ship and sailed away. Thus ended the campaign of 1813-14 and the second republic of Venezuela.[3]

The two Venezuelan generals landed at Cartagena, but soon found themselves embroiled there in a civil war against the republican leader, Castilla.[4] Meanwhile a powerful expedition, consisting of nearly 11,000 men with a siege train, had been despatched from Spain under Field Marshal Pablo Morillo, whom the restored Ferdinand had ordered to re-

[1] Torrente, *op. cit.*, II, 73; Restrepo, *op. cit.*, II, 263.

[2] Torrente, *op. cit.*, II, 79; Restrepo, *op. cit.*, II, 258, 264.

[3] Restrepo, *op. cit.*, II, 278.

[4] *Ibid.*, I, 311.

conquer the rebellious colonies.[1] Morillo had occupied Margarita and Cumaná and had reestablished the royal power in Caracas.[2] He besieged and captured Cartagena, and then sent strong columns southward to overrun New Granada. Bogotá, the capital, was captured and occupied May 6, 1816, by the royalist forces under Col. Miguel de la Torre.[3]

Meanwhile Bolívar had escaped to Jamaica, where he tried in vain to secure British aid for the cause of the revolution. He did indeed obtain the adherence of Luís Brión, a native of Curaçao, who furnished several ships and later became admiral of the Venezuela navy.[4] Bolívar then sailed to Aux Cayes and Port-au-Prince where he received substantial assistance in arms and ammunition from Alexandre Pétion, president of Haiti, in return for a promise to release the slaves in all provinces which might be freed from Spain.[5] Port-au-Prince became the rendezvous for many republican fugitives, among whom were José Francisco Bermúdez, Mariano Montilla, Santiago Mariño, and Francisco Antonio Zea, as well as the sailors Luís Brión and Louis Aury.[6] This group of patriots worked together to organize an expedition of two hundred and fifty men, which set sail for Venezuela in seven vessels loaded with arms and ammunition for six thousand.[7] Before starting, this expedition was joined by

[1] Torrente, *op. cit.*, II, 161; *Annual Register*, 1817, "General History," 161.

[2] Restrepo, *op. cit.*, II, 304; *Iris de Venezuela*, Jan. 21, 1822.

[3] Restrepo, I, 413, 414, 417, 419; *Archivo Santander*, I, 243; Ravenga, "Memoir on the Republic of Colombia," British Museum, *Additional Manuscripts* No. 38296, folio 83; Antonio Rodríguez Villa, *El teniente general Don Pablo Morillo*, I, 479; Morillo, *Manifiesto*, 20; Palacio, *op. cit.*, 216; *The Times*, Nov. 3, 4, 1818.

[4] *The Times*, March 6, Sep. 21, Oct. 24, 1816.

[5] Torrente, *op. cit.*, II, 255.

[6] For the careers of Brión and Aury, see Chapter XIII.

[7] Felipe Larrazábal, *Vida del Libertador, Simón Bolívar*, II, 25, 26.

Manuel Piar, H. L. V. Ducoudray-Holstein and Gregor McGregor,[1] foreigners whose careers will later be recounted more fully.

On May 3, 1816 the little expedition landed at Juan Griego on the island of Margarita,[2] where arms were distributed to the islanders who had risen under their leader, Juan Bautista Arismendi, against the royalist commander whom Morillo had left in charge.[3] Bolívar proclaimed a new republic and accepted unanimous election as Supreme Chief. He then conducted an unsuccessful attack on Cumaná[4] and subsequently sailed for Ocumare, a port on the coast between Puerto Cabello and La Guaira. There he disembarked his expedition and began to gather recruits. On July 14, the republicans were defeated by the royalist commander, Gen. Francisco Tomás Morales, in the hills a short distance south of Ocumare. Bolívar returned to the ships to load his artillery and trains, leaving McGregor behind in command of the vanguard. Then, having received a false report that the enemy was in the town, Bolívar ordered the cable cut on the " Indio Libre ", on which he had embarked, and sailed away, abandoning McGregor and the remnant of his troops, about 600 men, to their fate.[5] McGregor, however, managed to break through the royalists and to conduct

[1] Ducoudray-Holstein was a French officer who had served throughout the French Revolution and under Napoleon. He joined the revolutionary army at Cartagena and was appointed chief of staff to Bolívar in 1815. In the *Memoirs of Simón Bolívar*, of which he was the author, he displays the utmost bitterness against his commanding general. (See Chapter XIII). Gregor McGregor was a Scotch adventurer whose further interesting career will be dealt with in Chapter VI.

[2] Torrente, *op. cit.*, II, 262; Restrepo, *op. cit.*, II, 338; *Bell's Weekly Messenger*, Aug. 24, 1817.

[3] *The London Chronicle*, Nov. 10, 1817; *The Times*, Sept. 16, 1817; Morillo, *Manifiesto*, 8; " Piezas Justificativas," 4, 6.

[4] Torrente, *op. cit.*, II, 265.

[5] *Ibid.*, II, 269; Restrepo, *op. cit.*, II, 347, 348.

the retreat southward up the Aragua valley, and thence turned northward to Barcelona. At El Alacrán, McGregor defeated a royalist force which threatened to bar his way, and entered Barcelona without serious loss. There, having been superseded in command by Piar, he resigned in disgust. Piar then inflicted a severe defeat on Morales who had been pursuing McGregor from Ocumare.[1]

Bolívar meanwhile had returned to Port-au-Prince, where he met Brión and organized another expedition. On Dec. 21, 1816, Bolívar and Brión sailed again for Margarita, where they landed on the 28th. Bolívar issued his usual proclamation convoking a congress and reestablishing the republic.[2] Arismendi, who had kept alive the spark of revolution in Margarita, had led a force of four hundred men to the mainland at Barcelona, where Bolívar joined him the last day of the year. Assuming charge there, Bolívar either devised a new plan of campaign or adopted one which was already developing at the hands of others. This was temporarily to abandon the much-fought-over coast and mountain region about Caracas and transfer the revolution to the rich valley of the Orinoco, where transportation was easy and abundant supplies of horses and cattle were to be had for the taking.[3] As a matter of fact, Piar had already conceived this plan and was just then busy besieging Angostura, though he had been repulsed in an attempt to capture it by assault.[4] Bolívar therefore joined Piar and, with their combined forces, aided by a fleet of river gunboats organized by Arismendi and commanded by Brión, succeeded in forcing the royalists out of Angostura and in capturing the forts at

---

[1] O'Leary, *Narración*, I, 357-358; *The Times*, Jan. 15, 1817; Palacio Fajardo, *op. cit.*, 166, 167, 170.

[2] Larrazábal, *op. cit.*, II, 56.

[3] *Ibid.*, II, 67; *The Times*, Jan. 18, 1817.

[4] *Ibid.*, II, 75; Restrepo, *op. cit.*, II, 393-395.

Old Guayana.[1] With these victories, control of the whole of the important province of Guayana was assured to the revolutionists. Bolívar established his capital at Angostura, instituted a high court of justice, nominated a council of state, and again set up a republic.[2]

Meanwhile, along the upper Orinoco and on the plains of the Apure, the royalist troops had been harassed and demoralized by repeated defeats inflicted by 2000 " llaneros " under the impetuous leadership of that remarkable patriot leader of cavalry, José Antonio Páez. Páez was a man of no education, but of much native ability and bravery. He had early established complete control over the tireless horsemen of the plains, leading them up and down with the speed and devastation of a prairie fire, annihilating the royalist detachments wherever he encountered them and leaving Morillo no peace, until he consented to withdraw from the district. Páez was one who valued his own independence, and who could ill brook interference, yet for the love he bore his country, he now consented to recognize Bolívar as supreme chief and to conduct his own operations under the Liberator's direction.[3]

Bolívar joined Páez at the beginning of 1818, at San Juan de Payará, above the junction of the Apure with the Orinoco, and instituted a campaign against the royalists, who were based on Calabozo and Caracas. His plan was to destroy La Torre who was advancing from Caracas and then, with

[1] Torrente, *op. cit.*, II, 353, 354; *The London Chronicle*, Dec. 1, 1817. Capt. C. Brown, *Narrative of the Expedition to South America which sailed from England in 1817, for the service of the Spanish patriots*, 71, 72.

[2] Restrepo, *op. cit.*, II, 407; Francis Loraine Petre, *Simón Bolívar, el Libertador*, 195; José Felix Blanco, *Documentos para la historia de la vida pública del Libertador*, VI, 151, 152.

[3] O'Leary, *Narración*, I, 383; Larrazábal, *op. cit.*, II, 118; *The London Chronicle*, June 4, 1817; José Antonio Páez, *Memorias del general José Antonio Páez, autobiografía*, I, 136.

the cooperation of Páez, to attack Morillo as he withdrew from Calabozo. This was a risky plan, however, as it involved placing the republican army between two strong royalist forces.[1] La Torre, retiring northward to gather supplies, was followed by Bolívar, but when the latter was marching through the ravine of El Sémen, near La Puerta, on March 15, 1818, Morillo with the main royalist army suddenly fell upon and defeated the republicans, capturing 1500 muskets, munitions, flags, and all their baggage, including even Bolívar's correspondence.[2] Morillo himself was wounded, but was later rewarded for this victory by being created Marquis de La Puerta. So demoralized was the army of Bolívar that, during his hasty retreat southward, the enemy broke into his camp and very nearly succeeded in killing the Liberator himself.[3] Fortunately, Bolívar managed to escape to San Fernando where his disorganized infantry received protection from the cavalry of Páez.[4] At the same time the bad news came that Bermúdez had lost Cumaná and that Mariño had been defeated at Cumanaçoa, leaving the royalists in full possession of the north.[5] In this situation it seemed that nearly all was lost and that the independence of the Republic of Venezuela was only a forlorn hope, impossible of realization.

[1] Restrepo, op. cit., II, 448; Torrente, op. cit., II, 356.

[2] Rodríguez Villa, op. cit., III, 506-508; O'Leary, Narración, I, 459-460; The British Monitor, June 14, 1818; The Morning Chronicle, July 13, 1818.

[3] O'Leary, Narración, I, 465; Larrazábal, op. cit., II, 142.

[4] Restrepo, op. cit., II, 459; Torrente, op. cit., II, 452; Alexander Walker, Colombia, being a geographical, statistical, agricultural, commercial, and political account of that country, II, 371; The Morning Chronicle, July 1, 1818.

[5] Torrente, op. cit., II, 460, 461; Larrazábal, op. cit., II, 146, 147; The London Chronicle, July 13, Aug. 7, 1818; Herman Albert Shumacher, Biografía del General Agustin Codazzi, 1; Rafael Altamira y Crevea, Resúmen histórico de la independencia de la América española, 79.

From this rapid summary it will be seen that, in spite of his superabundant energy and determination, Bolívar had three times seen the frustration of his hopes; first when Miranda capitulated in 1812; next when the short-lived republic of 1814 ended with the emigration to Barcelona; again in 1816 when Bolívar fled from Ocumare; and now in 1818 it seemed as though the defeat at La Puerta had put an end to the government at Angostura. But all hope was not yet lost, for help was coming from beyond the sea.

Bolívar had already received a suggestion from his chief of staff, Ducoudray Holstein, that a foreign legion be formed to utilize the services of the many foreigners who were eager to aid the patriot cause,[1] and had come to believe that if his native soldiers, with whose enthusiasm and valor he was well contented, could be made more efficient through training in European military methods and tactics, they would become invincible.[2] Therefore in 1816, after the retreat from Ocumare, when his hopes were at their lowest, he had instructed Luís López Méndez,[3] the Venezuelan com-

---

[1] H. L. V. Ducoudray-Holstein, *Memoirs of Simón Bolívar*, I, 340, 341.

[2] Galán, *op. cit.*, 11; Rafael Urdaneta, *Memorias del general Rafael Urdaneta*, 149 n., 153.

[3] Luís Seferino López Méndez was born either at Maracay or Rio Chico, Venezuela, on August 25, 1758. The exact place of his birth is not known, for the records are believed to have been destroyed by the burning of the church in which they were kept. The date, however, is correctly fixed, for it is given in the record of his baptism on file in the cathedral at Caracas. He came of a distinguished Venezuelan family, his father being Bartolomé López Méndez and his mother, Petronilla María Núñez. In due course Luís López Méndez was graduated as a Master of Philosophy. He married twice and by his second marriage had three sons and three daughters. On May 27, 1797, he was chosen mayor ("alcalde ordinario de primer voto") of Caracas. In 1804 his name figured in the lists containing the names of the principal citizens of the colony, which were sent to the Captain General of Venezuela. He was one of the principal actors in the first revolutionary movement in Caracas. Carlos A. Vivanco, "Documentos históricos: Oficio del Libertador al Señor Luís

missioner in London, to raise money, arms, and men in England.[1] These men were now beginning to arrive, and the first contingents reported to Bolívar just as his fortune seemed the blackest. The foreign legionaries had entered the stage to play their part in history.

López Méndez" in *Boletín de la Academia Nacional de Historia,* Quito, II, 280; Vicente Dávila, *Investigaciones históricas,* 169; Información genealógica Jurado López Méndez, folio 167; transcript from record of baptisms in the cathedral at Caracas; and information furnished by Col. Santos Jurado y López Méndez (greatgrandson of Luís López Méndez) of Caracas from his family manuscripts.

[1] Vivanco, *op. cit.,* II, 279, 286; *The Times,* May 22, 1818; *Present State of Colombia by an officer late in the Colombian Service,* 87; Charles Stuart Cochrane, *Journal of a residence and Travels in Colombia during the Years 1823 and 1824,* I, 459; C. Parra-Pérez, "La diplomatie de Bolívar" in *Revue de l'Amérique latine,* VI, 103.

CHAPTER II

WHENCE THE LEGIONARIES CAME

FOR nearly five years after Waterloo, England suffered from conditions similar to those which befell it during the like number of years immediately after the close of the Great War. The aftermath of war seems to be always the same. Unemployment and strikes were then, as a hundred years later, the order of the day. Though there was then no dole, the country was called upon to furnish aid in the form of increased poor relief.

According to an editorial published in the *London Chronicle*, January 1, 1817,

The commencement of the year 1817 finds this country in a very different situation from that in which it was beheld with pride and exaltation but a few seasons ago. . . . As soon as the combat was over it was universally felt that her capital was reduced in a dreadful proportion. The little that remained was rendered every day still less, and the source from which it might be renewed experienced a vast diminution by the daily consumption and inactive condition of thousands of people who derived the means of existence from various pursuits connected with a state of warfare. . . . Trade was reduced when the continental system was abandoned and mutual intercourse was allowed. Our workshops were overstocked. The season consumed a great portion of the fruits which are consigned to their protection. . . . One branch of trade has followed the destruction of another, and this empire which lately abounded in wealth is reduced to a condition already alarming.[1]

[1] *London Chronicle*, Jan. 1, 1817.

31

By the end of that year the state of trade with America, due to the overstocking of the American markets, was so depressed that imports there from Sheffield and Birmingham were selling at fifty per cent of the cost of manufacture.[1] In the previous year 4770 fewer vessels were employed than in 1815, with a consequent reduction in tonnage of 826,000.[2] Manufacturers were forced to reduce their output. In the weaving districts of Yorkshire one-third of the cloth-dressers were put on part time, and one-third were discharged. In the Birmingham iron trade 27,500 of the 84,000 workers were being supported in idleness as parish paupers. Those who were fortunate enough to remain at work were forced to do so at reduced wages. The wages of miners dropped from eighteen shillings to ten shillings per week. The cotton-weavers in Lancashire, who in 1800 had received thirteen shillings a week, now received only four shillings, threepence, half penny per week, out of which they must spend a penny, half penny for repairs to their looms.[3] In the parish of Langton Matravers 419 out of 575 inhabitants were receiving parochial relief, and at Swanage not one in seven was able to support himself.[4] A statement was made in Parliament that 2000 of the 18,000 journeymen tailors in Westminster were believed to be " wholly destitute of work ".[5]

These reductions in wages were replied to by petitions, strikes and riots. The striking weavers of Nottingham asked for an increase in wages.[6] In Manchester a meeting of strikers arranged to send a like request to London.[7]

[1] *London Chronicle,* Dec. 3, 1817.

[2] *Hansard's Parliamentary Debates,* 1817, XXXV, 1007; XXXVI, 569.

[3] *Ibid.,* p. 1010; *The Times,* March 14, 1817.

[4] *Hansard's Parliamentary Debates,* 1817, XXXV, 907.

[5] *Hansard's Parliamentary Debates,* 1817, XXXV, 1011.

[6] *The Times,* Sept. 15, 1817.

[7] *Ibid.,* March 13, 1817.

Twelve thousand five hundred distressed mechanics of Birmingham signed an address and petition to Parliament, for a chance to labor to earn their living.[1] Most of these pleas were neglected by that body, which instead adopted measures of coercion and punishment against the strikers.[2] When there was a " turnout " among the pit-men of Newcastle and vicinity for an advance in wages, troops were used to compel the men to work; but most of the men had by that time gone to America, and there were not enough left even to load the colliers for the London market.[3] The coal miners at Paulton, Somersetshire, struck rather than work at wages which were not sufficient to support their families.[4] The iron-workers at Merthyr-Tydfil, South Wales, refused to continue on reduced wages and put out the fires.[5] So great was the fear of labor disturbances that a meeting of merchants, bankers and traders of London was called to organize resistance to the mass disaffection against the government and peace of the country.[6] In the House of Lords, on motion of Lord Liverpool, a committee was appointed to consider and remedy the state of the Poor Laws.[7]

Efforts were made both by the government and by private charities to better the condition of the poor and unemployed, but not always with distinct success. A law was passed imposing a fine of twenty pounds for each case in which an employee was given less than the legal rate of wages. Instead of helping matters, this law increased the distress of both laborers and employers, especially in the silk industry

[1] *Hansard's Parliamentary Debates*, 1817, XXXVI, 21, 23.

[2] *Ibid.*, p. 1379; *The Times*, May 15, 1817.

[3] *The News* (London), Aug. 31, 1818.

[4] *The Times*, Mar. 4, 1817.

[5] *Ibid.*, Feb. 11, 1817.

[6] *Ibid.*, Feb. 1, 1817.

[7] *Hansard's Parliamentary Debates*, 1817, XXXVI, 299.

in Spitalfields, where it made competition with French silks impossible.[1] In the North Riding of Yorkshire the apportionment of the poor rates worked particular hardship on those called upon to pay them, for the mine operators responsible for much of the distress avoided payment of their share because they were mere investors and not residents.[2] In other cases freeholders escaped payment because of the impossibility of enforcing collection.[3] After the Home Department had issued a new form on which parish officers must report their poor rates for the years 1800 to 1817,[4] the total cost of the poor rates raised during the years 1813, 1814 and 1815, as reported by the select committee, was shown to be £8,164,496.[5] Yet numerous half-clothed mendicants crowded the cities, for whose relief it was suggested that they be given work sweeping the streets.[6] In the House of Lords a bill was passed to relieve unemployment, by advancing money to parishes for carrying on public works and thereby giving employment to the poor.[7]

The state of the poor in Ireland was particularly shocking. In Dublin alone 60,000 were in need of parochial aid, and in Chesterfield a meeting was called by the mayor to consider means for alleviating the distress of the poor.[8] In despair of finding the wherewithal to live at home, the impoverished people of Ireland emigrated to America in large numbers. To mention only a few instances occurring during the year

[1] *Hansard's Parliamentary Debates*, XXXV, 1011; *The Times*, Sept. 6, 1817.

[2] *London Chronicle*, May 5, 1818.

[3] *Hansard's Parliamentary Debates*, 1817, XXXV, 908.

[4] *The Times*, Nov. 5, 1817.

[5] *London Chronicle*, Mar. 25, 1818.

[6] *The Times*, Dec. 17, 31, 1817.

[7] *Hansard's Parliamentary Debates*, 1817, XXXVI, 931, 932.

[8] *The Times*, Jan. 11, 1817.

1818, on April 30 and May 5 two shiploads of emigrants sailed from Dublin. In Carlow many families sold out preparatory to embarking. On May 6 forty-five families left Limerick, and on the following day nearly one hundred families abandoned Tipperary County. From Waterford three ships sailed full of these poor people; from Castlecomber seventy laborers deserted from the Kilkenny and Queens County collieries; and from Belfast many fled in the direst poverty.[1] In the House of Lords, the Earl of Darnley called attention to the distressed state of the people in many parts of Ireland owing to the scarcity of provisions; and in the House of Commons, Sir J. Newport introduced a resolution for inquiry into the state of Ireland.[2] In 1820 the Chancellor of the Exchequer stated that £100,000 had been expended out of an appropriation made in 1817 for the relief of the public distress in Ireland and proposed a further grant of £500,000 for giving employment on public works.[3]

Just as in the case of the present dole, the support of the poor and unemployed fell as a heavy burden on the taxpayer. In the House of Lords, Earl Stanhope in calling attention to the great distress caused by the lack of employment of the lower orders, stated that every man except the agriculturist paid one-third of his income, and the agriculturist paid one-half. The cost of relief during the first five months of 1820 equaled the entire expenditures for that purpose during the whole of the year 1792.[4] In spite of these efforts of the government the distress had continued throughout the intervening years, and in 1820 labor still remained discontented. The *Leeds Mercury* reported " agitations " and the *Wake-*

[1] *London Chronicle*, May 26, 1818.

[2] *Hansard's Parliamentary Debates*, 1817, XXXV, 905; XXXVI, 1076.

[3] *Ibid.*, 1820, N. S., I, 1105; *London Chronicle*, June 17, 1820.

[4] *Hansard's Parliamentary Debates*, 1820, N. S., I, 398, 404; *London Chronicle*, May 16, 1820.

field Journal printed accounts of a riotous assembly at Grangemoor and of riots at Haddersfield and neighboring mining districts.[1] The unemployment among seafaring men and longshoremen became an increasingly difficult problem for London, in spite of numerous meetings held in the city to devise measures to alleviate their distress.[2]

Another cause for the increase of unemployment was, to a certain extent in 1817, and to an even greater extent in 1819, the reduction of the army and navy. The editorial already quoted from the *London Chronicle* continued on this subject: "The peace threw back on the country an immense number of mariners and soldiers who increased expenditure and made no return by their labors."[3] This statement was rather an anticipation of events to come than a true report of what had already occurred. As a matter of fact, on the first of January, 1817, the British army had not yet been materially reduced by demobilization from a war footing. During that month, however, it had been decided that the allied army in France should be reduced one-fifth by the end of the year, and that 6000 men were to be returned from the British contingent.[4] Likewise, before the end of the year, another reduction of one-fifth of the allied army was being predicted in Flanders.[5] As late as 1816 the government had found it necessary still to keep 75,000 men in active service in Flanders, and in addition 25,000 men on the peace establishment for Great Britain, with 3000 extra during the continuance of the army in France.[6] The British Army List

[1] Reprinted in the *London Chronicle*, Apr. 24, 1820.

[2] *London Chronicle*, Jan. 6, Jan. 31, Dec. 26, 1818, Jan. 9, 1821.

[3] *Ibid.*, Jan. 1, 1817.

[4] *The Times*, Jan. 15, 1817; *British and Foreign State Papers*, IV, 826.

[5] *The Times*, Aug. 25, 1817; *Bell's Weekly Messenger*, Sept. 21, Dec. 7, 1817.

[6] British Museum Additional Manuscripts 38366, folios 36, 153, Liverpool Papers, CLXXVII.

on January 1, 1817, showed a strength of 9,017 officers, 9,614 sergeants, 3,852 drummers and trumpeters, and 143,479 rank and file.[1]

According to the first plans for the reduction of the army, every battalion under the Duke of Wellington was to be greatly reduced but none was to be disbanded. Staff and other officers were to be reduced in proportion.[2] It was not until 1818 that the decision was reached to withdraw the army of occupation from France, and even then 60,000 men of the allied troops were to be retained in Flanders at the expense of France.[3] However, late in that year, vessels began arriving at English ports almost daily, bringing back troops for demobilization; and by the end of 1818, cavalry, foot-guards and infantry had been reduced by 31,402 which, with other reductions in the dragoons and supernumerary officers, brought the grand total to 33,000.[4] The navy also suffered reductions during 1818; for the List of the Royal Navy, corrected up to September 30, showed only 13 admirals, vice-admirals and rear-admirals employed out of a total of 183; only 62 captains out of a total of 852; and only 494 lieutenants out of a total of 3,923.[5] A comparison of the reports of public expenditures submitted to Parliament for the years 1818 and 1819 indicated a reduction in naval expenses of £48,652 and for the army of £97,820 during the latter year.[6] On November 10, 1818, Wellington issued his general order of farewell on the return of his troops to Eng-

---

[1] *British Army List*, 1817, quoted in *The Times*, Apr. 16, 1817.

[2] *The Times*, January 30, 1817.

[3] *The British Monitor*, Apr. 5, 1818; *Morning Chronicle*, July 16, 1818.

[4] *Morning Chronicle*, Nov. 2, 5, 1818; *London Chronicle*, Oct. 29, Dec. 31, 1818. *Annual Register*, 1818, Chronicle, 167, 168.

[5] *London Chronicle*, Oct. 6, 1818.

[6] *Hansard's Parliamentary Debates*, 1818; XXXVIII, Appendix lxiii; 1819, XL, Appendix xlvi.

land.[1]   One London newspaper claimed that there were
500,000 ex-soldiers to be absorbed by a population of
25,000,000.[2]

These thousands of officers and men, thus suddenly thrown
out of employment, must look elsewhere for a means of
earning their livelihood. Many of them had been engaged
in military work for so long that they were unfitted for
civilian pursuits. Some of them looked longingly to other
parts of the world for an opportunity for continuing their
military careers.

A further factor that bore on the situation was a demand
on the part of British merchants and manufacturers for new
markets in which they might hope to dispose of their accumu-
lating stocks. Such a market was to be found in the revolted
Spanish colonies in America. If they could gain their independence, the close restrictions of the Spanish system of
mercantilism would be broken, and the new states would
open their markets to the world, or at least to those nations
which were friendly to them. So it behooved Great Britain
to keep on good terms with the Spanish-American states, and
to aid them as much as possible, without becoming involved
in a controversy with Spain.[3]   The British government was
willing to act at the request of the king of Spain as a media-
tor between that ruler and his rebellious colonies, but only
on condition that Spain would adopt there a liberal policy
toward foreign commerce.[4]   This, nevertheless, did not

[1] Duke of Wellington, *Supplementary Despatches*, XII, 826.

[2] *The Times*, April 5, 1817.

[3] *The London Champion*, Apr. 6, Aug. 3, 1817; *Bell's Weekly Messenger*,
Aug. 17, Dec. 21, 1817; *Cobbett's Weekly Political Register*, Feb. 14,
1818; *The Times*, Aug. 25, 1817; Dominique de Fourt de Pradt, *Des
Colonies et la révolution actuelle de l'Amérique*, 225, 226; William Burke,
Additional reasons for our immediately emancipating Spanish America, 18.

[4] Public Record Office, London, F. O. 72/216, San Carlos to Foreign
Office, March 8, 1818; *ibid.*, San Carlos to Castlereagh, July 3, 1818;

satisfy the British merchants, for it meant that they must compete for the new markets with France and the United States.[1] If, however, with the aid of British men and money the insurgents should gain their independence, the new republics might be so grateful that they would grant exclusive privileges to British commerce.

Brougham, in a speech in Parliament, strongly deprecated an agreement which England had made with Spain, not to furnish arms to the revolted provinces.[2] A letter, dated Port of Spain, November 11, 1816, and published in a London paper, stated that " the lovers of liberty and the friends of commerce, in short every staunch Englishman ", would be glad to know that the American patriots would listen to no mediation except on the basis of independence.[3] An editorial in the *Morning Chronicle* rejoiced that, if England took no part against the South Americans, the success of their cause would not be long doubtful, since the Spanish government could not continue the struggle much longer, and that the end of Spain's tyranny in the New World was at no great distance.[4] The same paper congratulated the Spanish Americans on their success.[5]

The *British Monitor* proclaimed in an editorial that it

ibid., F. O. 72/228, San Carlos to Castlereagh, Sept. 28, 1819; F. O. 72/216, M. Pizarro to Sir Henry Wellesley, Jan. 10, 1817; F. O. 72/204, Confidential Memo., Spain, Aug. 28, 1817. Hereafter F. O. will refer to the Foreign Office and W. O. to the War Office documents in the Public Record Office, London.

[1] Wellesley Papers, XXI, series I, British Museum, Ad. Mss. 37294, folio 138; *Morning Chronicle*, July 14, 1818; Robert Semple, *Sketch of the present state of Caracas*, 151; Miguel Cabrera de Nevares, *Memoria sobre el estado actual de las Américas y medio de pacificarlas*, 45.

[2] *Hansard's Parliamentary Debates*, 1817, XXXV, 1195; *The Times*, March 20, 1817.

[3] *Morning Chronicle*, Dec. 25, 1818.

[4] *Morning Chronicle*, Sept. 24, 1818.

[5] *Ibid.*, July 23, 1818.

could not be said that Great Britain had no interest in war between Spain and its colonies. Every Christian nation had an interest that war should not continue indefinitely to desolate the world, and every commercial nation had an interest in knowing with whom it was free to form commercial relations.[1] Another writer insisted that it was to the paramount interest of Great Britain to plant in South America a nation of customers, whose trade would one day become even more important than that of the United States.[2] Editorials in *Bell's Weekly Messenger* called attention to the fact that in this matter the Ministry of England did not represent the sentiment of the people. The former seemed disposed to assist Spain in the subjugation of its colonies, whereas the prosperity of the latter depended on a continuance of free trade with those dependencies. The commerce of Birmingham was reviving under the calls of the Spanish-American patriots; a return to the system of monopoly under the rule of Spain, or even any long interruption of the existing free trade, might produce incalculable mischief to British merchants and the commerce of the nation; yet this valuable public interest was in danger of being sacrificed by the Ministry.[3] Thus the influence of mercantile interest was brought, with more and more insistence, to bear on the government, to aid in extending British trade with the former Spanish colonies.

Here, then, in a nut-shell was the situation on both sides of the ocean. In England was a nation trying to readjust its economic balance disturbed by war; where the mills were idle because there were not enough customers to buy their products; teeming with an idle population into which constantly increasing streams of discharged soldiers were being

[1] *British Monitor*, Apr. 25, 1819.
[2] Col. Francis Hall, *Colombia: its present state*, 5.
[3] *Bell's Weekly Messenger*, Nov. 30, Dec. 21, 1817.

poured. On the other side of the Atlantic were peoples anxious to buy these surplus stocks, if only they could open their markets by gaining their independence; who had already begun their fight for independence and had gained considerable success; who were too young and weak to feel sure of being able to keep what they had gained; and who asked for foreign aid in men and money. Here were two distressing conditions so related that the simplest solution was to let each one remedy the other. In this way both would be the gainers. In England popular sentiment, backed up by mercantile interest, favored giving encouragement and sending aid to those struggling for independence. In South America a market was available for unemployed military talent. The outcome was obvious. Already incidents had occurred to illustrate the tendencies working toward a solution.[1]

As early as 1797 Henry Dundas, Secretary of War, had instructed Thomas Picton, governor of Trinidad, to give his attention to devising means of liberating the portion of Spanish South America near that island and the latter had opened the ports under his jurisdiction to the inhabitants of Venezuela and had offered them assistance in gaining their liberty.[2] The governor of Barbados also permitted recruiting for the insurgents to be carried on there. Admiral Sir Alexander Cochrane, commanding the Windward station, assured the patriots of support in both ships and men, and Admiral Dacres at Jamaica gave orders to his cruisers to afford them every possible protection.[3]

In 1798 Francisco de Miranda had arrived in London as a self-appointed envoy of the revolutionary elements, and

[1] Palacio Fajardo, *op. cit.*, 15; Cabrera de Nevares, *op. cit.*, 46; *London Chronicle*, Jan. 12, Feb. 6, 1818.

[2] Palacio Fajardo, *op. cit.*, 16-18; José M. Antepara, *South American emancipation: documents historical and explanatory*, 218-220.

[3] Antepara, *op. cit.*, 23; Burke, *op. cit.*, 51, 52.

had remained in England for seven years interviewing statesmen and merchants in an effort to secure aid in men and ships for revolutionizing the Spanish colonies. Although Grenville steadfastly opposed Miranda and influenced the cabinet against him, Pitt seemed at times to lend him his ear. During these years Miranda made his home at 27, Grafton Street, Fitzhugh Square, London, and for part of the time was supported by a small pension from the British treasury. Among the other Spanish colonial malcontents working with him were Pedro de Fermin Oriba Vargas in London, Manuel Gual and an individual named Caro in Trinidad, and one called Iznardi in South America. Joseph Pavia, from Mexico, was a fellow-conspirator in London, but was too jealous of Miranda to work with him loyally.[1] Miranda also tried to induce Rufus King, the American minister, to assist him in securing aid from the United States; and when in 1805 Miranda finally abandoned hope of obtaining help from England, he sailed for the United States and there managed to procure sufficient resources to enable him to outfit his ill-fated " Leander expedition " of the following year for the attempted invasion of Caracas.[2]

As a matter of fact, the British government had decided to help Miranda, a force of 10,000 men under Sir Arthur Wellesley having been organized at Cork for that purpose. When Napoleon invaded Portugal, and the latter called for help, the force was deflected to that country and later to Spain where it took part in the Peninsular War.[3] England's

[1] Antepara, *op. cit.*, 13; Archivo Miranda in Academia Nacional de Historia, Caracas, Colombia Negociaciones III, varia correspondencia XXIII; William Spence Robertson, *Francisco de Miranda and the revolutionizing of Spanish America*, 319-322, 340-346, 358, 359, 463.

[2] Robertson, *op. cit.*, 322, 329, 339, 358, 360, 369; James Biggs, *The History of Don Francisco de Miranda's attempt to effect a revolution in South America*, 1-8, 257-259 and *passim*.

[3] Antepara, *op. cit.*, 25; Palacio Fajardo, *op. cit.*, 59; British Museum, Ad. MSS. 37852, folio 22, Memo by Arthur Wellesley, Feb. 15, 1807.

alliance with Spain changed official British policy with respect to giving aid to the Spanish colonial insurgents; hence the governors of the West Indian islands were directed to maintain strict neutrality between Spain and its colonies as long as the former acted in the name of Ferdinand VII.[1] The home government itself limited its interference to offers of mediation. Unaware, however, of this change in policy, in 1806 General Beresford and Commodore Popham had set out from Cape Town with an expedition against the vice-royalty of La Plata, which had captured and temporarily held the cities of Buenos Aires and Montevideo.[2] Although this expedition was unauthorized by the home government, it was thoroughly in accord with British popular sentiment.

By 1815 British speculators had established at Trinidad an arsenal for discarded war materials, bought in European markets, for sale to the Venezuelan patriots.[3] Hislop, an English merchant established in Cartagena, had arrived in Jamaica to seek the protection of England for the colony where he resided.[4] On July 19, 1817, the merchants of Kingston sent a memorial to the " Council of Trade and Foreign Plantations ", urging that, inasmuch as the importance of trade between Jamaica and the Spanish colonies had increased so largely since the revolution, naval convoys should now be provided for merchant vessels sailing from British West-Indian ports to South America, to protect them against pirates and privateers and United States brigs-of-war.[5]

[1] *Bell's Weekly Messenger*, Aug. 31, 1817; *Niles Weekly Register*, II, 54, 57.

[2] Walker, *op. cit.*, II, 331; Pierre J. S. Dufey, *Abrégé de l'histoire des révolutions de l'Amérique meridionale*, II, 63. William Spence Robertson, *History of the Latin American Nations*, 138.

[3] Chesterton, *op. cit.*, 151; Ciro Bayo, *Exámen de próceres americanos*, 112.

[4] Palacio Fajardo, *op. cit.*, 143.

[5] *London Chronicle*, Sept. 3, 1817; Semple, *op. cit.*, 152.

It was not long after this that the sympathetic British public took matters into its own hands to atone for the hesitancy of the government. A group of merchants clubbed together to fit out the ship " Cumberland " as a privateer for Chile.[1]   The " Northumberland " was overhauled at Liverpool and outfitted to carry an expedition of three hundred men under Col. Murray. The " Sprightly " was loaded with 2000 muskets, and over 10,000 uniforms, 2000 muskets, 6000 sabres, 2000 lances, 4000 pistols, with the requisite powder and bullets, were shipped as merchandise on the " Perseverance " at Deptford. The " Sir Henry Stanhope " and other vessels were made ready to carry an unusually large complement of passengers to South America.[2]   Other merchants raised a fund equivalent to 100,000 Spanish dollars (piasters) to equip an expedition to Chile. Lord Cochrane, a former British naval officer, was to sail on the " Lucy " to command the Chilean navy. Admiral Brown and a renegade Spanish general, Renovales, were concerting arrangements with a committee of merchants in London for equipping a force against Mexico composed of Spanish deserters, French military men, and English half-pay officers with cadres of regiments of all arms, twenty pieces of heavy artillery, some field artillery, 6000 muskets, and 5000 carbines.[3]

Mexico, Chile and La Plata were not the only South American provinces seeking aid from England. In 1810 the Junta of Venezuela had sent Simón Bolívar and Andrés Bello, as well as Luís López Méndez, on a diplomatic mission to London to conduct negotiations on behalf of that young republic. The commissioners had sailed from La

[1] F. O. 72/216, San Carlos to Castlereagh, Jan. 28, 1818.

[2] *Ibid.*, Feb. 5, 1818.

[3] F. O. 72/216, San Carlos to Castlereagh, Jan. 23, 1818; *The British Monitor*, Jan. 31, 1819; Rodríguez Villa, *op. cit.*, III, 699.

Guaira about the middle of June, 1810, and arrived at Portsmouth, England, on July 10. Although they were not received officially as envoys of a recognized nation, they met Sir Richard Wellesley, the Secretary for Foreign Affairs, at his home and persuaded him to affix his signature to four conventions, whereby England was to furnish naval protection to Venezuela in case of invasion of the latter by France, and to recommend to Spain a reconciliation with Venezuela; commercial relations were to be maintained between Venezuela and Spain, and Venezuela was to remain faithful to Ferdinand VII. After completing the negotiations, Bolívar and Bello returned to America, leaving López Méndez as the sole commissioner or agent for the Venezuelan government.[1]

López Méndez established himself in Miranda's house at 27, Grafton Street, which had already become known as the London rendezvous for Venezuelan sympathizers.[2] When therefore he received the call for help from Bolívar, he must have felt that the time was ripe to utilize the favorable public sentiment so evident all about him; for in spite of the fact that he had only his private funds with which to finance operations,[3] he plunged whole-heartedly into the work of raising expeditions to send to the aid of his hard-pressed native land.

[1] Vivanco, *op. cit.*, II, 280; O'Leary, *Narración*, I, 25; Parra-Pérez, *op. cit.*, 2; Amunátegui, *op. cit.*, 77, 79, 88, 90.

[2] Vivanco, *op. cit.*, II, 280.

[3] The sums advanced by López Méndez and the debts incurred by him on his own responsibility for the benefit of Venezuela amounted to £7,080. The total value of the elements of war furnished by English speculators through his efforts was claimed to be more than two million "pesos." *Información genealógica, Jurado-López Méndez*, 168; Archivo Nacional, Caracas, Gobernación de Guayana, 1817, II; Archivo Nacional, Bogotá, Secretaría Guerra y Marina, Historia, III, 855, 928, 929; *Gaceta de Colombia*, March 7, Aug. 5, 1824.

CHAPTER III

Mustering of the Vanguard

GRAFTON STREET extends from Gower Street, across Tottenham Court Road and past the southeast side of Fitzroy Square to Cleveland Street. Only some five blocks in length, it lies in a neighborhood of eminent respectability, betokened by compact lines of three-storied brick houses protected in their exclusiveness by green blinds and black iron area-railings. These houses present doubtless much the same appearance to-day as they did a hundred years ago, and Fitzroy Square itself probably has changed little. It still remains a small circle of sunken meadow, not so prettily kept as the many other neighboring squares in Bloomsbury, with their neatly-raked gravel walks and their trimly-clipped lawns. Yet hunt as one may, number 27 is not to be found. Either the houses on Grafton Street have been renumbered and 27 has for some reason been omitted, or else a new one has been built on the spot where, a century ago, stood the house in which Miranda lived, and which later was occupied by Luís López Méndez. There at all events is the neighborhood in which toward the end of May, 1817, López Méndez began his efforts to secure British aid for his native country.

In the contract which he drew up the Venezuelan agent offered to officers and non-commissioned officers of the British army, either active, retired or discharged, promotions of one grade, and pay equal to the same grades in the British army; the pay of officers to commence from the day of arrival in South America, and that of enlisted men, from the date of embarkation in England. In addition to their pay,

46

they were to receive immediately upon arrival at a port in Venezuela, as bonus and reimbursement for the expenses of their equipment and voyage, a sum amounting to $200 each to officers and $80 each in the case of non-commissioned officers. A few privates were to be accepted for the artillery only, but all other privates were to be enlisted in Venezuela from among native South Americans. A guarantee was included that none of the officers and non-commissioned officers was to be transferred from a given corps to another organization without his consent, and that all those incapacitated by wounds received in service should be amply compensated by the government.[1]

No sooner had López Méndez let it be known that this contract was ready for signature, than his office was thronged with naval and military officers eager to sign.[2] Gustavus Hippisley, a half-pay lieutenant of British cavalry, was the first to accept the terms, and to him were given the rank of colonel and the duty of organizing the First Venezuelan Hussars, which he was to command.[3] Other applicants appointed colonels were Henry Wilson, who was authorized to raise the Second Venezuelan Hussars (Red Hussars), and William Hewett, the Second Venezuelan Lancers. The First Venezuelan Lancers was to be recruited by Lieut. Col. Donald McDonald; but so impatient was he to get to the scene of action that he sailed before his regiment was fully organized, leaving its completion to Col. Hippisley.[4] Upon their

---

[1] G. Hippisley, *A Narrative of the Expedition to the River Orinoco and Apure in South America, which sailed from England in November, 1817. and joined the patriot forces in Venezuela and Caracas,* 529-533. Figures with the dollar sign here and elsewhere refer to Spanish dollars, except when specific reference is made to the United States.

[2] *Bell's Weekly Messenger,* Sept. 14, 1817.

[3] Hippisley, *op. cit.,* 53,529; F. O. 72/204, San Carlos to Castlereagh, Nov. 19, 1817.

[4] Hippisley, *op. cit.,* 9, 10, 17, 18, 52, 53. Hippisley had begun his mili-

arrival at headquarters in Venezuela these regiments were
all to be assembled in a British brigade, the command of
which, Méndez promised, would be given to Hippisley, who
would thereupon be promoted to the rank of brigadier-
general.[1]

Robert Skeene, a retired lieutenant-colonel of British cavalry, temporarily accepted the same rank in the First Hussars.
The majors of the regiment were selected from captains and
former captains in the British army; the captains, from
lieutenants of cavalry, and the lieutenants from cornets in
active service or from lieutenants of infantry on half-pay.
The junior ranks were filled by appointing discharged sergeants of cavalry; and a few gentlemen, who had never held
commissions, were likewise appointed cornets.[2]   So keen was
the competition for commissions in the First Hussars, that the
colonel was offered money for promotion.[3]   López Méndez,
furthermore, was to guarantee payment for the equipment
of non-commissioned officers and privates.   Two contractors,
Thompson and Mackintosh, thereupon undertook to provide

tary career as a cadet at the Royal Military Academy, and had been an
officer of cavalry since 1787. He had served as aide-de-camp and brigade
major to a general officer, as major of a corps of cavalry and as adjutant of a regiment of militia. Henry Wilson had been a lieutenant in
the Light Dragoons, but had left the army four years before. William
Hewett at the age of twenty-one had enlisted in the Dragoon Guards and
been promoted through the grades of corporal, sergeant and quartermaster.
In 1812 he was commissioned an ensign and later a lieutenant in the
Royal Veteran Battalion. Donald McDonald had been aide-de-camp to
Gen. Ballesteros, had received the Waterloo Medal and in 1816 had been
placed on half-pay as a lieutenant. W. O. 25/762, folios 1, 44. *British
Army List 1817; Campaigns and Cruises in Venezuela and New Granada,*
I, 1.

[1] Hippisley, *op. cit.*, 14.

[2] *Ibid.*, 6, 7. Since 1807 Lieut. Col. Robert Skeene had been on duty
with the Maidstone Cavalry Depot. *British Army List 1817;* F. O.
72/204, San Carlos to Castlereagh, Nov. 19, 1817.

[3] Hippisley, *op. cit.*, 12.

Hippisley's regiment with clothing, arms, saddlery and similar accoutrements, as well as to procure a ship to convey the
troops to the shores of Venezuela. Everything was promised to be in readiness by August 20, 1817.[1]
    The other colonels also, in their desire to expedite the
organization of their respective regiments, had arranged for
their full equipment with Thompson and Mackintosh, making themselves personally liable for the expense; but later at
the request of the contractors, López Méndez assumed responsibility for the debt in the name of the Republic of Venezuela.[2] The contractors, in their eagerness to make a big
profit, soon realized that they had undertaken too much and
were forced to ask Hippisley for an extension of time. At
a meeting of the colonels it was decided, therefore, not to
attempt at first to equip more than three cavalry corps of 400
officers and non-commissioned officers each. Skeene, who
had been promoted to colonel, was to command the Second
Venezuelan Hussars and Col. Hewett was to serve as his
lieutenant-colonel, whereas Col. Wilson was to take Skeene's
place as lieutenant-colonel of the First Hussars.[3] This arrangement, however, did not suit Col. Wilson, who decided
to make himself responsible for the equipment of a regiment
of his own.
    Meanwhile the López Méndez factory of colonels had not
been idle, and Col. Donald Campbell, an experienced infantry
officer, had been authorized to raise a cadre of officers for a
rifle regiment;[4] while Lieut. Col. J. A. Gilmour had com-

[1] Hippisley, op. cit., 5, 11, 13.

[2] Blanco, op. cit., VIII, 600; The British Monitor, Nov. 22, 1818;
Gaceta de Colombia, March 7, 1824.

[3] Hippisley, op. cit., 18, 20, 22.

[4] Ibid., 11; F. O. 72/204, San Carlos to Castlereagh, Nov. 19, 1817.
Since July 17, 1815 Donald Campbell had served as ensign in the First
Foot (Duke of Kent's). War Office 25/62, folio 146. In this as in
other cases where an officer's previous record has been quoted from

menced to raise a brigade of artillery.[1] Col. Campbell had
been so expeditious that he was one of the earliest to embark
his regiment aboard a ship which he had succeeded in chartering through his brother. Learning, moreover, that Col.
Hippisley was experiencing delay in this matter, Col. Campbell offered to secure a vessel for him also, but Thompson
and Mackintosh insisted on being allowed to carry out their
contract to supply the ship.[2]

The " Prince ", which the contractors eventually furnished, proved to be too small to carry the entire regiment;
and, since Col. Hippisley refused to allow his command to
be divided, he gladly accepted the proffered aid of Col.
Campbell, who secured for him the " Emerald ". This
vessel had been a French corvette, captured by the English
and rebuilt for the merchant service. It was such a fine ship
that López Méndez agreed to purchase it as a frigate for his
government, publicly announcing it as such.[3]

Other vexatious delays then occurred. Esdaile, who was

the *Army List* or War Office records, care has been exercised to find the
correct name, but where there are so many officers of the same name the
possibility of error has been realized. For example, there were found
in the War Office records fourteen officers by the name of Campbell who
appeared to be of the proper rank at that time. In the *British Army
List* of 1825 there were nineteen officers with the name Ferguson, and
fifty-eight Wilsons who held commissions either active or on half-pay
below the rank of captain. Of these there were four Georges, five
Henrys, five James, six Thomases and so on. Eight Donald McDonalds
appear on the *Army List* for 1817. While there were a number of
Duncan and Donald Campbells, only one of them appeared to be of the
proper rank. It is the record of this one which is given above.

[1] Col. J. A. Gilmour had been a corporal of artillery, where he had
demonstrated such mechanical ingenuity that he was later promoted to a
commission in one of the West India regiments. Hippisley, *op. cit.* 24, 52.

[2] Hippisley, *op. cit.*, 15.

[3] *Ibid.*, 28, 36, 49; F. O. 72/217, San Carlos to Bathurst, Oct. 15, 1818.
James Hackett, *Narrative of the Expedition which sailed from England in 1817, to join the South American Patriots,* 75.

the sub-contractor for the uniforms, lost faith in the promises of López Méndez when bad reports of conditions in South America began to come in, and after completing the uniforms for Campbell's Rifle Corps, backed down on his agreement to furnish those for the First Venezuelan Hussars and First Venezuelan Lancers. Upon Thompson's adding his personal guarantee for the payment, Doolan, an army clothier, accepted the contract.[1]

This matter of uniforms, be it said, was considered of the utmost importance. Col. Campbell adopted a uniform similar to that of the Rifle Brigade in the British service, and Col. Gilmour satisfied himself with one similar to that of the Royal Artillery; but Col. Wilson, evidently with an eye to scenic effect rather than to suitability for a campaign in the tropics, chose a scarlet jacket with light blue facings and gold lace pipings, and scarlet pantaloons with broad gold stripe for full dress; and a similar uniform of blue and gold for service.[2] Col. Wilson may have expected the Red Hussars on parade and in the ball-room to dazzle all observers, but he did not allow for the effect of a tropical sun or for the waters of the Orinoco on all this gorgeousness. Col. Hippisley, not to be outdone, decreed that the First Hussars be handsomely uniformed in a dark green jacket with scarlet collar, lapels and cuffs, figured gold lace around the collar and cuffs, an ornamental Austrian knot on the arm, a lace girdle, and dark green trousers edged with similar gold lace down the sides, crimson sash and Wellington boots. The head-gear for the fatigue uniform was to be a forage cap, and for the dress uniform, a shako. The officers' uniform was the same as that of the non-commissioned officers, with the addition of a blue camlet cloak lined with red baize.

[1] Hippisley, *op. cit.*, 26, 27.
[2] *Ibid.*, 23; Hackett, *op. cit.*, xii, xiv.

The cost for the complete outfit for an officer was to be forty pounds.[1]

In order that López Méndez might meet the officers of all the regiments, it was decided to invite him to partake of a cold collation, at which the entire corps should be present. Mackintosh had obligingly offered the use of his drawing-room for the occasion, where the officers were seated, arranged in a circle in order of rank and seniority, awaiting the arrival of their guest whom few of them had seen, and whom most of them knew only as "General Méndez". All was hushed expectancy, when the door was thrown open and in walked an elderly colored man, dressed in an elaborate uniform of drab and scarlet facings, and with his head well powdered. Then, so an eye-witness described it, the "whole line of officers, with regularity and precision, rose spontaneously and formed the circle, and after a graceful bow from all, in which motion and time combined, the whole remained steady to receive the personage in uniform, who, all astonished at the reception given him, advanced no further, yet with two or three very genteel bows in return complimented the entire circle." As soon as Col. Hippisley could recover from the laughter which convulsed him, he relieved the suspense by informing the officers that the personage whom they had mistaken for "General Méndez" was only the negro George, a faithful servant of a gentleman who had loaned him for the occasion. Though "General George" himself grinned with delight at the mistake which had occasioned him so honorable and so flattering a reception, the officers sheepishly regained their seats, and when the real López Méndez made his appearance, hesitated to resume the circle with the alacrity and dignity which had been planned. Nevertheless, the introductions were accomplished, and López Méndez, through his interpreter, assured the officers that the Venezuelan government

[1] Hippisley, *op. cit.*, 12, 13.

would welcome them with love and gratitude, and would fulfill with liberality all the promises he had made.[1]

Mess dinners and other parties were of frequent occurrence. The regimental messes entertained one another, and a farewell dinner was given in honor of "Señor Méndez", and the agents of other South American states. At one of these dinners the new regimental standard of the First Venezuelan Hussars was displayed at the head of the table. It showed a yellow field ornamented with green and gold fringe around the edges. In the center was a belt, or garter, with the motto, " Unión, Constantia, y Valor ", and within the belt were the words, " 1° Huss de Venezuela ". In the field around this circle were seven blue stars, emblematic of the provinces composing the state. Col. Campbell's regiment, moreover, possessed a fine band which played at dinners, balls, and other suitable occasions.[2]

In spite of all this apparent cordiality and good feeling, the spirit among the colonels was sadly lacking in cooperation. Col. Campbell was the only one who seemed to feel that the other colonels were his brothers-in-arms; for although he was ready first and was anxious to sail, he magnanimously offered to wait for Col. Hippisley. Among the other colonels, however, jealousy was rife, and the question of seniority tended to embitter their relations toward one another. Col. Skeene tried to get the start of the others by sailing first, so that he might claim seniority on account of priority of arrival in Venezuela. Skeene, to be sure, had been a lieutenant-colonel in the British army whereas Hippisley was only a lieutenant; but, as will be remembered, Skeene's first commission in the Venezuelan service had been that of lieutenant-colonel under Hippisley's command.[3] Hip-

[1] Hippisley, *op. cit.,* 31, 32, 33.

[2] *Ibid.,* 64.

[3] *Ibid.,* 47, 53.

pisley claimed seniority over all because of the fact that he
had been the first to obtain his contract from López Méndez,
and over all, except Skeene, by virtue of having held senior
rank in the British service.

Among further provoking delays that prevented the regiments from embarking when they had hoped to was the act
of Thompson and Mackintosh in keeping many of Col. Hippisley's stores aboard the rejected " Prince ", which had
been reengaged by Col. Wilson for his Red Hussars, and
refusing to allow Col. Hippisley to have them until their
arrival in the West Indies.[1]   Col. Wilson's own regiment
was not yet ready, so it was decided that the " Prince " was
to follow as soon as possible after the fleet, with the remainder of the arms and saddlery.   It was also necessary to
make alterations in the cabin of the " Prince " for the ac-
commodation of two ladies, inasmuch as Mr. Mackintosh
decided to go along to look after his stores and to take his
bride and sister-in-law with him.[2]

Under such conditions it was impossible to conceal the
preparations for the expedition, and apparently no attempt
was made to do so.   Articles of equipment were displayed in
shop windows; outfitters appealed in newspaper advertise-
ments to those planning to go to South America; officers
strutted about in uniform in public places; the band played
at balls and dinners, and practiced regularly in Chelsea every
morning near the residence of a general officer.[3]   Even in
the coffee-houses in the city notices were posted, inviting passengers to go on board vessels waiting to sail direct for
South America.[4]   Apparently the government was deaf and
blind, until Col. Hippisley received warning from someone

[1] Hippisley, *op. cit.*, 65, 66.

[2] *Ibid.*, 28, 44.

[3] *Ibid.*, 25.   F. O. 72/204, San Carlos to Castlereagh, Oct. 12, 1817.

[4] *Bell's Weekly Messenger*, Oct. 12, 1817.

in a high position in the government to be speedy in his preparations and arrangements, not to make any unnecessary bustle, and above all to hasten his departure from England.[1]

All this went on while the Duke of San Carlos, the Spanish minister, was bombarding the Foreign Office with specific complaints. On October 12, 1817, he wrote a confidential letter to Lord Castlereagh, the Foreign Secretary, protesting against the embarkation from British ports of officers and munitions destined for South America, and requesting that the Prince Regent suspend temporarily permission to export arms and munitions to the West Indies, and that he prohibit officers on half pay from making long voyages. " Lately ", he declared,

it seems that all the population is engaged in this occupation of sending one or another expedition to aid the insurgents. The " Two Friends " has been followed by the " Gladwyn " and the " Morgan Rattler ", and to-day they prepare the " Prince ", the "Amelia Wilson " and other vessels to convoy at least four cadres of officers and non-commissioned officers and complete equipments for regiments of hussars and lancers, and even for three brigades of artillery. In fact we can say that all ships which sail for St. Thomas, San Domingo, and other points in the West Indies, with cargoes of arms and ammunition, have on board half-pay officers in charge of these succors for the insurgents.

He then named the agents of the insurgents residing in London, who were instrumental in organizing these expeditions and the firms of tailors who were engaged in outfitting them at Charing Cross, on Cheapside, across from St. Paul's, and elsewhere under the very nose of the government. The Spanish envoy also called attention to an article in the *Times* of the day before, stating that daily posters in the cafés invite officers on half-pay to follow the cause of the insurgents,

[1] Hippisley, *op. cit.*, 25.

and to an advertisement printed in the *Morning Post,* suggesting that those who wished to go to South America should get their equipment at B. Hindman, No. 34 Noble St., Fetter Lane, Cheapside. He concluded by urging that the severest penalties should be inflicted on agents of the insurgents, if it should be proved that they were violating the law.[1] A month later the Duke of San Carlos again wrote to Viscount Castlereagh, furnishing him a list of the names of English officers who had publicly embraced the cause of the American insurgents, by entering their service as leaders of corps, and protesting against the failure of the government to prevent the sailing of the ship " Two Friends ". He also demanded the prohibition of the exportation of arms and ammunition intended for South America and the West Indies, excepting such as might be needed by the English garrisons.[2]

Apparently these complaints produced at least a show of energy on the part of the government, for the War Office issued orders that half-pay officers must certify on their pay-vouchers that they were not employed in any other office by H. B. M.'s government or by any foreign government;[3] and on Nov. 17, 1817, the Prince Regent issued a proclamation, prohibiting British subjects from taking part in the contest between Spain and the Spanish provinces.[4] This action came so tardily that many of the officers were unaware, until too late, of this prohibition against engaging in the patriot service, and flattered themselves that a tacit consent had been given to their proceedings.[5]

[1] F. O. 72/204, San Carlos to Castlereagh, Oct. 12, 1817; *British Monitor,* June 6, 1819.

[2] F. O. 72/204, San Carlos to Castlereagh, Nov. 19, 1817.

[3] F. O. 72/204, San Carlos to Castlereagh, Nov. 12, 1817; Circular 378, W. O. Oct. 24, 1817, quoted in *The Times,* Oct. 28, 1817.

[4] *British and Foreign State Papers,* Foreign Office, IV, 488.

[5] Brown, *op. cit.,* 171. The Foreign Enlistment Act was not passed until July, 1819. *Cf.* chap. v, p. 111.

On account of the prolonged delay in sailing, officers and non-commissioned officers ran short of funds, and Col. Hippisley was compelled to advance, out of his own pocket, a shilling a day for each non-commissioned officer for his subsistence, and the various sums required by the officers to pay for their equipments. These loans were practically forced from Hippisley by the officers, with threats that otherwise they would have to resign.[1] Several non-commissioned officers of the First Hussars indeed deserted from the ship just before sailing, but their loss was easily filled from among the many discharged British soldiers who applied for their places. In this case, as in others, Col. Hippisley exercised great care not to take aboard any deserters from the army, requiring all applicants to show their discharges and recommendations from their former commanding officers, before they were accepted for enlistment.[2]

As a final blow, just as the " Emerald " was about to drop down the river, it was discovered that Senior Surgeon White, who had been selected to manage the officers' mess, was absent without leave, and that no mess stores were aboard. Surgeon White, it seems, had collected the sum of fourteen pounds from nearly every officer for the purpose of laying in mess-stores for the voyage, and after having embezzled the funds, had pretended to have himself arrested, so that his fellow officers and victims might not be able to find him before the ship sailed. Fortunately, a friend of Major English of the Hussars, when he learned of the situation of the mess, did what he could to remedy it by sending aboard a quantity of provisions, together with a crate of crockery to replace the table-service which Surgeon White had failed to provide. Yet in spite of this help and that of

[1] Hippisley, *op. cit.*, 29, 41, 43.
[2] *Ibid.*, 62.

the father of one of the officers, who also contributed something to the mess-stock, the slimness of their mess dinners gave the officers good reason to curse Surgeon White long before they even reached Madeira.[1]

It was not until December, 1817, that the five regiments comprising the first contingent embarked aboard their ships preparatory to sailing. An account by James Hackett, a lieutenant in the artillery brigade, gives the clearest idea of their situation at the time. He states that the First Venezuelan Hussars, Col. Hippisley, thirty officers, and 160 non-commissioned officers sailed on the " Emerald " (500 tons), Capt. Weatherly, with a crew of thirty; the First Venezuelan Rifle Regiment, Col. Campbell, thirty-seven officers, and nearly 200 non-commissioned officers, on the " Dowson " (400 tons), Capt. Dormor; the First Venezuelan Lancers, Col. Skeene, 220 officers and non-commissioned officers besides casual officers from some of the other regiments, on the " Indian "; the Brigade of Artillery, Col. J. A. Gilmour, ten officers, and about eighty non-commissioned officers and men, on the " Britannia " (400 tons), Capt. Sharper, with a crew of twenty-one; and the Second Venezuelan Hussars (Red Hussars), Col. Wilson, twenty officers, and a hundred non-commissioned officers and men, on the " Prince " (400 tons), Capt. Nightingale.[2]

In addition to the troops and their equipment, these ships carried as freight large quantities of military stores sent out by London merchants on speculation and on the understanding that they would be purchased by the insurgents. The " Britannia " also carried the guns for the artillery, consisting of five light 6-pounders and one 5½-inch howitzer, with

---

[1] Hippisley, *op. cit.*, 35, 66-70. White had been assistant surgeon of the Second Surrey militia from which regiment he had been forced to resign.

[2] Hackett, *op. cit.*, pp. xii, xiii, xiv, xv; *cf.* also Galán, *op. cit.*, 12, whose figures differ only slightly from the foregoing.

the necessary ammunition. In charge of a cargo of fire-arms on the " Britannia " an armorer was sent as sales agent; and on that same ship there also embarked a printer, with a valuable and extensive printing apparatus, who expected to find employment at Bolívar's headquarters.[1] The ships did not all set sail together. As each one was ready, it dropped down the river to Gravesend, Margate or the Downs, or to some other point where it might meet both wind and tide favorable to carrying it to sea. Any gloom which may have been produced by melancholy leave-takings was soon dispelled by the bustle of departure, and the excitement of making new acquaintances. As the anchors came up, joke and song sped from lip to lip and all was mirth and happiness. Their thoughts were of a speedy return, and their hopes were brightened with visions of wealth and glory to be gained.[2]

All of this would indicate that the popularity of the cause of South American independence and the difficulty of obtaining work in England, set forth in the preceding chapter, were thoroughly substantiated. Although reasons of the sort might account for the eagerness with which so many hastened to grasp the opportunity when offered, it might be well to examine somewhat more closely the motives which actually inspired certain of these individuals to join the cause of the South American patriots. Let them testify for themselves. Chesterton, a captain and judge-advocate, says: " In this country (England) it is only necessary to represent a nation fighting for liberty, to excite a generous sympathy." [3] Hackett, who went as a first lieutenant in the Venezuelan Artillery Brigade, remarks: " the termination of the late war and the consequent reduction of the British army, com-

---

[1] Galán, *op. cit.*, 3; Hippisley, *op. cit.*, 48.

[2] Hackett, *op. cit.*, 2, 3, 5; Robinson, *op. cit.*, 3, 5, 10.

[3] Chesterton, *Narrative*, 1.

pelled me to resign the hopes I had entertained of procuring a commission in the military service of my own country; and the kind and earnest exertions of my friends having failed to promote my interests in any other capacity, I was led, in the month of September, 1817, seriously to turn my attention toward the contest in South America, as presenting a fertile field for honourable enterprise." [1]   Brown, a captain in the Artillery Brigade, writes: " I resolved to contribute my feeble efforts towards the emancipation of the oppressed and, as I then imagined, a deserving people ".[2]   Hippisley observes: " The shouts were now for independence; and success to the Spanish-American patriots and a glorious triumph to their cause came from the mouth of nearly every Briton! It was not sufficient for me to wish them success: I felt I might do more; and I determined to lend my personal assistance in promoting it." [3]   Of Francis Burdett O'Connor his grandson writes: " His ardent love of liberty and of the republic, his aspirations and democratic ideals, caused him to abandon his land, his possessions, his fortune and his health to come in search of a new fatherland in those parts of a new world where the great Bolívar had just proclaimed the liberty and emancipation of the Spanish colonies." [4]   Still another writes that his brother " was dazzled by representations of immortal glory that awaited the liberators of millions of human beings, pining under the united influence of religious and political slavery ".[5]   Such at least were the sentiments which these writers claimed had inspired their acts.

[1] Hackett, *op. cit.*, iv, v.

[2] Brown, *op. cit.*, 1.

[3] Hippisley, *op. cit.*, 3.

[4] Francisco Burdett O'Connor, *Independencia Americana: Recuerdos de Francisco Burdett O'Connor*, 9.

[5] M. Rafter, *Memoirs of Gregor McGregor*, vii.

This may have been so; yet one may question whether thoughts of the kind were strong enough to influence any but a few to leave their homes, and risk their lives in far-away lands, for the sake of giving liberty to a foreign folk. It is the part of human nature to claim the best motives for one's acts. *The British Monitor,* in commenting favorably on Hippisley's book which it published in instalments, explained that " his object in joining the Patriots was with a view of providing very handsomely for his family ".[1] This, from a friendly witness, seems at least plausible. J. H. Robinson, who became a surgeon and inspector of hospitals in the patriot army, admits that he joined because López Méndez offered him " an excellent appointment ".[2] An English traveler in Colombia, who while there saw many of those who had come in the Legion, says of them: " They had heard of America as the country of gold and silver; they had read of the mines of Peru and Mexico, and they conceived that little more was necessary than to present themselves, to acquire some share of those riches the Spaniards had kept so long for themselves." [3] A contemporary writer, the Abbé de Pradt, who was an earnest advocate of independence for the Spanish colonies in America, asked: "Who can doubt that a long list of men will not hasten toward the same countries, the same battles, and the same termination of the inactivity which wearies them, of the misery which degrades them, and of the calm which leaves them in such idleness?" [4] The following comment on his comrades in arms, by an anonymous writer who accompanied McDonald in the ship, " Two Friends ", is so candid as to smack of

[1] *British Monitor,* Sept. 12, 1819.

[2] J. H. Robinson, *Journal of an expedition 1400 miles up the Orinoco and 300 miles up the Arauca,* 3.

[3] Walker, *op. cit.,* II, 433.

[4] de Pradt, *op. cit.,* 361.

the truth: "Alike to them whether they were to fight for or against his Catholic Majesty; whether they were to loosen or rivet the chains of slavery; enough for them that they were an object of enterprise to be removed from the dunning of tradesmen and the precincts of a prison." [1] This same writer gives as his own reason for going: " The loss of a beloved parent and some circumstances of a painful and distressing nature, over which I had neither control nor influence, induced me to seek relief to my feelings in absence from my country; and this contest, which my prejudices in favor of national liberty had led me to respect, caused me to listen with attention to proposals at once imposing and seductive." [2]

These several motives must have been compelling, for they seemed to outweigh the warnings which soon began to appear. The king of Spain decreed that foreigners taken in his dominions in America, in the act of carrying arms and under the banners of the insurgents, would be considered, treated and punished as were the respective classes of the insurgents themselves, and would not be included in any acts of pardon granted to Spanish subjects.[3] The newspapers urged caution. The *Morning Chronicle* was accused of having " exclusive possession of all the important and favorable proceedings of the insurgents ", of deceiving the people of England and keeping them ignorant of the real state of affairs in Venezuela, so that " listening only to the generous sympathy of their characters, they are led away by the sophistry of those who profit by the delusion ". The other

[1] *Narrative of a Voyage to the Spanish Main in the Ship " Two Friends,"* p. 16.

[2] *Narrative of a Voyage to the Spanish Main in the Ship " Two Friends,"* 4.

[3] F. O. 72/216, San Carlos to Castlereagh, June 15, 1818; *The British Monitor,* June 21, 1818; *British State Papers* VI, 1134.

papers were wiser in not accepting such prejudicial reports.[1]
The Times deprecated the great efforts which were being
made to allure officers and to raise men for South America.[2]
Bell's Weekly Messenger warned those who contemplated
engaging on the side of the insurgents that the penalty for
such interference in civil war was death without the opportunity of appeal, and that those who eagerly rushed into the
contest in the expectation of winning a glorious death, were
taking the risk of meeting the ignominious end of a criminal.[3]

Thus it will be seen that the motives were varied. Some
were unreasonable; some, rational and even laudable. Motives of a purely personal sort; others, selfish, unselfish and
whimsical—all were there. Yet in the background of their
minds seemed to hover a spirit of altruism engendered by the
popular appeal of love of liberty. It bore an analogy to the
attitude of Frenchmen of a generation earlier toward American independence. Here the correspondence of Grimm and
Diderot tells of the effect on the French public of those
" general and exaggerated maxims that fire the enthusiasm
of youth and would make them run to the world's end and
abandon father, mother, brother to come to the assistance
of an Esquimaux or a Hottentot." [4] After all, perhaps the
characterization that appeared in an editorial of the time, in
which this eagerness to rush into unknown dangers was
called "the South American mania" appears most to befit the
situation.[5] Certainly the promises made by López Méndez
were hardly sufficient in themselves to have caused officers

[1] *Narrative of a Voyage in the Ship "Two Friends,"* 191, 192.

[2] Sept. 20, 1817.

[3] Jan. 18, 1818; see also Cabrera de Nevares, *op. cit.*, 29, 30.

[4] J. J. Jusserand in Introduction to James Breck Perkins, *France in the American Revolution*, xiii.

[5] *Bell's Weekly Messenger*, Jan. 18, 1818.

in active service to give up honorable careers in the British army; nor did the increase in pay in the case of half-pay officers seem a valid inducement to risk the competence that their government was paying them.   If they were looking for hardship or adventure, they certainly encountered plenty of it within the next few years.

CHAPTER IV

EARLY CAMPAIGNING ON TROPICAL SHORES

FROM those days in December, 1817, when the five ships conveying the first contingent set sail from the shores of England, misfortune followed in their wake. Calms succeeded by violent storms delayed their progress, food and water ran short, and mutiny was rife.[1] It seemed as though the elemental forces of nature were combined with the perversity of mankind in a plot to prevent their reaching Bolívar in time to bear him aid.

The first serious disaster occurred shortly after their departure, when a blinding gale drove the " Indian " upon the Ushant Rocks. The ship went down dragging with it to a tragic end Col. Skeene and his regiment. Of all the passengers and crew only five escaped. Thus, long before it had a chance to meet the enemy, the First Venezuelan Lancers suffered annihilation.[2]

By good fortune the " Dowson ", which was to have been the consort of the " Indian " during the voyage, managed to weather the storm and put into the port of Fowey in Cornwall for shelter. Frightened by the dangers of the sea, sev-

[1] Robinson, *op. cit.*, 11, 15; Hippisley, *op. cit.*, 73, 85.

[2] Robinson, *op. cit.*, 9; Hackett, *op. cit.*, 9. One of those rescued was Capt. John Johnston, an officer of the Second Hussars temporarily attached to the Lancers. After his escape from shipwreck he made his way to the West Indies, joined Col. Donald McDonald with whom he reached Angostura on the ship " Grace ", and eventually became a major and commanding officer of the Albion Battalion. Archivo Nacional Bogotá, Sección República, Secretaría de Guerra y Marina, Historia, XXXV, 886.

eral officers and non-commissioned officers seized the opportunity to desert, before the " Dowson " finally sailed from its last English port on January 2, 1818. The appearance of the troops may be judged from the question put by a bumboat-man, who was about to board the ship before she sailed : " Pray, sir, is this a convict transportation ship?" [1]

After weathering the storm, the ships made for the Madeiras in the hope of replenishing their supplies. There disappointment was their only greeting, for the island authorities refused them permission to land. Col. McDonald and his followers aboard the " Two Friends " had left such a trail of riot and disorders, during their stay in port a few weeks previously, that no more uniformed British adventurers were wanted in those peaceful isles. Only a stock of wines and a few of the most essential refreshments were allowed to be placed aboard, before the ships were ordered again to put to sea.[2]

On their arrival at their rendezvous, at St. Bartholomew in the West Indies, the colonels were warned that a Spanish spy was lurking there to obtain information as to their movements.[3] Not only was there no representative of Bolívar to meet them with instructions as to their ultimate destination, but rumors were rife that all ports in Venezuela were again in the hands of the royalists, and that the insurgent cause was in the direst poverty and had everywhere met defeat. Any ship carrying troops or munitions to the mainland was reported liable to seizure by vessels of the royal blockading squadron. If the attempt were made, wholesale execution of the English officers and men as filibusters seemed inevitable. The masters of the ships refused to

[1] Robinson, *op. cit.,* 4, 6, 8, 10, 15.

[2] Hippisley, *op. cit.,* 541; *Narrative of the Ship "Two Friends,"* 313, note a.

[3] Hippisley, *op. cit.,* 99.

jeopardize the property of their owners and to risk almost certain capture. Efforts to replenish their supplies at other islands proved futile. Bad news bred uncertainty and un-certainty bred discontent; discontent aroused ill-humor, and ill-humor turned to jealousy. Adding to the lack of har-mony, Col. Hippisley took this occasion to assume the rank of brigadier-general and to attempt to give orders to the other colonels. The spirit of jealousy and suspicion spread downward through all the officers until quarrels among them became of daily occurrence. Duels were fought over trifles. The officers of the First Hussars forced Capt. Hippisley, son of the colonel, and Lieut. Braybrook to fight a duel which neither wished to fight and over a matter for which both were willing to apologize. Lieut. Braybrook was killed. Al-though the tragic ending to this affair cast a gloom over all the officers, it did not result in any better feelings among them.[1] Loyalty to their commanders or to the oaths which

[1] *Morning Chronicle*, March 28, 1818; *Hippisley's Writings, My First Love and Last Duel, Second Episode.* This book contains the following articles by Capt. (later called lieutenant colonel) Gustavus Hippisley: *Adventures in Colombia; Republican Perfidy; The War of Extermination in Spanish America; My First Love and Last Duel,* and *The Ruse de Guerre.* These articles evidently had been printed in magazines from which the author had cut the pages containing them. In 1848 Lieut. Col. Hippisley had them bound into a volume which he had offered for publication as his collected writings. From a memorandum on the flyleaf it is evident that no publisher had accepted the offer and the volume had been returned. It is now in the private library of the well-known Venezuelan bibliographer, Dr. Manuel Segundo Sánchez, of Caracas. Lieut. Col. Hippisley had come to Venezuela as a captain in his father's regiment. He was not a model officer, and his ideas were evidently colored with vindictiveness toward the Venezuelans and his own superior officers. While his writings do not purport to be more than stories based on his own experience, they give an interesting picture of the lives of the British troops, and in their essential facts are corro-borated by O'Leary, Robinson, and documents found in the National Archives at Caracas and Bogotá. These stories, moreover, are chiefly valuable as showing how the climate combined with other hardships to work on the nerves of the foreigners, making them irritable, morose, querulous and in many respects inefficient.

they had taken ceased to exist. The fires of enthusiasm had been quenched, and the hissing steam scattered the ashes of their hopes. The governor of Grenada, to whom many of the men applied for a release from their engagement, told them that they had formed no engagement which they were not at liberty to break, if they chose.[1] Funds were running short. The situation looked hopeless. Under such conditions, to hold the organizations together any longer seemed impossible.

The supercargo of the " Britannia " thereupon announced his intention to proceed to Port-au-Prince to sell his armament and munitions. Col. Gilmour, only too aware that a brigade of artillery without its guns was useless, yielded to the inevitable [2] and, after receiving the approval of a council of his officers, issued an order disbanding the organization. A small detachment of four officers and fifteen men managed to keep together and eventually reached Angostura as the sole representatives of the artillery. Several of the disbanded officers and men were attached to Col. Hippisley's regiment and about twenty others joined Col. Campbell's; but most of them were left to wander destitute among the West Indies, hoping in some way to pick up a passage home.[3] A few even, rendered desperate by their condition, were persuaded by an adventurer named Hudson to join him in a proposed piratical raid against the city of Santa Marta, for the purpose of securing plunder.[4]

The reports of the hopeless state of the insurgent cause so discouraged the officers of the First Venezuelan Rifle Regi-

---

[1] Robinson, *op. cit.*, 40, 41 ; Hackett, *op. cit.*, 48, 49, 52.

[2] Hackett, *op. cit.*, 49, 98.

[3] Hippisley, *op. cit.*, 196, 201 ; Brown, *op. cit.*, 2, 3, 4, 6, 65; *Bell's Weekly Messenger*, Nov. 30, 1817.

[4] Hippisley, *op. cit.*, 202, 203, 207; Hackett, *op. cit.*, ii, 91; Brown, *op. cit.*, 3, 8.

ment that that organization was quickly reduced to a skeleton by desertions and resignations. Some of them, taking possession of the " Dowson ", sailed with it to join the squadron of the patriot Admiral Brión. The regimental band was dispersed throughout the West Indies, and many of the musicians were glad of the opportunity of enlisting in the navy or in the British West India contingents. Fever added its havoc among the few who still remained with the colors. After the death, from yellow fever, of his son, Duncan, Col. Campbell himself resigned and sailed for home. Major Robert Pigott then assumed command of the remnant of the regiment, and with the surviving ten officers and proportionate number of men managed, after overcoming many difficulties, to reach Angostura, the seat at the time of the revolutionary government. They were assigned to serve under Gen. Páez near San Juan on the Arauca. In 1818, Pigott, who by that time had been promoted to a colonelcy, was sent down the Orinoco to the Caroni Missions, to fill the vacancies in his command with Indian recruits. He enlisted four hundred Indians and, in four months, had trained them so well that they were able to take the field. For having brought his regiment to such a high state of discipline, he received the thanks of Bolívar.[1] Col Pigott's riflemen took part in many an engagement under Páez along the Apure. In a skirmish at Ligamara, Col. Pigott had a horse shot under him. Eventually, however, he succumbed to the climate, and was forced to resign because of ill-health. Under his successor, Lieut. Col. Arthur Sandes, the Rifles became the crack regiment of the guards. This regiment was known also as the " First Rifles ", the " Rifle Battalion ", and sometimes as the " Black Rifles ". It remained in service until the last battle of the war of independence was won. Many

[1] Brown, *op. cit.*, 29, 41, 42, 180; Hackett, *op. cit.*, 118; Robinson, *op. cit.*, 171; Brown, *op. cit.*, 84, 85, 100.

of its officers were the most distinguished among the legionaries.[1]

Discord broke out in the Second (Red) Hussars when their ship, the " Prince ", was seized because of some violation of the customs regulations by its owner, James Mackintosh, and the regiment split in two.   Part of the regiment followed Major Graham and joined the Rifles.   Many of the officers resigned and remained at St. Bartholomew.   When Col. Wilson finally reached Angostura after many vicissitudes, only a small fraction of the Red Hussars remained under his command, although a few men from the disbanded artillery brigade had joined him.[2]

The " Emerald " was detained at Grenada by the customs officials because of irregularities in her papers and complaints against her captain, but was released after ten days.   After arriving at St. Lucia the captain refused to take his vessel into further danger and sold it to Admiral Brión for use as flagship of the Venezuelan navy.[3]   The First Venezuelan Hussars had now become so reduced by sickness, resignations, and desertions that Col. Hippisley was able to crowd them all aboard the small schooner " Tiger ", which, under the able guidance of Capt. Hill, an Englishman who had joined the naval service of Venezuela the year before, at last set sail for the Orinoco.[4]   Thus although 500 officers and non-commissioned officers had arrived at St. Bartholomew in the " Britannia ", " Dowson ", " Prince ", and " Emer-

[1] Brown, *op. cit.,* 91, 95, 100; C. S. Cochrane, *Journal of a residence and travels in Colombia during the years 1823 and 1824,* I, 467; *Present State of Colombia,* 92, 93.

[2] Hippisley, *op. cit.,* 196, 201; Hackett, *op. cit.,* 31, 73; Brown, *op. cit.,* 6, 50.   Major Graham died soon after entering the Orinoco.

[3] Hackett, *op. cit.,* 75, 107; Brown, *op. cit.,* 22; *Present State of Colombia,* 89.

[4] Hippisley, *op. cit.,* 639; Brown, *op. cit.,* 19; Hackett, *op. cit.,* 114.

ald ", not over 150 of them persevered in their attempts to reach Venezuela.

The town of Angostura, now Ciudad Bolívar, their destination, was located on the side of a steep hill on the southern bank of the Orinoco at a point where the river narrows to a width of approximately two miles. At that time it contained about 5,000 inhabitants. The streets, running parallel to the river and at right angles to it, extended to the crest of the hill, which was surmounted by a fort and lookout station. About halfway up was the plaza, containing, as usual in Spanish-American towns, the cathedral, public buildings and barracks. In this case the cathedral was a mere unfinished shell, for the work upon it had been stopped by the revolution, and the governor's palace, a plain one-story brick building standing opposite, was in use by the congress of the republic. The barracks, a long range of low buildings, formed with the " calabozo ", or prison, one end of the plaza. Most of the houses of the town were flimsy shacks, composed of bamboo watlings plastered with mud, but the better-class residences were fairly substantial structures, of whitewashed stone and brick, with flat tiled roofs and handsome green balconies. One of the finest houses was that occupied by James Hamilton, a Scotch merchant who had been of material assistance to the cause of the revolution by furnishing the army generous supplies of arms and other stores, for which he had not yet received any payment more substantial than the thanks of Bolívar. About three-quarters of a mile outside of town was the hospital, a large building surmounted with turrets, and at the top of the hill near the fort was the " Campo Santo ", or burying ground. Smallpox was endemic in the vicinity, and, due to the proximity of a swamp, yellow fever and various other tropical diseases were prevalent. Because of the devastation of war, moreover, agriculture in the outlying region had been sadly neglected, the fields being overgrown with tangles of brush, in which little piles of human bones were not an unusual sight.[1] The appearance of the town at all events did not create a favorable impression upon the new recruits from England.

After the arrival at Angostura of Colonels Hippisley and Wilson with the remnants of their regiments, all the hussars were consolidated in one brigade known as the "British Brigade", under Col. Hippisley, and various English officers who had come independently or who had originally belonged to the other regiments, were attached to the First Hussars. Among them was Lieut. Col. James Rooke,[2] who had already for some months been serving as aide to Bolívar. There were also one major, two captains, six lieutenants, and one surgeon, none of whom was a cavalryman. Nor at that time were men or horses provided by the republic. Considerable difficulty attended the process of reorganization, for many of those who resented the non-payment of the bounty which they had expected immediately upon landing, refused to take the oath of allegiance to Venezuela; but after Gen. Montilla had renewed the promises of payment at the first oppor-

---

[1] Robinson, *op. cit.*, 80, 81, 82, 85, 94; Chesterton, *op. cit.*, 113, 114; *Campaigns and Cruises*, I, 28, 30, 32, 33; *Journal des voyages, découvertes et navigations modernes*, III, 374; Brown, *op. cit.*, 96; Shumacher, *op. cit.*, 15, 16, 17.

[2] Lieut. Col. James Rooke was the son of Lieut. Gen. Rooke. He had reached the rank of major in the British army before he had retired and had held the post of deputy chamberlain to the Prince of Orange. He had been among those who had come out in 1817, and had been twice wounded at La Puerta. The *British Army Lists* for 1816 and 1817 show him on English half-pay as a lieutenant of the Staff Corps of Cavalry disbanded and reduced in 1814. Academia Nacional de Historia, Bogotá, *Boletin de historia y antigüedades*, XIII, 38; Cayo Leonidas Peñuela, "Jaime Rooke", in *Repertorio Boyacense*, No. 64, VI, 779, 780; VII, 777; M. L. Scarpetta and Saturnino Vergara, *Diccionario Biográfico de los campeones de Nueva Granada, Venezuela, Ecuador i Perú*, 542; *Recollections of Service*, I, 21; W. O. 25/65 folio 60; Ramón Azpúrua, *Biografías de hombres notables de Hispano-América*, III, 226.

tunity, and had ordered them arrested and stripped of their uniforms, both cavalry regiments eventually consented to take the oath.[1]

After the reorganization at Angostura, Col. Hippisley received orders to report with his brigade to Bolívar at San Fernando de Apure. The voyage up the river was made in open " flecheras ",[2] in which some of the women and children who had accompanied the expeditions from England were crowded in with the officers and men.[3] On arrival at San Fernando a scene of frightful confusion met their startled gaze, for the insurgent army was in wild retreat before the Spanish forces of Morillo. Bolívar, on the point of embarkation down the river, declared his intention of sending the English troops back to the West Indies, for there was no use in exposing them to certain destruction in a lost cause.[4]

Gen. Páez, who had been left in command by Bolívar, managed at length to restore a semblance of order among the disorganized insurgents; but the newly-arrived English troops were allowed to do as they pleased. Left without

[1] Hippisley, *op. cit.*, 291, 303, 315, 574; Archivo Nacional, Caracas, Gobernación de Guayana, IV, 482.

[2] " Flecheras " were large, deep canoes with sides built up by stretching hides along them, much used by the Indians on the Orinoco and along the coast. Their name, signifying " arrow-boats ", was given to them because of their speed whether propelled by sails or by paddles. Although quite safe at sea, they were peculiarly adapted for shallow waters. *Recollections of Service*, I, 204, II, 48; Geo. L. Chesterton, *An Autobiographical Memoir*, II, 181; *Campaigns and Cruises*, I, 37.

[3] Hippisley, *op. cit.*, 4, 327, 330; *Present State of Colombia*, 90, 91. From general orders issued to the British Army in Belgium it is evident that the presence of women and children with troops in the field was no unusual thing at that time. British Museum, Egerton MSS. 9842, folios 44, 45. Hippisley, however, had forbidden his own officers to bring their wives from England.

[4] Brown, *op. cit.*, 85.

rations, or shelter, or any authority to direct their movements, they readily found access to stores of liquor abandoned by the fleeing inhabitants of the town.   Officers as well as men became drunk and riotous.   Even Majors Ferriar and Trewren so far forgot the responsibilities of their rank as to lead gangs of rioters in search of the liquor.[1]   Col. Wilson declared himself in command of the brigade and with liberal promises of loot and laxity of discipline, gath‹ ered about him a gang of drunken followers.   Joining Col. Wilson in defiance of the authority of Col. Hippisley, the two majors encouraged the men in their drunkenness, and led them about shouting, " Viva General Páez ".[2]   The mutineers declared that they would serve no longer under Bolívar, but would remain at San Fernando instead under Páez.   They ransacked the " flecheras " and looted the army chests, clothing, private property of the officers, and the regimental stores.   Even Col. Hippisley's own orderly sergeant, once a member of the Duke of Brunswick's Hussars, stole all the bugles which were the colonel's private property.[3] In the confusion Bolívar slipped away secretly from San Fernando.   Col. Hippisley tried to follow him, but was unable to stem the desertion.   He succeeded, however, in re-embarking with nine officers, twenty-two non-commissioned officers and one trumpeter who still remained faithful to him.[4]

Upon his return to Angostura, Col. Hippisley tried to curry favor with his few remaining followers by listening to their complaints, and busied himself in transmitting them together with his own to Bolívar and the other patriot generals.   The non-commissioned officers urged him to send them to any

[1] Hippisley, *op. cit.*, 392, 396, 399, 595.

[2] Hippisley, *op. cit.*, 399, 591, 592.   *Campaigns and Cruises*, I, 112.

[3] Hippisley, *op. cit.*, 402, 404.

[4] *Ibid.*, 400, 404, 407 ; Brown, *op. cit.*, 85 n.

British island, asserting that none of the promises made to them had been fulfilled, and that they were unaccustomed to such poverty, hardships and privations as those which they were then being compelled to endure.[1] After he had brought the matter to the attention of the Venezuelan military authorities, he received promises of better rations to officers and men.

Although Bolívar appears to have done his best to redeem these promises, giving as good pay and rations as the resources of the republic afforded, he found that his treasury was not rich enough to satisfy the clamor of these homesick and disappointed foreigners, and was forced to permit the most vociferous of them to repudiate their agreements and return home. Hippisley himself resigned, but not until his resignation had been repeatedly submitted was it accepted. The indignant colonel was then given his passports to leave Venezuela.[2] When he arrived in London, he had López Méndez arrested for non-payment of the debt due him by the Republic of Venezuela.[3] Suit was brought against the Venezuelan agent for the recovery of freight charges.[4] An attempt also was made later by Mackintosh to collect from Colombia through diplomatic channels £186,475 plus six per cent interest due for furnishing equipment for the regiments sponsored by López Méndez.[5]

[1] Hippisley, *op. cit.*, 633; *British Monitor*, Jan. 10, 1819.

[2] Hippisley, *op. cit.*, 632; Brown, *op. cit.*, 51, 89; *Cartas de Bolívar, 1799 a 1822*, 228, 231, 232.

[3] Hippisley, *op. cit.*, 518, 519, 652.

[4] *Morning Chronicle*, Nov. 2, 1818.

[5] F. O. 18/16, Castillo to Consul Henderson, May 19, 1825; Henderson to Planta, June 9, 1825. On his return to England, Hippisley resumed his rank in the army. A suggestion was made that he be court-martialed for engaging in the war in South America, but for some reason no such action was taken. *British Army List for 1825*, 538. Eventually he went to Paris where he met McGregor, on whose behalf he proposed to re-

After the departure of Bolívar and Hippisley from San Fernando, Col. Wilson had tried to tamper with the loyalty of Gen. Páez, suggesting that he shake off his allegiance to his superior officer and declare himself commander-in-chief.[1] A few days later Col. Wilson arranged a grand review at which he led the right of the line, parading his Englishmen in their gaudy new uniforms. After the review a proclamation was read and signed, declaring Páez captain-General of the army. Páez seemingly gave his consent to this act of disloyalty, accepting Wilson's offer to raise a large corps in England for service under him. Wilson was then sent to Angostura with letters of recommendation to Bolívar. On his arrival there he was immediately thrown into prison for his misconduct. He demanded a trial, but as it was difficult to find enough British field officers to compose the court, he was eventually dismissed from the army, and was either deported from the country or suffered to escape from the fortress of Old Guayana where he was confined.[2] On his way home Wilson did all he could to injure the cause for which he had worn a uniform. While at Port of Spain he wrote a letter to Sir Ralph Woodford, governor of Trinidad, begging his interference on behalf of more than two hundred Englishmen who had joined the insurgent cause before the issue of the prohibitory order. He accordingly asked that

turn to Colombia in aid of the latter's plans for the colonization of Poyais. Because of alleged fraudulent transactions in connection with this scheme, Hippisley was arrested with McGregor in 1825 and confined in the prison of La Force (see Chapter VI, p. 156, n. 1). G. Hippisley, *Acts of Oppression Committed under the Administration of M. de Villéle, Prime Minister of Charles X*, 4, 6, 27, 28, 37, 38.

[1] Hippisley, *op. cit.*, 442; *Campaigns and Cruises*, 112, 113.

[2] O'Leary, *Narración*, I, 484, 485; Hippisley, *op. cit.*, 445, 446; Robinson, op. cit., 76; Karl Richard, *Die Republick Colombia; Briefe an seine Freunde von einem hanoverischen Officier, geschrieben in dem Jahre 1820*, 48, 49; *The Times*, Jan. 13, 1819.

official to secure the liberation of these men, then held in Venezuela practically as prisoners, since passports were allowed to none but a few officers who had agreed to spread glowing reports and to seduce more men to come.[1]

After reaching Cork, Wilson, established with his staff at the Munster Hotel, busied himself in circulating discouraging statements, to the effect that in no instance had the engagements of López Méndez been fulfilled; that pay was out of the question; that officers were forced to sell their clothes and go about in a state of nudity; that letters home telling the truth had been opened and other accounts in cleverly imitated handwriting had been substituted; and that extracts from them, published in the *Morning Chronicle,* were forgeries.[2] He also accused that individual of having carried out a most complicated and successful system of swindling, of which the British Empire had been the dupe. As for those who had been entrapped into joining the insurgents, their bravery had been belittled and ignored in official reports of engagements, and contempt had been the only reward for all their sacrifices.[3] In defending himself against these accusations, López Méndez stated that he had never acted in his private capacity, but always as the accredited agent of Venezuela; that he had never entrapped any officers to go, but that all had volunteered their services eagerly; and that there had been two classes of volunteers, first those who went independently and paid their own passage, and second, those who agreed to organize regiments. The members of this latter class had failed in their contracts to provide enough men and had commissioned too many officers without

[1] *London Chronicle,* Jan. 18, 1819.

[2] *London Chronicle,* Jan. 15, 1819, quoting an extract from a Cork newspaper not named or dated.

[3] *British Monitor,* Jan. 17, 1819, quoting an extract from the *Cork Advertiser.*

previous service. Of the first class scarcely twenty officers had actually arrived at Angostura, although the government of Venezuela had paid $300 apiece toward their passage and expenses. Many had committed excesses at Margarita Island, compelling the government to take severe measures. Others had stolen the vessel in which they came and had dispersed themselves throughout the West Indies. He concluded with the statement that Hackett's *Narrative of the Expedition which sailed from England in 1817 to join the South American patriots* was a tissue of lies.[1]

Subsequently it came out that Wilson was a spy who had been engaged by the Spanish minister to stir up treason against Bolívar. López Méndez reported that he had transmitted proof of correspondence between Wilson and the Spanish minister, and that the secretary of the latter had paid two bills drawn by Wilson as a bribe for his aid to the royalist cause.[2]

After Hippisley's resignation, Lieut. Col. Rooke, who was living at that time in Angostura, was appointed to the command of the First Venezuelan Hussars. Later he was sent to the mission station near San Fernando to recruit his regiment to proper strength among the Indians there.[3] He and Gilmour were the only colonels who had offered their services to the patriot cause and still remained with it after a year's trial.[4] Meanwhile other officers had arrived at Angostura and San Fernando to join Bolívar, some of them re-

---

[1] Letter from López Méndez, published in the *British Monitor*, Jan. 24, 1819; O'Leary, *Documentos,* XVI, 303.

[2] Hippisley, *op. cit.,* 515, 516; *Morning Chronicle,* Dec. 25, 1818; Urdaneta, *op. cit.,* 144, 145, n.; José D. Monsalve, *El Ideal político del Libertador, Simón Bolívar,* I, 200, 201.

[3] Hippisley, *op. cit.,* 280, 286, 611; Brown, *op. cit.,* 89, 95; Chesterton, *op. cit.,* 159.

[4] *British Monitor,* Dec. 13, 1818; *Boletín de la Academia Nacional de Historia,* Quito, IV, 304.

porting from time to time as individuals, others arriving with the semblance of an organization. Among the latter was Lieut. Col. J. Needham, who came the preceding summer in charge of a corps of lancers which Col. Strenowitz had organized at Brussels, from Hanoverians who had served under Wellington.[1] This body had arrived by way of the United States, where one of their number had betrayed them to the Spanish consul at Philadelphia. On the complaint of this official they had been committed for trial on the charge of violating the neutrality laws, but had eventually managed to obtain their release. With Needham came also ten British officers and non-commissioned officers, Capt. J. D. Perkins, Capt. J. B. Holland, Capt. Ferriar,[2] Lieut. Richard Stacy,

[1] *Wellington's Despatches,* XII, 783; Hippisley, *op. cit.,* 242, 243, 396, 476. Col. Strenowitz with his staff remained in Europe. See also Carlos Schoffer in " Süd und Mittel Amerika," translated and reprinted in *El Universal,* Caracas, June 12, 1911.

[2] The name of this officer is variously spelled as Ferrier, Ferrer, Ferriar, Farriar, and Farrar. The last is advocated as the correct one by Dr. Vicente Dávila, director of the national archives at Caracas, who points out in his *Investigaciones históricas,* 174, 175 that in documents found in Gobernación de Guayana, **VIII,** 75, 98, 104 and XIV, 133, 136 the officer had signed his name " J. D. Farrar ". This seemed conclusive until other documents were discovered in the national archives at Bogotá, Secretaría de Guerra y Marina, Historia, VII, 414 and DCCLXXX, 860, in which the signatures appear as " T. J. Ferriar " and " J. Ferriar ". It is possible that this officer may have changed his signature to conform to that by which the Spanish Americans insisted upon addressing him. This was very common especially with the first names. Several of the foreign officers also changed their last names. A notable case is that of Illingworth who changed his signature to " Illingrot ". Another possible explanation is that there were two brothers, or men of similiar family name, who signed their last names differently. This explanation seems to be confirmed by the document published as a footnote to L. Florez Álvarez, *Campaña Libertadora de 1821,* pages 200, 201, in which Sergt. Maj. Juan Ferrier states his service and asks for promotion. On this letter is an endorsement recommending the promotion, signed at Achaguas, June 18, 1820, by H. Ferrier, ex-commandant of the British Legion. This is probably a misprint for T. Ferrier, who was John's

Lieut. James Stacy, Lieut. Charles Webster, Surgeon Robert
Fry, Sergeant-Major Benjamin Pearkes and Sergts. John
Williams and Peter Hogan.   Another member of the group
was the commissary, Frederic Bruix, said to be a Cossack
nobleman, but in reality a Frenchman.[1]

Among the stragglers who drifted in from time to time
were three French officers, one of them was a captain decorated with the order of the Legion of Honor.   At one time
an Italian, Col. Jenaro Montbrune, held the post of adjutant-
general, and another, Lieut. Col. Manfredo Bertolazzi, acted
as chief of staff.[2]   A group of twenty British officers, among

brother and commanding officer.   It will be noticed that at this time both
brothers signed their names " Ferrier ".   O' Connor, *op. cit.,* 56, says that
Lieut. Col. Ferrer of the Carabobo Battalion was the brother of the
Col. Ferrer who was killed at the battle of Carabobo.   There seems to
be much confusion as to this name among Spanish-American authors;
for on page 160 of the work above quoted, Florez Álvarez gives the name
of the commanding officer of the British Battalion as Rafael Ferrier.
Level, *op. cit.,* 375, names Rafael Farrier as being in command of the
artillery on the Apure, and Santana, *La Campaña de Carabobo,* 163, shows
Col. Tomás Ferriar as the commanding officer of the British Battalion
at the battle of Carabobo and Sergt. Maj. Juan Ferriar also with that
battalion.   Montenegro in his *Geografía general,* IV, 364, n. names Col.
Juan Ferrier as commanding the British at Carabobo.   To the present
writer it seems best to follow the signatures found in the national
archives of Bogotá and record the name of the colonel who was killed at
Carabobo as Thomas Ferriar and that of his brother, the former British
commandant at Angostura who later was promoted to colonel commanding the Carabobo Battalion, as John Ferriar.

[1] *Bell's Weekly Messenger,* Dec. 14, 1817; *London Chronicle,* Dec. 14,
1817, March 23, 1818; *The Times,* Dec. 9, 1817; *British Monitor,* Jan.
4, 1818; Archivo Nacional, Bogotá, Guerra y Marina III, 936; J. Needham
to Bolívar, Calabozo, March 29, 1818, Archivo del Libertador, in private
collection of Dr. Vicente Lecuna of Caracas.

[2] Archivo Nacional, Bogotá, Hojas de Servicios, XXX, 247, 248;
La Nación, Caracas, Nov. 23, 1910; Hippisley, *op. cit.,* 429, 436, 446, 484.
Jenaro Montbrune had joined the navy of Venezuela in 1815 and had been
transferred to the artillery brigade at Cumaná two years later.   From
1817 to 1819 he was adjutant general of the division of Urdaneta and of

whom was Col. Donald McDonald, also arrived after having been reported massacred when their ship, the " Grace ", had been captured by the royalists.[1] At the battle of Villa de Cura " thirteen English officers with the infantry did wonders. They led the infantry in a style that would not have passed unnoticed at Waterloo. To their example was owing the success of the first part of the day." [2] At least so the *London Chronicle* expected its readers to believe, when it published the above extract from the journal of two English officers, a lieutenant-colonel and a captain in the insurgent cavalry. As early as March 16, 1818, moreover, at the disastrous battle of La Puerta, Bolívar had with him ten or twelve English officers, and a few men, with whose conduct he was highly delighted.[3] In a bold attack near the Arauca River, Capt. Grant, a Scotch volunteer under Páez, killed five of the enemy with his own hand.[4] At the battle of Ortíz eight English officers were put to death by the enemy after they had been wounded and taken prisoners. Capt. Noble McMullen escaped a like fate, by pretending to be a surgeon and non-combatant.[5] Bolívar indeed had granted commissions to many Englishmen and Irishmen and formed them into a Guard of Honor. In this guard had been Lieut. Col.

the province of Guayana. Lieut. Col. Manfredo Bertolazzi was chief of staff at the battle of Rincón de los Toros. After the battle he was taken prisoner and shot by the royalists.

[1] *London Chronicle*, Oct. 6, 1818, quoting from *Dublin Evening Post,* Sept. 30, 1818; Archivo Nacional, Caracas, Gobernación de Guayana, VIII, 94.

[2] *London Chronicle*, July 6, 1818; J. Needham to Bolívar, Calabozo, March 29, 1818, Archivo del Libertador, in private collection of Dr. Vicente Lecuna of Caracas.

[3] O'Leary, *Correspondencia de extranjeros notables con el Libertador,* II, 218; Hippisley, *op. cit.,* 568.

[4] *London Chronicle*, July 14, 1819.

[5] Hippisley, *op. cit.,* 289; *Campaigns and Cruises,* I, 86, 87; Archivo Nacional, Bogotá, Secretaría Guerra y Marina, Historia, III, 558.

Rooke and Captains Charles Smith and Samuel Collins, the last-named in the " Sacred Squadron ", as well as Lieut. Peter James Hope who had been captured at El Sémen.[1]

In spite of the annoyance caused by the actions of Hippisley and Wilson and by the complaints and behavior of many of the others sent by López Méndez, Bolívar was so well pleased with the conduct of the men who had arrived earlier and independently that he approved of a plan suggested by Rooke for filling up the vacancies in the First Venezuelan Hussars, to whom he had awarded the motto: " Siempre fiel a la autoridad suprema " (Always loyal to the supreme authority).[2]   The plan was to send officers to round up and bring to Angostura the numerous deserters, stragglers, and stranded volunteers, who were wandering about the various islands of the West Indies.   To this duty he had assigned Lieut. Col. James T. English,[3] accompanied by Cornet Dewey.   Owing, however, to the wreck of the brig-of-war " Colombia ", on which these officers had sailed, they had failed in their quest, and had returned empty-handed.[4]

So anxious was Bolívar to secure the services of more of the British that he then authorized Lieut. Col. English to return to England to recruit as many men as he could.   He was to receive the rank of brigadier-general and be paid fifty

[1] Archivo Nacional, Bogotá, Guerra y Marina, Hojas de Servicios, XI, 243, XLII, 501; Archivo Nacional, Caracas, Ilustres Próceres de Independencia, Hope, Peter James (folio not yet filed or numbered) ; Level, *op. cit.,* 303.

[2] Peñuela, *op. cit., Repertorio Boyacense,* no. 64, VI, 779.

[3] Lieut. Col. James T. English was second-in-command of the First Hussars. He had been sent ahead with an advance party to report to Bolívar and to arrange for the reception of the regiment at Angostura. It was reported that before obtaining his commission as lieutenant colonel, English had been an army contractor who had become bankrupt. *British Monitor,* June 13, 1819; Hippisley, *op. cit.,* 67, 147; Restrepo, *op. cit.,* II, 595, 596, note 40 a ; Hackett, *op. cit.,* 81.

[4] Hippisley, *op. cit.,* 323, 480.

pounds sterling for every man he landed in South America.[1] Capt. George Elsam, who had brought a few officers from Trinidad and had remained only a week at Angostura, was also authorized to recruit a thousand more men in London under the same conditions as to payment, although the rank he should receive was to be that of colonel.[2]

Elsam sailed at once on the schooner " Tiger "; so energetic was he that frequent ships arrived from England and from various ports in the West Indies, bringing groups of aspirants for commissions in the patriot service and men ready for employment of any kind ashore or afloat. On February 13, 1819, the frigate " King George ", from London brought eighty-four infantrymen, six officers and ninety-four sailors. It also carried a cargo of lead for bullets.[3] On March 6, the " George Canning " came with Capt. Barnard, Lieut. McGuire, and Sergts. Reynolds and Dombroskie, with a detachment of men.[4]

In addition to enlisting British subjects, Elsam accepted many German veterans of the Napoleonic wars, who offered their services to him. Adventurers calling themselves " South American Patriots " were successful in securing a number of recruits in Hamburg, until their activities were checked by the Senate of that city. At the request of the Spanish minister, a number of young men who had enrolled themselves in the service of the insurgents were arrested just as they were on the point of embarking. Two vessels, however, well loaded with recruits, managed to effect their escape.[5]

[1] Hippisley, *op. cit.,* 428.

[2] Elsam had formerly been an ensign in a distinguished corps of volunteers. He had sailed from England with the Second Hussars; Hippisley, *op. cit.,* 473, 475.

[3] Archivo Nacional, Caracas, Gobernación de Guayana, VII, 32.

[4] *Ibid.,* VIII, 77; Blanco, *op. cit.,* VI, 602.

[5] *British Monitor,* Dec. 13, 1818.

As soon as his men were recruited and vessels were secured, Col. Elsam sent them to Venezuela, and as each detachment of his forces arrived at Angostura, it was attached to one of the battalions of foreigners.[1] On January 12, 1819, 154 men under Col. Munro and Major J. D. Ferriar arrived at Old Guiana, whence they were transferred to the command of Col. Rooke at Angostura.[2] Nine days later a courier arrived, announcing the coming of the " Tartar " and the " Perseverance ", with 300 English troops aboard sent by Elsam, who had also dispatched the " Hunter " with supplies and equipment for the army, including the delayed uniforms of the Red Hussars.[3] Two companies under Captains Charles C. Johnson and Thomas Manby [4] touched first at Margarita Island before proceeding up the Orinoco. Here Manby received a letter from Bolívar, assuring him that everything promised by Col. Elsam would be fulfilled. Since Col. Elsam had àsked that no change be made until his arrival, the roster of the English corps would for the present remain unchanged. Piqued at being overslaughed in his expected promotion in the battalion in which he was serving, Manby resigned from that organization, although he expressed willingness to accept a position elsewhere.[5]

[1] Richard, *op. cit.*, 2 ; Cochrane, *op. cit.*, I, 467, 468.

[2] Archivo Nacional, Caracas, Gobenación de Guayana, VIII, 75 ; Vicente Dávila, *Investigaciones históricas*, 174 ; *cf. supra*, p. 79, n. 2.

[3] Hippisley, *op. cit.*, 320 ; Simon de Schryver, *Esquisse de la vie de Bolívar*, 177. Bingham collection of manuscripts (Yale University Library) Bolívar's letters No. 5, Bolívar to Guillermo White ; Feb. 9, 1819 ; Archivo Nacional, Caracas, Gobernación de Guayana, VIII, 74 ; *London Chronicle,* Oct. 14, 1819.

[4] The *British Army List* for 1815 shows Thomas Manby as an ensign in the Twelfth Regiment of Foot, and the *Half Pay Warrant Book* for 1817, shows him as a lieutenant on half pay. W. O. 25/2996, p. 67 ; Urdaneta, *op. cit.,* 150. In 1817 Charles C. Johnson was a captain in the Eighty-Fifth Foot (Gordon's) W. O. 25/65, folio 430.

[5] O'Leary, *Documentos*, Vol. XVI, p. 214. Archivo Nacional Caracas, Gobernación de Guayana, VII, 76 ; Archivo Nacional, Bogotá, Guerra y Marina, Historia, I, 667.

It was not until April that Col. Elsam with 192 more men at last joined his command, the size of which had now reached 700 men, part of whom were cavalry.[1] Col. Elsam was not destined to lead this force into battle, for he died soon after landing. Several companies under Capt. Charles James Minchin[2] were sent from the Apure to Margarita Island, but 350 of them (twenty-one of them officers) died of malignant fever while they were aboard ship in transit.[3] The 150 who reached Margarita were then assigned to serve under Col. Johannes Uslar[4] who had been the original commander of the Hanoverians.[5]

[1] O'Leary, *Documentos*, XVI, 251, 302; *London Chronicle*, May 21, 1819. Archivo Nacionàl, Bogotá, Guerra y Marina, Historia, VII, 414; *British Monitor*, Oct. 24, 1819.

[2] When not yet twenty-one years old, Charles James Minchin secured his parents' consent to go to South America and with his brother, William Milton Minchin, sailed on the " Hero ", arriving at Guayana on April 19, 1819. Within six months his brother William had died there. Azpúrua, *op. cit.*, III, 425.

[3] *Ibid.*, Galán, *op. cit.*, 14.

[4] Johannes Uslar, whose full title was Baron von Uslar-Gleichen, was born in Lockum, Hanover, in 1779 and was sent by his parents to England, where he studied in the Royal College at Windsor. In 1802, as a sub-lieutenant of dragoons he joined the King's German Legion for the Peninsular campaign and as a captain fought at Waterloo. After the Napoleonic wars he remained in England, where he attained the rank of major in one of the most exclusive regiments in the British army. In September, 1818, he cooperated with López Méndez in a plan to organize a German Legion. After leaving von Clauditz in charge at Hamburg, Uslar himself raised 300 Germans and English, all of whom were veterans. Aided by a commercial house in Hamburg. he sent his men to Venezuela in the " Gambler " and the " Plutus ". He himself sailed in the latter, in spite of the fact that the Spanish consul had induced the Hamburg authorities to order the arrest of both himself and von Clauditz. Archivo Nacional, Caracas. Ilustres Próceres de Independencia, XCIV, 306; Schoffer, *op. cit.* in *El Universal*, Caracas, June 12, 1911; *El Luchador*, Caracas, May 10, 1912.

[5] For a list of officers at Angostura who were assigned to Col. Uslar's command, see Appendix A.

These arrivals had first been assembled at Angostura, where they had temporarily been cared for under the orders of Major J. D. Ferriar, British commandant at that place,[1] who had supplied their deficiencies as well as possible by the issue of such clothing and equipment as reached him from time to time, kept them furnished with rations contributed by the inhabitants, supervised their discipline, and eventually forwarded them up the river in detachments to join the various battalions of foreigners. Major Ferriar's task must have been a far from pleasant one, for he had to bear the brunt of the first complaints on account of poor rations and quarters and lack of pay. Worst of all, he had to take care of the women and children who had followed their husbands and parents from England and had been held back at Angostura at a safe distance behind the lines. With more than a dozen of these on his hands he would have been a busy man, had he had no other troublesome duties to perform.[2] Pay was often in arrears, and even when it was distributed at the rate of half a month's pay per month, it came in the form of money made locally out of some base metal washed with silver which the tradesmen refused to receive, except at a large discount.[3] Rations were issued according to rank, but failed to satisfy the recipients.[4] By way of further misfortune, an unusual proportion of sickness prevailed at Angos-

[1] Archivo Nacional, Caracas, Gobernación de Guayana, VII, 155, 156; *cf.* also *supra*, p. 79, n. 2.

[2] Archivo Nacional, Caracas, Gobernación de Guayana, VII, 206, 207, XIV, 133. For a complete list of the foreign officers, enlisted men, women and children under the command of Major Ferriar at Angostura on June 16, 1819 see Appendix B. For a list of Irish women and children at Angostura, not dated but probably in 1820, see Appendix C.

[3] Archivo Nacional, Caracas, Gobernación de Guayana, VIII, 86; Lieut. Col. Hippisley's Writings, *Eve of Saint Simon*, 155, 156; Archivo Santander, III, 300.

[4] Archivo Nacional, Caracas, Gobernación de Guayana, II, 72, 76, 79, 85, 99, 101, 103, VII, 172.

tura because it was the base to which the sick and wounded were transferred from most of the organizations at the front.[1]

Since this town was a convenient place in which to rest from the fatigues and dangers of actual campaign, there were many malingerers. Captains Hippisley and Lancay were among the most troublesome of them. Though reported by Dr. Edward Kirby, the surgeon, as fit for duty, the former declared that he would be unable to join his command for more than a week, and Major Ferriar seemed unable to compel him to do so.[2] The surgeon also maintained that Capt. Lancay was not suffering from any particular disease, even if he did complain of affliction with great debility whenever with the army. Then evidently to square himself with that officer, the surgeon added that the climate was bad for this particular ailment, and advised anyone really suffering from it to take a sea voyage.[3] Dr. Kirby also reported Major Trilby as unfit for duty due to rheumatic gout, recommending his removal to the hospital where he might " be kept from indulging in the cause of his complaint ".[4] The surgeons in general seemed to have been the last straws for the long-suffering major, who ordered one of them under arrest. In his defense the latter pleaded that he had always strictly cared for his sick in spite of deficiencies of medicines, but that he had refused to attend Major Ferriar because he " poured upon me a shower of most opprobrious and vile epithets ".[5]

Courts-martial were not infrequent. Lieut. John Brown was tried for neglect of duty in not properly guarding Col.

[1] Archivo Nacional, Caracas, XIV, 211, 214, 216; XII, 59.
[2] *Ibid.*, VII, 153, 157.
[3] *Ibid.*, VII, 158.
[4] *Ibid.*, VII, 154.
[5] *Ibid.*, VIII, 100.

Wilson during his imprisonment at Old Guayana.[1]   Lieut.
Fitz-Thomas was court-martialed for attacking at night and
wounding one Máximo Seferino.[2]   The self-same Capt.
Hippisley, who was too ill to join his command in the field,
was found guilty of conduct unbecoming an officer and a
gentleman in drinking at the same table with two non-commissioned officers and two creole shopkeepers, and in striking Sergeant William Delany of the Guard of Honor of
Gen. Páez.[3]

Not only at Angostura, where they first met the people
for whom they had come to fight, but at the stations also
to which they were later sent for recruiting in the Orinoco
valley or for field training along the Apure, did the legionaries complain of hardship and ill-treatment.   No matter
where they went they were discontented and disappointed at
what they found.   With bright visions of wealth and glory
rudely shattered, they began to realize that this was real war,
and no longer a crusade of knights errant or a species of
foreign picnic party.   They might well have known that an
army fighting in the tropics would have to endure even
greater hardships than those inseparable from any war.
They should have expected unusual suffering and been prepared to meet it cheerfully.   But they had so deluded themselves and had been so deceived by their own commanders
that when they stood face to face with the truth, it gave them
a shock to correspond.   Discouraged and disheartened, they
rent the air with their ululations.

As to the truth of the conditions which they met, it is
hardly fair to judge from the reports which they wrote while
in this state of mind.   Considerably later the accounts of
their experiences became more cheerful and appreciative.

[1] Archivo Nacional, Caracas, IV, 481, 486, 490.

[2] *Ibid.*, XII, 139, 215.

[3] *Ibid.*, VIII, 83.

Yet since friends at home had these early complaints as the only basis on which to form an opinion, it might be well now to examine them, with due allowance for prejudice.

In the first place, these men from Europe could not understand the Spanish-Americans and disliked them accordingly. The attitude was quite mutual. On their part the Spanish-Americans looked upon the strangers with suspicion, and showed their dislike at having to give up so many of their best posts to foreign officers.[1]

The people of Angostura, as of the rest of the province of Guayana, seemed haughty toward these folk from abroad, whose presence they appeared to resent as that of interlopers and needy adventurers. They despised the English in particular as heretics; at least so the latter felt was the manner of their reception. Although the Venezuelans publicly hailed the legionaries in proclamations, as " generous strangers ", many of the colonial officers showed themselves jealous of their allies and suspicious of their motives in coming.[2] The English, on the other hand, did not consider themselves welcomed with the cordiality to which they believed they were entitled in sacrificing themselves for the people of so benighted a land. Capt. Hippisley, whose own record it will be remembered was none too good, asserted that " the English were objects of narrow-minded prejudice " and deemed " intruders in the country in whose defense they had bled. They were insulted by the inhabitants, who derided them as slaves purchased for hides and tallow," fancying that the troops had been sent from England in exchange for mules and bullocks exported from Venezuela.[3]   Ignor-

---

[1] Schoffer in *El Universal,* Caracas, June 12, 1911.

[2] Brown, *op. cit.,* 88, 89; *The British Monitor,* Jan. 18, 1818; Robinson, 122; *London Chronicle,* Feb. 14, 1821; *The Times,* April 18, 1817; Sept. 7, 1818; *Campaigns and Cruises,* I, 69; Chesterton, *Narrative,* 117.

[3] Lieut. Col. Hippisley's Writings, *Eve of Saint Simon,* 155; Robinson, *op. cit.,* 198.

ance of each other's language also heightened necessarily the feeling of mutual suspicion and misunderstanding.

By way of exemplifying this reciprocal attitude, it may be said that, shortly after his arrival at Angostura, Col. Hippisley was invited to attend a banquet of welcome given by the local commandant, Gen. Montilla. Neither the general nor his staff knew much English. During the banquet Gen. Montilla, flushed with wine and imperfectly understanding a friendly remark of Col. Hippisley, imagined himself insulted and ordered the latter placed under arrest. For a while it looked as if a combat might ensue between the officers of the two services. Fortunately Col. Hippisley accepted his incarceration with composure and forbade his officers from making any attempt to release him by force. The affair was subsequently allowed to blow over as a misunderstanding, after Gen. Montilla, acting on cooler and wiser counsels, rescinded his order.[1] While this incident may be taken as a striking, rather than an altogether typical instance of the sentiment between the creoles and their European allies, it does indicate a lack of cordial cooperation.

Their reception accordingly was not calculated to arouse the enthusiasm of the British soldiers who had come so far to fight for liberty. In fact their ardor tended steadily to cool at what they saw; and every day the conditions under which they were forced to live increased their disillusionment. Those who had been soldiers before expected as a matter of course that an active campaign would necessitate the endurance of hardships. When they were actually in the field they were reconciled to spending many a night in the open; but while they were doing garrison-duty at the headquarters of the army, under the very eyes of the commander-in-chief, they did feel that they might at least be quartered in proper barracks, rather than in mere open sheds, destitute

---

[1] Hippisley, *op. cit.*, 252, 257, 261.

of every convenience, even of beds, and where they were compelled to stretch themselves upon a thin straw mat spread between them and the stone or brick floor.[1] Even this slim comfort could not be long enjoyed, for the houses so swarmed with fleas and other vermin that sleep was impossible, and relief could be found only by abandoning whatever shelter the roof afforded and throwing themselves on the bare ground outside. The officers, too, found the ground the best couch obtainable, except for those few lucky ones who were invited by British residents to become their guests, or for those who were wise enough to sacrifice some article of clothing in barter for a hammock to sling between two trees.[2] In European campaigns officers at least had been accustomed to having tentage issued them if no better accommodations were available.[3]

For a short time after their arrival at Angostura they were fairly well off so far as food was concerned, for they had brought with them flour and other supplies which had remained unconsumed during the voyage.[4] As soon, however, as these stores were exhausted they were compelled to subsist on the rations furnished by the insurgent authorities. These consisted of two pounds of beef per day for each officer, and one pound for each man. Bread was not to be thought of. Maize and plantains were never issued. It was meat, meat, and nothing but meat, without even salt.[5] And such meat! Large herds of wild cattle ranged the plains and, since culti-

---

[1] Hippisley, *op. cit.*, 273; Richard, *op. cit.*, 90.

[2] Chesterton, *op. cit.*, 24; Robinson, *op. cit.*, 91.

[3] British Museum, Egerton Mss. 9842, G. O. 1, April 12, 1815, Army General Orders, British Army in Belgium.

[4] Brown, *op. cit.*, 89; W. J. Adam, *Journal of voyages to Marguaritta (sic) Trinidad and Maturin,* 113.

[5] Richard, *op. cit.*, 90; Chesterton, *op. cit.*, 150. *Autobiografía del General José Antonio Páez,* I, 96.

vation of the fields had ceased, furnished the sole food supply of this part of the country. When a distribution of rations was necessary, a bullock was lassoed and tied to a stake. It was then killed by stabbing in the neck. Very often no attempt was made to bleed the animal properly before it was skinned. The flesh was then torn and scraped off the bones with utter disregard of precautions to keep it clean. The fact that it might be covered with sand and grit as well as flies, when issued to the ultimate consumer, apparently received little consideration by those in charge of the operation. To secure this ration, even the officers must go for it themselves, and each one carried home his chunk of beef in the heat of the day to cook it as best he could without utensils.[1] Then, when the best pieces had been issued out for immediate roasting, stewing or boiling, the remainder, consisting generally of the muscular tissue, was cut into long narrow strips and hung in the sun to dry for several days. When these strips had become as hard and dry as rope they were considered properly cured, and could be kept indefinitely. Meat so prepared, called " tasajo ", constituted the national food. Sometimes the curing process was accelerated by rubbing the strips of meat in salt, but salt was a luxury seldom to be had. This constant diet of saltless beef, washed down with stagnant or muddy water, not only seemed tasteless and insipid to the Europeans, but caused them much suffering from intestinal disorders.[2]

In addition to sickness brought on by the lack of proper food, the legionaries also suffered their share of the mortality due to the ordinary tropical diseases and the periodic scourges of yellow fever, which devastated Angostura and other places along the Orinoco valley. Sergeant-Major Thomas Higgins

[1] Letter to *Cork Advertiser* reprinted in *British Monitor*, Jan. 17, 1819.

[2] Robinson, *op. cit.*, 106, 166, 172, 235; O'Leary, *Narración*, I, 531; Hippisley, *op. cit.*, 296; Brown, *op. cit.*, 91; Richard, *op. cit.*, 272.

was the first of the Hussars to die from this cause. His death occurred in April, 1818, while the troops were still on board the vessel bringing them to Angostura. Immediately after landing Lieut. Plunkett was taken mortally ill, and two of the men also. From that time on two or three died almost every day; and the fever carried off so many natives as well that there was not wood enough to make coffins for them. Among those who perished of yellow fever at Angostura were Captain Brown of the Second Hussars and Major Mahony and Colonel Trewren, formerly of the First Hussars. A German sergeant was fatally poisoned by eating " coco de mono " (monkey-nut).[1] Edward Winton, a merchant of Angostura who had loaned money to the patriot government, was even allowed to die in penury. Supported awhile by the charity of the British, he might have gone to his grave without a shroud had not his black washerwoman, poor as she was, furnished it as a last remembrance of her master.[2] The effects of Capt. Poole, another officer who succumbed to the unhealthful climate, were sold to pay for supplies furnished during his last illness.[3]

Hardly less serious were the infections caused by the bites of insects. When walking along the river banks or through the bush it was almost impossible to avoid the myriads of minute insects, called " chegoes " or " jiggers ", which attached themselves to the men's legs and burrowed into the skin, beneath which they laid their eggs. The first symptom was an intolerable itching and the appearance of a small pustule with a black speck in the center. If this pustule were allowed to break, the eggs would hatch and the sore spread

[1] Hippisley, *op. cit.*, 244, 561; *British Monitor*, Oct. 24, 1819; *Campaigns and Cruises*, I, 140, 152; Richard, *op. cit.*, 257.

[2] Lieut. Col. Hippisley's Writings, *Republican Perfidy*, 521.

[3] Elsom to Olivares, Aug. 22, 1819, Archivo Nacional, Caracas, Gobernación de Guayana; also IX, 142, 144, 150.

so rapidly as often to cause gangrene and even loss of the limb. The only cure was to cut out the pustule, taking care not to break it, and to fill the incision with the ashes of a cigar or cigarette. An even more serious swelling was that caused by the " maldita " which covered the arms, hands, legs and feet with ulcers that ate to the very bone, attended with inflammation, foul discharges and excruciating pain.[1]

The sufferings of the legionaries from these diseases were greatly aggravated by their ignorance of how properly to clean and care for the sores, which rapidly became dangerous and, in some cases, incurable.[2] When the British soldier went to the hospital he enjoyed no comforts there and received little attention from the creole doctors who could not understand his needs, or even from his own English and Irish doctors who lacked the medicines on which they were accustomed to rely. Lying unattended on the hard ground, sweltering with the heat, without water, and driven to desperation by the attacks of swarms of sand-flies and mosquitoes, those who came to the hospital ill with fever welcomed death as a relief from their miseries.[3]

If he had had a little money in his pockets, the foreigner might have mitigated his hardships and kept up his strength by eking out his rations with cassava bread, eggs or the liquor known as " aguardiente "; but since neither officers nor men received the money that had been promised them, the men had to go without any of the little comforts which money might have bought, and the officers had to sell the expensive articles of equipment with which they had supplied

[1] Robinson, *op. cit.*, 177, 178, 221; *Campaigns and Cruises*, 42. Chesterton, *op. cit.*, 90, 154.

[2] Chesterton, *op. cit.*, 25; Adam, *op. cit.*, 84; Richard, *op. cit.*, 90. Archivo Nacional, Bogotá, Guerra y Marina, Historia, III, 472, 473.

[3] Robinson, *op. cit.*, 235; Chesterton, *op. cit.*, 90.

themselves in London.[1] The creole soldier expected to have
to serve without pay. To the Europeans this was the severest hardship and the bitterest cause of discontent. They
complained that all they could get was what they could plunder.[2] At one time it was decided that pay should be granted
to colonels and captains at the rate of ten " cut dollars " per
month, to lieutenants eight and to cornets six; but, they
asserted, even these amounts were not paid until the end of
the second month after they were due. A month's pay indeed was scarcely enough to purchase a few small loaves of
cassava bread.[3]

In their efforts, accordingly, to ward off hunger, the needy
officers sought purchasers for their surplus clothing and
equipment, but found that their Spanish-American brothers
in arms were hard to bargain with, and would pay only a
small fraction of the value of the articles. A saddle and
bridle that cost seven guineas in Dublin brought about fifteen
shillings. Capt. Adam was forced to sell all his books to pay
the expenses of an official mission upon which he was ordered. Hippisley received only a hundred " cut dollars "
from the disposal of most of his outfit. Bolívar himself
bought Col. Hippisley's cap and his cocked hat with a feather
in it.[4] Gen. Manrique acquired so much that he was able
to appear every day in a new uniform.[5] The British, on

[1] Hippisley, *op. cit.*, 295; Chesterton, *op. cit.*, 118; *London Chronicle*,
Jan. 15, July 21, 1819; *British Monitor*, Jan. 17, 1819; Robinson, *op. cit.*,
108; *Journal des Voyages*, XII, 30; Ducoudray-Holstein, *op. cit.*, II, 82.

[2] *London Chronicle*, March 23, 1818; Alexander Walker, *Colombia*, II,
433, 580; Archivo Nacional, Caracas, Gobernación de Guayana, X, 1;
Archivo Nacional, Bogotá, Guerra y Marina, Historia, III, 846, IV, 140;
Richard, *op. cit.*, 270.

[3] Brown, *op. cit.*, 89-91. A " cut dollar " was approximately equal to
two shillings, sixpence.

[4] Adam, *op. cit.*, 20, 50; Chesterton, *op. cit.*, 116, 118; Hippisley, *op. cit.*,
295, 447.

[5] O'Connor, *op. cit.*, 59.

their part, were soon reduced to the clothes they had on.
The once gaudy uniforms became threadbare.   It was considered a remarkable feat that any of the officers still pre-
served two legs to their once gold-laced pantaloons.[1]   A pair
of cotton drawers soon stood between many an English
gentleman and nakedness.[2]   On one occasion, so it is said,
Col. Rooke appeared at a banquet with his coat pinned
together with thorns to hide the absence of collar and shirt.
When Bolívar told his servant to give the Englishman a shirt,
the servant replied that Bolívar himself had only two, the
one he had on and another in the wash.[3]

When their shoes wore out, both officers and men went
barefoot.   Even colonels marched without shoes.   A story
is told of Capt. John Thompson, who happened by good luck
to have kept an extra pair of boots which were the admiration of his companions.   The fact that he alone of all the
officers did not have to go barefoot gave the gallant captain
such a feeling of guilt, because he was not sharing their
hardships, that one day he threw the boots into the river,
remarking that though they were worth their weight in gold,
he was ashamed to be better off than the rest.[4]   When a
colonel had but one shirt, he did not think it beneath his
position to be seen washing it in the river.   Officers formed
regular parties for the purpose of laundering their clothes on
the rocks in the river at midnight, detailing one of their
number to scare off the alligators.[5]

Among the creole troops at Angostura there were more

---

[1] Robinson, *op. cit.*, 150, 162, 163.

[2] *London Chronicle*, Jan. 15, 1819, *British Monitor*, Jan. 17, 1819;
Chesterton, *op. cit.*, 116.

[3] Col. John Potter Hamilton, *Travels through the interior provinces
of Colombia*, I, 232; *Boletín de Historia y Antigüedades*, XIII, 37.

[4] Michael G. Mulhall, *The English in South America*, 303, 304.

[5] Brown, *op. cit.*, 931; Robinson, *op. cit.*, 124.

officers than men. To those used to the discipline of the British army they suggested a mere gang of unfortunate blacks who had been given their liberty in order that they might be shot at by Spaniards or starved to death in the service of the Republic.[1] They did not make a favorable impression certainly on their new comrades in arms. The privates were principally young negroes and mulattoes, most of them mere boys, seemingly not more than thirteen or fourteen years of age, tottering under the weight of their muskets and wearing nothing more than a piece of linen around the loins. Some might wear old military jackets, but would be without pantaloons. Some would be bareheaded, while others might wear straw hats or hairy caps.[2] A uniform one stage more advanced consisted of a pair of Indian trousers reaching to the knee, a blanket with a hole cut in the middle, through which the head was thrust, a large straw hat, feet and legs bare. Such indeed was the uniform worn by Gen. Páez himself.[3] Most of his " llaneros " fought practically naked, and were armed only with a twelve-foot lance, but his guard of honor consisted of three hundred men, dressed like British dragoons.

The ships that brought the legionaries carried quantities of surplus uniforms, sent out by the military contractors for sale on speculation, and subsequent vessels continued to increase the stock; so that, although the foreigners themselves were allowed to go in rags, the scarlet uniform of the British army, awkwardly worn by native soldiers, became no unusual sight throughout the army of the Apure. On the other hand,

[1] Brown, *op. cit.*, 116, 188-192; *Mémoirs du Commandant Persat, 1806 à 1844,* 41.

[2] Brown, *op. cit.*, 72; Chesterton, *op. cit.*, 149, 150; Rev. H. S., *Journal Written on Board H.M.S. " Cambridge" by the Chaplain,* 59-61; Shumacher, *op. cit.,* 15.

[3] Brown, *op. cit.*, 86.

a scabbardless bayonet or a cartridge-box might be slung across a bare back, and a sword might be fastened around the waist with a piece of string. The native officers, who formerly had been content to go barefoot, and to wear nothing but a shirt hanging outside of a pair of short drawers, soon shone resplendent in British uniforms, worn regardless of their proper rank insignia.[1]

Other observers, less prejudiced than those whose pride had been hurt by lack of appreciation, whose pockets were empty from lack of pay and whose stomachs were aching with hunger, looked upon the patriot army with more favorable eyes. One who saw them in Caracas described the regulars as dressed in jackets of Russian sheeting with Osnaburg pantaloons, shirts and shoes. Their apparel was generally in good condition, whole and neat; their leather caps were of the French pattern and polished; their belts and accoutrements well cared for. Each regiment wore its own special color on the facing of its uniforms. The officers were well mounted. This same observer noticed favorably the exemplary attention and silence of these troops, and their excellent marching. He also praised the quality of the military music rendered by the fife and drum corps and bands.[2] A letter, moreover, printed in the *London Chronicle* gave information as to the condition of the patriot forces at San Juan, stating that the discipline and clothing of the creole troops equaled all that could be expected. The necessity of living continuously on beef and a small quantity daily of cassava bread, as a lifelong habit was not, of course, the hardship to them which the European soldiers considered it.[3]

[1] Robinson, *op. cit.*, 137, 163, 164, 194; Chesterton, *op. cit.*, 118, 151; Brown, *op. cit.*, pp. 115, 133 note, 139; *Campaigns and Cruises*, I, 67; *Recollections of Service*, I, 164; Rodríguez Villa, *op. cit.*, III, 246, 698; IV, 11, 51, 108.

[2] William Duane, *A Visit to Colombia in the Years 1822 and 1823*, 53, 54, 100.

[3] *London Chronicle*, July 5, 1819.

Col. Francis Hall, who traveled through Venezuela shortly after the end of the war of independence on a mission for the British government, gave it as his opinion that probably three-fourths of the deaths among English soldiers was ascribable to drink.[1]   A letter published early in 1818, from a young man who had enlisted and sailed on the "Britannia" assured the mother of the writer that he did not regret his expedition.   For certain extra services which he had performed Bolívar had advanced him $200.   The payment, however, had not been made in money, but its equivalent in indigo, coffee and cocoa, which were to be used in lieu of cash for the payment of the troops.[2]   W. C. Jones wrote a cheerful letter to his father describing conditions in the village of Achaguas, telling him that the only inconvenience was the excessive dryness of the soil and the quantity of dust which necessitated keeping the doors and windows closed during the day.   He also said that the soldiers made money by catching wild ducks which they sold for a "real" each and armadillos which brought two "reals" apiece.[3]

Evidently there were two sides to the story.   Because of them it is difficult to obtain an impartial conception of the conditions of service which the members of the foreign legion encountered during the first months after their arrival. As has been shown, most of the accounts covering this period were written by men who became discouraged or disgruntled at their early hardships, and abandoned the cause before they could adjust themselves to the unusually hard conditions of campaigning.   Naturally, the most vociferous complaints came from the weaklings or otherwise unfit who, after their premature return to England, kept the book-stalls supplied with harrowing accounts of the hardships and in-

[1] Hall, *Columbia, Its Present State*, 107.

[2] *Morning Chronicle*, April 22, 1818.

[3] *Journal des Voyages*, XIII, 392-394.

justices they had endured.   Quite obviously Hippisley, Brown, Hackett and Chesterton all believed they had good reasons for venting their spleen against Bolívar and his generals, and other writers were more or less swayed by personal motives.[1]   It is unfortunate that the more earnest soldiers, who remained true to their engagements, did not have equal opportunities for enlightening the news-hungry public of England about the true conditions of the war in South America.

The Morning Chronicle charged that Hackett's book had been written for political purposes, and under feelings of pique and disappointment, by one who went only halfway on his voyage.   His picture of Venezuela did not agree with that given in the intercepted despatches of Morillo.   Many of the adventurers who had gone during the past eighteen months were young men of character and respectability, but a large proportion were not of that description.   Many of the latter had repudiated their contracts and deserted.   Those who had actually joined the patriot army were perfectly satisfied with the conduct of the native officers.[2]   To clinch the argument, next day was printed an unsigned letter, dated Maturín, Aug. 5, 1818, in which the author stated that he had every reason to be satisfied with the treatment he had experienced since his arrival in Venezuela.   He enjoyed the situation of aide-de-camp to Capt. Gen. Mariño and felt every desire to continue on that duty.   He advised those army officers in England who at the time were unemployed that they could do no better than to repair to a theatre where

[1] Walker, *op. cit.*, II, 434; *London Chronicle*, Nov. 29, 1819; Restrepo, *op. cit.*, II, 596, note 40 ª, calls Hippisley's book " a horrible libel against the Liberator and against almost all the patriots of Venezuela "; Galán, *op. cit.*, 13, 14, says " Hippisley resigned and left for Europe, his heart full of hatred toward the Liberator, which is proved by the libels which he published."

[2] *Morning Chronicle*, Nov. 16, 1818.

their talents and courage would be brought into action and ultimately rewarded. A few young men, contemporary with himself in that service, had left it in disgust, but they had not given it a fair trial, and were therefore incompetent to judge.[1]

Subsequently another letter was published, certifying that the reception and treatment of the British officers had been everything that could possibly have been expected. It was written declaredly " to contradict the numerous erroneous reports already circulated by discontents (*sic*) who have left the service " and was signed by James Rooke, Col. Commandant, and by R. L. Vowell, Captain, First Venezuelan Hussars; Thomas E. Smith, Captain, Red Hussars; Thomas Foley, Inspector General of Military Hospitals, and George Bryan, Surgeon of the division of Gen. Sedeño.[2] *The Morning Chronicle* had previously called attention to the character and reputation of those from whom the loudest complaints were heard, saying that many who had never been more than lieutenants expected to become colonels. Others by their intoxication and malpractices not only disgraced themselves, but created such disgust among their respectable companions that the latter were ashamed to be seen in their company. The scurrilous and unfounded attacks in some of the London prints were written either by persons who had not the courage to go to the spot or else by others whom the better elements gladly saw depart, as they themselves felt disgraced by association with such worthless deserters and malcontents.[3] The accounts which they published were no doubt written either to excuse their premature return home, or to vent their spite on those against whom they fancied they had

[1] *Morning Chronicle,* Nov. 17, 1818.
[2] *Ibid.,* Dec. 3, 1818.
[3] *Ibid.*

grievances. The sufferings and injustices set forth in these accounts must therefore be largely discounted, except where they are substantiated by the hospital records, or by the memoirs of those braver spirits who stuck it out to the end.

Difficult though it may be to sift the complaints of disgruntled ones, or to check accurately the exaggerations of protagonists, it can safely be said that those of the legionaries who went to South America as pioneers did not find conditions as favorable as they had been pictured; that many gave up in despair at the earliest discouragements; that those who remained faithful to their bargain in spite of hardships, were the bravest and best among these adventurers; but that all of them, heroes and weaklings alike, were early confronted with a sad disillusionment.

The chief cause of complaint appears to have been lack of pay. Yet, as a matter of fact, such complaints were not entirely justified; for the records of the army paymaster show that although pay-days did not come regularly each month, payments to the troops were made from time to time even during the years 1818 and 1819.[1] Collections also were taken up " for the benefit of the English troops who have come to help us destroy the enemy of the Patria ".[2]

There is, however, no question that the conditions of the campaign in South America were such as to necessitate the endurance of hardships much greater than even the oldest soldiers had encountered on the battle-fields of Europe. In the European armies well-organized commissary and medical departments served to mitigate the rigors of warfare. Good roads enabled wagon transportation to accompany the armies of Great Britain and of France, and to keep them supplied with clothing, equipment, cooking utensils, and

[1] Archivo Nacional, Caracas, Gobernación de Guayana, VIII, 104, 106; X, 2, 3. For an example of one of the pay-rolls, see Appendix D.

[2] *Ibid.*, IX, 25.

sometimes even tentage.[1] In South America, on the other hand, wheeled transportation was almost unknown in the army, for the roads over the plains or across the mountain heights, were mere trails, so bad at times that even pack animals could not keep up with the troops. No matter how long the campaign, each soldier had to carry on his own back or on that of his horse, all the equipment, food, and comforts which he would require throughout the entire time. A change of clothing was an unheard-of luxury. When the clothes with which he began the march fell apart from dirt, sweat and hard usage, he simply went naked, for there was nothing on hand with which to replace them.[2]

The native soldiers in reality were no better supplied or treated than were the British, but the latter suffered more because they were unused to the privations and hardships necessitated by the campaign. The Europeans suffered terribly from the tropical climate which laid them low with fever and dysentery, while the natives felt no differences from the conditions to which they had always been accustomed. Folk who had been brought up from childhood on a diet of beef dried in the sun felt perfectly immune to hunger, as long as the strips of meat lasted which they had stowed under their saddles to be seasoned by the salt sweat of the horses. At times even the beef supply failed, and then the native soldiery contented itself with sucking a stalk of sugarcane. The sweet liquid, drawn out of the woody pith, failed utterly to appease the cravings of hunger of the Europeans.[3] The British soldier could not justly complain that he did not

---

[1] Brown, *op. cit.*, 114; British Museum, Egerton Mss. 9842, G. O. 1, Apr. 12, 1815, Army General Orders, British Army in Belgium.

[2] *Present State of Colombia*, 71, 73; Benjamin Vicuña Mackenna, *El Wáshington del Sur*, 35.

[3] Hippisley, *op. cit.*, 296; Brown, *op. cit.*, 101; Restrepo, *op. cit.*, II, 521; *Recollections of Service*, I, 114.

get as good treatment as his creole fellow, but conditions that did not cause even inconvenience to the native seemed like unbearable hardships to the foreigner.

Thus, combined with a modicum of truth, several half-truths, many exaggerations, and even some falsehoods, accounts of what the " South American adventurers " [1] were encountering came back to England. The widespread circulation of gloomy reports and complaints by returning members of the early contingents did not, however, affect adversely the continued recruiting by Elsam, nor did it seem to dampen the ardor of those whom English sought to enroll under the banners of his new British legion.

[1] *The British Monitor*, Dec. 6, 1818.

CHAPTER V

A British Contingent and Its Prowess

FORTUNATELY for Col. English and Capt. Elsam, they found on their return to England that recruiting was a relatively easy matter; for just at this time the allied armies had been withdrawn from France and Belgium, many regiments had been demobilized,[1] and London, Liverpool, Manchester, Dublin and Brussels were full of discharged soldiers, yearning for the free companionships of the army, and eager for a renewal of their lives of adventure.[2] There was therefore no trouble in finding men, but governmental opposition, or at least the appearance of it, must be reckoned with.

It will be remembered that, when López Méndez began his efforts to raise the first contingents, no positive orders against that procedure had been issued. Two years later the Prince Regent's proclamation, which had been published just about the time the first regiments had sailed, was in full effect.[3] Orders in Council had repeatedly been issued, prohibiting the exportation of munitions to South America.[4] The Treasury had sent instructions to commissioners of cus-

---

[1] *British and Foreign State Papers*, IV, 826, VI, 8; *London Chronicle*, Oct. 28, 1818.

[2] *Bell's Weekly Messenger*, Sept. 21, Dec. 14, 1817; Chesterton, *Autobiography*, II, 37; Wellington's *Despatches*, XII, 731.

[3] *Bell's Weekly Messenger*, Nov. 30, 1817; *London Times*, Dec. 1, 1817; *British and Foreign State Papers*, IV, 488, 489; VI, 130; *London Champion and Sunday Review*, Dec. 14, 1817.

[4] *British and Foreign State Papers*, IV, 140, 731, 732; V, 227, 1024; VI, 510; *London Chronicle*, July 14, 1819; *British Monitor*, June 6, 1819.

toms to enforce the royal proclamation and the neutrality laws, and to stop the illegal preparations which were being made in British ports for sending out officers and men for the service of the insurgent troops in the Spanish-American provinces.[1] The War Office issued a circular, stopping the pay of half-pay officers who might accept commissions under other governments without royal permission; [2] a petition of a lieutenant-colonel on half-pay for permission to raise a " British Legion " to consist of 5,000 men for service under the War Ministry at Naples was rejected by the king; [3] and a general order from the War Office forbade any officer to leave the United Kingdom without special permission from the Prince Regent.[4] Judged by its official acts, the British government was doing its full duty toward preserving its neutrality, but actually the enforcement of its published orders was perfunctory.[5]

This seemingly formidable array of laws and orders indeed was useless in the face of popular disapproval. Recruitment and preparations for sailing proceeded without effective hindrance from officials sworn to enforce the laws. What really happened was, that the authorities contented themselves with giving warnings, instead of acting. Even in the War Office British officers applying for leave to serve in South America, were informed that leave could not be granted for such a reason but if the officer had other reasons for asking leave, it might be granted, and no inquiry would

[1] *British and Foreign State Papers*, V, 1224; *Bell's Weekly Messenger*, Oct. 12, 1817.

[2] *Bell's Weekly Messenger*, Nov. 2, 1817; F. O. 72/204, San Carlos to Castlereagh, Nov. 12, 1817.

[3] *The Gentleman's Magazine and Historical Chronicle*, Jan.–June, 1821, XCI, 178.

[4] *Bell's Weekly Messenger*, Oct. 12, 1817.

[5] *Ibid.*, Aug. 31, Nov. 30, 1817; Chesterton, *Autobiography*, II, 30.

be made as to how he spent his time while on leave.[1] Referring to the Foreign Enlistment Act, Wellington himself said: " The strongest suspicion that a vessel building in the ports of England is destined to be armed elsewhere, or that a particular cargo of arms is destined for the purpose of arming the very vessel in a foreign port, would not justify the government in detaining the vessel or seizing the arms. The vessel being unarmed and the arms entered in the customs as cargo, the law applies only to what can be proved." [2] When an officer of the Coldstream Guards applied for a warrant to search the " Duncombe ", a ship lying off Blackwell, for three deserters of his regiment intending to join the insurgents in Venezuela, on the ground that several of his men had already sailed and he wished to stop the practice, the officer was put off by the Lord Mayor, who replied that he was sorry, but the vessel was not lying within his jurisdiction, so that he would have to refer the matter to the Thames police.[3]

That the Duke of San Carlos was plentifully supplied with information as to what was going on has already been referred to in connection with the organization of the first contingents. In spite of his failure to stop these proceedings, the Spanish minister kept repeating his requests for stricter enforcement of measures to prevent aid being sent to the insurgents. On January 23, 1818, he reported that he had information that the following ships with arms and ammunition for the insurgents had already sailed: the " Indian ", the " Prince ", the " Britannia ", the " Emanuel ", the " Amelia ", the " Emerald ", the " Gladwin ", and the " Morgan Rattler "; and that the " Grace ", which had been

---

[1] *Bell's Weekly Messenger*, Sept. 14, 1817.

[2] Edith Walford, *The Words of Wellington Collected from his Despatches, Letters, and Speeches*, 183, 184.

[3] F. O. 72/228, San Carlos to Castlereagh, Jan. 3, 1819; *British Monitor*, Jan. 3, 1819.

detained by the customs, had been released and was again advertised to sail.[1] On April 13 he invited attention to the insufficiency of measures taken to prevent the sending of aid to the insurgents, and requested the Foreign Secretary to exert his personal influence to enforce the regulations. He stated that a Spanish brig-of-war had reported that many officers had arrived in America recently; and that Lord Cochrane and Sir Gregor McGregor were preparing new expeditions in England; that Renovales had not yet gone; but that successive shipments of arms and munitions from the insurgent agents in London had reached Venezuela, Chile and Rio de la Plata.[2]

To avoid the monotony of too frequent repetition of these complaints of the Duke of San Carlos, it will be sufficient to state that on April 22, 1818, he furnished proof of the arrival in America of the expeditions complained of, by enclosing an extract from the *Morning Chronicle* of that date,[3] and on May 2 and May 25 he called attention to his repeated complaints and his previous letters, which had failed to produce the result he desired of checking the flow of aid to the insurgents.[4] Meanwhile accounts of these same expeditions were appearing in the London newspapers,[5] and their echoes were coming back from America. Gen. Morillo, the Spanish Commander-in-Chief in Venezuela, reported to his minister of war that adventurers of all nations, especially the English, were daily increasing the forces of the enemy. The rebel troops were completely equipped with English arms and uniforms and were gathering a surplus of supplies and arms.[6]

[1] F. O. 72/216, San Carlos to Castlereagh, Jan. 23, 1818.

[2] F. O. 72/216, San Carlos to Castlereagh, Apr. 13, 1818.

[3] *Ibid.*, Apr. 22, 1818.

[4] *Ibid.*, May 25, 1818.

[5] *London Times*, Apr. 11, 1817; *Morning Chronicle*, Mar. 28, 1818; *British Monitor*, Jan. 31, 1819; *Bell's Weekly Messenger*, Oct. 12, 1817.

[6] Rodríguez Villa, *op. cit.*, III, 699, IV, 10, 25.

The wide diversity of the complaints of the long-suffering Duke of San Carlos gives a further clue to the previously indicated trend of British sympathies. Sometimes he protested against the conduct of the captain of H. B. M. frigate "Active" in protecting an insurgent privateer near Vera Cruz;[1] sometimes against the seizure of the Spanish ship "Paloma" by an insurgent privateer manned by British subjects, and the condemnation of this ship by a prize court at the port of Dingle, Ireland;[2] sometimes against calumnious editorials in London newspapers directed against the Spanish monarch and government;[3] and finally he transmitted a copy of the *Morning Chronicle* for October 3, 1818, which showed that the editor was growing bolder because of not having been punished for his previous offensive articles against the King of Spain. The Spanish Minister would now put it squarely up to the Prince Regent whether or not to prosecute.[4]

The British government was impaled on the horns of a dilemma. It must either maintain the strict obligations of neutrality, while at the same time appeasing home sentiment by appearing to favor the insurgents; or it must convince Spain that it was doing its utmost to perform its duty as a neutral, while it was not really doing so at all. The desire for votes being a weightier factor than fear of complications with Spain, it decided to adopt the latter course. It succeeded in performing the difficult feat of facing both ways at once. It smiled blandly at the Spanish Minister, prom-

[1] F. O. 72/217, San Carlos to Castlereagh, Aug. 16, 1818.

[2] F. O. 72/204, San Carlos to Castlereagh, Nov. 3, 13, 19, 24, 1817; F. O. 72/216, May 14, 1818; F. O. 72/204, Castlereagh to San Carlos, Dec. 20, 1817; F. O. 72/216, Feb. 20, June 27, July 18, 1818.

[3] F. O. 72/217; Castlereagh to San Carlos, Sept. 9, 1819; F. O. 72/217, San Carlos to Bathurst, Sept. 24, Nov. 9, 1818; *Morning Chronicle,* Sept. 9, 24, 1818; *The News (London) Sunday,* Sept. 20, 1818.

[4] F. O. 72/217, San Carlos to Bathurst, Oct. 13, 18, 1818.

ising to close its gates at his request, while at the same time managing to indicate to the British public with a wink that one of the gates was still left open, just a crack wide enough to slip through.

The Foreign Office indeed employed its best talent in concocting evasive replies to the complaints of the Spanish minister. It informed him that, in the opinion of the legal advisers of the crown, when editors were tried for libel they were seldom convicted, and that the acquittal of the editors of the *News* and *Morning Chronicle* would produce much more mischief than the articles which had been published against the King of Spain.[1] The Foreign Office assured the Spanish Minister that there was " no reason to fear that the practice of entering into foreign service will extend . . . . because no particular permission or approbation has been given to English officers for entering into the service which forms the subject of this complaint", and because they would lose their pay if they did so.[2] The Duke of San Carlos, moreover, was advised of the impossibility of instituting criminal proceedings to prevent the sailing of the ships and expeditions complained of, " since the licences for the shipments of arms issued have been conformable to statutes, and there is no law which restricts the number of men which may be carried aboard." [3] Nevertheless Castlereagh had ordered an investigation into the violations of the order against the exportation of arms, and promised to report the result to San Carlos.[4] In accordance with this promise, Castlereagh transmitted a report that Capt. Woodbine, late of the Colonial Marines and Commissary to the Indian

[1] F. O. 72/217, Foreign Office to San Carlos, Oct. 16, 1818.

[2] F. O. 72/204, San Carlos to Castlereagh, Nov. 12, 1817; Circular 378, W. O. Oct. 24, 1817; *The Times*, Oct. 28, 1817.

[3] F. O. 72/217, Foreign Office to San Carlos, Dec. 9, 1818.

[4] F. O. 72/216, Castlereagh to San Carlos, Feb. 9, 1818.

Tribes, had proceeded to Jamaica to purchase arms and ammunition to assist the insurgents,[1] for which information San Carlos returned his thanks to the Prince Regent.[2]

Nevertheless, fearing that the Spanish minister might require something more than promises, after the issue of the Prince Regent's proclamation, the solicitor of the treasury was instructed to call upon that envoy for such evidence as the latter might care to furnish in the legal proceedings to be instituted against such persons as might have combined for a conspiracy to violate this proclamation.[3] On May 26, 1819, the War Office put out a circular, directing that there be transmitted to the Secretary of War a list of all British officers, half-pay or otherwise, who might be holding appointments in the Spanish or Portuguese service, or in the service of any foreign power.[4] A bill also to prevent the enlistment of British subjects in foreign service was introduced into Parliament by the attorney-general, came to its second reading on June 3, 1819, and passed a month later.[5]

The opposition aroused by this Foreign Enlistment Act may be inferred from the introduction of a petition from merchants, ship-owners, and traders of Liverpool, who opposed it on the ground that a highly beneficial trade was then being carried on with the patriots of South America, which would be interrupted and thrown into the hands of other nations by the irritation liable to be produced in that region;[6] and by a protest and petition signed by London merchants at a meeting held May 22, 1819, at the old George

---

[1] F. O. 72/216, Castlereagh to San Carlos, Feb. 11, 1818.

[2] F. O. 72/216, San Carlos to Castlereagh, Apr. 16, 1818.

[3] F. O. 72/228, Castlereagh to San Carlos, Feb. 3, 1819.

[4] *British Monitor,* May 30, 1819.

[5] *Hansard's Debates,* 1819, XL, 908; *British and Foreign State Papers,* VI, 130.

[6] *Hansard's Debates,* 1819, XL, 909; *British Monitor,* June 6, 1819.

and Vulture Inn, Lombard Street (made famous by Dickens).[1] The Foreign Enlistment Act in fact passed its second reading by a majority of only thirteen.[2]

Castlereagh continued his efforts to appease San Carlos by transmitting to him a copy of a letter from the Home Department, stating the measures taken for the enforcement of the Foreign Enlistment Act, and by assuring him that similar orders had been issued by the Admiralty and Treasury.[3] Although the Duke of San Carlos was aware of the lack of effect of these measures of the British government, he was required by the rules of diplomacy to pretend to be very grateful, so he wrote repeatedly to Castlereagh thanking him for issuing the proclamation prohibiting the exportation of arms, and transmitting with pleasure the thanks of H. M. the King of Spain for the measure taken by the Prince Regent to cut off supplies of men, arms and ammunition, which were being conveyed from England to the insurgents.[4]

So English and Elsam, undeterred by any serious fears, prosecuted their work of gathering recruits with almost as much publicity as formerly, except that they sent the men away in small detachments on various vessels, instead of embarking them by organizations, as was done in 1817. Bills were posted in public places inviting enlistments. Soldiers were induced to desert from the British army. George Tucker of the 20th Regiment of Foot and Samuel Turner of the 39th Regiment of Foot testified that they had been induced to enlist by Gen. English's promise of three hundred acres of land on arrival in America, or $500 and free pas-

[1] *British Monitor,* May 23, 1819.

[2] *Hansard's Debates,* 1819, XL, 908.

[3] F. O. 72/288, Castlereagh to San Carlos, Aug. 16, 1819.

[4] F. O. 72/204, San Carlos to Castlereagh, Nov. 30, 1817; F. O. 72/216, San Carlos to Castlereagh, Feb. 18, Apr. 16, 1818. *Bell's Weekly Messenger,* Dec. 7, 1817.

sage home after five years, or after independence should have been secured. They had then received tickets and orders to repair on board the ship " Jupiter ", lying at Blackwall. William Cunningham made an affidavit telling how, while in a public-house one night, he had been approached by a sergeant, who offered him a bounty of $80 on arrival in Venezuela, pay at the rate of two shillings per day, allowances the same as in the British army, and after five years' service, $500 and return passage, or fifty acres of land. After treating them to several rounds of drinks, and when some of them were no longer entirely sober, the sergeant had inveigled Cunningham and a party of nine others aboard the ship "Duncombe", which was anchored off Blackfriars.[1]

Account has already been given how Col. Elsam sent to Venezuela ship after ship loaded with officers and men, until 700 of his recruits were gathered there. Meanwhile Col. English was rapidly filling the ranks of the body that was to bear the name, " British Legion ". Everything possible was done to increase the popularity and pride of the new organization. As an inspiring motto, the phrase " Morir o vencer " (" Die or conquer ") was adopted. A legion anthem was composed to the tune of " Ye Gentlemen of England ", the words of which were published in the newspapers, and the music of which was constantly played by the band which formed part of the legion. For the support of this band and for the colors, officers were required to subscribe ten pounds each.[2]

The offers made by English were especially alluring. He promised the officers one-third more pay than that of the same rank in the British cavalry, with all the allowances of the British army. When independence should have been

[1] F. O. 72/228, San Carlos to Castlereagh, Jan. 22, 1819; Chesterton, *Autobiography*, II, 26.

[2] *Ibid.*, II, 29, 30.

gained, officers were to receive grants of land and bonuses ranging from $3,000 for a sub-lieutenant to $10,000 for a colonel; while enlisted men were to be paid two shillings per day with clothing and rations, a bounty of $80 on landing, and at the end of the war to receive a grant of land and $500.[1] The organization of the British Legion differed from that of the troops raised in 1817. Its ranks were fully recruited in England with privates as well as officers and non-commissioned officers, whereas, it will be remembered, the earlier regiments left England as mere skeleton organizations of officers and non-commissioned officers only, the privates, except in the case of the artillery, to be recruited in Venezuela.

The first of the British Legion to embark was Major Beamish's Irish battalion, which sailed from Cork on July 17, 1818. Major Beamish died on the voyage out and was succeeded in command by Capt. Mardyn. After touching at Margarita Island to bury Major Beamish, the ship continued on up the Orinoco and disembarked the troops at Angostura, whence they were to march to join the command of Col. Rooke which was then at the headquarters of Bolívar.[2] Twelve ships subsequently sailed, bearing that portion of the legion which was under the command of Lieut. Col. Blossett, and arrived at Margarita early in February, 1819.[3] Other ships sailed from time to time with smaller detachments. The strength of the British Legion at that time, as shown on its muster rolls, was 1,050 effective men. It had been outfitted by the firm of Herring and Richardson with expensive uniforms, similar to those worn in the British army. These same contractors had also fitted out the ships and stored them

[1] Chesterton, *Narrative,* 34.

[2] *Recollections of Service,* I, 9, 11, 22.

[3] *Ibid.*, I, 9; Brown, *op. cit.*, 160; O'Leary, *Documentos,* XVI, 314. Archivo Nacional, Caracas, Gobernación de Guayana, VIII, 74, XIII, 75.

with provisions for the voyage.[1] The report which reached Bolívar, to the effect that English and Elsam, having accomplished their missions in England, would sail at about the same time and that the two expeditions would aggregate four thousand men, armed, uniformed and fully equipped,[2] was an exaggeration. It was not until the very last that Col. English took his wife with him and sailed, with only a few hundred men, on the headquarters ship " Francis and Eliza " (20 guns) convoying the " Duncombe ".[3] While the " Francis and Eliza " was anchored off Trinidad, the governor, Sir Ralph Woodward, prepared to go aboard and induce as many men as possible to quit the expedition, by telling them the bad state of affairs in Venezuela, but refrained when Gen. English threatened to fire on his boat if he came.[4]

An official despatch, dated Jan. 13, 1819, to Admiral Brión, commanding the patriot navy, informed him of the expected arrival of the expedition under English, and directed him to coöperate with Gen. Urdaneta in receiving and organizing the newly-arrived troops. Margarita Island was selected as the rendezvous, because of its strategic importance near the coast of Cumaná and because of the shelter it afforded the patriot fleet. Furthermore Margarita was the only area along the north coast of Venezuela which, at that time, remained under the control of the patriots.[5]

Upon the arrival of Col. Blossett's battalion the British Legion found Margarita Island anything but a happy home. Quite inadequate provision had been made for the health and comfort of the troops. In addition to the natural disadvan-

[1] Chesterton, *Narrative*, 5; *Recollections of Service*, I, 8.

[2] O'Leary, *Documentos*, XVI, 208.

[3] Chesterton, *Narrative*, 3, 6; Ducoudray-Holstein, *op. cit.*, II, 84.

[4] Chesterton, *Narrative*, 7; *Recollections of Service*, I, 49.

[5] Chesterton, *Narrative*, 12, 13; Rafael Sevilla, *Memorias de un oficial del ejército español*, 36; Urdaneta, *op. cit.*, 150, 151.

tages of this hot, unhealthy island, with its poverty of suitable quarters and equipment and its lack of potable water, there existed a fatal absence of coöperation between the higher military authorities.   Gen. Arismendi, the commander of the island, resented the fact that the command of the newly arrived troops had not been given to him, and placed especial obstacles in the way of Gen. Urdaneta.   Moreover, the requisitions made by the latter upon Angostura remained unfilled, because the poverty of the Republic made it impossible to comply with them.[1]

The troops accordingly were allowed to find quarters as best they might in the fishing shacks along the beach at Juan Griego and in the miserable clusters of huts scattered about the island and dignified with the name of villages at Norte, Juan Griego, Asunción, and Pampatar.[2]   The men found these abodes so filthy and swarming with fleas that they preferred to sleep on the bare ground in the open air.   Having no change of clothing, they were compelled to continue wearing their single shirt and canvas pantaloons for a longer period than was comfortable, or else to go naked while washing them.   Water had to be carried long distances, and even the best of it was so foul as to be almost undrinkable.[3]   The issue of rations was conducted in an uncertain and irregular manner, and on some days was forgotten altogether.   The bonus that had been promised officers and men on landing was also forgotten, and no pay whatever was forthcoming. So hard pressed to obtain food were the men that they cut the lead buttons from their uniforms and palmed them off on the natives as money in payment for bread and fruits.

[1] Chesterton, *Narrative,* 20, 21, 22, 23; *Recollections of Service,* 1, 58; *British Monitor,* Jan. 18, 1818; Marqués de Rojas, *Simón Bolívar,* 185; Urdaneta, *op. cit.,* 153, 154.

[2] Brown, *op. cit.,* 37; Chesterton, *Narrative,* 8, 9.

[3] Brown, *op. cit.,* 122; Chesterton, *Narrative,* 24, 25; *Recollections of Service,* I, 30.

The sympathetic merchants of the island then took up a collection from which they donated two dollars to each soldier. The men, thinking this a trick to defraud them of what was rightfully due, refused to accept this donation until they had been assured it was not from the government.[1]

When on April 7, 1819, Gen. English himself at last arrived, it was expected that conditions would improve. These hopes were destined to remain unrealized, for the general was too indolent and selfish to trouble himself about the comfort of his officers and men. If he made any efforts to secure better treatment from the Venezuelan authorities, he certainly did not press them vigorously enough to produce results. Gen. Urdaneta claimed that the promises which English had made in order to secure recruits were impossible of fulfillment, and that the latter had known as much at the time, and had made them on his own responsibility.[2]

Gen. English treated his officers in a haughty and overbearing manner which inspired them with hatred, while at the same time he took no pains to gain their respect. As a last resort, thirty-six of the officers signed a round-robin protesting against the inefficiency in the issue of rations, and received a severe reprimand for their insubordination. The men joined in open mutiny, refused to parade and threatened to desert to the Spaniards. To quell the mutiny, Gen. English ordered the lash to be used upon the ringleaders and all the men to be drilled six hours a day in the hot sun until they should become better disciplined.[3] Many of the officers asked for their passports to return home. A few of these were granted, but most of them were peremptorily refused.[4]

[1] Chesterton, *Narrative*, 19, 24, 25, 26; O'Leary, *Documentos*, XVI, 315.

[2] Chesterton, *Narrative*, 15, Urdaneta, *op. cit.*, 153, 154.

[3] Chesterton, *Narrative*, 16, 17, 18; Brown, *op. cit.*, 161.

[4] Brown, *op. cit.*, 169, 183, 184, 192; Archivo Nacional, Bogotá, Guerra y Marina, Historia, VII, 003; Archivo Nacional, Caracas, Gobernación de Guayana, XVI, 189, and Ferguson to Zea, June 27, 1819.

As if all these troubles were not enough, the new British arrivals brought an even more serious one with them. Typhus fever, which was then raging in England and Ireland, had broken out on the " Duncombe " and the " Francis and Eliza ", and had not abated by the time these vessels reached their destination.[1]   Many soldiers suffered from a severe flux brought on by drinking the contaminated water, and others fell victims to the yellow fever which was rampant on the island.   Disease spread rapidly and fatally. During the continuance of the fever all work was suspended by the natives.   Within five weeks 250 of them, men, women and children, died.   For convenience the military hospital was located halfway between Juan Griego and Norte.   Here nearly a quarter of the English troops, including two medical officers, were confined with the fever.   Col. Blossett's command was soon reduced to 500, and of these only half were fit for duty.[2]

Other English troops on the island at that time belonged to the artillery.   They consisted of three officers and fifteen men who had remained with Col. Gilmour after the disbandment of his brigade.   These men, as will be recalled, had managed to make their way up the Orinoco in small boats and had reported to Bolívar, by whom Col. Gilmour had been confirmed in his rank and directed to form a siege-train at Margarita.   Nearly a hundred natives had been recruited on the island, and by assiduous drill under the energetic colonel a fairly efficient artillery detachment had been created.[3]   The artillerymen were sheltered under canvas which had been used by the British army in the Peninsular War until it was

[1] Chesterton, *Narrative*, 6.

[2] Chesterton, *Narrative*, 9, 10; Brown, *op. cit.*, 144, 162, 163; O'Leary, *Documentos*, XVI, 263.

[3] Brown, *op. cit.*, 56, 95, 111, 140; Archivo Montilla, III, Urdaneta to Montilla, May 27, 1820.

worn out. It had then been condemned as unserviceable, and had been bought up by the patriots. Although the tents were mildewed, full of holes, and of no protection against the scorching sun or the incessant rain, yet they were made to serve for months more as the only shelter for these artillerymen, who had now been long enough in the country to have become inured to " patriotic living ", as they called it.[1] Col. Gilmour was appointed chief of staff to Gen. Urdaneta, but after a stay of four months on the island was forced to leave on account of sickness, and was relieved by Col. Mariano Montilla. Lieut. Woodbury was attached to the artillery and assigned to duty as adjutant of the general staff.[2] There was also stationed at Margarita the detachment of 150 Hanoverians under Col. Uslar which had arrived at the same time as Col. Elsam's troops. In spite of the difference in nationality, some of them had been incorporated in the British Legion.[3]

Bolívar's object in assembling these troops on Margarita Island was to utilize them in making a raid on the north coast in order to distract the attention of the Spanish commander from Bolívar's own campaigns along the Apure and into New Granada. Urdaneta and Mariño were directed to commence active operations in the northeastern provinces of Venezuela. Mariño and Bermúdez were to head off Mo-

[1] Brown, *op. cit.*, III, 114, 115, 161.

[2] O'Leary, *Documentos*, XVI, 252; Urdaneta, *op. cit.*, 152, 155; Brown, *op. cit.*, 137, 138, 181; Richard, *op. cit.*, 55.

[3] Chesterton, *Narrative*, 21, 22; Six Hanoverian brigades had been attached to the British army in Brussels. British Museum, Egerton Mss., 9842, Army G. O. Apr. 25, 1815. Among the Hanoverian officers under Col. Uslar were Major Freudenthal, second in command, Dr. Nordman, and Capts. Billersbeck and Holst. Of these Capt. Holst., who had been appointed aide-de-camp to Gen. Urdaneta, lost his life in the attack on Cumaná, Dr. Nordman died later at Maturín, and Capt. Billersbeck also succumbed to the hardships of the campaign. Richard, *op. cit.*, 55, 108; Urdaneta, *op. cit.*, 153; also *cf.* Appendix A.

rillo's left wing at Barcelona, while Urdaneta was to sweep down with his expedition from Margarita, effect a junction with them, and occupy Caracas, or at least, to hold all territory on the north coast which he might succeed in liberating from the royalists.[1]   In accordance with these instructions Urdaneta began to mobilize his division, which was to be composed of the British Legion, 800 men; Uslar's corps of Hanoverian riflemen augmented with creoles, 200 men; a column of Margaritans, 500 men; and Gilmour's siege-train of four guns.[2]   However, the liberty-loving Margaritans, who had repeatedly and willingly shed their blood in defense of their homes, now refused to leave their island for a campaign on the mainland, even under their beloved leader, Arismendi.   This general, sympathizing with the attitude of his people, declined to furnish the force called for by Urdaneta. The latter accused Arismendi of stirring up the mutiny, relieved him from command of the island, and sent him to Angostura a prisoner under guard of British troops.   Not until then, and until he had used squads of Englishmen to round up native recruits, was Urdaneta able to raise a quota of 300 Margaritans.[3]

At last on July 14, 1819, the whole force of approximately 1000 English and Hanoverians and 300 natives embarked aboard the ships of Admiral Brión's squadron and sailed for the mainland.   Barcelona, the first objective, was easily taken, although the small royalist garrison of less than 500 men was allowed during the night to escape into the mountains.   The total loss of the attacking force, which was

[1] Mariano de Briceño, *Historia de la isla de Margarita*, 179, 181; Marqués de Rojas, *op. cit.*, 177; Urdaneta, *op. cit.*, 159, 160.

[2] O'Leary, *Documentos*, XVI, 317.

[3] Urdaneta, *op. cit.*, 154, 155, 156; Chesterton, op. cit., 23; Briceño, *op. cit.*, 182; Gil Fortoul, *Historia constitucional de Venezuela*, I, 286; Brown, *op. cit.*, 177; *Recollections of Service*, I, 61-63.

led by Col. Uslar, was only two officers and eleven men.[1] After their entry into the town the patriot troops were suffered to range it as they pleased. They found that the inhabitants, in the haste of their departure, had failed to remove from their houses and shops quantities of spirits of all kinds, principally rum. It was not long before the British, and some of the natives, were in a state of brutal intoxication and entirely beyond control.[2] The commanding general blamed the British especially, saying that so many of them were stretched out dead drunk in the streets and houses, that the section of town they occupied looked like a battlefield after a defeat. He furthermore stated that the 150 Germans under the cool and circumspect Col. Uslar, and the creoles with them, were his only reliance for restoring order and covering the approaches to the city against a surprise by the enemy.[3] Officers were little better than the men and seized the opportunity for looting. Even the officers of Urdaneta's staff led in sacking the church and in stripping it of everything which could be converted into money.[4]

A stay of fourteen days was made at Barcelona, as Urdaneta expected to be joined there by Gen. Bermúdez with supplies of cattle and horses from the plains. The royalists evidently had learned of this plan, for they sent in early one morning a raiding party of horsemen, which pretended to be the advance guard of Bermúdez. Galloping up the streets and shouting " Viva la patria ", they succeeded in reaching the center of the town, when suddenly they threw off their disguise, wheeled about, and dashed out again unscathed, after lancing the patriot sentries and others who happened to

---

[1] *British Monitor,* Sept. 5, 1819; Chesterton, *Narrative,* 27, 29; Cochrane, *op. cit.,* I, 503; Walker, *op. cit.,* II, 418.

[2] Chesterton, *Narrative,* 31, 32; *Recollections of Service,* I, 76, 77.

[3] Urdaneta, *op. cit.,* 161; *El Luchador,* Caracas, May 10, 1912.

[4] Chesterton, *Narrative,* 50; Urdaneta, *op. cit.,* 162.

be in the streets.   They also took prisoner several soldiers and an officer of rank.   Urdaneta repeatedly tried to put himself in communication with Bermúdez, but his messengers were evidently captured by the enemy, for no replies were received.[1]

Although the royalist force which had retired to Espírito, a day's march from Barcelona, was understood to be less than half the size of that which the patriots had, Urdaneta refused to order an advance.   Discontent at their inactivity was increased among the foreign troops by the fact that provisions had run short.   At this time a proclamation, printed in English, from the Spanish commander-in-chief, Morillo, was distributed among the British soldiers, urging them to desert to the royalists.[2]   Induced by this appeal, between thirty and forty deserted with the intention of going over to the enemy.   Of the five who were recaptured, one was shot while attempting to escape.   The other four were tried by court martial and sentenced to be shot.   When led out for execution, these unhappy creatures fell on their knees and begged for mercy.   Gen. Urdaneta relented to the extent of allowing them to draw lots to determine which would suffer the penalty, and then had the two unlucky ones executed in the public plaza.   This scene, enacted in the presence of the division, drawn up under arms, had a discouraging effect on such others as contemplated desertion at that time.   A few days later, information was received that all but eight of those who had escaped had been recaptured by a party of creoles under Col. Montes, and had been treacherously butchered.[3]

[1] Urdaneta, *op. cit.*, 162, 163; Chesterton, *Narrative*, 45, 46; O'Leary, *Documentos,* XVI, 423, 424.

[2] Chesterton, *Narrative*, 42, 43; Urdaneta, *op. cit.*, 163; Rodríguez Villa, *op. cit.*, IV, 108.

[3] O'Leary, *Documentos*, XVI, 424; Morillo, *Manifiesto*, 41, 42; Chesterton, *Narrative*, 48, 49, 55; Urdaneta, *op. cit.*, 163; *Recollections of Service*, I, 91, 92.

After a spiritless pursuit of the Spanish squadron by Admiral Brión which resulted in nothing, Gen. Urdaneta reembarked his division and sailed for Cumaná, abandoning Barcelona without having been able to inform Gen. Bermúdez of the fact. The latter, believing that the patriot forces still held the town, hastened his march in accordance with his orders to effect a junction with Urdaneta at Barcelona. He brought with him several hundred head of cattle and horses, but only two rounds of ammunition per man, in the expectation that he would be able to replenish this from the stores of munitions on Brión's fleet. Bermúdez was attacked by the royalists, who overwhelmed him in his helpless position and forced him to evacuate Barcelona forthwith. In his retreat to the mountains he suffered severe losses, and arrived at Cumanacoa with only a small remnant of his command.[1]

Upon arrival off Cumaná, the British Legion was landed and, after having been joined by a creole force of approximately 200 men under Col. Montes, was marched past Cumaná in order to take up a position in the rear of the city. The troops were forced to struggle through a dense growth of low thick bush, which effectively shut off all breeze. The weather was so oppressively hot, and the march so fatiguing that Capt. Holst, a German and aide-de-camp to Urdaneta, died of exhaustion. After fording a river, the road led to a sandy plain near the town, where the troops bivouacked without shelter of any kind against the heat of the tropical sun. Although the only water available was stagnant and brackish, the men were too exhausted to go back to the river for better. Communication might have been maintained with the fleet, yet Admiral Brión sent ashore no provisions. Col. Montes, however, had driven down from the hills a few

---

[1] Chesterton, *Narrative*, 33, 39, 40, 52, 94, 95; Urdaneta, *op. cit.*, 163, 166; *Recollections of Service*, I, 104.

bullocks, which were slaughtered and furnished the only food the troops could get.   An issue was made at the rate of one pound of beef per man.[1]

Great was the disgust of the foreigners when they learned that Urdaneta again refused to order an attack, and that Brión was anxious to take his fleet out of danger.   Gen. English and other officers waited upon Gen. Urdaneta in a body and remonstrated with him, urging that their men would assuredly mutiny if ordered to march further without being given a chance at the enemy.   Lieut. Col. Lowe, brigade major of the Legion, who had just completed a reconnaissance of the defenses of the city, offered to lead one hundred men, supported by a six-pounder, to an attack on Fort Agua Santa, which he considered the key to the position.   Gen. Urdaneta refused to accept this offer, pretending that he could not dispense with the services of Col. Lowe from his staff duties.   The general had no intention of besieging Cumaná, as he had already made up his mind that now the sole object of his expedition was to penetrate into the interior of the country.   However, in order to give the troops occupation, to distract them from these complaints and to satisfy the officers, he ungraciously told Gen. English that, if he was willing to assume the entire responsibility for the attack, he might take charge.   English hesitated to accept this burden, but when urged by his staff to do so, finally ordered the attack on Agua Santa to be made that very night.[2]

Agua Santa was a block-house surrounded by a deep ditch, and built on top of a commanding hill on the side of the town facing the Gulf of Cariaco.   This hill was steep and rugged without any road leading upward.   Notwithstanding

[1] Chesterton, *Narrative*, 54, 56, 57, 58; Sevilla, *op. cit.*, 241.

[2] Chesterton, *Narrative*, 58, 59; *Recollections of Service*, I, 114, 115; Urdaneta, *op. cit.*, 164.

the fact that the attack was set for two o'clock in the morning of the fifth of August, Col. Montes, who was to have furnished guides, delayed for some reason in sending them until nearly daybreak.[1] Lieut. Col. Harrison commanded the assaulting party of 150 men of the grenadier and light companies, while Major Freudenthal with 100 Hanoverian riflemen supported him. So poorly had the arrangements been made that neither scaling-ladders nor pioneer tools had been provided, nor had any plan of the fort been furnished. The duty of preparing the attack with preliminary artillery fire should have been entrusted to the siege-train, but no orders to that effect had been issued.[2] Two of the guns had been landed at Barcelona under a detachment of sailors, who, after struggling painfully to drag them through the mud, had abandoned them up to their hubs in the tidal flats.[3]

When the guides did finally come, they led the attacking party up the wrong hill. When the treachery was discovered, Major Freudenthal cut one of them down but the other escaped. It was then necessary for the troops to descend again; but before they could climb the right hill they were discovered by the royalist garrison who opened fire upon them.[4] Although there were only two guns mounted in the fort at the time, the sudden discharge of these with salvos of grape for a moment disconcerted the attack. The defenders kept up a continuous fire of musketry through loopholes, and from time to time opened the ports to fire the guns or to hurl out hand-grenades. Meanwhile the attackers slowly advanced in extended order, sheltering themselves behind projecting rocks until they had gained the protection of the

[1] Chesterton, *Narrative*, 60, 61; *Recollections of Service*, I, 115.

[2] Chesterton, *Narrative*, 62, 63; O'Leary, *Documentos*, XVI, 425; *Recollections of Service*, 116, 117.

[3] *Recollections of Service*, I, 72, 73; Chesterton, *Narrative*, 27, 28.

[4] *Ibid.*, 61.

ditch. There they halted, somewhat sheltered from the fire of the guns, which could not be depressed sufficiently to reach them, although in grave danger from the hand-grenades. One section of the bottom of the ditch was by these converted into a veritable volcano. The glacis was drenched with a stream of lead. So heavy was the fire that a house in the rear, which had been chosen as a temporary dressing-station, was demolished with such rapidity as scarcely to permit the removal of the wounded. Further advance was found to be impossible, since through lack of artillery preparation the walls of the block-house remained intact. Had the troops been provided with scaling-ladders, the result might have been different.[1]

After the combat had thus been prolonged for two hours, Gen. Urdaneta, deeming further attempts at attack to be a useless waste of life, ordered a withdrawal. In vain did Gen. English and Col. Blossett entreat him to push the attack further. Col. Blossett had gone forward to the front line and had reported that, owing to the shelter afforded by the ditch, the men were not suffering severe losses and that there was still hope for success. Urdaneta, however, remained immovable and ordered the signal for retreat to be sounded.[2]

When Major Davy who was with the advance heard the bugle, he refused to believe it was intended for him, but continued to press the assault. Just at that moment a squad of sailors arrived with scaling-ladders which were quickly put into place. The men, led by Capt. Saddler of the light company, began swarming up. The captain had reached the top step of the ladder when again the bugle was blown. Just as he looked around to inquire what it meant, he was struck by a musket-ball in the head, and fell backwards dead.[3]

[1] Sevilla, *op. cit.*, 242, 243; Chesterton, *Narrative*, 63.

[2] Chesterton, *Narrative*, 64; O'Leary, *Documentos*, XVI, 425; Urdaneta, *op. cit.*, 164.

[3] *Recollections of Service*, I, 119, 120.

Lieut. Peters and Lieut. Lyons, however, followed by their men jumped to the ramparts and were driving the enemy before them when a third time the bugles were sounded. The order could no longer remain unheeded. Major Davy ordered the fighting to stop and the men to descend the ladders again. In obeying this order, a number of men lost their lives. As Lieut. Peters and Lieut. Lyons attempted to reach the ladders, the former was instantly killed, and the latter fell mortally wounded, only to be murdered with his own sword by a royalist who wrenched it from him.[1]

In their retreat from the ditch the British Legion suffered much more heavily than in the advance, for the royalists immediately resumed their posts and reopened a heavy fire upon the backs of the men as they withdrew. At the same time a detachment of seventy royalists was sent in pursuit, with orders to harass the retreat as far as the main body and to take prisoners if possible.[2] Three British officers had given up their lives in vain and seventy-seven more officers and men were stretched dead or dying on the ground. Almost all the wounded eventually died, for in that climate even trifling wounds brought on lockjaw, and serious wounds meant certain death. The royalist loss was only five killed and sixteen wounded. Thus ended in disaster the glorious attack which should have brought laurels of fame.[3]

The only success won by the British that night was the dispersal of two companies of royalist troops returning to Cumaná from the garrison of Cariaco in ignorance of the state of affairs. Many of these men were killed, and a captain and three men were captured. According to the custom of the " war to the death " in vogue at that time, these prisoners were stripped naked, bound together, and then

---

[1] *Recollections of Service*, I, 121, 122; Chesterton, *Narrative*, 65.

[2] Sevilla, *op. cit.*, 244, 245.

[3] Chesterton, *Narrative*, 64, 65; *London Chronicle*, Oct. 21, 1819.

were stabbed in the back of the neck until they were dead, much to the horror and disgust of the British.[1]

It was later learned that even if Agua Santa had been captured, it could scarcely have been held, for it would in all probability have been leveled to the ground in five minutes by the guns of Fort San Antonio which dominated it.[2] Since, however, Gen. English had been allowed the command on this occasion, he was blamed, even by his own men, for the disastrous retreat. The disgrace and shame so weighed on his mind that he is said to have died of remorse. However that may be, Gen. English was sent back to Margarita on account of illness, and died there shortly after from fever.[3]

Before the fleet returned to Margarita, the troops were transported to the harbor of Madera, whence Urdaneta began his march inland to join Bolívar. His route was to take him via Cumanacoa and thence into the interior of the " llanos " to his destination at Maturín, where in accordance with the instructions of Bolívar he was to intern himself with the British Legion in a situation where it would be impossible for it to rebel. There the foreigners were to be mingled with the troops of the country, so that they might be trained to adopt the native customs, food and mode of living of the Venezuelans.[4] As a first step in this process of disciplining, 350 of the men had been assigned to duty as marines aboard the ships of Admiral Brión's squadron.

The permission to return to Margarita, be it said, had been readily granted to Gen. English, because Gen. Urdaneta

[1] Sevilla, *op. cit.*, 245; Chesterton, *Narrative*, 66, 67; *Recollections of Service*, I, 125, 126; O'Leary, *Documentos*, XVI, 426.

[2] *Recollections of Service*, I, 122, 124; Chesterton, *Narrative*, 175.

[3] *London Chronicle*, Dec. 2, 1819; Chesterton, *Narrative*, 70; Ducoudray-Holstein, *op. cit.*, II, 113, 114; Urdaneta, *op. cit.*, 165; Francisco Burdett O'Connor, *Independencia americana*, 22.

[4] Restrepo, *op. cit.*, II, 520; Urdaneta, *op. cit.*, 165.

felt that his presence was an embarrassment rather than a benefit to the division. In the opinion of the division commander, that officer lacked every quality of command and energy of spirit to repress the disorders of his foreign soldiers. After the departure of Gen. English, Col. Blossett succeeded to the command.[1]

The march to Maturín accordingly began on August 19, 1819, and lasted ten days. It was conducted without rest, in the height of the rainy season, and under discouraging conditions, which were exaggerated in the minds of the Englishmen already dispirited by their defeat at Cumaná. The fine uniforms with which they had left England had, by this time, been worn to shreds and failed to protect them against the cold and wet of the mountains. Their rations were of the most meager sort, some days being limited to a stalk of sugar-cane per man. While the native troops managed to subsist on this, the foreigners soon became so weak they could hardly drag one foot after another.[2] To add to the hardships of the march, the rains had converted the roads into morasses of mud into which men and horses sank above their knees; and small streams, which under ordinary conditions were mere brooks, had been swollen so that they overflowed their banks. Those who were too weak to breast the swirling current were carried down, drowned by the muddy waters. Nevertheless the column was hurried along without rest, for it was pursued and incessantly attacked by strong royalist detachments which hung upon its flanks and rear. Those men who fell exhausted were left behind either to starve, to fall a prey to " tigers ",[3] or to be put to death by

[1] Restrepo, *op. cit.*, II, 520; Urdaneta, *op. cit.*, 165, 166; Brown, *op. cit.*, 165.

[2] Chesterton, *Narrative*, 69, 70; *Recollections of Service*, I, 131, 134; Briceño, *op. cit.*, 183; Urdaneta, *op cit.*, 166.

[3] The Spanish word " tigre," meaning tiger, is commonly used in South America to designate the animal known in English as the " jaguar ".

the enemy.   Many preferred the prospect of death rather
than to return to the ranks and prolong their agony.   The
overcoming of one obstacle meant only the necessity of
grappling with another.   Owing to the fact that Admiral
Brión's squadron had sailed in such a hurry as to leave behind many of the sick intended for transportation to Margarita, these unfortunate men, who were hardly able to stand,
had to struggle along with the column as far as possible.
When at last they fell exhausted, their clothing was stripped
from them for reissue to the well men, and the poor wretches
were left behind naked and helpless.   Out of 140 who reported at sick call at Cumanacoa and were there abandoned,
only thirty ever rejoined.[1]

Had they been cheerful and inspired by hope of victory
and reward, the men might have lightened their distress by
joking over their discomforts.   But a defeated army finds it
hard to joke, and an army without pay never does.   A care-
free soldier loves to complain, though his growl is received
by his comrades with a smile; but when all growl at once
and no one smiles, then mutiny is in the air.   Keeping a
soldier's stomach or his pockets empty is the surest way to
drive away his smiles.   The British resented the fact that
their promised pay had never been received; their spirits
faded away with their strength; lacking food, they became
weary, worn, and discouraged; they could see no hope ahead.

As day after day went by and the difficulties of the road
became harder and harder, the men lost all sense of loyalty
to the cause which they felt had not treated them justly.
They preferred to brave the dangers of the forest alone, and
dropped out of the column when they saw an opportunity.
Many even deserted to the enemy, feeling that nothing could
be worse than their present condition.   Emboldened by the

---

[1] Chesterton, *Narrative*, 68, 76, 77, 80; *Recollections of Service*, I, 134,
137, 138; José M. Rivas, *Biografía del ilustre prócer, General Rafael
Urdaneta*, 155.

success of individuals in getting away, whole squads tried to scatter into the woods. Companies refused longer to advance. It was feared that the British Legion would desert *en masse*. A strong rear guard was then formed of Venezuelan troops, with orders to scour the woods for deserters, capture them and force them back into the column. One day the march led over the lofty, cloud-capped " Impossible " Hill, so called because of the steepness of the trail and the discouragingly difficult preliminary ridges and ravines, each higher or deeper than the one before, which caused the weary traveler to despair of ever reaching the true summit. This proved the last straw, and one of the British battalions refused to continue. The rear-guard was brought up to force them forward, and a regular battle ensued. Not until sixteen of their number had been killed did the mutineers yield and consent to resume the march. His eyes opened by this incident to the seriousness of affairs, Urdaneta ordered the horses and mules of the officers to be killed and issued as meat, in order to feed the men into a better humor.[1]

At last on August 24 they reached Maturín, but the abundant supplies which had been promised them there proved to consist entirely of beef and cassava. To the officers were issued three pounds of beef and a two-pound loaf of cassava bread per day, but the rations of the men were limited to half that quantity. The officers displayed an unsoldierly spirit in not sharing the hardships of their men. They even attempted to fare better, at the expense of those who looked up to them for protection. The higher the rank of the officer, the less he appeared to appreciate the responsibilities of his position. A consignment of wines, rum, porter and flour, which had been sent by some merchants of Trinidad

[1] Chesterton, *Narrative*, 72, 81, 84; *Recollections of Service*, I, 134, 140; George W. Crichfield, *American Supremacy*, I, 37; Rivas, *op. cit.*, 154, 155; Restrepo, *op. cit.*, II, 520; Urdaneta, *op. cit.*, 166; Carlos Benedetti, *Historia de Colombia*, 547.

as a present for the use of the British Legion, somehow managed to arrive at Maturín, but it never reached the men. The field officers kept all these luxuries for their own exclusive use. Not even the company officers were allowed to share them, except on rare occasions when they dined as guests of the field officers' mess.[1]

With such conduct on the part of their officers it is not surprising that the spirit of the men was not of the best. The only real relief which they experienced after their arrival at Maturín was a chance to rest and recuperate from the hardships of their march. Most of the luggage of the Legion had been carried off in the ships of Admiral Brión, leaving both officers and men destitute of the few comforts which they had hoped to retain. Even a change of clothing was impossible. The shacks in which they were quartered were overrun with rats which lived in the straw walls. Swarms of sand flies added to their miseries, and the arms and legs of many were festering with sores caused by the "maldita". Surgeon Murphy reported that the sick were dying for lack of medicine, and urged Gen. Urdaneta to send a " flechera " down the river to obtain a supply from Trinidad, but the general was apparently too busy gambling for high stakes with Gen. Valdés and Col. Montilla to bother himself about such a matter.[2] The strength of the British Legion had become reduced to 400, only 233 of whom were effective. The vacancies in the higher grades were filed by promotions, and Lieut. Woodberry became adjutant general with the rank of colonel, the field officers being Col. Blossett in command, with Lieut. Col. Harrison, and Majors Davy, Carver and Ditton.[3]

[1] Chesterton, *Narrative*, 85; *Recollections of Service*, I, 153, 154, 155; Adam, *op. cit.*, 82, 83, 84; *Apoteósis de Bolívar, Ofrenda del Estado Bermúdez en el primer Centenario del Libertador, 237.*

[2] Chesterton, *Narrative*, 68, 85, 87, 90; Adam, *op. cit.*, 82, 83; *Recollections of Service*, I, 154, 155.

[3] Adam, *op. cit.*, 70.

The spirit of the organization became so poor that even the officers secretly plotted means of deserting. Some tried to escape by boat to Trinidad; others, when refused permission to resign, left the command without authority to seek better posts with headquarters at Angostura. Duels among them were of frequent occurrence. Col. Stopford, an attached field officer, communicated with Angostura, and tried in vain to secure a promise from the congress that it would consider the claims of the British based on the recruiting promises of Gen. English.[1] Gen. Tomás Montilla, chief of staff to Urdaneta, answered that the members of the organization were the property of the Republic, which had arranged to pay a certain sum for their services. If they did not give those services willingly, they would be compelled to do so. The fact that no pay had been received made no difference. They were still the property of the Republic and must so remain.[2] Gen. Urdaneta requested to be relieved from command of the division, saying " six months with this division is worse than ten campaigns; it has cost patience, constancy, and even self-respect to keep the division together ".[3]

Gen. Urdaneta was thereupon transferred to a command in New Granada, and his division was left under the orders of Gen. Mariño, who was kinder to the British, increased their rations of cassava bread, and distributed $1.50 to each man and a few dollars to each officer.[4] Bolívar, feeling that his own presence was necessary at Maturín, made frequent journeys thither in the intervals when his attention could be spared from the organization of the congress of Angostura.

[1] Chesterton, *Narrative*, 92, 120; Richard, *op. cit.*, 106; *Recollections of Service*, II, 46, 47.

[2] Chesterton, *Narrative*, 91.

[3] O'Leary, *Documentos*, XVI, 426; Rivas, *op. cit.*, 156.

[4] Chesterton, *Narrative*, 97, 98; Urdaneta, *op. cit.*, 167, 168; Rivas, *op. cit.*, 156, 159; O'Leary, *Narrative*, I, 545; *Documentos*, XVI, 394; *Recollections of Service*, I, 167, 168.

Finally, to keep the British remnants more closely under his own eye, he ordered them transferred to the army of Páez on the Arauca.[1]

Páez, in command of the army of operations of the west, which at this time consisted of about 5,000 well-armed, uniformed and disciplined troops, was actively engaged in a campaign against Morillo's 3,000 royalists; but as his tactics consisted principally in raids and sudden onslaughts against detachments of the enemy, in which the speed and endurance of his creole lancers were utilized to the utmost, he did not always call upon his infantry to join in these forays. At the capture of La Cruz, he sent the infantry back, because they experienced difficulty in crossing a ford. The famous victory of Queseras del Medio was entirely a cavalry fight, in which Páez with 150 horsemen captured 1000 of all arms of the enemy. Serving in his army there was such a superabundance of British officers that Páez had formed from them a mounted guard of honor, in which they retained their rank as officers but did duty as privates.[2]

In March, 1819, reorganization was effected by Bolívar. This placed the entire foreign force under the command of Col. Rooke, comprising the Dragoons of the Guard of Bolívar, the artillery under Lt. Col. Thomas Ferriar, and the two Rifles battalions, the first under Col. Pigott, made up largely of native troops although officered by Britons, and the second under Major John Mackintosh,[3] which was at the outset composed entirely of British and Germans.[4]

[1] O'Leary, Documentos, XVI, 206, XVII, 201; Apoteósis de Bolívar, 237; Niles Weekly Register, II, 123; Urdaneta, op. cit., 171.

[2] O'Leary, Documentos, XVI, 207; London Chronicle, Oct. 21, 1819; Páez, Autobiografía, I, 182, 183, 184, 193; Chesterton, Narrative, 117; Level, op. cit., 316.

[3] John Mackintosh, who had been commissioned as sergt. major, Aug. 15, 1818, had begun his service in the campaign of the lower Apure, and had taken part in the action of Trapiche de Gámara under Bolívar. Archivo Nacional, Bogotá, Guerra y Marina, Historia, XXX, 912.

[4] Peñuela, op. cit., in Repertorio Boyacense, no. 64, 780.

Early in June Col. Rooke, with the Second Battalion of Rifles [1] and a detachment from the First Battalion, had followed Bolívar in his campaign into New Granada. This left behind the remaining foreigners under the command of Lieut. Col. Ferriar. These were consolidated with the British Legion when it arrived, enlarging it to two battalions of infantry (eight skeleton companies) and a squadron of dismounted cavalry. As shown on a report of strength, dated at Achaguas, Jan. 7, 1820, the English (sic) Legion at that time was assigned to the first column of the infantry division and contained fourteen officers, one of whom was sick, and 130 non-commissioned officers and men, twenty-five of whom were sick.[2]

During 1819 and 1820 Páez was unremittingly engaged in conducting guerrilla operations against Morillo, in order to deceive him as to what was really going on in New Granada and to prevent him if possible from detaching a sufficient force to interfere with Bolívar's campaign. Altogether these months were busy ones for the British soldiers, who were kept marching and countermarching; making raids and surprises against royalist outposts; taking prisoners; herding cattle; foraging for rations; shipping munitions; building barracks and drilling recruits; [3] yet they had enough leisure

[1] See Chapter VIII. After the battle of Boyacá the name of the Second Battalion of Rifles was changed to "Albion Battalion". Previously it had also been called "English Rifles" and "Cazadores Británicos". *Present State of Colombia,* 95. Col. Carlos Cortés Vargas, "De Arauca a Nuncia" in *Memorial del Estado Mayor del Ejército de Colombia,* September 1919, number 89, p. 229; Archivo Nacional, Bogotá, Guerra y Marina, Historia, VII, 414; General Order signed by Carlos Soublette at San Juan de Payará Jan. 20 (1820) in private archives of Dr. Vicente Lecuna, Caracas.

[2] O'Leary, *Documentos,* XVII, 28, 29; Archivo Nacional, Caracas, Gobernación de Guayana, XIV, 136.

[3] Páez, *op. cit.,* I, 193, 197; Peñuela, *op. cit.* in *Repertorio Boyacense,* No. 64, 780; L. Florez Álvarez, *Campaña Libertadora de 1821,* 92-144.

while at Achaguas to suffer from sickness, from too frequent desertions, and from internal discords.

The climate seemed to enervate the mind of Col. Blossett, so that he became irritable and apathetic toward the interests and comforts of those under his command. He was easily accessible to flattery and influenced by sycophants. This weakness was taken advantage of by Brigade Major Traynor,[1] a former sergeant whom Col. Blossett promoted to captain and brigade major. This officer was arrogant and overbearing toward those who had formerly ranked him, and it was said that he influenced the colonel toward adopting such severe and unjust measures that the men under his command were ready to revolt. Then having prepared the fuse, Traynor touched the match to it by ordering Lieut. Risdale into arrest for not preserving proper discipline in a fatigue party. According to the account told by another officer, this young lieutenant had been ordered to supervise a detachment which was working unwillingly in the hot sun. Many of the men were under the influence of liquor and when Risdale, who was popular with them, was placed in arrest, they gave vent to their indignation by abandoning their work and running about crying " Down with Blossett ".[2] In the heat of their excitement they attacked some creole officers of the garrison and wounded Lieut. Col. Davy who attempted to check them. Then Traynor, acting with his usual arrogance and lack of discretion, instead of firmly quelling the trouble when it was nothing more than a drunken row, egged the men on to the commission of real acts of mutiny. The next day six sergeants were ordered executed

[1] Capt. John Traynor served in the patriot army for a little over three years from 1819 to 1822, in the British Legion, in the " Columna Sagrada " and in the " Bravos de Orinoco " Archivo Nacional, Caracas, Illustres Próceres de la Independencia (folio not yet numbered).

[2] Lieut. Col. Hippisley's Writings, *Eve of Saint Simon*, 158, 161.

as ringleaders of the revolt, but Capt. Hadskinson,[1] of the light company, refused to give the order to fire the volley. Next an offer of promotion to a lieutenancy was made to any sergeant who would see that the order was carried out, and Sergt. Gill agreed to fulfil it. In the meantime, however, the six sergeants made a break to escape, but were cut down by creole troops as they ran. The execution of Lieut. Risdale and of the two privates who had wounded Lieut. Col. Davy was nevertheless carried out as planned, and accomplished nothing except to increase the spirit of gloom and resentment throughout the whole command.[2]

Col. Blossett indeed seemed to grow steadily more morose and irritable. About this time there arrived at Achaguas a battalion of an " Irish Legion " which had been raised by Gen. D'Evereux.[3] When its commanding officer, Col. William Middleton Power,[4] claimed that he had been promised the rank of brigadier-general, Col. Blossett, who had been a fellow officer of his in the same regiment in the British army, could not control his jealousy and tried to undermine

---

[1] Capt. Richard St. John Hadskinson was born in England in 1798 and entered the army of Venezuela at the age of twenty. He served as an officer of the British Legion and the Boyacá Battalion in the campaigns of Oriente, Apure and the province of Caracas. At one time he was detailed as official instructor for the valley of Aragua. Archivo Nacional, Caracas, Ilustres Próceres de la Independencia LXXXV, 113; Vicente Dávila, *Diccionario biográfico de ilustres próceres de la independencia suramericana*, II, 253.

[2] Lieut. Col. Hippisley's Writings, *Eve of Saint Simon*, 163-166; Level, *op. cit.*, 375, 376.

[3] *Cf.* Chapter VII.

[4] William Middleton Power had been a major in the British army in Egypt, in the same regiment in which Col. Blossett was then serving, the 28th Regiment of Foot. He had obtained from D'Evereux the colonelcy of the First Regiment of Light Infantry, Irish Legion, with the promise of a commission as brigadier general. Bolívar refused to confirm this appointment on the ground that the congress alone could grant such high rank. Archivo Nacional, Bogotá, Guerra y Marina, Historia, VI, 771.

the latter's character with the commanding general. Failing in this, Col. Blossett sought every opportunity to offer insults to Col. Power. The latter stood these as long as he could do so without being called a dastard by his brother officers. At last Col. Power called Col. Blossett to account and killed him in the ensuing duel. Thereupon Col. Power felt obliged to resign from the service and asked for a return of his commission and a settlement of his accounts.[1] After the death of Col. Blossett, Lieut. Col. Thomas Ferriar succeeded to the command.[2]

The British Legion as such did not arrive in time to be engaged in the actual campaign of Boyacá, although Bolívar had contemplated postponing this campaign until its arrival;[3] but it facilitated his operations in New Granada by its apparently fruitless attacks on Barcelona and Cumaná and its heart-breaking march to Maturín. Urdaneta's raid on the north coast had served a useful purpose by distracting Morillo's attention away from New Granada, and by causing him to hold most of his force in a position to protect Caracas, for the safety of which he feared.[4] The concentration of 1819-1820, under Gen. Páez, of the British troops had brought the major portion of the legionaries together for the first time. Before very long they were to be augmented by more individuals and further organizations which continued to gather in the Old World, preparing to cross the sea to do their part in the liberation of the New.

[1] Lieut. Col. Hippisley's Writings, *Apparition Adventures*, 631; Level, *op. cit.*, 337; Archivo Nacional, Bogotá, Guerra y Marina, Historia, 771, 773-777.

[2] *Present State of Colombia*, 99; Dávila, *op. cit.*, 175; Archivo Nacional, Bogotá, Guerra y Marina, Historia, II, 504. For a complete roster of the officers of the British Legion at Achaguas, on Dec. 23, 1820, see Appendix E.

[3] Bingham Mss. Bolívar Letters No. 5. Bolívar to Guillermo White, Feb. 9, 1819.

[4] O'Leary, *Narración*, I, 523; *Documentos*, XVI, 282; *Bell's Weekly Messenger*, Oct. 24, 1819.

CHAPTER VI

Two Militant Scotchmen on a Venture

Notwithstanding the numbers who eagerly flocked to the house in Grafton Street, Fitzroy Square, where the London agent of Venezuela received their signatures upon his contracts, all did not move smoothly with López Méndez. Opposition developed in an unexpected quarter, and many of his recruits were weaned away from him by the efforts of José María del Real, diplomatic agent from New Granada. Rather than consider López Méndez as a fellow worker in a common cause, del Real treated him as an upstart rival. Instead of coöperating with each other in securing recruits and raising a loan for the benefit of their common cause, the two agents preferred to dissipate their energies in repudiating each other, and in airing their quarrels in the public press. In such efforts they were ably seconded — López Méndez, by the fertile brain of William Walton; and del Real, by the clever pen of an international soldier of fortune, Col. Francis Maceroni.[1]

[1] *Morning Chronicle*, Nov. 3, 4, 8, 1818; *British Monitor*, Nov. 8, 1818; W. Davidson Weatherhead, *An Account of the Late Expedition against the Isthmus of Darien under the Command of Sir Gregor McGregor*, 3; *Narrative of a Voyage in the Ship " Two Friends,"* 3; Hippisley, *op. cit.*, 3, 4; Francis Maceroni was the author of *An Appeal to the British Nation on the Affairs of South America, particularly as regards those of New Granada*, esp. 4, 28, 29, 30, 39; *Memoirs of the life and adventures of Colonel Francis Maceroni*, esp. II, 432-434, 444; and *Prospectus of a Loan for the Service of the Federated Governments of Venezuela and New Granada, and Proposed in Conformity to the Express Powers and Instructions of the Supreme Government of the Same*. William Walton was secretary, interpreter, compiler of news and propagandist for López Méndez. He kept the *Morning Chornicle* supplied with news of the

139

In this connection it has already been shown how the Spanish government, through the Duke of San Carlos, had become aware of all the stir of preparations against it. The Spanish commander-in-chief in America was warned of the British aid which was coming to the insurgents. In 1818 the Spanish Minister of War informed Morillo that an expedition was preparing to sail from England, under one Gregor McGregor, with eight hundred men and a great train of artillery, embarked on many transports and convoyed by a 30-gun ship-of-war. With an expenditure of 500,000 pounds sterling, Scotch capitalists, it was said, had outfitted this expedition, the object of which was, not to join any particular insurgent force, but to raid the cities on the Spanish Main and capture Vera Cruz.[1]

This Gregor McGregor [2] was just at that time one of the

insurgent cause in Venezuela. The information on which he based his articles came from William White of Trinidad, who in turn received it direct from his friend, Bolívar. In one of his letters Bolívar urged White to send as much information as possible to Méndez and Walton, " so that the news of patriot successes may influence the opinion of the English people." As part of his propaganda, Walton published in London a pamphlet entitled the *Present State of the Spanish Colonies.* Of this book Bolívar wrote: it " is a compilation of what Spanish-American writers have published and deserves credit for the influence it will bring, but it will receive little appreciation because of its poor style and composition." Walton appealed to Bolívar for payment of his expenses and services in propaganda, parliamentary lobbying and raising expeditions and aid for the insurgents. As a reward for his services, Bolívar accordingly contemplated appointing him consul for Venezuela in London. Bingham Collection of Mss., Bolívar Letters, Bolívar to William White, Nov. 22, 1817, June 24, 1818, *Cartas de Bolívar,* 1799-1822, 229; F. O. 72/216, William Walton to Bolívar, July 15, 1817.

[1] Rodríguez Villa, *op. cit.,* III, 357, 674, 696.

[2] Gregor McGregor, born in the highlands of Scotland, had entered the British army at an early age. After reaching a captaincy, he had been obliged to sell out his commission, because of a misunderstanding with his commanding officer. Then, after a short period of service as a major in the Portuguese army, he had again been forced to withdraw for insubordination and unmilitary conduct. On his return to Edinburgh, he

chief sources of controvery between López Méndez and del Real. Without any valid commission or authority from Bolívar, or from any other insurgent government as far as is known, he had assumed the rank of major general and the title of " Commander in Chief of all the Forces, both Naval and Military, destined to effect the Independence of the Floridas, duly authorized by the constituted authorities of the Republics of Mexico, Buenos Ayres, New Granada, and Venezuela '" and with a force of 150 filibusters, raised in the West Indies and the United States, had captured Amelia Island, at the mouth of the St. Mary's River, adjacent to the Spanish province of East Florida. By the sale at a dollar per acre of 3,000 acres of land which he promised to capture in Florida, he obtained funds from merchants in Savannah, and on June 25, 1817, had sailed from Charleston with the

had assumed the titles of colonel and count, and had become known as Sir Gregor McGregor. In 1812 he embarked for Caracas, and became a colonel of cavalry under Miranda, who had raised the standard of revolt against Spain. He there married Josefa Lovera, a niece of Bolívar. Upon the collapse of Miranda's revolution, McGregor escaped to Cartagena, where he led armies of the insurrection in a campaign in the southern provinces of New Granada. When Bolívar again aroused the forces of revolt in Venezuela, McGregor joined that leader and took part in the expedition against Margarita Island and the capture of Carúpano. In 1816, after Bolívar's defeat at Ocumare, McGregor gained distinction by keeping the patriot army together and conducting an able retreat for thirty days, leading his army safely into Barcelona. *Cf.* Chapter I. Feeling that his services had not been adequately recognized, McGregor then resigned his commission and went to Margarita Island, where he was persuaded by Gen. Arismendi to go to the United States and raise a force for the capture of Florida. O'Leary, *Documentos,* XV, 85, 90; *Narración,* I, 357-359; Rafter, *op. cit.,* 19, 20, 22, 24, 42, 65, 81, 87; *The Times,* Jan. 2, 15, 1817; *Bell's Weekly Messenger,* Aug. 24, 1817; Cochrane, *op. cit.,* I, 370; *View of South America and Mexico by a citizen of the United States,* 87; *Exposición documentada que el General Gregorio MacGregor dirigió al Gobierno de Venezuela y resolución que a ella recayó,* 1, 2, 3, 4; Palacio Fajardo, *op. cit.,* 169; Hippisley, *Acts of Oppression,* 21; Archivo Nacional, Bogotá, Guerra y Marina, Historia, VII, .008; Archivo Nacional. Caracas, Ilustres Próceres, XLIX, 46.

vanguard of his expedition. On July 9 he had led fifty-four of his men, charging through a swamp, in an assault on the fort of Fernandina. So surprised had been the Spanish garrison that without having fired more than a single gun, the fort had been hastily evacuated.

In order to secure the conquest of Florida, McGregor should have marched at once to attack St. Augustine, but instead he contented himself with establishing a form of government for Amelia Island with himself at the head. As soon as his treasury became exhausted he had been glad to accept an offer of Commodore Louis Aury, formerly of the French navy, and had turned over to him the empty treasury and the government of the island on condition that the latter should assume his debts. Col. Irwin, however, formerly an officer in the American militia, who had been appointed adjutant general and treasurer, resented the change and treated his former commander in such an insolent manner that McGregor felt constrained to abandon his men and to return to his base at Aux Cayes, whence he sailed for England.[1]

After his return to England from this abortive expedition against Amelia Island, McGregor had persuaded López Méndez to advance him 1,000 pounds on the strength of his promise to raise a new force and transport it to America. When the money had been spent without the materialization of the promised expedition, the Venezuelan agent had had McGregor arrested for debt; but a wealthy merchant, named Newte, had opportunely come to the rescue and paid the sum necessary to open the gates of the prison. McGregor

[1] The Times, Aug. 16, 29, 30, 31, Sept. 2, Oct. 8, 1817; London Chronicle, Mar. 26, 1819; Bell's Weekly Messenger, Aug. 10, Dec. 14, 1817; Narrative of a voyage in the ship "Two Friends," 85, 86, 87, 96, 150; American State Papers, Foreign Affairs, IV, 130, 292, 450; British and Foreign State Papers, IV, 814; Annual Register, 1817, "General History," 160; Rafter, op. cit., 91, 95, 100, 107, 109.

had then offered his services to the representative of New Granada. When del Real accepted his offers and announced himself as the patron of Gen. McGregor, the dispute between the two diplomats had become so acrimonious as to threaten the success of the cause which both represented.[1]

Thus, aided by the influence of del Real, supported by the funds of Newte and advertised by the glowing periods of Col. Maceroni, McGregor spread far and wide alluring accounts of the gold and glory awaiting in America those who should invest in his offerings or should follow his banners. Applicants for commissions gathered from England, Scotland, Ireland, France and the Netherlands.[2] Captaincies were eagerly bought for 50 pounds, and lieutenant-colonelcies for 150. It was said that for a sufficiently large cheque on a Lombard Street bank, Col. Maceroni stood ready to bestow the baton of a field-marshal. Fashionable military tailors competed in designing glittering uniforms, and offered to equip the general gratis, in return for his patronage and favor. McGregor became a lion of the hour and was visited by many of high social position, among whom were the Dukes of Kent and Sussex.[3] Money poured into his coffers from dupes whom he sent away to various ports to wait for ships which never sailed. In Dublin, Col. Eyre raised the " Regiment of Hibernia " from the sale of commissions in which he collected 13,000 pounds. The difference between this sum and the 7,000 pounds which he spent for chartering ships went to swell the profits of McGregor's venture. For

[1] F. O. 72/217, San Carlos to Bathurst, Nov. 3, 1818; F. O. 72/228, San Carlos to Castlereagh, Jan. 22, 1819; *Morning Chronicle*, Nov. 2, 1818; *British Monitor*, Jan. 10, 1819; *Exposición documentada*, 4; Maceroni, *Appeal*, 9, 10, 11, 20, 21, 25, 26, 27, 33; *Present State of Colombia*, 101.

[2] F. O. 72/217, San Carlos to Bathurst, Oct. 15, 1818; *British Monitor*, June 13, 1819; Rafter, *op. cit.*, 119, 140; Maceroni, *Appeal*, xxx, xxxi.

[3] F. O. 72/217, San Carlos to Bathurst, Nov. 3, 1818; Rafter, *op. cit.*, 119, 122, 123; *Narrative of the Expedition under Gen. McGregor against Porto Bello, by an officer who miraculously escaped*, 7.

the "Wilhelmina Catherina" was paid 2,000 pounds, for the "Mary and Eliza" and the "Henry" 1,800 pounds each, and for the "Little Frank" 1,400 pounds. These ships were not large enough to carry safely all those who clamored to be allowed to go, or the supplies put on board sufficient for the long voyage; but owing to the laxness of the inspections by port officials, excessive numbers, including wives and children, were permitted to embark.[1]

Besides this Hibernia Regiment, there were other regiments, comprising hussars, lancers, light infantry and artillery. During December, 1818, three more vessels loaded with troops sailed from Gravesend, the "Onyx", "Peterburg" and "Monarch". Each was provided with medicine-chests and two or three surgeons. There were also sent a number of smiths, armorers, carpenters, and gardeners supplied with seeds. On the "Monarch" were shipped two portable printing presses, with compositors to operate them. Among McGregor's assistants was Col. Rafter, who raised and organized the rifle regiment of Salabarrieta.[2] Some military men joined these regiments, "but the greater number of officers consisted of young gentlemen of respectable families, who not having been educated for any particular profession, and unable to procure commissions in the service of their native land, embraced with delight a mode of life which, uncertain and adventurous in the extreme, was particularly in unison with their young and romantic minds ".[3]

Recruits poured into Col. Maceroni's orderly room at the Nag's Head, Orange Court, Leicester Square, attracted by

[1] Rafter, *op. cit.*, 124, 128, 129, 131.

[2] Maceroni, *Memoirs*, II, 436, 437; Weatherhead, *op. cit.*, 3, 5; Rafter, *op. cit.*, 158, 160; Col. Rafter had been a captain in the regular army, and had served for eleven years in Holland, the West Indies, Spain and Portugal; Archivo Nacional, Bogotá, Guerra y Marina, Historia, VII, 385, XVI, 945.

[3] Rafter, *op. cit.*, 144.

alluring hand-bills which promised to soldiers enlisting the same pay and allowances as in the British army; corporals to be appointed sergeants and sergeants to become color-sergeants. Furthermore, all soldiers were to be paid $80 on landing in America, to receive their full share of all prize money, and after five years' service, to become the possessors of grants of one hundred acres of land each.[1] Francis Beggs was granted a commission as lieutenant colonel, in return for which he agreed to raise a regiment of infantry, to provide transports, provisions, bedding, and other requisites, and to have everything ready in a year. He was to consider himself under the direct command of " General " Maceroni and was to submit a report of expenses to be paid by credit on the government of New Granada. Unfortunately, however, before he could do this, two of Maceroni's officers ran away with the " Flora " which Beggs had chartered and provisioned at his own expense, and the latter had to pay out 2,000 pounds more for the charter of another vessel.[2] Subsequently Maceroni transferred his attention to the continent. He sent Baron Beauregard to raise an expedition in Belgium, and he himself in France purchased on two years' credit three armed vessels of 250 tons each and 10,000 stand of arms. He also engaged 150 French and Belgian officers and a band of musicians whom he assembled in Antwerp ready for embarkation. Nothing came of these preparations, however, for Del Real lost his courage and refused to sign the contracts.[3]

McGregor himself sailed on the "Hero" (18 guns) from

[1] F. O. 72/228, San Carlos to Castlereagh, Jan. 22, 1819; *British Monitor*, Jan. 10, 1819.

[2] Archivo Nacional, Bogotá, Guerra y Marina, Historia, XXXV, 845, 848. Francis Begg had been a lieutenant on half pay in the Sixth Regiment of Infantry of the British Army.

[3] Maceroni, *Memoirs*, II, 443, 444. Baron de Beauregard had been the director of the imperial arsenal and cannon foundry at Turin.

the Downs on Nov. 18, 1818, and arrived at Aux Cayes, Haiti, about two months later. There he was joined by the officers and men who had preceded him. In the force assembled at Aux Cayes were English, French, Germans and Poles, many of whom were " self exiled from that country which they could no longer serve ".[1]   This motley army was characterized in the Jamaica papers as a " collection of outlaws whom the government had permitted to embark, in order to decrease the poor rates and to save the expense of their passage to Botany Bay ".[2]   A London editorial said:

Some of these half-pay officers—these dressed up dandies— these stuffed turkies (*sic*)—these walking wine vaults, indeed, disgrace the name of Britons. It is a pity a few more of these animals did not join McGregor's band. We could dispense with them. Those who fight under Bolivar's standard might allege some excuse, but surely nothing can be said in favor of those who joined McGregor's standard.[3]

The merchants of Haiti were somehow induced to contribute 300 stand of arms and fifty casks of gunpowder. President Boyer was won over by promises that the negro slaves in the liberated Spanish provinces would be given their freedom, and agreed to provide a schooner to accompany the expedition.[4]   Reduced by desertions to 350, the force sailed from Aux Cayes about the middle of March, 1819. A stop of three weeks was made at the island of San Andrés, of which McGregor took formal possession to hold as a depot for his sick and wounded.[5]

[1] Rafter, *op. cit.*, 142, 143, 144; Weatherhead, *op. cit.*, 3, Archivo Nacional, Bogotá, Guerra y Marina, Historia, XVI, 946.

[2] Rafter, *op. cit.*, 169.

[3] *British Monitor*, July 4, 1819.

[4] Rafter, *op. cit.*, 147; *British Monitor*, June 13, 1819.

[5] *Narrative by an Officer*, 8, 29, 30, 32, 33, 36; *Exposición documentada*, 4; C. Rodríguez Maldonado in *Boletín de Historia y Antigüedades*, Bogotá, V, 265.

Thence the little squadron sailed for the north coast of the Isthmus of Panamá and, on April 9, 1819, arrived off the harbor of Porto Bello. This is a long, narrow bay formed between two promontories which jut out westward into the Caribbean. The town of Porto Bello was on the southern side of the harbor near the head of the bay. The entrance to this harbor was protected by two stone forts, San Jerónimo, adjacent to the town, and San Fernando, across the harbor. The forts were believed to be mounted with 113 heavy guns, besides howitzers and mortars. In the orders for the attack, Col. Rafter was directed to make an assault with the light infantry and lancers upon the rear of the forts, while McGregor himself, and Colonels O'Hara and López, with the reserve and the artillery, should remain aboard the " Hero " to fire upon the forts, in order to divert their fire from Col. Rafter. The latter landed his men on the sea side of the western promontory and marched them across it through an almost impenetrable jungle until he arrived within sight of Fort San Jerónimo. Although the royalists retreated, skirmishing, Col. Rafter made no immediate assault, but lay on his arms all night while the "Hero" kept up an intermittent fire. During the night the garrison completed its withdrawal, so that when the assault was made at daybreak the capture was easily accomplished. After all firing had ceased, the reserve was landed on the east side of the harbor and took possession of Fort San Fernando, without opposition. The garrisons had abandoned the forts without even destroying the guns or removing the powder.[1]

McGregor did not go ashore until the enemy had withdrawn and the town had been captured. Then the doughty

[1] *Narrative by an Officer,* 37, 39, 40, 41; Maceroni, *Memoirs,* II, 437, 439; *London Chronicle,* June 19, Aug. 9, 1819; Maldonado, *op. cit.,* 265; Archivo Nacional, Bogotá, Guerra y Marina, Historia, XVI, 946; Extract from *Kingston Chronicle,* April 22, 1819 printed in Blanco, *op. cit.,* VI, 676.

general stepped into his barge, preceded by a band of music playing the air, " See the Conquering Hero Comes ". On landing, he triumphantly stalked ashore and installed himself in the palace of the fugitive governor where he had the Spanish flag spread out on the floor, and boastfully tramped back and forth several times across it. The royalist garrison, which was said to have numbered 466 but probably not over ninety men of whom only forty were fit for service, had been able to offer an ineffective resistance, and after one of their number had been killed had abandoned the town to Col. Rafter, retiring to Panamá. The loss among the attacking party had been one killed, one wounded, and one missing.[1]

The reputation gained by McGregor from this far from brilliant exploit was soon shattered. Deceived by the ease with which he had overcome a small force of royalists, McGregor relaxed all semblance of discipline, and failed to observe even the commonest military precautions. He allowed his men to mingle freely with the inhabitants and to give themselves up to licentiousness and dissipation. The officers, dined and wined by the principal residents, neglected their duties. Efforts to scout the adjacent country were abandoned, and even the interior guards were suffered to quit their posts. Meanwhile McGregor busied himself issuing proclamations to inform the world how the "Army of New Granada " had covered itself with glory, and designing decorations to be worn by the members of his newly created " Order of the Knights of the Green Cross ". The booty captured at Porto Bello comprised six Spanish ships with their cargoes, and government stores consisting of tobacco, cocoa, cochineal and other merchandise valued at 20,000 pounds. Although it had been agreed that Col. Maceroni

---

[1] Rafter, *op. cit.*, 195, 196, 200; Blanco, *op. cit.*, VI, 676, 677; Maceroni, *Memoirs,* II, 438; *London Chronicle,* June 17, 1819; *British Monitor,* June 6, 1819.

was to be reimbursed for his expenses in outfitting the expedition out of such booty as might be captured, McGregor neglected to send any of this back to England.[1]

When information of this condition of affairs in the captured city reached Gen. Horé, the royalist commanding general of the Isthmus, he raised a force of 500 men, consisting of the Battalion of Catalonia with militia and volunteers, marched forty-seven miles through the jungle, and, early in the morning of April 30, fell on Porto Bello. The English were taken completely by surprise, many of them lying drunk in the streets, and were not aware of the approach of danger until the enemy were in the very center of the town. Col. Rafter alone kept his head and rallied fifty of his men in Fort San Jerónimo. Col. O'Hara, Capt. Acton and Lieut. Stewart were murdered in their beds. McGregor, who was asleep when the enemy entered his quarters, made no effort to join his men, but dressed only in his nightshirt and accompanied and protected by a single staff officer, Capt. Colclough, he jumped out of a window into the sea and swam to one of his ships. When safely aboard, he ordered the ships to slip their cables and escape from the harbor.[2]

Col. Rafter, although he saw himself abandoned by his commander with the fleet, nevertheless made a brave but hopeless attempt to hold out all night. At last he consented to capitulate, on condition that he and his men should be sent to Jamaica or some other British island. Gen. Horé, however, in violation of these terms, marched his captives to Panamá, where he kept them in prison and subjected them to hardships and indignities.[3] Many died in prison, while

[1] *British Monitor*, June 20, 1819; Rafter, *op. cit.*, 207, 215; *Narrative by an Officer*, 47, 48; Maceroni, *Memoirs*, II, 438, 440.

[2] *Narrative by an Officer*, 49, 50, 51, 52, 53, 54, 55; Walker, *op. cit.*, II, 414, 415; Maldonado, *op. cit.*, 266.

[3] Rafter, *op. cit.*, 217, 218, 219, 222, 235; Morillo, *Manifiesto*, 219-

Col. Rafter and eleven others were executed for attempting to escape. The remainder were sent across the Bay of Panama to a " village of Chinamen ", where they were employed on public works and spent weary days carrying heavy logs and stones, while at night they were confined in stocks so that they were unable to rest their tired muscles. Their hopes of obtaining their exchange were shattered by the refusal of the viceroy to accept the cartel which Bolívar proposed. It was therefore nearly the end of 1820 before they were released on the demand of the captain of a British man-of-war. Then no more than five officers and twenty-five men remained alive to enjoy their liberation.[1]

McGregor, after abandoning his men to their fate, fled to Aux Cayes,[2] where he found reenforcements awaiting him. Col. Eyre had arrived from Dublin with two vessels and 500 men of his regiment. The "Lovely Ann", provided by Col. Maceroni, had managed to slip out of Gravesend three days before the Foreign Enlistment Act went into effect, and

220; Rodríguez Villa, *op. cit.*, IV, 36, 37; *Present State of Colombia,* 103-107; *Narrative by an Officer,* 42, 43; *London Chronicle,* June 29, July 2, 5, 19, 1819; Gen. Horé is said to have been an Irishman, named Hoare, a native of Wexford.

[1] Rafter, *op. cit.*, 241; Weatherhead, *op. cit.*, 118; Chesterton, *Narrative,* 135; O'Leary, *Narración,* I, 582; *Narrative by an Officer,* 53, 54, 55; Archivo Nacional, Bogotá, Guerra y Marina, Historia, VII, 385, XVI, 946; Galán, *op. cit.*, 14, 15.

[2] McGregor subsequently explained that his defeat at Porto Bello was due to the treachery of one of his officers, who had engaged with the Duke of San Carlos to deliver him into the hands of the Spanish. McGregor further stated that he had earnestly exhorted Col. Rafter to defend the fort near the town, while he himself with the ships saved the garrison and ammunition of the fort on the opposite side of the harbor. In spite of these instructions, the colors were hauled down by Col. Rafter, within a quarter of an hour. This letter written by McGregor to the *Edinburgh Star* Sept. 28, 1821, is printed in full as an Appendix to G. Hippisley, *Acts of Oppression committed under the administration of M. de Villéle,* 111, 112.

had brought forty officers, French, Italian and British, sixty-one soldiers and eight women, under Col. de Lima and Lieut. Col. Berridge. The schooner " Amelia ", loaded with 750 muskets, 500 pistols, and 400 barrels of powder, had been despatched from London by Newte, and had arrived safely at its destination. In addition to the foregoing, there were several hundred recruits who came from New York and Jamaica.[1]

The members of this expedition had been rendered enthusiastic by the news of McGregor's first success at Porto Bello, and were so keen for further conquest and glory that McGregor was forced to think up some new objective upon which to expend their energy. He therefore concocted a plan to attack the town of Rio Hacha on the north coast of New Granada, where he hoped to make himself master of the waterways and valleys controlling the strategic approaches to the interior. With the aid of Lieut. Col. William Norcott, one of the new arrivals, McGregor set to work to organize the reenforcements, but experienced difficulties, owing to the fact that news of the true state of affairs at Porto Bello had begun to leak out, and because the 80 dollars promised as a bonus on arrival at Aux Cayes, had not been distributed. A battalion of the 1st Lancers mutinied and might have had matters all their own way, had not Lieut. Col. Rafter, another new arrival and a brother of the colonel captured at Porto Bello, surrounded and overawed them with his rifle corps. In spite, however, of these delays, the three small vessels " Amelia ", " Alerta " and " Lovely Ann " weighed anchor and sailed from Aux Cayes on September

[1] Rafter, *op. cit.*, 260, 270, 290; *London Chronicle*, July 23, 1819; *British Monitor*, July 25, Nov. 14, 1819; *The Times*, April 16, 1819; Weatherhead, *op. cit.*, 3; Maceroni, *Memoirs*, II, 435, 442. Col. de Lima was a Portuguese officer, who had been aide-de-camp to Marshal Soult.

27, 1819, with sixty-one officers, one hundred and seventy-six men, and nineteen women and children.[1]

On October 5, the attack on Rio Hacha took place. Night was chosen as the time for putting the troops ashore, but, as usual, McGregor, himself, remained aboard ship, asleep. The attack was led by Lieut. Col. Rafter with the Rifle Corps of Salabarrieta on the right, Lieut. Col. Norcott with the Regiment of Hibernia in the center, and Major Atkinson leading a detachment of skirmishers along the beach. After a five hours' running fight, the defenders were driven out and the city was captured, with a loss of fifty on the royalist side and of seventy-eight officers and men killed and wounded out of the 210 of McGregor's men engaged. The skirmishers advancing along the beach suffered heavily, and Major Atkinson fell mortally wounded. The attack of the right and center was delayed by the ruggedness of the terrain, yet the rocks among which they advanced afforded good shelter and reduced the number of their losses. In the thickness and obscurity of the jungle, the troops became scattered and out of hand, but when daylight disclosed the city below them, they found that the enemy had fled. When he saw the flag of the independents waving over the captured city, McGregor had himself cautiously rowed ashore and reassumed command.[2]

Here, as on the former occasion, he allowed discipline to be relaxed among his own troops, and admitted the inhabitants freely into his councils. To show his confidence in them, McGregor even went so far as to issue arms to the townspeople, on their promise to join the cause of independ-

[1] *Narrative by an Officer*, 18, 19, 24, 25; Rafter, *op. cit.*, 146, 156, 273, 290, 302; Maceroni, *Memoirs*, II, 444; Archivo Nacional, Bogotá, Guerra y Marina, Historia, XXXV, 931; Lieut. Col. Rafter was the author of the *Memoirs of Gregor McGregor,* here quoted.

[2] Rafter, *op. cit.*, pp. 322, 327, 329; *London Chronicle*, Dec. 27, 1819; Maceroni, *Memoirs*, Vol. II, pp. 445, 446; *The Times,* May 10, 1820.

ence. The victors fell into idle ways, spent their time in carousing, and refused to perform their military duties. The men sold their ammunition to obtain liquor, and even the outposts became drunk. The state of affairs was so bad that a number of officers, fearing for the safety of the expedition, decided to desert before it should be too late. Five days after the capture of the city, Colonels Norcott and Rafter, with Surgeon General Nuchett, Surgeon Hunt, Capts. Gilbert, Cox and Low, and Lieuts. Davis and Mullion took possession of a captured schooner and sailed away to Jamaica. On arrival at Kingston, the schooner was replevined by the authorities and the deserters were abandoned to destitution. For years they wandered in poverty through the West Indies, while the two colonels were the only ones ever to reach home.[1]

The same fate that had befallen Porto Bello wiped out the garrison at Rio Hacha. Disgusted with the insolence and license of the foreigners, the townspeople, now well armed rose against their captors, and in a short fight almost annihilated them. McGregor, with a few of the women and children, managed to escape to the ships and abandoned their wounded comrades to their fate. The garrison of the fort blew it up either by gross carelessness, or purposely in order to avoid surrender. All the rest of those left behind were taken prisoners, and were later driven down to the beach, where they were executed in cold blood. Only their whitened bones, rolled about by the high tides, were left to tell the tale.[2] As a final act of perfidy, when Captain Hudson of

[1] Rafter, *op. cit.*, 349, 362; *London Chronicle*, Dec. 27, 1819; Archivo Nacional, Bogotá, Guerra y Marina, Historia, XXXV, 931; *Acts of Oppression*, 19; Maceroni, *Memoirs*, II, 446.

[2] Rafter, *op. cit.*, 371, 372; *Present State of Colombia*, 108; Maceroni, *Memoirs*, II, 448, 449, 450, 451, 452; *Niles Weekly Register*, XVII, 301, Jan. 1, 1820; Galán, *op. cit.*, 15. In a letter to the Editor of the *Courant* dated Edinburgh, October 17, 1821, McGregor explained that while at

the brig " Hero " fell sick McGregor sent him ashore at Port-au-Prince with the high-sounding title of " Rear Admiral of the White to the Free and United Republic of New Granada ", and then ran away with his ship, leaving Hudson to appeal to the Admiralty for redress.[1]

McGregor's utter failure was entirely due to his own conceit, indolence and timidity. He was not lacking in ability, and was clever enough when he chose to be. It required no mean genius of a sort to induce others to work for him, and to persuade so many to follow his standards. After the collapse of his schemes at Amelia Island, his agents had been able to charter eleven vessels, and to send out 344 officers, 1,696 men, ninety-nine women and forty children. It is a sufficient comment on his selfishness, that of these 2,000 souls who entrusted themselves to his guidance only three are known to have reached home again, and one of them was McGregor. Even Col. Maceroni characterized his conduct as that of an imbecile and infamous mountebank.[2]

Rio Hacha he had organized the inhabitants as national troops, principally to protect the town from the depredations of the European troops (his own!) who were from the first moment intent upon plunder. These European troops, he believed, with the exception of their native bravery, were the most unfit class of men that could possibly have been selected for such service. (Yet, McGregor, himself, had selected them.) He further explained that the defeat at Rio Hacha was due to the desertion of Colonels Norcott and Rafter and to the madness of the remainder, who, fearing that they were to be deserted by their officers, turned the guns of the fort on the town. Col. Rodríguez, the commander of the national troops, then called to his assistance a royalist force near the town. To complete the catastrophe, the fort was blown up by a drunken soldier's discharging his musket into the magazine. This letter is reprinted as an appendix to *Acts of Oppression,* pp. 114, 115, 116, 120.

[1] *London Chronicle,* Sept. 9, 1819; *The Times,* Sept. 25, 1819. Hudson may have been the same as the one who tried to induce Colonels Campbell and Hippisley to join him on a raiding expedition against the north coast of New Granada, although no proof has been found to substantiate this assumption.

[2] Maceroni, *Memoirs,* II, 436, 437, 452, Appendix i; *Appeal to the British Nation,* v.

In early life, when serving under the orders of a superior, McGregor had had the reputation of being a brave officer.[1] When he led the famous retreat from Ocumare, he had been considered efficient.[2] As he grew older, however, his energies were more and more devoted to self-advertising. In this he was remarkably successful; but in his obvious efforts to take care of himself he neglected his followers and lost their respect and loyalty. If his men had not realized that they were fighting in a cause in which failure meant certain death, they would not have fought as well as they did, for the bravest of men will lose heart when they suspect that their leader is a skulking coward. McGregor must have known that he did not deserve the success which his men had won for him at Porto Bello and Rio Hacha, and he must have feared that his men were aware of it too, so it is probable that he hoped to win back their good-will by allowing them to do as they pleased. Having once relaxed discipline, he could not recall his men to their duty, and was unable to enforce any precautions against attack. His own statements show that he was afraid of his men.[3] Under such circumstances, his ultimate defeat was inevitable.

During his remarkable career McGregor enjoyed more than his share of good fortune. He had many successes which he did not merit. For his mistakes he had only himself to blame, and his final failure was fully deserved. The fate, into which he dragged so many helpless followers, was

---

[1] Rafter, *op. cit.*, 380.

[2] *Exposición Documentada*, 9, 10; Flinter, *op. cit.*, 192. Even for his celebrated retreat, according to Restrepo, McGregor does not deserve all the praise. The credit should rather be given to Col. Carlos Soublette, his chief of staff, who suggested all the measures adopted, and to the other generals who helped with their advice. Restrepo, *op. cit.*, II, 583, note 21a. Palacio Fajardo, *op. cit.*, 170.

[3] *Narrative by an Officer*, 47, 48; *British Monitor*, June 20, 1819; also *cf.* p. 153, n. 2.

not indeed deserved by them. Their misfortunes were the rungs of the ladder on which he was climbing toward success. But it was a rickety ladder and finally fell apart. Gregor McGregor has left no permanent mark on history. His career is that of an unusually successful adventurer, which at last ended in ruin.[1]

Neither the capture of Porto Bello nor that of Rio Hacha had any part in the plans of Bolívar at this time, nor did

---

[1] After the loss of Porto Bello and Rio Hacha, Bolívar became anxious to rid himself of McGregor, and made no objection when the king of the Mosquito Coast offered him a concession of land there. On the strength of this concession, McGregor announced himself as "cacique" of Poyais, opening offices in London and Scotland to collect funds for the exploitation of a colonization scheme. For a while success crowned his efforts and he was able to live in style and to inveigle numbers of unfortunates into investing their all in his colony. Whole families went out as colonists to the Mosquito Coast, only to find that none of the money entrusted to McGregor had been expended in preparations for their welfare. The farms which they had bought turned out to be jungle and swamps. They found themselves abandoned without food or shelter in an unhealthy land. Large numbers of them succumbed to their hardships, and were carried off by starvation and fever. McGregor went to France to dispose of more of his land and bonds, and was arrested in Paris for alleged irregularities in connection with a concession of 256 square leagues to the Compagnie de la Nouvelle Neustrie. After having been held prisoner in La Force for several months he was in 1826 tried before the Cour Royale and acquitted. Reports of the failure of the colony of Poyais eventually reached Scotland and the bubble burst. McGregor was a ruined man. In 1839 he returned to Venezuela in the hope of obtaining a pension for his services in the army of liberation. His appeals resulted in his restoration to the grade of major-general in the Venezuelan army with one-third of the pay of his grade. He was also the recipient of a grant of money from the government which saved him from dire poverty and enabled him to make his home in Caracas until he died there on December 4, 1845. *Acts of Oppression*, 80, 81, 95, 123, 125; *Exposición Documentada*, 9, 10, 24; O'Leary, *Correspondencia*, XII, 240; Vicente Lecuna, *Papeles de Bolívar*, 12; *Dictionary of National Biography*, XXXV, 95; Eduardo Posada, *Apostillas a la historia colombiana*, 225, 226. Ramón Azpúrua, *Biografías de hombres notables de Hispano-América*, II, 367; Archivo Nacional, Caracas, Ilustres Próceres, XLIX, 46; Maldonado, *op. cit.*, 264-269.

their loss delay in any respect the ultimate acomplishment of independence. Had McGregor invaded Santa Marta in accordance with Bolívar's wishes, he might have coöperated with the latter's plans for the liberation of New Granada, but he made no attempt to advance inland after his occupation of Rio Hacha. He had furnished valuable aid to Bolívar when the army of the patriots was weak and hardpressed, but his real services to the revolution had ended with his resignation from the army of Venezuela, in 1816. The capture of Amelia Island and the raids on Porto Bello and Rio Hacha were the acts of a pirate and filibuster. After 1817 McGregor was no longer a patriot, but a selfseeking adventurer and promoter of tricky enterprises. Bolívar had lost faith in him and characterized his efforts as " ambitious pretensions ", which he feared might work harm to the true cause.[1] After 1816 McGregor held no commission under the revolutionary government; yet because he had once been regularly employed in the patriot army, and because he claimed high-sounding titles,[2] the cause of independence had still to bear the onus for his misdeeds. His exploits received wide notoriety in the London papers;[3] and in the United States his seizure of Amelia Island was considered a most odious and dangerous act of foreign adven-

---

[1] *London Chronicle,* June 17, 28, 1819; *Exposición Documentada,* 4, *Annual Register,* 1819, "General History", 241; O'Leary *Documentos,* XVI, 390; Bingham Collection of Mss., Bolívar Letters No. 5, Bolívar to Guillermo White, Feb. 9, 1819; Ms. plan of campaign signed by Mariano Montilla and L. Brión, March 6, 1820 in Archivo General Montilla. This archive, consisting of three volumes of official and private papers, (folios not yet numbered) of Mariano Montilla, is now at Caracas in the possession of the Misses Uztáriz Montilla.

[2] *London Times,* Aug. 16, 1817.

[3] *London Times,* Aug. 29, 30, Sept. 2, 1817; *London Champion,* Aug. 31, 1817; *British Monitor,* June 13, 20, July 4, Oct. 3, 1819; *London Chronicle,* Mar. 26, June 19, July 2, 1819.

turers [1] who had no standing either with Spain or the insurgents.

McGregor's method of recruiting, and his public quarrels with López Méndez did not increase the respect of the English people for the government of Venezuela; and his wild and extravagant promises that those who joined him should "after five years be possessed of an ample provision for themselves and families for ever" [2] could dazzle only a few irresponsibles, and cause substantial business men to look with suspicion upon all opportunities for investment in South America. On the whole, it may be said that McGregor's activities resulted in more damage than benefit to the cause for which the legionaries were fighting in South America.

Neither McGregor himself nor his men as a body can be called real legionaries. Presumably individuals who landed with him on the mainland, or were abandoned to wander penniless about the West Indies, did drift to Venezuela, and eventually did join their compatriots among the foreign legionaries. Since it is impossible to trace the antecedents of all these Englishmen who fought under Bolívar, and since numbers of foreign recruits joined him independently from time to time, it is but fair to assume that some of these wanderers and soldiers of fortune were the stragglers left behind by previous expeditions. Col. James Rooke was said to have been one of them. [3]

As a possible source of recruitment, McGregor's irregular forces are therefore of interest. There is indeed one clear trail which leads direct from Amelia Island to Angostura.

---

[1] *American State Papers, Foreign Affairs,* IV, 130, 292, 450, *Bell's Weekly Messenger,* Jan. 4, 1818; Message of President James Monroe, Jan. 13, 1818, in James D. Richardson, *A Compilation of the Messages and Papers of the Presidents,* II, 23, 24.

[2] Rafter, *op. cit.,* p. 140; F. O. 72/228, San Carlos to Castlereagh, Jan. 22, 1819.

[3] *Recollections of Service,* I, 121; also *cf.* Chap. I, p. 72, n. 2.

It will be worth while to follow this trail, for the man who made it unquestionably forms a connecting link between the legionaries and McGregor. This man was Donald Mc-Donald.[1]

It will be remembered that Lieut. Col. Donald McDonald, of the First Venezuelan Lancers, had been the first officer among those commissioned by López Méndez to sail from England to join the patriots. In spite of the fact that he had accepted his commission as lieutenant colonel in the Venezuelan army from that agent, McDonald had hopes of obtaining higher rank by arriving early and reporting to Bolívar as an independent volunteer.[2] Therefore he had not waited for the other colonels appointed by López Méndez but, having entrusted the organization of the Lancers to Hippisley, had sailed on July 31, 1817, from Portsmouth on the ship " Two Friends ", with about one hundred other candidates for promotion in the armies of Venezuela and New Granada.[3]

After the vessel had been released from detention at the Liverpool custom-house for navigating contrary to law, the voyage over was enlivened by excessive drinking and, since Col. McDonald had no ability or interest in maintaining discipline, quarrels and brawls among his officers were frequent. These led to the giving and accepting of challenges. By mutual consent most of the duels were postponed until the opponents might stand on firm land again; but two Irishmen, an officer and the apothecary, unable to restrain their

---

[1] Another important person linked with McDonald was Capt. Henry Weir, who served throughout the War of Independence and later became a general in the Colombian Army. Galán, *op. cit.,* 12; Archivo Nacional Bogotá, Guerra y Marina, Hojas de Servicios, XLVIII, 747.

[2] Hippisley, *op. cit.,* 9, 10; *Campaigns and Cruises,* I, 1, 2, 5.

[3] Hippisley, *op. cit.,* 10; *Narrative of a Voyage in the " Two Friends,"* 12; F. O. 72/216, López Méndez to Bolívar, April 15, 1818.

wrath, insisted on facing each other at once, regardless of how much the deck of the ship might heave beneath their feet. Such conditions were not conducive to accuracy of aim, and six shots were fired without either contestant being hurt. The duel was abandoned and became thereafter the standing joke of the voyage, since all but the contestants had known that corks had been substituted for bullets. Even McDonald and the captain of the ship had their quarrel, because the latter had advanced the sum of thirty pounds to save the former from imprisonment for debt at Portsmouth, and McDonald had forgotten to repay his benefactor.[1] While ashore at Madeira, where the ship put in for supplies, the conduct of McDonald's followers was so scandalous as to cause the local authorities to vent their resentment on the regiments which followed and, as will be remembered, to refuse them permission to land.[2]

On arrival at the island of St. Thomas, McDonald allowed full reign to the promptings of his conceited and boastful nature. Having donned his most showy uniform, he paraded about the streets, introducing himself to the officials of the government and claiming the courtesies due his rank. He pretended that he had been authorized to precede some other British regiments, which were preparing to embark for South America, and that the Prince Regent had specially delegated him to assure the patriots of the lively interest felt by his Royal Highness and the British nation in their ardent struggle for independence. These boasts led to McDonald's downfall.[3]

The Danish Island of St. Thomas was at that time de-

---

[1] *Narrative of a Voyage in the " Two Friends,"* 31, 32, 33, 37 ; F. O. 72/217, *San Carlos to Castlereagh,* Sept. 5, 1818.

[2] *Narrative of a Voyage in the " Two Friends,"* 31, 313, note A ; Hippisley, *op. cit.,* 541.

[3] *Narrative of a Voyage in the " Two Friends,"* 38, 41.

pendent for supplies on the neighboring Spanish island of Porto Rico. If the Spanish governor should hear that the Danish governor was harboring enemies of Spain, he might retaliate by placing an embargo on the shipment of supplies to St. Thomas. Fearing this eventuality, the Danish governor issued orders for the expulsion of the " Two Friends " from St. Thomas. The captain of the vessel, heartily tired of his passengers, took advantage of this order, and quietly slipped away one night, abandoning McDonald and many of his officers who were carousing ashore.[1] The "Two Friends" made for Margarita Island, where it met a most unwelcome reception from Gen. Arismendi. The general refused to receive the few officers who still remained aboard, as he wanted men to fight in the ranks, not officers to be given commands. In spite of the fact that Arismendi had the vessel in his power and had stripped it of its guns, it managed to escape before he could confiscate all its supplies. The ship sailed to Aux Cayes, where it ran on a rock and was lost.[2]

Abandoned by his ship on an unfriendly island, without food or shelter or any money to procure them, the plight of McDonald and his companions was pitiable indeed. Even the English inhabitants of St. Thomas refused them help. Some of the officers died from starvation and exposure. The remainder were now not only unable to return to England, but even found small chance of continuing their journey to the mainland where the insurgents held no ports except Angostura. All reports about the insurgent cause were discouraging, for in St. Thomas it was generally believed to have collapsed in utter failure.[3]

---

[1] *Narrative of a Voyage in the " Two Friends,"* 48, 55.

[2] *Ibid.*, 183, 184, 185; Rafter, *op. cit.*, 109; *London Chronicle*, Feb. 6, 1818.

[3] *Narrative of a Voyage in the " Two Friends,"* 5, 47, 48, 50, 51; *Bell's Weekly Register*, Dec. 7, 1817.

At this juncture, an American sea captain, named Lane, of the schooner " Mary ", who was on his homeward voyage, offered to convey McDonald and about thirty of his followers as far as Amelia Island, where they would be able to report to Gen. McGregor for further instructions. During this voyage, after leaving Turk's Island McDonald tried to persuade the captain to alter his course for the purpose of capturing a Spanish fortress on the island of San Domingo, but when a council of war convinced him that he had no arms, except swords and pistols, with which to make the attack, McDonald was compelled to abandon his crazy idea.[1]

On arrival at Amelia Island, McDonald found that McGregor had already gone and that, as already narrated, the independents were divided into two hostile factions, striving for control. With a few boys he at first sided with the French party headed by Commodore Aury, but most of the officers joined the American faction under Col. Irwin.[2] A few of the latter deserted and managed to escape to Charleston, whence they made their way back to England. In the absence of other instructions, and early realizing that there was no opportunity for gaining glory under the state of anarchy which existed at Amelia Island, McDonald thought it best to continue to Venezuela and report to Bolívar.[3]

---

[1] *Narrative of a Voyage in the " Two Friends,"* 54, 72, 73, 74.

[2] *Ibid.,* 78, 91, 95, 98, 99, 100; *The Times,* Oct. 30, Dec. 5, 1817.

[3] *Narrative of a Voyage in the " Two Friends,"* 80, 97, 114, 145, 147, 186; *London Chronicle,* Dec. 3, 1817; Rafter, *op. cit.,* 109, 111, 113, 114; Brown, *op. cit.,* 36; The occupation of Amelia Island by Commodore Aury lasted for only a few months longer. The Spanish Minister to the United States, Luís de Onís, protested because the expedition of McGregor had been permitted to sail from an American port, and the Federal Court of the District of South Carolina issued a warrant for the apprehension of the latter. President Monroe even ordered a ship of war to sail with a commission of three prominent citizens along the southern coast to suppress these operations against the interests of the United States. A detachment of American troops and a squadron were sent to capture

Having persuaded Commodore Aury to furnish them passage, McDonald and twenty of his officers then sailed for St. Thomas, whence they reembarked for Angostura in the ship " Grace ", arriving early in 1819.[1]

While ascending the Orinoco River, McDonald's incorrigible vanity induced him to put on his elaborate uniform for some boat excursion ashore. A party of Indians, thinking his uniform too magnificent for anyone connected with the patriot army, mistook him for a royalist officer and shot arrows at him. McDonald and one of his companions were killed. This disaster occurred near the junction of the Apure River with the Orinoco, where McDonald was on his way to report to Bolívar at Calabozo. Those of his companions who survived were subsequently accepted into the patriot army at Angostura. The news of the death of his fellow officer was received by Col. Hippisley on his arrival.[2]

While the events narrated in this chapter have a dramatic interest, it must be borne in mind that they were only side issues in the history of the legionaries. Donald McDonald died too soon to perform any important service, and Gregor McGregor did more harm than good by his theatrical performances. Meanwhile, however, still another contingent was being raised in Ireland.

Amelia Island. On Dec. 22, 1817, Aury was summoned to surrender. He protested against this demand as unworthy of the United States, but yielded to superior force and withdrew. *American State Papers, Foreign Affairs*, IV, 130, 450; *London Chronicle*, Feb. 4, 1818; *Bell's Weekly Reigster*, Feb. 8, 1818; Richardson, *Messages of the President*, II, 23, 24.

[1] *Narrative of a Voyage in the Ship " Two Friends*," 101, 107, 110; Archivo Nacional, Caracas, Gobernación de Guayana, VIII, 90, 91. Among these were Captains John Johnston and Henry Weir. *Cf.* p. 159, n. 1; also Chapter IV, p. 65, n. 2.

[2] *Narrative of a Voyage in the Ship " Two Friends*," 186; Hippisley, *op. cit.*, 151, 245, 246; Brown, *op. cit.*, 98, 99, note; *Campaigns and Cruises*, I, 49; Level, *op. cit.*, 433; Rodríguez Villa, *op. cit.*, III, 698; Hackett, *op. cit.*, 55; Robinson, *op. cit.*, 148.

CHAPTER VII

The Irish to the Fore

The year 1819 was a busy one in recruiting for the legionaries. López Méndez and del Real continued their efforts to secure officers, and Gen. English and the agents of McGregor were combing the country for recruits. In London William Walton had opened a recruiting office at 7 Carmarthen Street. Others had been established by Col. Maceroni at 17 Norfolk Street and 11 Upper Brookstreet. At 24 Downing Street, under the very shadow of the Foreign Office, a man named Jonté, representing Buenos Ayres, had long been receiving applications from those who were eager to go to South America.[1]

There was still another personage whose efforts produced a vital effect on the subsequent history of the legionaries. This was John D'Evereux, an Irishman who had been forced into exile because of the part he had taken in the uprising of 1798 in Ireland, and had become a citizen of the United States.[2] While employed as supercargo of a vessel loading at Cartagena, he had been introduced to Bolívar, for whom he had offered to raise an Irish Legion of 5,000 men, and to provide the requisite arms, ammunition and military stores, on condition that he be given command with the rank of general of division, and authorized to promise inducements similar to those offered by Gen. English. He was, moreover, to be

[1] F. O. 72/204, San Carlos to Castlereagh, Oct. 12, 1817; F. O. 72/217, San Carlos to Bathurst, Nov. 3, 1818; *Narrative of a voyage in the ship " Two Friends,"* 4.

[2] O'Connor, *op. cit.,* 13; *View of South America and Mexico by a citizen of the United States,* II, 112.

164

paid $175 for each soldier whom he imported into Venezuela.[1] D'Evereux had then returned to Dublin, where he had assumed the rank of major general and had commenced the work of issuing commissions in the Irish Legion.[2]

Most of the officers enrolled had served in the British army, but a number of them were raw and inexperienced, and " were mere infants in the art of war ".[3] Although many of the non-commissioned officers and privates were veterans, little care was exercised in selecting the best material and nearly all who applied were accepted. It was a force more noted for its bravery than for its discipline.[4] The ranks were easily and quickly filled, now that the army had been returned from France and disbanded. By enlisting for service in Venezuela, the men saw not only the certainty of an immediate livelihood, but also the prospect of further excitement and adventure, with a possible chance of making their fortunes in the Eldorado across the seas. They were, alas, soon to learn that the rewards would be hunger, poverty, hardship and sickness for all, and a hasty grave in a hostile land for many.

The glowing accounts of wealth and glory spread broadcast by McGregor and Col. Eyre in their recent efforts to secure recruits had aroused in Dublin a furious desire to enlist, of which the recruiting officers of the Irish Legion took full advantage. Competition between them and those who were recruiting for the Regiment of Hibernia was keen, and soon the rivalry spread to the men themselves. Bitter fights between parties from the rival organizations were of

---

[1] Ducoudray-Holstein, *op. cit.*, II, 84; *Niles Weekly Register*, May 8, 1819, XVI, 191, 192; *London Chronicle*, Jan. 21, 1820; Richard, *op. cit.*, 72.

[2] Rafter, *op. cit.*, 132, 133; *Present State of Colombia*, 108, 109.

[3] Adam, *op. cit.*, 155.

[4] *Recollections of Service*, I, 174; Walker, *op. cit.*, II, 433.

frequent occurrence in the city streets. A newspaper account describing one of them was headed " War between the soldiers of McGregor and those of Bolívar ", and narrated how soldiers who had embarked for South America under the respective banners of McGregor and of D'Evereux had gone ashore at Gravesend, got drunk and engaged in a fight with swords and bayonets, in which some of the participants were dangerously wounded. Another report of police-court proceedings told how D'Evereux himself had appeared as complainant against the brother and brother-in-law of Mc-Gregor, charging them with having attacked him in bed. The defendants pleaded that they had been merely demanding redress from the plaintiff for insulting remarks, which he had written impugning the conduct of McGregor. D'Evereux accepted the apology of the defendants, " and all parties bowed to the magistrate and retired ".[1]

The brilliant uniforms of the lancers of D'Evereux aroused the jealousy of the more soberly clad Hibernians, and weaned from the latter regiment many prospective recruits. This unfair poaching on his own preserves so aroused the anger of Col. Eyre that he challenged D'Evereux to fight a duel. That prudent commander, however, doubtless believing that his blood was too precious to be spilled at so early a date, deemed it advisable to withdraw to Liverpool,[2] where he opened an office for the sale of lands in South America. After he had sent out a shipload of emigrants to the Orinoco, the notoriety of this method of gaining wealth for himself aroused the opposition of the new agents from Venezuela, Fernando de Peñalver and José María Vergara, whose remonstrances stopped his proceedings.[3]

[1] *British Monitor*, Jan. 10, Aug. 15, 1819.

[2] Rafter, *op. cit.*, 128, 132, 134.

[3] Rafter, *op. cit.*, 134; *London Chronicle*, Feb. 1, 1822; *Journal des Voyages, découvertes et navigations modernes*, V, 239. Fernando de

In Dublin, Liverpool and London the offices of D'Evereux were swamped by applicants for commissions in the Irish Legion, by the issue of which D'Evereux made considerable profit for himself. In the sale of commissions his charges increased according to the rank which the commission was supposed to confer; and little difficulty was encountered in persuading inexperienced and modest young applicants for ensigncies that they were justified in accepting commissions as majors or even as colonels. The imposing personality and eloquent tongue of Gen. D'Evereux qualified him eminently for the rôle of a successful salesman of military commissions.[1] Even the great Irish patriot, Daniel O'Connell, was so charmed by this eloquence that he announced publicly that " he never knew a man better suited to such circumstances than Gen. D'Evereux ". He even bought a commission for his own son, Morgan O'Connell, whom he sent with a special letter to Bolívar, asking that the son be permitted to serve on the staff of the Liberator.[2] O'Connell also persuaded the " Irish Friends of South American Independence " to invite D'Evereux to a banquet to be given in his honor at Dublin on July 20.

In his acceptance of this invitation D'Evereux styled himself as "John D'Evereux, member of the Order of Libera-

Peñalver and José María Vergara, sent by the congress of Angostura to secure a loan in Europe, arrived in London on Nov. 20, 1819, where they established themselves as joint agents of Venezuela with López Méndez. After the arrest of López Méndez for debt (*cf.* Chap. IV, p. 75), Peñalver succeeded in obtaining his release. In April, 1820, Peñalver returned to Colombia, leaving Vergara in London to examine the accounts of López Méndez and to cooperate with him in securing additional elements of war and influencing public opinion in favor of the insurgents. *Boletin de la Acadêmia Nacional de Historia,* Quito, II, 282, 283.

[1] Ducoudray-Holstein, *op. cit.,* II, 85; *Recollections of Service,* I, 173; *British Monitor,* Oct. 17, 1819.

[2] Daniel F. O'Leary, *Correspondencia de extranjeros notables con el Libertador,* II, 36, 37; Adam, *op. cit.,* 153; O'Connor, *op. cit.,* 55.

tors, Major General of the army of the Republic of Venezuela and New Granada, commanding the Irish Legion".
Two thousand guests, comprising some of the most distinguished patriots of Ireland, were present and Lord Cloncurry
was in the chair.[1]   The celebrated orator, Charles Phillips,
made a fervid speech in which he stated that, although Spain
might solicit British neutrality, Ireland at least had given her
answer by sending a legion of her chosen youth " to un-
manacle the slave, to unscepter the despot, to erect an altar
on the Inquisition's grave, to raise a people to the altitude
of freedom ", and when their answer should come back " in
thunder on the waters, every age and every clime would
bless their memories ".[2]   The " Irish Friends of South
American Independence " then presented an engraved sword
to D'Evereux, addressing him as the companion of Bolívar
in war as in peace.   D'Evereux replied in a strain of affect-
ing emotion, and " took a comprehensive view of the state
of liberty in Spanish America ".   In responding to a toast
to Bolívar, he thanked the company in the name of his friend,
the gallant and magnanimous President of the Republic of
Venezuela.[3]

No opportunity to advance the social prestige of the
Legion was neglected.   Military levees were held at Morrison's in Dawson St., at which Gen. D'Evereux, accompanied
by his staff, forming a vast circle, all in glittering new uniforms, graciously received select representatives of the rank,
fashion, and beauty of the city.   Patriotic ceremonies aroused
enthusiasm at these assemblies.   When the " lady of Chancellor O'Connell " presented a stand of colors to the First
Lancers, she was very impressive, though evidently much

---

[1] *Morning Chronicle*, July 21, 25, 26, 1819; *Niles Weekly Register*,
XVII, 53-57; Blanco, *op. cit.*, VI, 722.

[2] *Phillips' Speech on South American Liberty*, 2, 3.

[3] *Correo del Orinoco*, May 6, 1820; *London Chronicle*, July 26, 1819.

affected toward the conclusion of her address; and when
Mrs. Putland presented their colors to another regiment, she
assured the colonel that the women of Ireland relied on his
gaining for them triumph and glory. Col. McDonald, in
reply, promised for himself and for his regiment, that they
would shed the last drop of their blood, before the touch of
an enemy should pollute their standard.[1]

The social and personal prestige of D'Evereux and his
officers was supplemented by the employment of recruiting
sergeants and glaring hand-bills in Dublin and other cities.
Before the end of the year 1819, the rolls of the Irish Legion
showed 1,700 names.[2] Subsequently more were recruited;
but despite the assertion of one contemporary,[3] the total
number sent out by D'Evereux at different times probably
did not amount to 2,100.

As rapidly as the regiments were filled they were dispatched on their voyage. Five were ready to sail from
Liverpool about May 1. Haste was necessary because of the
Foreign Enlistment Act. Ten regiments sailed from Dublin
on the very last day before the Act went into operation. In
the hurry of departure the preparations were not always
perfect. One vessel was so overcrowded that it was stopped
by a revenue cutter off Dunleary, and all men in excess of
the number permitted by regulations, were removed. Fifty
men of Col. Meade's regiment, who mutinied because of the
scarcity and bad quality of the food supplied them, were put
ashore from the "Laforey" at Waterford, much to the
indignation of the inhabitants, who objected to the turning
loose among them of so many destitute wretches, at a time

[1] *Morning Chronicle*, July 25, Aug. 6, 1819.

[2] *London Times*, "South American Supplement," May 30, 1912; *Niles Weekly Register*, XVI, 175; XVII, 40, 80; Carlos Navarro y Lamarca, *Compendio de la Historia General de América*, II, 744 note.

[3] Ducoudray-Holstein, *op. cit.*, II, 85.

when it was so hard to provide sustenance for hundreds of their own industrious population.[1]

In organizing the regiment of fusileers, Col. Lyster promulgated the rule that no man was to be received who had not served in the army, or who was under five feet eight inches in height. This regiment, known as " Gen. D'Evereux's Own ", embarked from Liverpool. From that same port the ship " William " sailed on July 5, 1819, with thirty-two officers and 200 men, under Major L'Estrange. The major, who was a cabinet-maker in Dublin, had never been in the army, and was totally ignorant of even the simplest duties of an officer.[2] That same month the " Hannah " sailed from Dublin, having on board one hundred officers and one hundred and one men, among whom was the young lieutenant-colonel of the Tenth Lancers, Francis Burdett O'Connor, in whose memoirs considerable information is given.[3] The commanding officer of the Tenth Lancers, Col. William Aylmer, was also second in command of the Irish Legion.[4]

The commander of the Legion, D'Evereux himself, remained behind in England and Ireland, living sumptuously on the contributions of his dupes, until the return of some of those whom he had cheated, exposed him to danger of being arrested or shot, so that he was forced at last to go. Assuming the rôle of a shipwrecked merchant, returning home with his crew, D'Evereux managed to charter the coal brig "Ariel", in which he sailed from Liverpool with a staff con-

---

[1] *Morning Chronicle*, July 25, Aug. 6, 1819.

[2] *Ibid.*, July 20, Aug. 4, 1819; *British Monitor*, Dec. 5, 1819.

[3] O'Connor, *op. cit.*, 16, 17, 18.

[4] Col. Aylmer had been a lieutenant-colonel of cuirasseurs in the service of Austria against Napoleon, and had been assigned to special duty in England, at the request of the Prince Regent, to instruct the hussars of the British army in continental tactics. O'Connor, *op. cit.*, 14, 15.

sisting of two aides, one colonel, one major, one surgeon, one chaplain, and twenty-two privates, but did not reach Margarita Island until many months after his Legion had departed.[1]

On their arrival at Juan Griego, on the island of Margarita, the early detachments of the Irish Legion found that no preparations had been made to receive them. Neither Admiral Brión nor Gen. English had been informed of their arrival, and the commander of the island was having difficulties enough in supplying the English and native troops already there. The unsuitability of Margarita Island as a mobilization center had already been shown by the sufferings of the British Legion. Similar sufferings were experienced by the men of the Irish Legion, but to an even greater extent because their officers were either too inexperienced to know how to mitigate them, or else too indifferent to exert themselves to do so. Col. Aylmer was in a state of constant inebriety, on account of despair, it was said. Col. Meade was imprisoned because of attempting to obtain rations in an improper manner. Three of the surgeons were taken from the troops and assigned to duty aboard ship. The inspector general of hospitals, Costello, had been a minor apothecary, and none of Gen. D'Evereux's staff had ever served in any military capacity. The men were drilled six hours a day in the hot sun, and were forced to do this on a ration of only one pint of oatmeal (subsequently changed to a third of a pint of rice), and half a pint of new rum per day.[2] Owing to the deficiency of huts or buildings for their shelter, the troops were so widely scattered throughout the interior that even when the hard-pressed commissary officers were able to

---

[1] *Recollections of Service*, I, 176, 177; Ducoudray-Holstein, *op. cit.*, II, 85; Archivo Nacional, Bogotá, Guerra y Marina, Historia, I, 666.

[2] Adam, *op. cit.*, 9, 14, 121; *British Monitor*, Dec. 5, 1819; *London Chronicle*, Jan. 21, 1820.

procure rations, they were unable to distribute them promptly. In their search for water the men had to walk long distances over narrow trails, hedged in and often overgrown by a species of prickly pear, the thorns of which pierced the soles of their shoes, and the venomous juice of which caused inflammation in the wounds.[1] Many were thus incapacitated from the performance of their duties, but many more succumbed to diseases brought on by the unhealthiness of the water and by the heat and humidity of the climate.

The Irish blamed the Venezuelan authorities for the terrible hardships which they were forced to endure, but the responsibility should have been placed entirely on D'Evereux, who sent his troops off without making any arrangements for their reception, designated Margarita as their destination, without consultation with or notification to the military authorities of Venezuela, and above all, failed to accompany his men to look after their needs.[2] He had deceived his men with promises of one-third more pay than that given in the English army,[3] although he must have known that the native troops were accustomed to serve without pay. As a matter of fact, Bolívar was utterly unable to pay any troops, for at that time he had barely $1,000 in his treasury.[4]

As in the case of the previous arrivals, the failure to receive any pay made the lack of proper rations even more difficult to endure. Had D'Evereux sent his troops to Angostura, where Bolívar expected them and was better prepared to receive the men, undoubtedly the Irish Legion would have been spared much of the hardships, sickness and loss of life which it suffered at Margarita. On account of lack

---

[1] Chesterton, *Narrative*, 9, 10; O'Connor, *op. cit.*, 23.

[2] Adam, *op. cit.*, 156, 157; *Present State of Colombia*, 110.

[3] O'Connor, *op. cit.*, 22.

[4] Walker, *op. cit.*, II, 433; J. T. Mosquera, *Colombia*, II, 58; Chesterton, *Narrative*, 129.

of instructions regarding the Irish Legion, Admiral Brión refused to afford the members any assistance, as he doubted whether they would be acknowledged as allies. It was stated that he and the other chiefs at Margarita used starvation as a natural remedy, to get rid of the incompetents. They hoped in this way that the most useless of the adventurers would be weeded out, and that only the fittest would survive.[1] Subsequently Bolívar, on December 14, 1819, issued a proclamation to the Irishmen, stating that Venezuela had scarcely sufficient means with which to reward them, but that the promises made by Gen. D'Evereux would be fulfilled.[2]

As soon as the members of the Irish Legion landed, they received such gloomy reports from those of the British Legion who were still on the island that the joy at arrival was at once turned to despair. The condition of these Englishmen was indeed truly deplorable, for most of them were invalids who had been left behind. Many of them were dying of fever, lying on the bare ground, naked and without care, and those who had recovered looked to be mere shadows of their former selves. The first duty which the Irish Legion was called upon to perform was to march to the mournful strains of the regimental band in attending the funeral of Gen. English, who had succumbed to the fever only the night before.[3] So obviously bad were the conditions which they viewed, and so great was the depression engendered thereby, that thirty or forty of the officers, including three lieutenant-colonels, Harvey, MacLaughlin, and Minchin, and all the officers of the lancers refused to remain, but returned to Ireland on the same vessels in which they had come.[4]

[1] *Present State of Colombia,* 110; *London Chronicle,* Jan. 21, 1820.

[2] *London Chronicle,* Mar. 3, 1820; Walker, *op. cit.,* II, 443, 444; O'Leary, *Documentos,* XVI, 563; Chesterton, *Narrative,* 129, 130.

[3] Adam, *op. cit.,* 16.

[4] O'Connor, *op. cit.,* 21, 23.

In spite of Bolívar's proclamation, contentment was not established among the Irishmen, for promises seemed rather unsubstantial sustenance, when the ration supplied them was so scanty that they had to fish for sardines to ward off starvation.[1] Weakened by lack of proper food, they soon fell victims to the climate. The scarcity and badness of the water encouraged their natural inclinations to drink stronger beverages, and drunkenness increased the virulence of the fever. Many lay for days unattended in some empty hut, others crawled to the beach to cool their fevered blood in the salt waves, one dragged himself under a field gun to die in its grateful shade. Their fate was pitiable. Every day many left their barracks for the hospital, and every day more left the hospital for the grave.[2]

Scattered as it was throughout the island, the Legion soon lost what little discipline it might once have had. Men who had entered into a military life with no idea of continuing in it, but solely with a view to making enough money to enable them to get out again as quickly as possible, found intolerable whatever discipline the officers tried to enforce.[3] On one occasion a rumor was spread abroad that a chest containing prize-money captured by the fleet had been transferred from the ships to the headquarters on shore. Admiral Brión was no favorite with the Irish; for not only had he refused to supply them with rations from his fleet, but he had even deprived them of their beloved band, by retaining it aboard his flagship. Under such circumstances, when the rumor of the presence of the chest of money became whispered around, it did not require much urging to raise a mob

[1] O'Connor, op. cit., 24.

[2] Adam, *op. cit.*, 35, 36; O'Connor, *op. cit.*, 27; Chesterton, *Narrative,* 119; Archivo Montilla, Report of Sick in Irish Legion.

[3] Walker, *op. cit.*, II, 433. Archivo Montilla, Montilla and Brión, Agreement dated March 6, 1820.

with which to rush headquarters and attempt to seize the money. The officers were helpless in the emergency, and in order to calm the disorder, broke open the chest and distributed its contents among the mob, one peso to each soldier and an ounce of gold to each officer.[1]

Meanwhile, since Col. Uslar who had been sent by Gen. Mariño to take command of the Irish Legion had been captured by the royalists,[2] an Irish renegade named Jackson, attached to the staff of Admiral Brión, assumed the function.[3] Ignoring this person, on December 14, 1819, Bolívar assigned the Legion to the command of Gen. Mariano Montilla, who had traveled much in Europe and could speak the principal languages.[4] These orders further specified that Montilla should organize an expedition to harass the coast of Venezuela and New Granada from La Guaira to Porto Bello. Bolívar had originally intended himself to take command of it and to penetrate the province of Caracas while the army of the north attracted the attention of the enemy toward Barinas and Barquisemeto; but had decided to relinquish this plan in order to devote his personal attention to a more important campaign. The operations on the north coast, forming part of the plan, were therefore entrusted to

[1] O'Connor, *op. cit.*, 22, 25, 26.

[2] While crossing the Gulf of Cariaco he had been caught by the royalists who, after stripping and beating him, had exposed him in that condition to the scorching rays of the sun. He was long held a prisoner in Caracas, kept in chains and forced to clean the streets and perform other menial services. During the armistice of 1820-1821 he was released at the personal request of Bolívar, who subsequently appointed him to the command of a regiment of grenadiers of the guard. Chesterton, *Narrative*, 125, 187, 227; Cochrane, *Journal*, I, 495; Richard, *op. cit.*, 108. *Cf.* Chapter XIII.

[3] Adam, *op. cit.*, p. 39; *London Chronicle*, April 7, 1817.

[4] Urdaneta, *op. cit.*, 171; Archivo Montilla, III, Bolívar to Mariano Montilla, Dec. 14, 1819; Archivo Nacional, Bogotá, Guerra y Marina, Historia, VI, 572.

Gen. Montilla, with instructions, after threatening the coast, to occupy Caracas and then proceed to Rio Hacha and Santa Marta to coöperate with Gen. Urdaneta.[1]

Immediately on the arrival of Montilla, a vigorous reorganization of the Irish Legion was instituted. At Pampatar, the rifles under Col. Foster and a small detachment under Lieut. Col. O'Lalor, which was composed of men from the British Legion invalided back from Barcelona, were incorporated with a battalion of infantry under the name of " lancers ", although there was not a horse to be found in the place. Col. Francis Burdett O'Connor was appointed commandant of this body.[2] Early in March, 1820, Gen. Montilla felt that he had his command sufficiently in hand to begin the campaign, and on the sixth of that month sailed for the mainland aboard the ships of Brión's squadron, with about 678 men, two-thirds of whom were the Irish, although a number of creole officers and men had been incorporated into their ranks.[3]

It was soon learned that the destination of the expedition was Rio Hacha. On arrival before the batteries of that place, the Spanish flag was seen flying from the round tower. Fire was opened on the tower and the houses of the city, which was replied to uninterruptedly all afternoon by the shore batteries. Early next morning orders were issued for the attack. The disembarkation was carried out with difficulty in small boats through the surf. The Irish lancers

[1] O'Leary, *Narracion*, II, 22; Archivo Montilla, III, Bolívar to Mariano Montilla, Dec. 14, 1819; Blanco, *op. cit.*, VII, 222.

[2] Rafael Maria Baralt y Ramón Díaz, *Resumen de la historia de Venezuela desde el año de 1797 hasta el de 1850,* II, 5; O'Connor, *op. cit.,* 23, 27. Lieut. Col. O'Lalor had formerly belonged to the Irish Guard in Spain. For a morning report showing the strength of the Irish Legion at Juan Griego, March 4, 1820, *cf.* Appendix F.

[3] Baralt y Díaz, *op. cit.,* II, 6; Rojas, *op. cit.,* 192; Archivo Montilla, Montilla to Santander, March 22, 1820.

charged the round tower but encountered no resistance, as it had been abandoned by the enemy. Hauling down the royal ensign, the captors raised in its place their own standard, displaying the harp of Ireland in the center. A large quantity of munitions and fifty guns of all calibers were captured. Montilla then ordered his troops to take quarters in the city, which had been entirely deserted by the royalist troops and by the greater part of the citizens.[1]

While the division rested a few days at Rio Hacha, the time was improved by giving instruction to the troops. Not a cent of salary was forthcoming, however, and the only rations consisted of turtle meat. The animals furnishing this food were said to be so large that a single one supplied enough for a hundred persons. Their shells were used for the roofing of the houses, for which purpose, it was said, six shells sufficed. Melancholy sights which met the eyes of such as sauntered down to the beach were the scattered bones of those unfortunate men, women and children who had been massacred the year before, when McGregor fled from Rio Hacha and abandoned them to their fate.[2]

Early in March, 1820, the advance was begun from Rio Hacha, with the objective of effecting a junction near Maracaibo with a patriot division under Gen. Urdaneta. All organizations were very much reduced in strength, especially the lancers, which had disembarked at Margarita 800 strong, but now left Rio Hacha with scarcely 260. These were organized in six companies under Col. O'Connor, and marched on foot. Col. Aylmer was in command of the entire legion, with Col. Jackson as chief of staff. The light battalion of Cundinamarca was under Major Rudd, while

[1] O'Connor, *op. cit.*, 30; *La Gaceta de Curaçao*, April 22, 1820. Archivo Montilla, Report of Montilla, March 23, 1820.

[2] O'Connor, *op. cit.*, 31, 32; *Correo del Orinoco*, June 17, 1820; *Present State of Colombia*, 108.

Lieut. Col. O'Lalor commanded the company of sharpshooters. A detachment of German pioneers formed the advance-guard. The country through which they marched was occupied by the Goajira Indians, who were strongly attached to the royalist cause, and were well supplied with arms and ammunition.[1]

Resistance was encountered in the villages of Moreno and Fonseca, where the Indians fired upon the column from the windows of the houses. On entering the latter village, the advance guard fell into an ambuscade, from which not a single man of the German detachment escaped. Their bodies were later found hacked to pieces and horribly mutilated. During this march many stragglers were cut off by the Indians. Water was scarce and the men suffered much from thirst. Those who dropped out of the column in search of water were invariably murdered. After arriving at the town of Valle de Upar, word was received that a detachment of the division left behind at Moreno had been surprised and wiped out. The Indians had set fire to the houses in which the men were sleeping, and although every possible resistance had been made, the detachment had been destroyed. Capt. Murray of the lancers had been almost decapitated, but had managed to escape to Rio Hacha. The destruction of this detachment cut off Montilla from his base.[2]

As a result of this disaster, the general summoned a council of war, which declared that under the circumstances it would be impossible to continue the advance through hostile country held by superior forces of the enemy to effect the junction with Urdaneta, as had been ordered by Bolívar. It was therefore decided to return to Rio Hacha. Col. O'Connor, fearing the bad effect of a retreat on the discipline of

[1] O'Connor, *op. cit.*, 23, 31, 32, 33; Baralt y Díaz, *op. cit.*, II, 5, 6; Archivo Montilla, Bolívar to Montilla, Dec. 14, 1819.

[2] O'Connor, *op. cit.*, 33, 34, 36.

the Irish, alone protested and insisted that the soldiers were eager to continue the advance. He assured Urdaneta that he knew the Irish better than the general did and that for his part, if a retreat were ordered, he could not respond for the preservation of order. As O'Connor had feared, no sooner was the withdrawal begun, than discontent and disorder broke out among the men, who bitterly complained at being forced to retreat. The conduct of the Irish troops worried Montilla, and their tendency to pillage and devastate the country through which they passed caused him to issue proclamations to the inhabitants to assure them that he was eager to retain their friendship and that he was not in any way connected with McGregor.[1]

The enemy followed close behind and reached Rio Hacha almost as soon as Gen. Montilla's division arrived. They invested the outskirts of the city and prepared to check any further attempts at an advance. On March 20, 1820, they suddenly attacked a patriot patrol near the suburb of Laguna Salada. The call to arms was sounded in the patriot lines, but the lancers were the only ones to rush out of their barracks and form on the plaza. O'Connor led his men against the enemy who occupied a strong position, with one flank resting on a lake and the other in a thick wood. When they had arrived within three hundred yards of the enemy's position, the lancers rushed forward with a loud cheer, forcing the enemy to withdraw in flight. One hundred and seventy Irishmen, supported by a company of sharpshooters and one small field gun, had, so it was said, defeated 1,700 royalists. Eager to pursue their opponents, the lancers were much disgusted when orders to the contrary were given. Montilla was highly pleased with their bravery; and in the course of

[1] O'Connor, *op. cit.*, 37; Archivo Montilla, Montilla to Santander, March 22, 1820; Montilla to Urdaneta, April 6, 1820, Montilla to the Duke of Manchester and Admiral Sir Home Popham, June 6, 1820; *La Gaceta de Curaçao,* April 22, 1820.

conversation stated that he had had no idea what kind of soldiers the Irish were, until he saw the little line of skirmishers charge with the bayonet into the smoke of battle. He had not believed such a charge possible, but now he realized that the division would have been able to cut its way through any number of Spaniards, and all his life he should regret that he had decided to retreat.[1]

On March 25th the division marched out of Rio Hacha to attack the enemy, which had reoccupied its former position. A detachment of native sailors, under Cols. Jackson and Stopford, led the advance guard. The main body was formed of the sharpshooters under Lieut. Col. O'Lalor and the Battalion of Cundinamarca under Major Rudd. Col. O'Connor, with his lancers, marched as rear guard. The advance guard walked into an ambuscade, and thirty sailors fell at the first volley. When the column came to a halt, Col. O'Connor led his lancers out of the path toward the right, and struck the royalists on the flank. He found the enemy formed in line, with his sharpshooters posted on both flanks. In the melee which ensued, Col. Aylmer was dangerously wounded, and Col. O'Connor slightly so in the right shoulder. This did not, however, delay his men, who deployed as skirmishers and, with a terrible " hurrah ", charged upon the enemy. The latter abandoned their lines, leaving them occupied only by the dead and wounded, mingled with barrels of rum and carcasses of cattle. An Irish officer named Finlay performed especially meritorious service in directing the fire of the artillery. Because of the lack of cavalry and the bad condition of the roads, Montilla did not deem it prudent to pursue the enemy but ordered a return to the city.[2]

During the march back nothing was heard but the growls of the soldiers, complaining that they had not been permitted

[1] O'Connor, *op. cit.*, 38, 39; Blanco, *op. cit.*, VII, 331.

[2] O'Connor, *op. cit.*, 41, 42; Baralt y Díaz, *op. cit.*, II, 7.

to pursue the defeated enemy. They were tired of marching through a country where there was no water to drink. They swore they would never make this march again, nor would they advance a step, except under the orders of their own officers. They accused the native generals of not being soldiers and not wanting to win victories. When they reached their barracks, they kept up their complaints, adding that the promises made to them had never been fulfilled, and that they had not received a single penny of pay since they left home. They then demanded that they be sent to some English island.

So loud was the uproar that it reached the ears of the commanding general. Next day Montilla, accompanied by his staff and officers of the legion, visited the barracks and harangued the men, who reiterated their complaints of the day before. They would not listen to the general, insisting that they be returned to Ireland. Montilla left, after assuring them that he would do what he could to send them away. Thinking that that was all they wanted, he made no attempt to redress their other grievances. Forthwith he directed the embarkation of all the malcontents aboard some merchant ships which were in the harbor, and ordered that they be taken to Jamaica. This was carried into effect on June 4, while the lancers, who were the only ones who had not taken part in the mutiny, enforced the embarkation of the rest. Some sailors during the night commenced sacking the houses and afterwards set fire to the citadel. This is the version of the incident, as given by O'Connor, although other accounts describe the mutiny as a much more serious affair, and blame the Irish for getting drunk and setting fire to the town.[1]

These accounts state that the Irish had been ordered to

[1] O'Connor, *op. cit.*, 43; *London Chronicle*, July 28, 1820; O'Leary, *Documentos*, XVII, 337, 343.

remain in their barracks until the merchant ships which were to transport them to Jamaica were ready to receive them, but in a few hours they broke loose in great disorder. They began to ransack the city for booty and to appropriate the few miserable trifles left behind by the inhabitants. Then they got drunk on liquor found in the houses and finished by setting fire to the town. They attacked some officers who tried to check them and continued committing disorders until they were forced aboard their transports. The city was reduced to ashes and the next day the fort was blown up. In further explanation of the conduct of the Irish to the governor of Jamaica, Montilla himself wrote: " The soldiers have combined dishonor with barbarity, for they requited the friendship and kindness of the inhabitants of Rio Hacha, who received them as brothers and furnished them provisions, by setting fire to the town." To the Minister of War he wrote: " their comportment has been contrary to all military discipline. Against my positive and repeated orders, they have pillaged places which offered no resistance. It was no use for me to make an example by shooting an individual caught in the act of pillage. They are not troops but merely a crowd of men." [1]

O'Connor, judging from the good conduct of his own lancers, believed that had Montilla handled the situation more tactfully, and had he taken the pains to investigate and remedy the causes of the complaints of his troops, there would have been no serious trouble with the Irish Legion. The lancers, when urged to remain loyal did so, and assisted in disarming and forcing their mutinous compatriots aboard the vessels. The lancers themselves were therefore not put aboard the transports, but were distributed among the war-

Archivo Montilla, Montilla to the Duke of Manchester and Admiral Sir Home Popham, June 6, 1820; Montilla to the Minister of War, March 20, 1820; Baralt y Díaz, *op. cit.,* II, 8; Blanco, *op. cit.,* VII, 332.

ships in the harbor and remained behind with Montilla.[1] Several of their officers, however, among whom were Majors Bourne and Clinton and Capt. O'Brien, refused to remain behind and joined the mutineers. O'Connor himself was ordered to take charge of the transports, and to conduct the mutineers to Jamaica where he was to turn them over to the British authorities. After having completed this duty, he and Col. Stopford were to return and resume their commissions in the patriot army.[2]

Col. Aylmer died of his wounds a few days after his arrival at Jamaica, and Lieut. Col. Hopkirk returned to England. Approximately 300 of the Irish were engaged in the mutiny and desertion. On their arrival in Jamaica many of the men enlisted in the King's Corps. The municipal council of Kingston voted to ship the remainder to Canada at the expense of the English government, and Sir Home Popham, the admiral commanding the naval station, arranged for their restoration to the rights of British subjects. After their arrival in Canada, the men were scattered, and never heard of again as an organization.[3] They took no further part in the operations of the Irish Legion. Bolívar, who had previously warned Montilla that at the first serious breach of discipline on the part of the Irish Legion he was to dismiss it from the service of the republic, wrote that he was not surprised at the conduct of the Irish, and was " pleased to be rid of these vile mercenaries ", who would do no killing until after they had first been paid for it.[4]

[1] O'Connor, op. cit., 54.

[2] Archivo Montilla, Montilla to Stopford and O'Connor, June 6, 1820; Montilla to the Duke of Manchester and Admiral Sir Home Popham, June 6, 1820.

[3] O'Connor, op. cit., 44, 45; Present State of Colombia, 111; London Chronicle, July 31, 1820.

[4] O'Leary, Documentos, XVII, 337; Larrazábal, op. cit., II, 260.

This, however, was by no means the end of the Irish Legion; for some hundred of the lancers whom O'Connor had managed to keep loyal, were disembarked again, and having been furnished with horses now for the first time, followed Montilla in his evacuation of Rio Hacha and took an important part in the siege of Cartagena and the campaign against Santa Marta. They formed part of the 160 men who were all that were left from Montilla's division after the Irish Legion had been despatched to Jamaica.

Nevertheless, with this diminutive force Montilla continued operations in the hope that by invading the Magdalena valley he might open communication with Bogotá, or at least might send to Bolívar the artillery and munitions which he had with him. Montilla thereupon sailed for Sabanilla, which he took by surprise, and later occupied Barranquilla, where he was aided by patriotic sympathizers in raising supplies and recruiting some additional men. Then with 400 infantry, sixty cavalry and four guns, he left Barranquilla to effect a junction at Tenerife with Col. José María Córdoba who, having cleared the Cauca valley, was operating along the Magdalena River. Having accomplished this, Montilla invaded the province of Cartagena and laid siege to the city of that name.[1] When the royalist garrison made a sally and captured Montilla's headquarters at Turbaco, a detachment of twenty-five or fifty Irish lancers bravely rallied, drove back the royalists, and covered the retreat of the patriots, who had already lost fifty of their men. In this stand, Lieut. Barnes of the artillery was killed while gallantly defending his gun.[2]

[1] Archivo Montilla, Montilla to the Commanding General of the Division of the Lower Magdalena, Dec. 22, 1820; Baralt y Díaz, *op. cit.,* II, 9, 11, 12; Larrazábal, *op. cit.,* II, 259, 260.

[2] O'Connor, *op. cit.,* 45; Walker, *op. cit.,* II, 479; *Present State of Colombia,* 112.

At Tenerife, Montilla had been joined by Colonels Jacinto Lara and José María Carreño who had come down the Magdalena valley with the Rifles Battalion. These were sent to capture the port of Santa Marta. Col. O'Connor was appointed chief of staff of this division and was accompanied by part of his lancers.[1] The bloodiest battle in which the Irish lancers were engaged was fought on November 12, 1820, when Fort Ciénaga, one of the defenses of Santa Marta, was captured, after the slaughter of 690 royalists. The royalist governor of this fort had distributed barrels of " aguardiente " to his men before the battle to incite them to make a stubborn defense. After the capture of the fort, Col. O'Connor was sent with a corporal and four privates of the lancers to receive the surrender of the city of Santa Marta. During this campaign many creole royalists deserted to the patriots, and finally the Spanish general, La Torre, was compelled to retire to Caracas. An armistice signed Nov. 27, 1820, by Bolívar and Morillo put an end to the campaign.[2]

Meanwhile during the month of June, 1820, another contingent of the Irish Legion had been arriving in Venezuela. This was a force of 387 men, which had been raised by Col. Gore in 1819 (200 for McGregor and 187 for the Irish Legion itself), and which had been sent up the Orinoco, instead of to Margarita.[3] During the rest of the year, under the command of Colonels Power[4] and Lyster, these troops

---

[1] Cochrane, *Journal*, I, 464; *View of South America*, II, 112; O'Leary, *Documentos*, XVII, 31; O'Connor, *op. cit.*, 48.

[2] O'Connor, *op. cit.*, 52; Walker, *op. cit.*, II, 479, 480; Blanco, *op. cit.*, VII, 251; O'Leary, *Documentos*, XVII, 575, 576, 577, 578.

[3] Archivo Nacional Bogotá, Guerra y Marina, Historia, VI, 771, 772, DCCLXXX, 861; Archivo Nacional, Caracas, Gobernación de Guayana, XII, 253, XIV, 200, 203, 207, 215; Navarro y Lamarca, *op. cit.*, II, 794; *Correo del Orinoco*, June 24, 1820.

[4] A certificate of service under the Duke of York showed that William

had remained with the army of Páez at Calabozo, ready either to follow Bolívar into New Granada, or to keep up operations against the royalists in Venezuela, to prevent their falling upon the rear of Bolívar's little army.[1] When the members of this detachment of the Irish Legion learned of the disgraceful conduct of their compatriots at Rio Hacha, they together with some members of the British Legion wrote to Bolívar a declaration of regret and assurances of loyalty dated at Achaguas August 25, 1820, which was signed by one representative of every grade from colonel to private.[2]

It will be remembered that Gen. D'Evereux had remained behind in Ireland and England until he was forced to leave. When at last he reached the West Indies, he was directed from Barbados to Rio Hacha, and from Rio Hacha to Jamaica in search of his orphan Legion. When the governor of Jamaica refused him permission to land any of his staff, he sailed for Sabanilla, where he at length found Brión and Montilla, and learned of the defection of his troops.[3] In the course of his wanderings D'Evereux arrived at Margarita, where he was received with great distinction by Arismendi. At a banquet given in his honor, he attended in the full-dress uniform of a field marshal. Continuing the same methods for raising his prestige as he had used in Ireland, D'Evereux

Middleton Power had served in the Forty Eighth Regiment of Infantry for twenty-two years as ensign, lieutenant, captain and major. He had taken part in the campaign in Holland in 1794-95, in the capture of Minorca, in Germany, and in the Egyptian campaign. He had been engaged in the capture of Copenhagen and in the battles of Burosa and Corunna, in the last of which he had been three times wounded. Archivo Nacional, Bogotá, Guerra y Marina, Historia, VI, 776. *Cf.* also Chap. V, p. 137, n. 4.

[1] O'Leary, *Narración*, I, 550; Walker, *op. cit.*, II, 477; Richard, *op. cit.*, 85.

[2] Walker, *op. cit.*, II, 477, 478.

[3] Ducoudray-Holstein, *op. cit.*, II, 86; Richard, *op. cit.*, 73.

rose to make a speech. He is reported to have spoken for two hours, promising that all Ireland was aroused in the cause of the patriots and that he himself was ready to kill every Spaniard in South America. He closed his peroration by drawing his huge sword from its diamond-studded scabbard and threatening to mete out destruction to the enemies of liberty, not only in Colombia, but in every part of the globe. The effect of this eloquent speech, however, was somewhat marred by the fact that D'Evereux spoke in English, which none of his hearers was able to understand.[1]

D'Evereux claimed a rank senior to that of Gen. Montilla, who refused to serve under him. Jealousy led to bitter words that might have resulted in a duel, had not friends persuaded D'Evereux to leave for Cúcuta, where the congress was sitting.[2] Just as he managed to arrive too late to take part in any engagement with the enemy, so he seemed somehow always able to dodge the duel which again and again threatened him. While at Cúcuta he managed to pick a quarrel with Gen. Antonio Nariño, the vice-president, whom he challenged for a supposed insult to the widow of Gen. English. The vice-president thereupon ordered D'Evereux confined in a dungeon. Thus again was this doughty warrior saved from getting under fire. In November, 1821, D'Evereux was honorably acquitted by a commission of inquiry sent by the congress, and was confirmed by Bolívar in the grade of major general. Orders also were issued for the payment to Mrs. English of her claims to a pension and to the arrears of her husband's salary.[3] When Bolívar met

---

[1] *Recollections of Service*, II, 81, 82.

[2] Ducoudray-Holstein, *op. cit.*, II, 87; *Recollections of Service*, II, 160-162; *London Chronicle*, Feb. 14, 1821; Archivo Nacional, Bogotá, Guerra y Marina, Historia, III, 350, 351.

[3] Ducoudray-Holstein, *op. cit.*, II, 88; *London Chronicle*, Feb. 1, 1822; Archivo Nacional, Bogotá, Guerra y Marina, Historia, VII, 153, 155; *Gaceta de Colombia*, Dec. 8, 1822.

D'Evereux at Barranquila, he received him cordially, absolved him from any blame on account of the defection of the Irish, and next year attached him to the general staff at Bogotá.[1]

D'Evereux had never had any previous military service except as an aide to his father and, as already observed, never took part in a single engagement with the Irish Legion. His sole connection with that body lay in organizing it as a speculation out of which he made a pretty profit.[2] He never saw the Legion after it left Ireland. And yet he has been called the " Lafayette of South America ".[3] Such a characterization needs no further comment.[4]

[1] Walker, *op. cit.*, II, 477; Archivo Nacional Bogotá, Guerra y Marina Historia, DCCLXXIX, 445, 622, 752.

[2] *Present State of Colombia*, 112; Richard, *op. cit.*, 186.

[3] *View of South America*, II, 113; José Maria Baraya, *Biografías militares*, II, 94.

[4] D'Evereux remained in the military service of Colombia for two years longer. During much of this time, however, he served on military commissions, since ill health prevented his exercising an active command in the field. By devoting much of his time to the purpose, he obtained liquidation of his accounts from the government at Bogotá and reimbursement for the munitions which the Irish Legion had brought with it, yet he permitted Mathew Macnamara, from whom he had bought the supplies, to appeal to the government for his own payment as well. Although D'Evereux remained in Bogotá on staff duty throughout these years, he took credit for one year, nine months and seventeen days field service (the entire period of the existence of the Irish Legion) and subsequently claimed that the loss of his sight, which he afterwards suffered, "began, as some field officers assure him, in the campaign of the Magdalena." In December, 1823, he was appointed Colombian envoy extraordinary to the courts of northern Europe, and sailed from Cartagena to England. In 1825, while travelling in Italy for his health, he was arrested by the Austrian authorities, who confined him in Venice on account of his political opinions and because of his having taken part in the revolution in South America. His friends hoped for the intervention of Great Britain, on the ground of his British citizenship, and of that of the United States, because he was travelling on a passport granted by the American minister at Paris. He was eventually released by Metternich

on the request of the Duke of Wellington, although three Italians, who had expressed kindly sentiments for him, were allowed to continue in prison. Returning to the United States, he lived there upon a pension which he received from the government of Venezuela until his death in 1854. He was buried in the National Pantheon at Caracas. Archivo Nacional, Bogotá, Guerra y Marina, Historia, XXXV, 864, 865, 911, DCCLXXIX, 722, 846; Hojas de Servicios, XIII, 979, 981; Azpúrua, *op. cit.*, II, 457; *The Times*, June 14, 1825, June 29, 1826.

CHAPTER VIII

PASSING THE ANDES TO FREEDOM

AT the beginning of the year 1819 Morillo's army of the Apure contained 17,000 men, while Bolívar had only 7,200 in the whole of Venezuela. Under these conditions Bolívar could not hope to carry on successful operations in that province. On the other hand, there was less disparity of forces in New Granada, where only 4,000 Spanish troops garrisoned the northeastern frontier and 3,000 men were distributed among Bogotá, Socorro, Mompox, Cartagena, Santa Marta, and other cities of the interior and the coast.[1]

Information was received that the division of the vanguard which had been raised by the patriots in the Casanare district of New Granada had been brought to a high state of efficiency and discipline by its commander, Gen. Francisco de Paula Santander. Bolívar, determined not to risk the fate of the republic on a general battle with Morillo, therefore was inclined to look favorably on the proposition of utilizing Santander's division in conjunction with his own for a campaign in New Granada, where it seemed probable that he might also receive aid and coöperation from inhabitants who were discontented with the royalist régime. Such an invasion would deprive the enemy of the resources of that rich country and would enable Bolívar to establish communication with the patriots in Chile.[2]

---

[1] O'Leary, *Narración*, I, 560; Level, *op. cit.*, 311, 312, 314; Torrente, *op. cit.*, II, 532; *Boletín de Historia y Antigüedades*, Bogotá, XII, 479.

[2] Bingham Collection of Mss., Bolívar Letters, Bolívar to Guillermo White, April 4, 1819; O'Leary, *Narración*, I, 541, 556; *Documentos*, XVI, 371, 389, Carlos Cortés Vargas, " De Arauca a Nuncia," in *Memorial del Estado Mayor del Ejército de Colombia*, No. 87, p. 228.

Within the next few months the English and Irish re-enforcements, described in the preceding chapters, continued to arrive at Margarita and Angostura. This augmentation to his forces came at an opportune time to enable Bolívar to think more seriously of using them in an expedition into New Granada. The approaching rainy season would make further operations in the lowlands of Venezuela impossible, and would undoubtedly induce Morillo to scatter his troops in small detachments in winter quarters. Therefore the moment seemed most propitious for an invasion of New Granada, and for carrying into execution the project which Bolívar had long held in contemplation.[1]

Bolívar's plan of campaign was to invade New Granada by way of Casanare with the division of Gen. José Antonio Anzoátegui and the infantry from the division of Gen. Páez.[2] At Casanare Santander was to effect a junction with him. Páez, who had advised against taking his plainsmen into the mountains, was to remain behind with his cavalry, to attract the attention of the enemy towards Cúcuta by a raid into that valley; and by continuing operations on the plains of the Apure, he was to form an effective cavalry screen, in order to prevent Morillo from obtaining any information as to the movements of the main army under Bolívar.[3] The attention of Morillo was further to be distracted by attacks on his rear; for Bermúdez with the army of the east was to threaten him constantly in Calabozo, while Urdaneta should make a descent on the coast and capture Barcelona and Cumaná. As has already been recorded, the English troops

[1] O'Leary, *Narración*, I, 541, 550; *Documentos*, XII, 413; Bingham Collection of Mss. Bolívar letters, Bolívar to Guillermo White, Feb. 9, 1819.

[2] O'Leary, *Narración*, I, 478, 541, 543; *Documentos*, XVI, 390.

[3] *Ibid.*, *Narración*, I, 544, 546, 548; *Documentos*, XVI, 390; Páez, *op. cit.*, I, 193; Lucila L. de Pérez Díaz, " La batalla de Boyacá, su importancia militar y política," in *Cultura Venezolana*, III, 319.

that had arrived at Angostura had been forwarded up the Orinoco to Páez, who had been instructed to incorporate them into his infantry, whereas those who had been assembled at Margarita formed the bulk of the force under Urdaneta.[1]

Realizing that secrecy was essential to the success of his plans, Bolívar did not reveal them to his subordinates until May 23, when on the march to Mantecal he held a council of war in the deserted village of Setenta. There grouped about him in a little ruined hut, reclining on the bare ground or seated on the skulls of oxen whitened by the rain and sun, were his generals, Soublette, Anzoátegui, Briceño Méndez, Carillo, Iribárren, Rangel, Plaza, Manrique, and the English colonel, Rooke.[2] Iribárren and Rangel refused to risk their horses in the mountains, and soon after withdrew with their squadrons. Col. Rooke, on the other hand, is reported to have assured Bolívar that if necessary " he would follow with the British Legion even beyond Cape Horn ".[3]

On May 26, 1819, the army began its advance from Mantecal. Bolívar's force was composed of four battalions of infantry (1300 men), the Rifles, Barcelona, Bravos de Páez and the British Legion, and 800 cavalry of the squadrons Husares, Llano Arriba, and Guías (Guides). The organizations containing foreigners in this army were the Rifles under Lieut. Col. Arthur Sandes and the British Legion (sometimes called the Albion Battalion) under Col. James Rooke. When he was joined later by Santander with two more battalions of infantry and two additional squadrons of cavalry, Bolívar's total force was brought up to 3,400. The spirits

[1] O'Leary, *Narración*, I, 477, 478, 545; *Documentos*, XVI, 202, 391, XVII, 35; Bingham Collection of Mss. Bolívar letters, Bolívar to Guillermo White, April 4, 1819; Gil Fortoul, *op. cit.*, I, 210.

[2] O'Leary, *Narración*, I, 543.

[3] *Ibid.*, 544, 551; Larrazábal, *op. cit.*, II, 200, 201; Manuel París R., *Campaña del ejército libertador colombiano en 1819*, 95.

of the troops were high at the prospect of an active campaign.[1]

The rainy season and the campaign began on the same day. Of course this contingency had been foreseen, and had really been one of the determining factors; but the resulting difficulties were sufficient to try the courage of the stoutest-hearted commander, and the spirits of the lightest-hearted men. The rains, which had begun with unusual rigor, fell in torrents. The landscape was blotted from view by an apparently solid wall of water. In this downpour their much-worn uniforms clung to their wearers in clammy folds. What little protection their coats and shirts might have afforded was sacrificed in a vain attempt to keep arms and ammunition dry. "Arroyos" (rivulets), which in summer were mere dusty gulleys, now overflowed their banks. Brooks, which a little while ago held barely enough water to quench the thirst of the traveler, became navigable rivers. At this time of the year it was always considered that the plains could not be crossed even by cavalry. The network of rivers in the province of Casanare, above the junction of the Apure with the Orinoco, was a serious obstacle to travel even during the dry season, but now the waters had so risen as to form a morass or lake over all this region. Conditions seemed impossible for any troops, especially for infantry, yet Bolívar, with noble determination, led his army forward.[2] For seven weary days the men were obliged to wade through water up to their belts. For hours at a time they were unable to halt, since there was no place where they could rest

[1] O'Leary, *Narración*, I, 547; París, *op. cit.*, 23-25; Level, *op. cit.*, 320; Blanco, *op. cit,*. VI, 682, Arturo Santana, "La batalla de Boyacá" in *Memorial del Estado Mayor del ejército de Colombia,* No. 6, p. 376; *Archivo Santander,* II, 141.

[2] O'Leary, *Narración*, I, 547, 552; *Campaigns and Cruises,* I, 157; Chesterton, *Journal,* I, 480.

or even stand in comfort. Lucky they thought themselves if, after the end of an exhausting day, they found a high spot where they could lie down in the mud. Time after time the column was delayed to rescue some comrade who had stepped into a concealed hole. To cross the many deep rivers it was necessary to construct rafts of hides to carry the ammunition and baggage. At such times Bolívar showed the kindliness of his nature, for he would swim his horse back and forth in order to carry with him those soldiers who were weak and the women who were following their husbands in the army.[1]

To all these dangers was added that of being eaten alive by the swarms of caribes, or man-eating fish which infested those waters. These fish, although small, were provided with broad, sharp teeth, and were so voracious that whenever they bit they took away a piece of flesh. The taste of blood, spreading in the water, attracted them by the myriads to feast on the legs and thighs of their helpless victim. When once a man was attacked, he was beyond hope, for in a few seconds they would strip all the flesh off his bones. The fish were even more feared than the alligators which, because of their sluggishness, could more readily be avoided.[2]

On arrival at Tame, where a junction was effected with the division of Santander, the men rejoiced because they were able to add to their meagre ration of dried beef, a little salt and some bananas.[3] It took a whole month in fact to cross the province of Casanare and reach the foot of the mountains. Bolívar wrote to his friend, William White,

---

[1] O'Leary, *Narración*, I, 551, 552; *Campaigns and Cruises*, I, 159; Level, *op. cit.*, 320; De Schryver, *op. cit.*, 206, 207.

[2] *Campaigns and Cruises*, I, 157, 158; Robinson, *op. cit.*, 133; Chesterton, *Narrative*, 154.

[3] O'Leary, *Narración*, I, 552, 560; *View of South America*, 101; *British Monitor*, Oct. 24, 1819.

" These marches have fatigued the English more than I feared." [1] On June 22, after leaving behind his baggage train, Bolívar then began the actual ascent of the cordillera. Five days later he arrived at Paya, having lost all his horses and many of his men from the dangers and hardships of this memorable march. [2]

During those five days new difficulties had been surmounted, even more terrible than those of the submerged plains of Casanare. The mighty wall of the Andes, piled range upon range, each one higher and more rugged than the one before, towered heavenward until the glittering summits touched the clouds. Upwards the tired soldiers climbed, gasping for breath in the thin air, their hearts beating as though about to burst. Their strength was exhausted by lack of proper food, their vitality sapped by the intense cold against which their threadbare tropical clothing afforded scant protection. The rain continued day and night in an incessant downpour, chilling the shivering men and glazing the steep trail with a sheathing of ice. As they climbed higher and higher they began to suffer a new and strange sickness, the " soroche ". This mountain ailment, caused by the rarefied atmosphere of those extreme altitudes, was manifested by severe pains in the head, nausea and an extreme drowsiness. Those who yielded to it and lay down

[1] Bingham Collection of Mss. Bolívar letters. Bolívar to Guillermo White, April 4, 1819.

[2] Professor Hiram Bingham (now United States Senator) who was inclined to be skeptical of the claims made by Spanish-American writers as to the difficuties of this march, took the trouble to make a personal test of them. After having followed the same route that Bolívar took from Mantecal to Bogotá, although not in the rainy season, he declared that " it was an undertaking that has few equals in military history ". He also wrote: " seldom have men been called upon to overcome such obstacles ", and " one cannot but marvel at their courage and admire the tenacity of purpose that upheld them." Hiram Bingham, *The Journal of an expedition across Venezuela and Colombia* in 1906-07, pp. 200, 223.

soon became livid in the face and, after suffering violent
paroxysms with foaming at the mouth and frenzied tearing
of the hair, died in a stupor, as in a fit of apoplexy. In such
cases the only hope was to keep the sufferer moving, for to
lie down meant certain death. It was the part of kindness
for one friend to beat and lash another to keep him from
yielding to this deadly drowsiness. In fact, this was the only
way in which many were kept alive. Before the army had
crossed the highest pass, fifty of the British alone had succumbed to these perils of the Andes.[1]

   Terrible as were the sufferings of the British, those of the
Venezuelans were even worse. To the British soldier, weakened as he was by lack of proper food, the exertion of the
climb was bad enough, and the " soroche " was a new terror,
but he knew something of the rigors of a cold climate; while
to the Venezuelan who had spent all his life in the tropical
lowlands, the bitter cold of these altitudes seemed unendur-
able torture, especially since he had become almost naked
after his campaign in the "llanos". Very rarely had a
soldier been able to keep his shirt or pantaloons and often he
was reduced to nothing but a breech-clout. Men accustomed
to cross the swirling rivers of the pampas, to tame wild
horses, to subdue in face-to-face combat the fierce bull, the
crocodile and the tiger, now lost courage before gigantic and
untamed nature, and many gave up the struggle and deserted.
Not a single horse survived this march, for they were accustomed to the springy turf of the plains, and the sharp, stony
trails lamed them so badly that even the most brutal drivers
could not force them to proceed. Instead, the poor beasts
lay down in the trail and, refusing to budge, obstructed the
march of those who followed. Even the sure-footed mules

[1] O'Leary, *Narración*, I, 565; *Present State of Colombia*, 96; Bingham,
op. cit., 271; *Campaigns and Cruises*, I, 165; *Recollections of Service*,
II, 135-137.

lost their balance when forced to carry the loads of the horses in addition to their own, and tumbled headlong from the precipices.[1] All along the trails were visible the bones of men and animals which had perished in previous attempts to cross, and now and again were passed small crosses fixed in the rocks by some pious hands in memory of former travelers who had died there.

Above the tree-line the only vegetation that flourished in the harsh soil was a sort of gigantic mullen the height of a man, flaunting small yellow flowers at the tips of its scrawny branches. This plant is called the " fraylajón " because of its fancied resemblance to a friar holding his funeral torch at the head of a bier. These sights added depression to the already exhausted spirits of the army.[2] Yet in spite of these hardships and discouragements, Col. Rooke never lost his optimism and good nature. He was always happy and joking. The climate of the Apure was the mildest and best he had ever experienced, until he undertook the passage of the Andes, when the climate there seemed to him to have no rival in the world![3]

At Paya occurred the first encounter with the enemy. Here an outpost of 700 royalists held a position of such great strength that they should have been able to hold at bay a division of at least 6000 men. Nevertheless this detachment was driven in and retreated to Lebranza Grande, on the main road to Sogamoso, where Barreiro was stationed with the third Spanish army.[4] This road he held in force, believing it to be the only practicable route for an invading

---

[1] O'Leary, *Narración*, I, 561, 566; Bingham, *op. cit.*, 196; París, *op. cit.*, 96.

[2] O'Leary, *Narración*, I, 560, 561; Chesterton, *Journal*, I, 481; Larrazábal, *op. cit.*, 337, 338.

[3] O'Leary, *Narración*, I, 555.

[4] *Ibid.*, 555, 564; *Archivo Santander*, III, 198.

army. Another circuitous trail across the Páramo (alpine plain) of Pisba was left unguarded, because it was considered, even by native mountaineers, to be too dangerous, and was reported so blocked by rocks, trees and landslides as to be absolutely impassable for troops.

Bolívar, however, led his men along the slippery paths and dizzy precipices of this trail toward Pisba, but had not yet succeeded in crossing the " páramo " when darkness forced a halt. On that dismal plain nothing grew but the scattered stalks of the " fraylajon "; only a sheep or goat could find sustenance there. At frequent intervals an icy drizzle charged with frozen needles swept across the barren expanse. There was nothing to break the force of the biting gale which blew so fiercely as to impede progress at every turn. A terrible night of rain, hail and cold was spent on this bleak and desolate spot. The lighting of fires was rendered impossible by the absence of firewood, and by the violent winds and rain. Officers and men huddled together to save themselves from freezing. Only with the greatest difficulty did they manage to keep their arms and ammunition dry. Those who had imprudently thrown away their rations, in order to keep their shoulders free for climbing, suffered the pangs of hunger. Worn out by sheer exhaustion, they slept or froze on that bleak mountain-top. Many succumbed to their sufferings and died during the night.[1]

From this point onward Bolívar's plan of operations for the next few weeks proves him to have been one of the really great commanders of history. In its rapidity of movement, its sudden changes of base, its secrecy and its utter unexpectedness, the strategy of his campaign was strikingly like

[1] O'Leary, *Narración*, I, 564; Bingham, *op. cit.*, 271; *Campaigns and Cruises*, I, 166; Lieut. Richard Bache, *Notes on Colombia taken in the years 1822-23*, 176, 177. In the Colombian Andes the word "páramo" is used to denote a mountain-top (not a snow-covered peak) or summit of a pass which owing to the extreme altitude has become a desert.

that of the famous Valley Campaign of Stonewall Jackson; and it accomplished the same purpose of bewildering and outwitting the enemy. Fighting in the mountains gave the royalist army acting on the defensive the enormous advantage of being able to occupy chosen positions fortified by nature. Such positions were impregnable to frontal attack. Bolívar therefore not only utilized the flank attack in all his tactical dispositions for every engagement, but throughout the entire campaign his purpose was to flank the enemy out of his strong positions before bringing on an engagement. Bolívar's objective was Bogotá, the capital of New Granada, which Sámano held with only a small force. Between the patriots and this objective was the main royalist army under Barreiro.

Two routes along the mountains to Bogotá were possible. The first of these was via Sogamoso, where Barreiro held his main force; the other was further west up the valley of Serinza to Paipa and thence to Tunja and the bridge of Boyacá. Barreiro's position at Sogamoso was central and enabled him to keep in touch with both these routes. His mission was to block them against the advance of an enemy, yet at the same time keep open his own communications with Sámano at Bogotá. Bolívar's problem was either to force his way through the Spanish defenses or to outflank them and get between Barreiro and Bogotá. This accomplished, he could march on the capital and capture it. Lieut. Col. José Barreiro was a brilliant young artillery officer, who was well qualified in the science of artillery fire, but had never had any experience with infantry or cavalry and was ignorant of the first principles of commanding the combined arms. Bolívar accordingly had to deal with an opponent who was not hard to outwit.[1]

[1] *Correo del Orinoco*, June 17, 1820; Torrente, *op. cit.*, II, 533; Restrepo, *op. cit.*, II, 596 n. 41 a.

Bolívar's first attempt to outflank Barreiro resulted successfully in his safe arrival at Socha on July 5. After trying by several frontal attacks at the Gameza River and Tópaga to dislodge his opponent from his natural fortress, Bolívar then continued his flanking movement to the valley of Serinza, where he rested and recruited his forces before attempting to force the main road to Bogotá.[1]   Here Col. Rooke, who had been left behind at Paya with the British Legion to bring up the ammunition and the sick and wounded, rejoined and reported to Bolívar, in his usual cheerful manner, that the English had not suffered at all in crossing the Páramo of Pisba.   When challenged by Anzoátegui with the fact that he had actually lost two officers and a quarter of his men, Rooke replied that he did not deny these facts, but that those men were the most useless in his command and deserved their fate, and he was glad to be rid of them.[2]

When Barreiro learned of Bolívar's entrance into the valley of Serinza, he feared for his own communications and allowed himself to be drawn from his strong position at Sogamoso in order to throw himself across Bolívar's road at Paipa.   On July 25, Bolívar resolved to attack this position before Barreiro could assemble all his forces to oppose him. The two armies met at a narrow defile called the Pántano de Vargas.   The royalists had the advantage both of numbers and position.   Bolívar was in a difficult situation, hemmed in by the pántanos (or swamps) of Vargas on his right and by the heights on his left.   When Barreiro's troops were seen crowning these heights, Santander was directed to protect the left flank of the patriots with his division, but was driven back with heavy loss.[3]   It seemed then as if there was no

[1] O'Leary, *Narración*, I, 567, 568; Torrente, *op. cit.*, II, 534; Level, *op. cit.*, 322; Santana, *Boyacá*, 377.

[2] O'Leary, *Narración*, I, 569, 570; Hamilton, *op. cit.*, II, 16.

[3] O'Leary, *Narración*, I, 570, 571; Elías Prieto Villate, Ms. description

hope for the patriots, caught as they were in a trap, had not Col. Rooke led his men in a spirited charge up the hills under a heavy fire, driving the Spaniards from the heights at the point of the bayonet. Col. Rooke fell wounded in the first charge, but his men did not lose heart, and twice again charged under the command of Major Mackintosh, who believed that nothing was impossible for British bayonets, until the enemy yielded to the persuasion of their cold steel.[1] Barreiro then ordered an attack against the center of the patriot line, which began to yield. Again the day seemed lost, when Bolívar, riding up to Col. Rondon, who commanded a squadron of " llaneros ", shouted, " Colonel, save your country!" On the instant Col. Rondon dug spurs into his horse and galloped down the road followed by only fourteen men who happened to be near enough to hear the order. These cowboys riding bareback, using pieces of rope for bridles and armed only with lances, charged after their colonel and drove back the well-equipped royalist cavalry who, crowded six abreast in the narrow lane, were unable in the confusion to use their pistols effectively.[2] The patriot infantry imitated the example of Rondon, and made such an impetuous attack that the enemy fled before them. The Second Battalion of Numancia of the Spanish army alone held its ground.

Night and a heavy shower put an end to the action, enabling Barreiro to withdraw his shattered forces to Paipa, while Bolívar returned to his old position at Corrales de

of the battles of Vargas and Boyacá written from accounts told by his father Javier Luís Villate, and Francisco Mariño Soler, who were eye witnesses and participants in the events, in Bingham Collection of Mss. at Yale University Library, 10.

[1] O'Leary, *Narración*, I, 556, 571; *Campaigns and Cruises*, I, 169; Archivo Nacional, Bogotá, Guerra y Marina, Hojas de Servicios, XXX, 918.

[2] O'Leary, *Narración*, I, 571; Prieto Villate, *op. cit.*, 12; Bingham, *op. cit.*, 273; Carlos Cortés Vargas. " Pántano de Vargas ", in *Memorial del Estado Mayor del Ejército de Colombia*, No. 145-146, p. 319.

Bonza. Although both sides suffered heavy losses, this battle was indecisive. On the patriot side, the division of Anzoátegui suffered most. All his battalions, after having consumed almost all their ammunition, were reduced to skeletons. After the battle, the clothing of the dead was distributed among those of the living who were the most naked.[1] Bolívar then found it necessary to remain in camp five days, filling his ranks with recruits from the provinces of Socorro and Pamplona, where he had appointed patriot governors.[2] On the other hand, so costly was the battle to Barreiro that thereafter he lost the advantage of having the initiative and of acting on the defensive, and was forced to retreat before Bolívar and give battle when the latter chose. " Pántano de Vargas may well be included among the decisive battles for liberty. On that field the Republic of Great Colombia was born." [3]

Among the casualties in the battle of Pántano de Vargas was Capt. Daniel F. O'Leary, then attached to the staff of the rear guard, who was slightly wounded. In the Rifles Major Sandes was twice wounded. In the British Legion, Sub-lieutenant McManus was wounded and Lieut. Kaisley killed.[4] Col. Rooke's wound was so serious as to necessitate the amputation of his forearm. With his usual cheerfulness and courage he joked with Dr. Foley the surgeon who was about to perform the operation, saying that that member was really too perfect to be thrown away. During the operation Rooke was like a marble statue. When the surgeon had completed his work, Rooke grasped the severed forearm in

[1] O'Leary, *Narración*, I, 572; *Documentos*, XVI, 427; Prieto Villate, *op! cit.*, 15; Jorge Martínez L., " Pántano de Vargas " in *Memorial del Estado Mayor del Ejército de Colombia,* No. 43-44, pp. 8, 9.

[2] O'Leary, *Narración*, I, 563, 573.

[3] Cortes Vargas, " Pántano de Vargas," 321.

[4] O'Leary, *Documentos*, XVI, 422; Cochrane, *op. cit.*, I, 487.

his other hand, and waving it above his head, cried " Viva la Patria ".   When asked whether he meant Ireland or England, he answered that he referred to the land which was soon to give him a grave.   Next day the brave Rooke was dead.[1]

Bolívar's object, as already stated, was to reach Bogotá, but he realized that Barreiro must be maneuvered out of his position before that object could be accomplished.   On August 3rd he crossed the River Sogamoso by the bridge of Paipa and established himself within half a league of the royalists, as though he contemplated initiating the attack. Barreiro would not be drawn from his position.   Nearly all next day the contestants stood face to face.   Late in the afternoon the patriot army recrossed the bridge and apparently began its withdrawal to quarters in Paipa.[2]   At eight o'clock that night Bolívar countermarched his army, crossed the Sogamoso again and marched south on Tunja by the road through Toca, some distance east of the main road. The small garrison at Tunja was taken by surprise and easily overcome, and by dawn of the 5th that place was in his hands.   Six hundred muskets were captured, and an arsenal well stocked with food, clothing and ammunition.   Best of all, the road to Bogotá lay open, for Barreiro had been left behind at Paipa, a day's march in the rear.   Had he practiced the most elementary principles of correct minor tactics, he would have kept his scouts hanging on Bolívar's flanks and rear, and would never for a moment have lost track of his adversary's movements.   Due to his neglect, however, Barreiro had been clearly outwitted and had let his enemy get between him and his base, a situation of which the Span-

[1] *Recollections of Service*, I, 21n.; Cortes Vargas, " Pántano de Vargas," 320; Peñuela in *Repertorio Boyacense*, No. 64, VII, 784; *Boletín de Historia y Antigüedades*, XIII, 38, 39.

[2] O'Leary, *Narración*, I, 573; Level, *op. cit.*, 323.

ish commander was not aware until the following morning when he received reports of the capture of Tunja.[1]

As soon as Barreiro learned the situation, he evidently resolved to retrieve his neglect and to place himself again between Bolívar and the capital, where there was only a small guard of 400 men with Sámano. He therefore hastened with all his command southward toward Bogotá, by the road which leads to the westward of Tunja via Motavita and Samacá. This road and the one through Tunja meet at the bridge of Boyacá, sixteen kilometers south of Tunja. Barreiro must have hoped to be able to march past Bolívar while the latter was busy at that place and to seize this bridge before the patriots could arrive there. If he should accomplish this, he could again interpose himself between Bolívar and the capital and could again recover the advantage of standing on the defensive in a selected position.[2]

The Boyacá River, near the bridge of that name, flows from west to east. Ordinarily it is a mere brook cutting its narrow way between steep banks, but at the time of the battle it had been so swollen by the rains that it spread out over its whole valley; and for most of its length the center of its channel was deeper than a man on horseback. At that time, also, approach to the banks was rendered difficult by a thick growth of trees and bushes.[3] The stream was crossed by a single narrow bridge only wide enough for the passage with difficulty of a squad of men abreast. South of the bridge

[1] O'Leary, *Narración*, I, 574; Prieto Villate, *op. cit.*, 29; Luís Acevedo T., "Batalla de Boyacá," in *Memorial del Estado Mayor del Ejército de Colombia*, No. 145-146, p. 326; Santana, *Boyacá*, 382.

[2] O'Leary, *Narración*, I, 574; Level, *op. cit.*, 323; Acevedo, *op. cit.*, 327.

[3] Elías Prieto Villate, "Apuntamientos sobre la campaña de 1819" in *Repertorio Boyacense*, series V, No. 43, pp. 111, 112. This article appears to be either directly copied from, or based largely on, the same author's manuscript in the Bingham collection of manuscripts, cf. p. 200, n. 3; Bingham, *op. cit.*, 245.

the right bank spread out into a tiny level dell, shut in on three sides by steep hillsides up which the road wound. North of the river low ridges of barren rock, covered with a thin soil in which grew clumps of stunted trees, stretched finger-like toward the bridge. Between these ridges shallow ravines strewn with broken rocks and thorny bushes provided good cover for a defense while presenting obstacles against an attack.

On the morning of August 7, 1819, Bolívar formed his troops in the plaza at Tunja and waited until he could determine whether Barreiro intended to march on Tunja directly across from Motavita or to continue on to Boyacá. He was too impatient to await the reports from his scouts and staff officers, so personally made a reconnaissance of the movements of the enemy. The moment he had definitely learned that the royalist army was headed for Boyacá, Bolívar gave the necessary orders, directing his troops to march south from Tunja to seize the heights above Boyacá and to surprise the enemy by an attack while they were crossing the bridge.[1]

At two o'clock in the afternoon the royalist advance guard reached the bridge just as the point of patriot cavalry appeared on the crest of the hill from which descended the road from Tunja. Since the remainder of the patriot army was concealed by this hill, Col. Jiménez, commander of the royalist vanguard, doubtless believed that he had to deal with nothing more than a simple observation patrol, and ordered some chasseurs against it for the purpose of sweeping it aside and of continuing his march unopposed. Boldly the royalist chasseurs advanced up the hill and opened fire against the little group of horsemen.

When the patriot commander heard this firing, he ordered

---

[1] O'Leary, *Narración*, I, 574; Prieto Villate, Mss. account, 40, 45; Bingham, *op. cit.*, 274; Santana, *Boyacá*, 379, 380.

forward his main body of infantry in close column to the great surprise of the enemy. Although the vanguard of the royalists had climbed part way up the hill in pursuit of the patriot cavalry his main body was in the hollow a quarter of a league more or less from the bridge. Instantly the patriot battalion, chasseurs of the vanguard, under command of Col. París, sent forward a company of skirmishers and with the remaining companies in column attacked the chasseurs of the enemy, obliging them to retire in haste to the shelter of the walled enclosure of a farmhouse [1] near the road-fork. Here they made a short but determined stand only to be driven back again. Having lost this position, the royalist vanguard crossed the bridge and seized the heights on the right bank of the Boyacá River.

Meanwhile the patriot infantry descended the gentle slope of the hillock to the plain, while the cavalry followed the road, advancing with the hope of occupying the bridge. When Barreiro saw this he attempted a flank movement to his right toward the bridge in order to join his vanguard, but this was stopped by the Albion (British Legion) and Rifle battalions rushing into the gap, while at the same time the patriot cavalry directed itself against the royalist center. Before this unexpected attack Barreiro stopped, changed his plan, rapidly scaled the ridge at his right rear and reformed his troops in line of battle with three pieces of artillery in the center. He stationed his infantry in line of battalions, and covered his flanks with his cavalry. From his rear guard he detached a squadron to cover the road from Samacá, and on his extreme right sent a battalion toward the edge of the ravine to open an enfilading fire on the patriot infantry.

Simultaneously the patriot main body deployed in battle

---

[1] This farmhouse known as "the historic house" or the "Casa de Teja", is still standing. The latter expression means "tile-roofed house" to distinguish it from the ordinary thatched houses of this vicinity.

formation along the main road on the slope of the ridge, the crest of which the enemy occupied. The right of the republican army was formed by the Second Division under Anzoátegui, who likewise commanded the center. This division was composed of the Rifle, Albion (British Legion) and Barcelona battalions. The cavalry then took battle formation in two columns, the dragoons being in one, while some of Rondon's men were in the other with the infantry of the Apure. The columns of militia and recruits from Tunja and Socorro were held in reserve.

Santander commanded the left wing with the First Division composed of the Battalion of the Line of New Granada, the Guides and the Chasseurs of the Vanguard. These troops confronted the royalist vanguard which continued to hold its position on the south side of the bridge.

North of the bridge the royalist sharpshooters in the ravine were the first to open fire, and then the battle raged at all parts of the line. In view of the heavy loss caused by their fire, Gen. Anzoátegui attacked them at once, forcing them to fall back on the main body. Then he ordered Plaza to force the royalist left, while he himself launched two dauntless battalions at its center. This was the most intense moment of the battle. The royalist gunners hurled an iron rain on the republican lines at the same time that repeated volleys from the infantry opened great gaps in the ranks of the Rifles and Albion battalions who, following their general, fearlessly charged to the crest of the ridge. In the charge the guns were captured and thereafter remained silent.

The Bravos of Páez now reinforced Anzoátegui, who had just ordered a bayonet charge against the Chasseurs of the King, who had deployed to the royalist left into a dale from which they had opened an enfilading fire on the republican hosts. The shock was terrible. The bayonets glittered for a moment before burying themselves in the breasts of the contestants. The stony soil greedily drank up their blood while the chasseurs ran back helter-skelter to the main body of their army on the crest of the ridge where Barreiro stubbornly held on. It was at this moment that Anzoátegui resolved to attack the exposed flank of the enemy, and began that celebrated enveloping movement which won the battle.

The bugles sounded, but their echoes were drowned by the thunder of pounding hoofs as the squadron of lancers, hitherto held impatiently in support, now charged against the double line of bayonets of the royalist center. In vain Barreiro called upon his men to stand firm; in vain he ordered his mounted grenadiers and the dragoons of González to make a counter charge against the patriot flank. In spite of heroic but fruitless efforts, the grenadiers were forced to flee loose-reined; the horsemen of González were thrown to the ground and pierced with wounds, and a reserve squadron, drawn up in line to receive with couched lances the shock of the patriot cavalry, was dispersed by the thrusts of the lancers. Meanwhile the rest of the royalist cavalry on the road to Samacá, which had not taken part in the battle, fled like cowards behind their leader, Col. Victor Serra.

Barreiro, abandoned by his center, ran at the head of two battalions to oppose the advance of Anzoátegui, who was hastening his enveloping attack. But it was too late. The patriot infantry decided the victory with a bayonet charge. Swept off their feet, the royalist battalions gave ground and tried to reform on another ridge, but the republican horsemen interposed and put these last remnants of the army to flight.

Meanwhile Santander on the left wing, after repeated and energetic attacks against the hostile infantry which stubbornly held the bridge sent Rondon and Carvajal with some of their cavalrymen to cross the Boyacá by an old ford lower

down the stream, in order to attack the royalists from behind and dislodge them from their positions. The movement, combined with a vigorous attack by the infantry in
front, brought about the complete rout of the enemy vanguard. Surrounded on all sides, the royalist army lay down
its arms and surrendered itself to the victors. Barreiro threw
away his sword and then gave himself up to a private of the
First Rifles. Only a few individuals of the royalist vanguard managed to elude their pursuers and reach Venta
Quemada, south of the river. Besides Barreiro and Jiménez,
there surrendered thirty-nine officers and 1,600 men, the entire royalist army, with its arms, ammunition, guns, horses,
baggage and colors. Not fifty men escaped. The entire
patriot loss was thirteen killed and fifty-three wounded; and
the battle had been won in less than two hours.[1]

[1] The foregoing interpretation of the official reports of the battle of
Boyacá is based on the reconstruction of the battle by the general staff
of the Colombian army on the hundredth anniversary of the battle, and is
substantially that accepted by Col. Arturo Santana of the Venezuelan
army and by Col. Carlos Cortés Vargas of the general staff of the
army of Colombia (*cf.* works by these authors in *Memorial del Estado
Mayor del Ejército de Colombia,* Nos. 6, 87 and 145-146, and by Major
Manuel París, R. in his *Campaña del ejército libertador colombiano en
1819*). Unfortunately the official report of the battle is vague and so
lacking in detail as to make possible more than one interpretation. There
have therefore developed two schools of opinion regarding the battle.
One of them, that of the general staff of Colombia, of the officers above
referred to, and of the well-known Venezuelan historian, Dr. Vicente
Lecuna (*Cf.* his *Documentos referentes a la creación de Bolivia,* I, p.
lxix), believes that the combat between the main bodies of the royalist
and patriot armies took place on the ridges north of the river Boyacá,
and that the only fighting which occurred south of the river was that
between the vanguards under the royalist Jiménez and the patriot Santander. The other school believes that Barreiro succeeded in crossing
the bridge with his whole army and that the entire battle, with the exception of the preliminary skirmish at the " Casa de Teja ", was fought south
of the river. To this school belong Gen. J. D. Monsalve, a retired major
general of the Colombian army and a historian of note, Restrepo the historian who was serving at the time on Bolívar's staff, Elías Prieto Villate
and Cayo Leonidas Peñuela. *Cf.* José Manuel Restrepo, *Historia de*

After the battle of Boyacá, Bolívar's march to Bogotá was unopposed. He entered the capital on August 10th, to find that acting-viceroy Sámano had hastily evacuated the city with his guard of honor, the Regiment of Cazadores of Aragon, the members of the " audiencia " (supreme court), and all the royalist civil and military employees.[1] The patriots entered the capital as victors amid acclamations, though not with the pomp and pageantry of a triumph. Rather they came as the worn-out survivors of an arduous campaign.

la revolución de la República de Colombia en la América Meridional. II, 537-539; Elías Prieto Villate, "Apuntamientos sobre la campaña de 1819", published in *Repertorio Boyacense,* series V, number 43, pp. 77-122, or the similar work by the same author in Bingham Collection of Manuscripts, folios 38-46; and Cayo Leonidas Peñuela, *Album de Boyacá,* I, 332-336. This latter school bases its belief largely on the accounts of old men, residents of the neighborhood, who either took part in or witnessed the battle. Senator Hiram Bingham in his *Journal of an Expedition across Venezuela and Colombia, 1906-1907* evidently accepts as the correct one the account of the battle given in the manuscript by Elías Prieto Villate. Both interpretations, moreover, conform to the official report and to the actual terrain and both may be accepted as possible; but the present writer, after a personal visit to the battlefield, is inclined to favor the interpretation of the general staff as being the most probable and most in conformity with the terrain. He has therefore based his description of the battle on this interpretation. It seems to him that, if the battle had been waged south of the river, the royalists could have retired safely upon Bogotá, since the position commanding the bridge, was so strong that a small rear guard could have held it long enough to delay the advance of the patriots, while the retirement of the royalist main body was being effected. If, on the other hand, the battle of the main bodies took place north of the river, when Barreiro found himself cut off from his own vanguard at the bridge and from the royalist base at Bogotá, toward which he had been retreating, his situation must have seemed so desperate as to justify his surrendering. The official report of the battle is printed in full in O'Leary, *Documentos,* XVI, 428-430. The account in the *Annual Register* for 1819, "General History", 243, describing the experiences of the British in the battle relates their activities as taking place north of the bridge.

[1] O'Leary, *Narración,* I, 580, *Documentos,* XVI, 431; *Campaigns and Cruises,* I, 172, 177; Larrazábal, *op. cit.,* II, 210; *British Monitor,* Nov. 14, 1819; *The Times,* Oct. 22, 1819.

" They came as spectres, and these spectres were those who were strong of body and soul, because the weak remained in the snow, in the torrents, on the mountain-tops, where there was no air for the lungs." [1] At the head of the column of victors swinging proudly into the central plaza were some companies of the British under Capt. Manby, among which there was not a single man who possessed a pair of shoes or stockings. Even the officers had nothing better to wear than cheap cotton slippers (alpargatas).[2] Ibáñez relates how " at the dedication of a column of victory in Bogotá, Bolívar was crowned with a laurel crown by Señorita Dolores Vargas. Bolívar replied in a happy speech, first taking off the crown and putting it on Santander and then Anzoátegui and finally held it toward the Rifles Battalion saying, ' Those soldier liberators are the men who deserve these laurels.' " [3]

These momentous and far-reaching results had been accomplished in a short campaign of only seventy-five days, beginning at the departure from Mantecal and ending with the battle of Boyacá.[4] In it the British troops had played an important part. Their arrival early in the year had made it possible for Bolívar to undertake the campaign into New Granada, which he had postponed until these reenforcements had come.[5] It is true the number of the foreigners who crossed the Andes with him was not large. A hundred and fifty were in Rooke's command, of whom one-third had perished before the Páramo of Pisba had been crossed. Only ninety took part in the battle of Pántano de Vargas.[6] There

[1] José Enrique Rodó, *Cinco ensayos*, 221.

[2] Hamilton, *op. cit.*, I, 217.

[3] Pedro M. Ibáñez, *Las crónicas de Bogotá y sus inmediaciones*, 262, 263.

[4] O'Leary, *Documentos*, XVI, 431.

[5] Bingham Collection of Mss., Bolívar letters, Bolívar to Guillermo White, Feb. 7, 1819, April 4, 1819.

[6] O'Leary, *Documentos*, XVI, 411; Cochrane, *op. cit.*, I, 478, 484; Luís Felipe Acevedo, "Batalla de Boyacá" in *Memorial del Estado Mayor del Ejército de Colombia*, number 87, p. 216.

may have been fifty more holding commissions in the Rifles or scattered in staff positions or in other organizations of the army. There were nearly 3,000 additional, it will be recalled, engaged under Urdaneta in the attacks on Barcelona and Cumaná. Although these attacks were not crowned with success, they did accomplish the part assigned to them in Bolívar's grand strategy, namely that of distracting Morillo's attention from the more important operations of Bolívar's main force invading New Granada. The services of the British Legion under Gen. English and Gen. Urdaneta, as already described, must therefore be credited with rendering material assistance to Bolívar in his campaign of 1819. Furthermore, the relative strength of the two armies must be taken into consideration. The sizes of the forces engaged in this war were so small that a hundred men more or less were enough to determine Bolívar's policy one way or another. The troops under Barreiro actually engaged at Boyacá amounted to only 2940, while those under Bolívar were only 2630. Thus the difference in the size of the two armies was only 310. It is true that Bolívar had 800 additional recruits gathered from the countryside a few days before, but these columns of Tunja and Socorro were held in reserve and took little part in the fighting.[1]

---

[1] Col. Luís Felipe Acevedo gives the following tables of organizations engaged in the battle:—

Royalists: Vanguard

Dragoons	160
2nd Battalion of Numancia	500
3rd Battalion of Numancia	350
Main body:—	
Dragoons	320
Battalion Chasseurs of Victory	480
Artillery	90
1st Battalion of the King	640
2nd Battalion of the King	400

As to the importance of the foreigners at the battle of
Boyacá itself, there seems to be some question which might
stand investigation. It has been customary for English
writers to attribute the victory of Boyacá largely to the
efforts of the British. Ducoudray-Holstein says: " This
battle of the 7th August decreed the fate of New Granada
and its success was attributed to the European troops ";[1]
but his statements are evidently not made from first-hand
knowledge, for he speaks of the battle as that of " Venta
Quemada" and calls Barreiro "Barasano".[2] Mulhall writes,
" Respecting the Battle of Boyacá we read in Miller's Memoirs as follows: ' It was fought on August 7, 1819, and is
called the birth of Colombia. In this battle the English
troops, under the command of Major Mackintosh, greatly
distinguished themselves. The gallant major was promoted
by the Liberator on the field.' "[3] In following up this quo-
tation, one finds in Miller's Memoirs the statement that the

Patriots: Vanguard:—

1st Battalion of Chasseurs	400
1st Battalion of the Line	410
Guides	200
Main body:—	
Battalion of Rifles	420
Battalion of Barcelona	300
Battalion of Bravos of Páez	300
British Legion	120
Lancers	300
Guides	100
Dragoons	80
Militia:—	
Column of Tunja	500
Column of Socorro	300

Acevedo, *op. cit.,* 216. The figures given in París *op. cit.,* 27, 67, agree
closely with the foregoing.

[1] Ducoudray-Holstein, *Memoirs of Simón Bolívar*, II, 118.

[2] *Ibid.*, II, 117.

[3] Mulhall, *op. cit.*, 294.

battle of Boyacá " was fought on August 7, 1819, and is called the birth of Colombia ".[1]   That is all there is in the text itself, for the remainder of the remark quoted about the English troops is relegated to a footnote.   Furthermore, Miller is not a primary source for the campaign in New Granada.   Koebel remarks that " The battle of Boyacá consolidated the reputation of the British whose ranks had now received more reenforcements ".[2]   It will be noticed that all of these writers are rather vague as to the achievements of the British in the battle, and that none of them gives particulars as to the services the English Rifles actually performed.   Bingham, however, is more specific, for he says: " The British Legion made a bold attack on the centre and caused a complete rout ".   Barreiro had " some light artillery on one of the hills and it required no little bravery on the part of the British Legion to make the frontal attack ".[3]

The trouble seems to be that all these writers, with the exception of Bingham, make their statements on little or no contemporary evidence.   Unfortunately the evidence which should be the most reliable, the official report of the battle, is so brief and vague as to give little information as to details, and other evidence seems to be limited to the treacherous memories of old men who claimed to have seen the battle, but probably did not understand what was taking place, even if, as is not probable, they were able to see it all or to remember correctly what they saw.   If we accept the interpretation of the battle, which places the scene of the action of the main bodies under Barreiro and Anzoátegui on the ridges north of the river, the British may be credited with having interposed themselves between the bridge and Barreiro and

[1] John Miller, *Memoirs of General Miller in the service of the Republic of Peru,* II, 288.

[2] William Henry Koebel, *British Exploits in South America,* 174.

[3] Bingham, *op. cit.,* 221.

having prevented the attempt of the royalist commander to effect a junction between his main body and his vanguard. The Rifles may also be credited with taking their part in the charge against the royalist artillery and in driving the royalist infantry from the ridge on which it made its last stand. While leading his company in this charge Capt. John Johnston was wounded in the arm.[1] If, however, the interpretation is accepted of the school which places the entire royalist force on the south side of the river,[2] it is not possible to credit the British with any particular deeds of prowess, for the battle must have been practically won by Santander, when he crossed with his vanguard and crumpled up the right flank of the enemy, before Anzoátegui with the main body could cross.

That Bolívar and his staff failed to value the services of the foreigners above those of their own compatriots may be judged from the meagre mention of the former found in the official reports and despatches concerning the battle. In the bulletin of the liberating army of New Granada issued from headquarters at Venta Quemada the day after the battle, the only special mention of them is found in the statement that a hostile movement toward the right was checked by the Rifles and an English company.[3] An order of the same source and date directs that " the following organizations are authorized to place on their colors the word ' Boyacá ':— First Battalion of Cazadores; First Battalion of the Line of New Granada; the battalions Rifles, Venezuela, Barcelona, Bravos de Páez, and English Rifles; also the squadrons Lancers of Llano-arriba, Guides of Casanare, and of Apure,

[1] Archivo Nacional, Bogotá, Guerra y Marina, Hojas de Serricios, XXX, 916; Cochrane, Journal, I, 490.

[2] *Cf.* p. 209, n. 1.

[3] O'Leary, *Documentos*, XVI, 428.

and the Dragoons." [1]　Thus every organization, without discrimination, which took part in the battle was granted the honor of inscribing the name on its colors — a common method of distributing honors wholesale after a successful campaign.　Moreover, in the bulletin of the battle, previously quoted, those mentioned as deserving special praise are Generals Anzoátegui and Santander; and the Bravos de Páez, First Battalion of Barcelona, Squadron of Llano-arriba, and even the columns of Tunja and Socorro, which had been held in reserve until the last moment.[2]　It will be noticed that the British do not appear among those singled out for special praise.

As for the battle of Pántano de Vargas, however, there is no question that the British did render distinguished service when they charged the heights.　Of this battle Bingham says: " The Spaniards took up a very strong position, but the British Legion attacked so fiercely that the result was a drawn battle."　Further on he says: " In many ways Pántano de Vargas was a more important victory than the Battle of Boyacá.　It was not definitive and is not so well known. Nevertheless it seems clear to me that it put the Spaniards on the defensive and gave Bolívar the upper hand.　Boyacá saw the end of the Spanish army in Colombia, but Pántano de Vargas was the decisive victory." [3]　O'Leary, in describing the battle writes: "All appeared lost, but Bolívar rallied the shattered centre and ordered Rooke with the British Legion to dislodge the enemy from the heights which they occupied.　The brilliant conduct of Rondon and the calm valor of the British troops won the victory, or rather saved from complete destruction the liberating army of New Gra-

---

[1] O'Leary, *Documentos,* XVI, 430.

[2] *Ibid.*

[3] Bingham, *op. cit.,* 214, 215.

nada."[1] In his general orders next day, Bolívar recognized
the valor of the British and conferred upon them the star of
the Order of Liberators.[2] Thus, although one cannot glorify
the British for winning the victory of Boyacá, they may be
credited with making that victory possible, by saving the
army of Bolívar a few days before, on an occasion of almost
equal importance, at the battle of Pántano de Vargas.

After the victory of Boyacá and the occupation of the
capital at Bogotá there still remained formidable royalist
forces scattered throughout other sections of New Granada.[3]
The important ports of Santa Marta, Barranquilla and Cartagena were held by them. La Torre threatened to invade
Cundinamarca by way of Cúcuta. Colonel Francisco War-
lata, under orders from Sámano, still controlled Antioquía
and was operating in the valleys of both the Atrato and
Cauca Rivers and along the upper Magdalena. In the south,
strong royalist guerrillas were terrorizing the country about
Pasto, Popayán, and even as far as Neiva.[4]

Most of the cities and important towns of Cundinamarca
were located in the mountains and received the bulk of their
supplies from the port cities on the Caribbean coast. In
southern New Granada, as in the present Republic of Colombia near the boundary of Ecuador, the chain of the Andes is
gathered in a confused knot of lofty peaks and ranges in the
vicinity of Pasto and Popayán. Thence they divide into
three branches and extend northward as the western, central
and eastern cordilleras. Between the Pacific Ocean and the
western cordillera flows the Atrato River, between the west-

---

[1] O'Leary, *Narración*, I, 572.

[2] O'Leary, *Documentos*, XVI, 422; Blanco, *op. cit.*, VIII, 6; Walker,
op. cit., II, 422.

[3] *Archivo Santander*, V, ii.

[4] O'Leary, *Narración*, I, 580, 581; *Archivo Santander*, III, 224, 271, 278,
298, 305; Rodríguez Villa, *op. cit.*, IV, 49; José Manuel Groot, *Historia
eclesiástica y civil de Nueva Granada*, III, 59, 60.

ern and central cordillera the Cauca River and between the central and eastern winds the Magdalena. Then as now these three rivers, of which the Magdalena is the most important, formed the only lines of communication between the mountain cities and the coast.

A hundred years ago this journey of nearly a thousand miles down the mountains to the rivers and down the rivers to the sea was difficult and dangerous in the extreme. Even today, with short lines of railway to carry the traveler from the capital down to the river, and around the dangerous rapids near Honda, it is still difficult, tedious and time-consuming. The Magdalena River is so shallow and treacherous along the greater part of its course and so liable to sudden floods on its lower reaches, that the shallow draught, stern-wheel paddle steamers often miss the channel and spend days and weeks hard and fast on a sand-bar or a gravel-bank until the rains raise the river again. Under the best conditions the traveler to-day is fortunate if he makes the journey from Bogotá to Barranquilla in ten days; but in the early years of the nineteenth century, when the only means of transportation in the mountains was the back of a mule, and on the river was a "bunga", or long flat-bottomed canoe, propelled by poleing,[1] the journey was a precarious one. In those days, therefore, one of the greatest problems of maintaining troops in the interior lay in keeping control of the long lines of communication necessitated by these river valleys.

To assure himself possession of New Granada, Bolívar accordingly had to wrest these valleys and coast cities from the royalists who still held on there. To do this, large mobile forces were necessary, so Bolívar's first care was to increase and reorganize his troops.[2] He appointed Gen. San-

[1] *Recollections of Service*, I, 204.

[2] *Archivo Santander*, III, 224; *Boletín de historia y antigüedades* (Bogotá), X, 56.

tander vice-president of New Granada, and made him responsible for recruiting in that province and for organizing and supplying all the armies operating both in the south and in the north.[1] Although Gen. Urdaneta was placed in immediate command of the troops in the north, Gen. Soublette was appointed chief of staff and director of operations in that zone, and was sent toward Cúcuta to drive back La Torre. Soublette was to capture the region about Cúcuta and to hold it with what veteran troops he had, while at the same time gathering recruits and training new organizations.[2]

Bolívar, far-sighted and expert as a statesman and organizer as well as a general and liberator, conceived the magnificent plan of uniting the provinces which he had freed and was yet to free into one powerful republic. He therefore made a hurried trip to Angostura and persuaded the congress to accept his plan. On Dec. 17, 1819, that body accordingly declared that Venezuela and New Granada were incorporated into a new and independent republic to be called " Great Colombia ".[3] The capital of this republic was to be at Cúcuta on the eastern slopes of the eastern cordillera in New Granada near the boundary of Venezuela and conveniently located for both the former provinces. Here Bolívar, elected president, made his headquarters, and here he reorganized his veteran army by filling it with recruits.[4]

Some of these recruits were formed into new organizations, while others were incorporated into the old battalions

[1] *Archivo Santander*, II, 281; O'Leary, *Documentos*, XVI, 456.

[2] *Archivo Santander*, II, 264, 265; O'Leary, *Documentos*, XVI, 482-485, 544, 545; Archivo Nacional, Bogotá, Guerra y Marina, Historia, DCCLXXIX, 156.

[3] O'Leary, *Narración*, II, 19; *Documentos*, XVII, 5-8.

[4] O'Leary, *Narración*, II, 21-23. Sergt. Major Flegel was sent to the town of Gibraltar on Lake Maracaibo to recruit and discipline the militia on the Venezuela side of the border. Archivo Nacional, Bogotá, Guerra y Marina, Historia, VI, 11.

which were reorganized to facilitate their training. The Second Battalion of Rifles under Col. Mackintosh was allowed to keep its former organization, but in order to indicate more clearly the character of its personnel and as a distinction for its conduct in the late campaign, it was officially renamed the "Albión Batallón". This name it proudly retained throughout the remainder of its existence. Having suffered least from the influx of recruits, it was soon ready to continue active operations and was sent under Gen. Valdéz to Popayán to the relief of the hard-pressed garrison there and to take part in the campaign of the south.[1]

The First Battalion of Rifles suffered more severely from the reorganization, inasmuch as all lieutenants and non-commissioned officers were detached and assigned to other organizations for the purpose of instructing recruits. Many of its foreign officers, however, continued with it and Lieut. Col. Arthur Sandes was left in command. It was, moreover, honored by being assigned to the guard of the president as the First Battalion of Rifles of the Guard.[2]

The order providing for this reorganization of the Albions and the Rifles directed that the vacancies caused thereby were to be filled from deserters from other organizations that might be in the province and from such recruits as might be necessary to bring the number up to five hundred. The recruits were to receive only their rations until they were well-disciplined, and then given half pay; but in order to check

[1] Walker, *op. cit.*, II, 585, 607; Major Jorge Zornosa, "Los Batallones Libertadores" in *Memorial del Estado Mayor del Ejército de Colombia.* No. 15, p. 14; Florez Álvarez, *op. cit.,* 46. *Vide* also Chapter X.

[2] Among the foreign officers serving with the Rifles Battalion at this period were Lt. Col. Arthur Sandes commanding, Sergt. Major Peacock, Major Friedrich von Clauditz, Capt. William Winter, Lieuts. Heinrich Mathias Witt, Pierre Bachelier, John David Tribolet, George Fatherstonhaugh, William Franklin, Moritz Gustav Richter, Carl August Heinrich Meinecke, Mons Larson, William Schacht, and Surgeon August Zinkernagel. Archivo Nacional, Bogotá, Guerra y Marina, Historia, I, 658; *Correo del Orinoco,* March 3, 1821.

their fault-findings and complaints, the English officers and non-commissioned officers were to receive full pay. Above all, the most rigorous discipline must be maintained and any disorders committed by members of these corps severely punished. For this purpose a court-martial must be kept in permanent session in each battalion.[1] It is evident that, while Bolívar valued the fighting qualities of his foreigners during campaign, he was not entirely sure of their good conduct when in garrison. With regard to the order that the Englishmen should receive full pay, Cochrane says that, although this order could not be carried fully into effect at all times, never again as in 1819 were they entirely without pay.[2]

Of the Rifles of the Guard, Level has said it was the bravest of all the veteran battalions. It was the steadiest in combat, but the most disorderly and turbulent in garrison. Magnificent in action, it was ever ready to sacrifice itself with boyish heroism which in time of peace displayed itself in a spirit of insubordinate discontent and undisciplined wrangling. The Rifles were the terror of the peasantry. It is true they did not loot and rob, but they were fond of good eating and drinking; and when they invited themselves to feast it was a calamity to their hosts. There was no drinking-place which they did not own as soon as they entered it. No dance was held at which some member of the Rifles did not monopolize the girls. The officers were as gallant as the men. " When the captain made love to the lady, the orderly left the maid nothing to complain of." Even in church the officers were sometimes boisterous and sacrilegious. The discipline of the Rifles does not speak well for the ability of Col. Sandes as a commanding officer; yet nothing could be said against his bravery as a soldier, for in the moment of danger the Rifle Battalion showed splendid conduct.[3]

[1] O'Leary, *Documentos*, XVI, 503, 508, 509.

[2] Cochrane, *op. cit.*, I, 494.

[3] Level, *op. cit.*, 389, 390.

While stationed at Bucaramanga, near Pamplona, this battalion was filled up with 400 recruits, half of whom promptly deserted, taking with them their uniforms and equipment. O'Leary says that during the years 1818 to 1822 it was necessary to furnish the Rifles with 22,000 recruits, in order to replace the losses from desertion and deaths in action and in hospital, and to maintain a strength of 600.[1]

At first the Rifles were assigned to the division of Gen. Anzoátegui, but that general contracted a fatal illness and died at Pamplona on Sept. 15, 1819.[2]   The Rifles had then been sent northward from Ocaña toward Tenerife as part of a division under Colonels Lara and Carreño which was to support Montilla.   It will be remembered that, after occupying Rio Hacha and Barranquilla, Montilla had penetrated to Tenerife where he effected a junction with Col. Córdoba. The latter commander had been one of those who had been sent northward from Bogotá to drive the royalists out of the river valleys and to open lines of communication to the north coast ports.   With his Division of Antioquía, Col. Córdoba had been sweeping down the Cauca valley toward Medellín and thence to the Magdalena valley, where he had captured Mompox and Tenerife.[3]   In his attack on the latter place he had been aided by Montilla and by Admiral Brión with ships and ammunition.[4]

[1] O'Leary, *Narración*, II, 123, 124, Carlos Cortés Vargas, *Participación de Colombia en la libertad del Perú*, I, 103, 104; Florez Álvarez, *op. cit.*, 40, 41; Archivo Nacional, Bogotá, Guerra y Marina, Historia, XXXVII, 911; Archivo Soublette, II, Documentos, 1822.

[2] Urdaneta, *op. cit.*, 168, *n.*; Florez Álvarez, *op. cit.*, 36, 37. Dr. Thomas Foley attended Gen. Anzoátegui in his last illness.

[3] Urdaneta, *op. cit.*, 173-175; *Archivo Santander*, IV, 6; "Documentos históricos" published in *Memorial del Estado Mayor del Ejército de Colombia*, No. 36, p. 294; "Diario de operaciones de la División de Antioquía", in *Memorial del Estado Mayor*, No. 103, pp. 27-30.

[4] *Cf.* Chapter VII; *Correo del Orinoco*, June 10, 1820; *Present State of Colombia*, 47.

The sufferings of the troops in this campaign of the Magdalena were almost as terrible as they were in the " llanos " of the Apure, for the recruits, bred in the high altitudes of cold and bleak Cundinamarca were oppressed by the heavy, humid atmosphere of the torrid lowlands of the river valley; they were filled with the germs of malaria by the nightly attacks of swarms of mosquitos; they were exhausted by floundering in the swamps and hacking their way through the jungle. More than half the troops succumbed to the rigors of this campaign and one column was compelled to leave 600 sick men behind.[1] The organizations that made this campaign of the Magdalena under Córdoba were the Battalions Upper Magdalena, Girardot, Antioquía and Mompox, in the last three of which a number of foreign officers were then serving.[2] The Rifles did not actually take part in the whole campaign, but they traversed similar country and endured similar hardships in their march down from Ocaña to Tenerife. At that place it will be remembered a junction was effected with Montilla.

Córdoba's division then accompanied Montilla's to lay siege to Cartagena, while the Rifles, augmented as will also be remembered by some lancers of the Irish Legion under

[1] " Documentos históricos " in *Memorial del Estado Mayor del Ejército de Colombia*, No. 36, p. 294.

[2] Peñuela, *op. cit.*, I, 390-392. In the Girardot Battalion were Lieut. Col. T. Minuth, Capts. James Loedel and James Lister and Lieut. John D. Murray; in the Antioquía Battalion were Capt. Joseph Doubourdieu and Lieut. Charles Brown; Lieut. Col. Dunlop commanded the Battalion of Mompox; and on staff duty or unassigned were Lieut. Col. John Traynor, Sergts. Major Edward Brand, D. Reinboldt, Otto Nagle and Dennis Egan, as well as Capt. N. Pueche. Archivo Nacional, Bogotá, Guerra y Marina, Historia, I, 674, 675-677; VII, 158; XV, 569, 573, 579, 585, DCCLXXX, 860. These records are lists of promotions or recommendations and are not rosters of the organizations; therefore they must not be considered as containing the names of all the foreigners who were attached to these organizations. There may or may not have been others.

Col. O'Connor, were sent to capture the city of Santa Marta. On arrival at the Rio Frio it was necessary to wade across, in the face of a well-directed fire from the opposite bank. The royalists then withdrew a league from the river to the crest of a perpendicular cliff where they tried to defend themselves, but were driven off by the Girardot Battalion, a company of the Rifles and some of the lancers. The demoralized enemy then raced back to the shelter of the palisades of Fort Ciénaga, two leagues in their rear, which the patriots at once invested. Sailors from the fleet were landed and captured the suburb of Sábanas. O'Connor was given command of the left wing while Col. Carreño took charge of the right. Twice the enemy sallied out from behind their palisades and rushed upon the bayonets of the patriots, but each time they were repulsed with heavy casualties. Eight hundred men of the Rifles took part in the attack. Of these, forty were killed and sixty wounded. The total enemy loss was five hundred.[1] This meant the practical annihilation of Sánchez Lima's force of defenders.

After the capture of Fort Ciénaga the road to Santa Marta was open, and the next day Col. Carreño marched upon it. On Nov. 11, 1820, that city surrendered. In this capture fifty siege guns and twenty-two field guns were taken by the patriots. In his report Montilla recommended for valor Lieut. Col. Sandes and Sergt. Major Peacock of the Rifles as well as Capts. Philam and Romero of the same battalion, who were wounded.[2] Bolívar gave his thanks to the troops, and authorized Montilla to promote especially deserving captains to brevet lieutenant colonels. Diplomas granting the use of chevrons of honor of the Army of the

---

[1] *Correo del Orinoco*, Feb. 3, 10, March 3, 1821; Urdaneta, *op. cit.*, 176; O'Connor, *op. cit.*, 30, 48-52; Groot, *op. cit.*, III, 90; *Present State of Colombia*, 61, 75, 79.

[2] *Correo del Orinoco*, March 3, 1821.

Magdalena were subsequently awarded to 170 members of the Rifle Battalion.[1] The possession of Santa Marta was especially important to the patriots, for it opened shorter lines of communication from the coast, not only to Cúcuta but also to the region about Lake Maracaibo.

It was intended that the Rifle Battalion should be sent into this region to Truxillo to be reincorporated in the Guards under the supervision of Urdaneta; but owing to the armistice which it will be recalled went into effect on Nov. 27, 1820, this transfer was delayed.[2] While awaiting these orders the Rifles suffered the loss of six or seven of their musicians who were transferred to San Juan near Achaguas for assignment to the British Legion. Evidently the Legion had by that time organized a band of which it was proud, for Sergt. Major Sasely, music major, had brought three clarinets, a flute and other instruments, while a box of band paraphernalia belonging to the Legion had been shipped from Margarita and had reached Angostura.[3]

In the spring of 1821 the armistice was broken by a revolt of the citizens of Maracaibo and by a misunderstanding on the part of Urdaneta who supported that revolt and then started on an independent expedition to Coro.[4] About the

[1] Archivo Nacional, Bogotá, Guerra y Marina, Historia, XVII, 6 Oct., 1821; Archivo Montilla, III (folio not numbered).

[2] Archivo Montilla, 1820, III, Sucre to Montilla, Dec. 22, 1820; O'Leary, *Documentos,* XVIII, 8.

[3] Archivo Nacional, Caracas, Gobernación de Guayana, XIV, 155. It is evident that English musical talent was appreciated by the patriots, for Music Major J. S. Canning was granted a salary of $20 a month for instructing the young musicians in the army, and a contract was entered into with George Kay and John Cummings of Jamaica to teach music to military bandsmen, whereby these instructors were to receive in addition to their salaries, quarters and expenses back to their homes in case the climate of Bogotá did not agree with them. Archivo Nacional, Bogotá, Guerra y Marina, History, XXXV, 857, 859, 894, 895.

[4] Urdaneta, *op. cit.,* 191-194; *Correo del Orinoco,* June 23, 1821; Archivo Nacional, Bogotá, Guerra y Marina, Historia, VI, 32.

middle of that year the Rifle Battalion at last received its order to join Urdaneta's division, which was then returning from Coro to Barquisimeto to concentrate for operations under Bolívar. The battalion returned from Ciénaga to Santa Marta, whence part of it embarked for Coro and the remainder marched overland across the Goajira peninsula toward Lake Maracaibo. Those who went by land were employed in suppressing a revolt of the Goajira Indians, whereas those who went by sea were delayed by the stranding of their vessel, so that the Rifles did not join Urdaneta until after his division had reached Pedregal well on its way to Barquisimeto. Soon thereafter Urdaneta fell sick and relinquished his command to Col. Antonio Rangel.[1] Under that officer and his successor, Col. Ambrosio Plaza, the Rifle Battalion was subsequently incorporated into the Third Division of Bolívar's army for the campaign of Carabobo.

[1] Urdaneta, *op. cit.*, 194-196; O'Leary, *Documentos*, XVIII, 36; O'Connor, *op. cit.*, 56; Archivo Nacional, Bogotá, Guerra y Marina, Historia, VI, 834; Level, *op. cit.*, 393; Florez Álvarez, *op. cit.*, 247; Archivo Montilla, III (folio not numbered).

CHAPTER IX

Struggling on the Plains for Liberty

Just as the campaign of Boyacá had separated the legionaries by taking some of them away into New Granada, so now the campaign of Carabobo was to bring many together again. The Albion Battalion, it is true, had gone southward to make history for itself and to end its days in glory, but the Rifles and the Lancers from the Irish Legion were marching back into western Venezuela. Foreign officers who had been detached to organize and train other battalions were gradually being concentrated in the Maracaibo Lake district, not far from their former comrades of the British Legion who had continued to serve under Páez near Achaguas.[1] It will also be remembered that Gen. Urdaneta had been directed to take command of the Colombian Guard,[2] which was being newly formed near Cúcuta from several veteran battalions that were stationed there or in the neighboring Venezuelan departments of Mérida and Trujillo which lay between the Achaguas, Lake Maracaibo and New

---

[1] Among the latter were Lt. Col. Thomas Harrison who had continued to serve with that portion of the British Legion which had remained with Páez, Capt. Jacob Vale Asbury, who was in the Guard of Honor of Páez and later in the Battalion Bravos Cazadores del Orinoco; Robert Fry who was Surgeon Major on the staff of Páez at Achaguas; and Dr. Foley, who had been chief of the hospitals of the patriot armies under Bolívar, Páez and Anzoátegui. Archivo Nacional, Bogotá, Guerra y Marina, Historia, III, 145-146; VI, 3; VII, 64; Archivo Nacional, Caracas, Ilustres Próceres, XCV, 245; XCIX, 219; Level, op. cit., 314. For a complete list of the English officers and soldiers who were still at Angostura in 1820, see Appendix G.

[2] Rivas, op. cit., 170, 181, 186, 191; Santana, Carabobo, 75.

Granada border.   All of these battalions of the Guard sooner or later contained foreigners.[1]

Interesting characterizations of the battalions are given by Gen. Lino Duarte Level.   " Vencedor," he says, " was the battalion of decisive charges, of last resorts, of rapid maneuvers.   It was composed of mountaineers from Venezuela and New Granada and had no foreigners in its ranks." [2]   The Battalion of Tiradores, he observes, was a combat corps and well trained in the school of fire.   It had one black page in its history, for it was the only organization that mutinied because of delay in receiving its pay, but it soon felt so ashamed of this that it returned to duty of its own accord. It formed part of the Army of the West under Páez on the Apure, and its men were both Venezuelans and New Granadans who lived on the frontier between Maracaibo and Cartagena.

The Grenadiers, remarks Gen. Duarte Level, further, were taught by Uslar calm, dignity and steadfastness.   This battalion had no use for trophies, triumphal arches, receptions,

[1] Lieut. Col. George Woodberry was appointed Adjutant General and Chief of Staff of the Guard; Col. Johannes Uslar, of the Grenadiers, likewise as senior colonel temporarily commanded the First Brigade of the Guard; Lieut. Col. Miller Hallowes was a company commander in the Battalion Vencedor en Boyacá; Sergt. Major Ludwig Flegel commanded the Boyacá Battalion in which Lieut. Schmeiden was second adjutant; subsequently after the Vargas Battalion had been broken up to form the Battalion of Tiradores, in which in 1820 Julius A. Reinboldt was a major, Sergt. Major Flegel was assigned to the command of a detachment of the Vargas; and as will be remembered there were a number of foreign officers besides Col. Arthur Sandes in the First Battalion of Rifles of the Guard.   Archivo Nacional, Bogotá, Guerra y Marina, Historia, VI, 11, 17, VII, 53, 54; X, 232, 250, 274, 357; Correo del Orinoco, Sept. 29, 1821; Santana, Carabobo, 184, 186; Level, op. cit., 426.

[2] Probably Duarte Level refers only to enlisted men and did not consider Lieut. Col. Miller Hallowes as being " in its ranks."   Level, op. cit., 410.

music or demonstrations. It learned from him to do its work in a truly German phlegmatic manner. It was always honorable and never a stain sullied its history. It was the cnly battalion which never failed in discipline. It fought well; it suffered without complaining; it never believed that it should be rewarded with anything but its normal pay. It had only two commanding officers, Plaza and Uslar. On Oct. 21, 1818, it was organized from recruits in the missions of Caroni. It served in the campaign of Apure and fought at the battle of El Semen. It took part in the campaign of 1819 and in the battles of Gameza, Pántano de Vargas and Boyacá. In the last, by order of Anzoátegui, it charged the royalist center. After Boyacá, still under the command of Plaza, it was recruited to one thousand. April, 1821, during the armistice, it marched to Barinas and was incorporated into the First Brigade of the Guard. August 11, 1821, Col. Uslar was appointed its commanding officer by Bolívar, who ordered that it should consist entirely of tall men, all of the same height (from 5 feet 10 inches to 6 feet) to form a strikingly brilliant battalion worthy of the chief who commanded it. The men chosen were to be models of athletic and muscular build all under twenty-five years and none under eighteen. Its uniform was like that of French grenadiers and its drill was a modification of Prussian and English drill regulations. It was in every way a noteworthy and imposing corps.[1]

Believing that the armistice which had been in effect since the previous November had lasted long enough to enable Spain to arrive at a decision to grant independence, and that a longer continuance would accomplish no good, but would cause undue hardship instead on the inhabitants of Venezuela by checking the natural flow of commerce and thereby

---

[1] Level, *op. cit.*, 402-407, 410, 425, 426.

causing scarcity of provisions, Bolívar, on March 10, 1821, wrote to La Torre, the Spanish commander in Venezuela, proposing that the armistice be ended. La Torre consented, laying the blame for the rupture on Bolívar. A little over a month later, on April 28, the armistice was declared at an end, and preparations for the renewal of operations were made by both sides.[1]

At this time the situation of the two armies may be roughly described as follows. The royalists occupied the north coast of Venezuela including the provinces of Coro and Caracas. The strength of their forces amounted to 11,000 men at the time. During the armistice Morillo had relinquished the command to La Torre and had returned to Spain. The latter had located his headquarters at Valencia, about halfway between Barquisimeto and Caracas; and by means of strong divisions stationed at Barquisimeto, Guanare, San Carlos and Calabozo, he controlled most of the territory north of the Apure River as far east as the junction of that river with the Orinoco.[2] The republican army held the whole line of the Orinoco and the provinces of Guayana, Mérida, Truxillo and part of Barinas. It also garrisoned the coast cities of Barcelona and Carúpano and the Island of Margarita, through which communication by sea was kept open.

In the center of his line Bolívar had 4000 men at Barinas, while Páez commanded 3000 British and native troops south of the Apure, near San Fernando and Achaguas. At the extreme left, Urdaneta was organizing a new division between Santa Marta and Coro, while Bermúdez, on the right

[1] *Correo del Orinoco*, April 14, 1821; Bingham, *op. cit.*, 276.

[2] Archivo Montilla, III, Sucre to Montilla, Dec. 22, 1820; Carey I. Crockett, " Carabobo," in *Journal U. S. Infantry*, XXV, 373-383; Santana, *Carabobo*, 43 44; Bingham Collection of Mss. Bolívar letters, no. 9, Bolívar to Guillermo White, May 6, 1821; *Annual Register*, 1821, "History," 261.

at Barcelona, was thrust in between the Spanish division at Cumaná and the main Spanish army.[1] It will thus be seen that, while the Spanish commander had the advantages of holding the inner lines and of keeping open his communications by sea with Spain, Bolívar, on the other hand, held the vast and rich Orinoco valley in which to support his army, and possessed uninterrupted lines of communication by the numerous rivers which watered this section. The wide dispersion of his forces, necessitated by the area to be covered, had also facilitated their living off the country during the armistice.

Two causes had heretofore prevented Bolívar from concentrating his forces. The first was the difficulty of supplying more than 4,000 men in any one locality; the second was the jealousy of his subordinates, who until Bolívar had gained his great prestige by the conquest of New Granada in 1819, were unwilling to curtail their independence by subjecting themselves to his orders.[2] Obviously, now that active operations had begun again, the proper thing to do was to seize the initiative, attack the enemy and either destroy him or drive him to his ships. First, however, it was essential for Bolívar to mobilize his forces. His plan of campaign was to concentrate the divisions of Páez and Urdaneta with his own near Guanare; then to advance against the enemy and risk a decision in combat. Meanwhile Bermúdez with the army of the east was to march on Caracas and create a diversion against the rear of the enemy, so that La Torre might be compelled to detach important forces from his army on the eve of battle and send them back for the protection

---

[1] *London Chronicle*, July 27, Aug. 6, 1821; *Archivo Santander*, VI, 174; *Correo del Orinoco*, May 6, 1821; Santana, *Carabobo*, 43; Bingham, *op. cit.*, 276; Walker, *op. cit.*, II, 499.

[2] Santana, *op. cit.*, 72; Vicente Lecuna, " La Campaña de Carabobo y la Diversión de Bermúdez " in *Hispania*, II, 859.

of the capital.[1] Because after the event this seems to have been the obvious thing to do should not detract from the credit due to Bolívar for the excellence of his strategy.

The campaign of 1821 began on April 28, when Bolívar sent Cols. Gómez and Plaza to clear the road from Guanare to San Carlos. The Fifth Division of the Spanish Army was driven out of San Carlos, where Bolívar established his headquarters to await the arrival of the divisions of Páez and Urdaneta.[2] To the commanders of both of these divisions orders were sent, directing them to join Bolívar at San Carlos instead of at Mijigual, the point of rendezvous designated in the original orders, and informing them that the attack on Caracas by Bermúdez had been successful in causing La Torre to withdraw his troops from the interior and to concentrate the First, Third and Fifth Divisions at Valencia.[3] La Torre was so alarmed for the safety of Caracas that he detached a corps under his second in command, Gen. Morales, for its defense. Bermúdez won several skirmishes, but at length was forced to yield to superior numbers and give up Caracas again to the royalists. Morales then had time to rejoin La Torre and with the greater part of his forces took part in the battle of Carabobo.[4]

Urdaneta, returning from Coro, had succeeded in reorganizing his division, of which the Rifles now formed an important part, and was on his way south again to comply with the orders of the commander-in-chief for the concentration. After Urdaneta, who it will be remembered was too ill to continue his march beyond Barquisimeto, had relinquished the command of his division to Col. Rangel, the

[1] *London Chronicle*, Aug. 24, 1821; Crockett, *op. cit.*, 375; Santana, *op. cit.*, 72.

[2] Santana, *op. cit.*, 80, 84; Rivas, *op. cit.*, 173, 190.

[3] O'Leary, *Documentos*, XVIII, 179, 297, 298.

[4] O'Leary, *Narración*, II, 79.

latter was instructed to join Bolívar at San Carlos.[1] First, however, he was to detach a force under Col. Carillo to make a feint toward San Felipe in order to draw more troops away from La Torre's main command.

Bolívar's army now received the organization with which it went into the battle. The three divisions were commanded respectively by Gen. Páez, Gen. Cedeño and Col. Plaza. The first division, under Páez, was composed of the British Battalion, the Bravos of Apure (with which the Hussars and Cazadores de Barinas had been incorporated), and six regiments of cavalry; the second, under Cedeño, formed of the Second Brigade of the Guards, the battalions, Tiradores, Boyacá and Vargas, with a squadron of cavalry; the third, under Plaza, contained the First Brigade of the Guards, the battalions Rifles, Grenadiers, Vencedor en Boyacá, and Anzoátegui, with one regiment and two squadrons of cavalry, their total strength being about 6500.[2]

La Torre had detached a division under Col. Tello toward San Felipe to oppose Col. Carillo's little raiding party. This reduced the Spanish main army to 5000 men. La Torre had kept this whole force, 3500 infantry and 1500 cavalry, encamped at Carabobo to protect the road to Valencia and Caracas, and instead of employing them to prevent the junction of Urdaneta and Páez, had supinely waited until Bolívar could unite his forces and advance to the attack.[3]

Shortly after dawn on June 24, 1821, when Bolívar at the head of his army arrived on the hill of El Vigia, he looked down upon the plains of Carabobo, five kilometers broad,

[1] Urdaneta, *op. cit.*, 195.

[2] Archivo Nacional, Bogotá, Guerra y Marina, Historia, DCCLXXIX, 923-989; DCCLXXX, 549; Santana, *op. cit.*, 163-165; Crockett, *op. cit.*, 377; Florez Álvarez, *op. cit.*, 96.

[3] Vicente Lecuna, in *Hispania*, III, 910; Manuel Castaños y Montijano, *Páginas olvidadas de la historia militar de España*, 56, 59.

and saw the whole army of La Torre in position to receive him. The early morning mists, breaking away below, revealed a confused mass of low, irregular hills enclosing and almost hiding the little Carabobo brook which meandered in and out among them, showing itself here and there by means of the brighter verdure which lined its banks. Beyond the brook the hills rose higher and higher until they culminated in a broad plateau on which could be distinguished the royal battalions drawn up in close ranks on both sides of the road that wound its way up to the plateau and then disappeared in a blur of dry grass and dust-laden atmosphere long before it reached the distant blue mountains. The white uniforms of the royalist troops and their glittering accoutrements made a picture which meant more to Bolívar than mere beauty. For the Spanish commander had chosen a position at the junction of the direct road to Tinaco and the old road to Pao from which he could effectually block the advance of the patriots by whichever road they might come.[1] Behind and around him stretched the level open savannas which provided an ideal maneuvering-ground for the cavalry that he held in readiness along the main road behind his heavy infantry battalions. In his front he had an open field of fire down hill, and he could have at his mercy any rash patriot troops who might venture to attack him from that direction.

Bolívar, realizing that under these conditions a frontal attack would be impossible, rapidly estimated the situation and determined to attack the right flank of the enemy from

[1] Santana, *op. cit.*, 112; Montenegro, *op. cit.*, IV, 361; O'Leary, *Narración*, II, 80. O'Leary says that Bolívar made his reconnaissance from the heights of Buenavista; but the present writer agrees with Dr. Lecuna that the hill at present known by that name is too far from the field of Carabobo to afford a view of all the royalist troops, and prefers to accept as the proper point of observation the hill marked " El Vigia " on the map in Santana, *op. cit.*, facing page 108. This hill is pointed out by residents of the locality, who call it Bolívar's hill.

the hills which dominated the plain on that side. Summoning Páez, Bolívar ordered him to lead his division away from the main road and to make a wide detour to the westward; to cross the Carabobo at a convenient point in the hills and then to swoop down upon the enemy's right flank and rear.[1]

At eleven o'clock in the morning Páez led out his division to obey these orders, preceded by the guide who had given the information. First came the Bravos de Apure, then the British Battalion and finally the cavalry. Leaving the main road, Gen. Páez conducted his division to the westward following the sinuosities of a narrow trail which led for the most part behind the shelter of the hills but which at first carried them across ground exposed to the fire of the enemy's artillery.[2] Eventually the trail descended between two small hills and debouched suddenly into the Carabobo brook. The bed of this stream is mostly dry and supports a scattering growth of scraggly trees and bushes, so that although it afforded some slight shelter from the fire of the enemy, it presented an obstacle to the patriot advance. When the Bravos de Apure peered around the corner of the last hill they suddenly found themselves on the edge of the brook. As they jumped down and attempted to cross they were staggered and blinded by a withering fire from the enemy on the opposite hillside. Owing to the comparatively level and open surface of the plateau north of the brook, the royalist battalions, Burgos, Barbastro and Hostalrich, had been able to arrive in advance of the patriots and to deploy along a defensive position on the edge of the plateau.[3] The Bravos

---

[1] Blanco, *op. cit.*, VII, 634.

[2] Santana, *op. cit.*, 113; Reports of Pedro Briceño Méndez and of Gen. José Antonio Páez in Vicente Lecuna, "Relaciones fundamentales de la batalla de Carabobo" in *Boletin de la Academia Nacional de Historia,* Caracas, IV, no. 16, pp. 369-394.

[3] Montenegro, *op. cit.*, IV, 362; Report of Pedro Briceño Méndez in Santana, *op. cit.*, 159.

dashed across the stream bed and began to climb the opposite bank where they received such a concentrated fire that
they broke and scattered to the shelter of the brook.

The British Battalion followed, rushed across the stream,
climbed the further bank and halted to take breath. As they
knelt and fired they took deliberate aim at the bobbing heads
of the enemy on the crest of the hill above them. In spite
of the rain of lead which was poured upon them at point-
blank range, they fired with the steadiness of troops on
parade. Lieut. Ashdown knelt, hugging the republican colors
to his breast, while the men around him held their ground
like a wall of steel. With the words " Steady men ", half
uttered on his lips, Col. Ferriar was one of the first to fall.
Major Davy took his place only to fall mortally wounded a
few moments later, as did also Captain Scott, the adjutant.
Thus they held on while the Bravos, under cover of their
fire, were enabled to reform behind them and then to creep
forward in prolongation of the line to the left. Two companies of Tiradores from the Second Division had also come
up on the right.[1]

By this time the ammunition of the British was getting
low, and in spite of their calls for more none was sent them
from the rear. At this critical moment of suffering from a
heavy fire which they were unable to return, when seventeen
of their officers had been killed or wounded and half of their
effective force was out of action, Capt. Minchin, although
wounded, jumped to the front and ordered a charge. The
whole line, British, Bravos, and Tiradores followed him.[2]
It was not a short and gallant dash to glory such as painters

[1] Report of the Chief of Staff of the royalist army in " Relaciones
fundamentales de la batalla de Carabobo," 392; Florez Álvarez, *op. cit.*,
173; Páez, *Autobiografía*, I, 206; *London Chronicle*, Dec. 24, 1821.

[2] Report of Páez in " Relaciones fundamentales," 381; Montenegro,
op. cit., 362.

and poets love to put into their thrilling pictures of a charge, but a slow painful climb up a steep hillside, during which the blazing sun made their temples throb, and the effort of dragging with them their muskets and packs used up in short, quick gasps what little breath was left in their lungs.

To climb those two hundred yards of sun-baked hillside takes all the strength and endurance that one who is unencumbered and ready for the task can muster. Even under the best conditions it is an exhausting undertaking, but when those British soldiers climbed that hill, they had to carry with them the extra weight of their muskets and equipment, their packs and their rations, and to do so in the face of a hostile fire which stretched one out of every ten of them dead or wounded on the ground.[1] Hot, thirsty, sweating and dirty, they had to leave behind them the shelter of the stream bed with its cool waters, to force their weary muscles and empty lungs to drag them ever upward into the heat and turmoil. No doubt many a man wished for a friendly bullet in the brain to give him an excuse to lie down and rest. It was a task that required not only heroic courage, but herculean endurance and bull-dog determination to keep on while the last spark of life and strength was left.

During the upward struggle the patriots necessarily slackened their fire or ceased firing altogether, and the enemy, relieved from the necessity of keeping themselves covered, rose and poured a murderous fire upon the struggling throng of men below them. It was in vain, however, for the royalist infantry was forced to yield to the onrushing might that irresistibly swept them off their feet. The front ranks fell back on those behind, the rear ranks gave way, and soon the three royalist battalions yielded their ground to the patriots. Just as the attacking lines gained the crest of the hill, Capt. Minchin fell gravely wounded. Promptly Major Brand

---

[1] Report of Bolívar in "Relaciones fundamentales," 370.

took command of the British Battalion and ordered it to form square to resist the attack of royalist cavalry which had come to the aid of the three battalions. Fortunately, however, by this time Páez at the head of his column of cavalry had crossed the brook higher up where the hills were less steep, and without waiting for the arrival of the remainder of the regiment, had ordered Col. Vásquez with thirty-four officers of the staff and a company of the guard of honor to charge the right flank of the enemy.[1]

Colonels Vásquez and Múñoz, then leading two mixed groups of staff officers and cavalrymen, dashed against the royalist cavalry and soon had them, as well as the broken battalions of infantry, fleeing across the plains. Páez with his rear guard pressed home the attack on the infantry, completed the rout of the Hostalrich battalion and accepted the surrender of the Barbastros who, seeing themselves surrounded by the patriots, threw down their arms.[2] The battle

[1] Report of Páez in "Relaciones fundamentales," 381; Montenegro, *op. cit.*, 362.

[2] Report of Briceño Méndez in "Relaciones fundamentales," 374. The above account of the battle of Carabobo is based on the official reports of Bolívar, Páez and Briceño Mendez, as printed in O'Leary, *Documentos,* XVIII, 337-339; and Santana, *Carabobo,* 158, 162; and collected by Vicente Lecuna in his "Relaciones fundamentales de la batalla de Carabobo" in *Boletín de la Academia Nacional de Historia,* Caracas, IV, no. 16, pp. 369-394; also on the above quoted works of Lecuna, Santana and O'Leary, supplemented by a personal examination of the battlefield by the present writer. These reports are generally clear and explicit and agree with one another. Although at first view the actual terrain did not appear to conform to the reports, because of modern changes in the roads, on closer examination it was found to do so in all essential particulars. The writer believes that he located the exact point of crossing of the Carabobo brook by the British Battalion. Just below the hill called "Pica de la Mona" another brook flows into the Carabobo brook forming a triangular peninsula between them. Ths triangle of land is about fifty yards across at its middle point, is nearly free from trees, and is completely exposed to fire from the heights above. It is however not extensive enough to allow of its being crossed by a battalion or even a

was won! In less than an hour the greater part of the royalist infantry and cavalry had been destroyed! Of the patriots (with the exception of two companies of Tiradores from the second division [1]) only the first division under Páez had been engaged.

On the main road the second and third divisions had waited in idleness the outcome of the enveloping movement. The Rifles, under Col. Sandes, at the head of the column in the road, found it hard to restrain their impatience to attack the Valencey battalion which blocked the road before them. At last their turn came. Seeing that all was lost, and that they alone were left to hold back the main body of the enemy, the Valencey Battalion under its brave commander, Tomás García, formed square about the artillery and began slowly to withdraw down the road toward Valencia. The Rifles followed them and at the fork of the road to Pao interposed themselves between the Valencey and Infante Battalions, which tried to effect a junction at this point. Meanwhile the Grenadiers attacked the Infante Battalion on the

company deployed in line of skirmishers. To reach the shelter of the hill up which the British charged, it was necessary for them to jump down, one after another, into the bed of the Carabobo brook, cross that is an extended line, climb up its further bank, cross this exposed peninsula in column of files or twos, and then jump down a second time into this other brook. Having crossed this, they were fairly well sheltered by the bank of the further brook and by the dense growth of trees and bushes which grew upon it and on the lower slopes of the hill, along which they could again deploy as skirmishers. Unless this or a similar junction of two streams higher up was the spot where these events took place, it is hard to explain the following doubtful passage, in the report of Briceño Méndez: "We had to defile a second time to cross a brook which separated the hill on which our army had deployed from that which the enemy dominated." This passage conveyed no meaning to the writer until he had actually found the locality above described, for there was nothing in the report to indicate where or when the patriots had defiled the first time.

[1] Santana, *op. cit.*, 115; *Correo del Orinoco*, July 25, 1821.

flank. There was a brief struggle in which Col. Plaza, the heroic commander of the third division, fell mortally wounded.[1]

By this time Bolívar and Páez had arrived with their victorious forces from the western sector of the battlefield and launched repeated cavalry charges against the Spanish square. The Valencey Battalion stubbornly held its formation, but found it necessary to withdraw more rapidly, and in order to do so was forced to abandon in the road its two pieces of artillery. Five hundred men of the Rifles and Grenadiers were then hastily mounted and sent in pursuit. The pursuit was continued through the streets of Valencia and as far as Naguanagua, where at last it was given up and the Valencey battalion was permitted to escape to Puerto Cabello. Of the entire army of La Torre engaged that day, this battalion and 1500 cavalrymen under Morales were the only ones to escape.[2] The patriots lost only 200 men altogether, and of this loss eleven officers and 119 men belonged to the British Battalion. Forty per cent of the royalist army was killed, wounded or captured. Besides the two pieces of artillery, a great number of muskets, flags and materials of war fell into the hands of the patriots. The power of Spain in Venezuela had been definitely broken. From Puerto Cabello, La Torre despatched 500 of his sick and wounded by transport to Curaçao and settled down to hold Puerto Cabello as a last stronghold and base for the Spanish fleet in Venezuela.[3]

[1] Santana, *op. cit.*, 116; Lecuna, *op. cit.*, in *Hispania*, III, 908; Castaños y Montijano, *op. cit.*, 581, 582.

[2] Letter from Josef Rodríguez Rubio (an officer of the Valencey Battalion) to his father Manuel Rodríguez Rubio dated July 30, 1821, from the private collection of Dr. Vicente Lecuna at Caracas.

[3] Santana, *op. cit.*, 118; Florez Álvarez, *op. cit.*, 176; *London Chronicle,* Sept. 5, 24, Dec. 24, 1821; Galán, *op. cit.*, 17; Level, *op. cit.*, 437. Although the accounts vary as to the casualties in the British Battalion, it is safe to say that this organization lost approximately a dozen officers and a hun-

As to the importance of the part taken by the British in the battle of Carabobo there seems to be no question. All authorities consulted agree that the brave stand of the British Legion enabled the Bravos of Apure to reform at the critical moment, and that their charge broke the ranks of the Burgos, Hostalrich and Barbastro battalions, making it possible for the cavalry of Páez to complete the destruction. The victory was won with the crushing of the Spanish right wing. The battle was decided by a part of the action in which not more than a fifth of the patriot army was engaged. Bolívar, in his official report of the battle dated June 25, 1821, says:

The distinguished Gen. Páez, at the head of the two battalions of his division and of the regiment of cavalry of the valiant Col. Múñoz, advanced with such intrepidity against the right of the enemy that in half an hour it was enveloped and totally destroyed. No honor can ever be great enough to recompense the valor of these troops. The British battalion commanded by

dred men. Lieut. Col. Edward Brand in a letter to the *London Chronicle* dated Santa Marta, Oct. 25, 1821, says: " we lost 10 officers out of 27 and 94 men out of 324." " Our colonel (Ferriar) and lieutenant colonel (Davy) fell on our first charge. My horse was shot under me, but fortunately I escaped. . . . Killed at Carabobo, June 24: Capt. James Scott, Sergt. William Blackburn, Corporals John McCartney and John Ryan; Privates John Ballnoby, William Drummond, James Simpson, John Maginis, Nicholas Ruddy, Robert Haydon, John Green, Stephen Aicken, John Hall, John Duffy, John Spearman, Andrew Grogan, Edward Carroll, Thomas Hammond, Frederick Hendricks, Edward Hinks, Thomas Clarke, Charles Baker, John Hudson, John Marsham, John Sills, Josea Tauro, Patrick Coghlan, Henry King, James Wingate and John Williams. Total killed: 1 captain, 1 sergeant, 2 corporals, 26 privates, Grand total killed 30. Wounded: Col. T. J. Ferrier (since dead) Lt. Col. William Davy, Capts. Charles Minchin and Charles Smythe (very dangerously), Lieuts. John Hands, Acheson Houston (since dead), John Hubble, James Mathews and William Talbot. Dead of their wounds, 1 colonel, 1 lieutenant, 3 sergeants, 1 corporal, 6 privates, total 12. Wounded: 1 lieutenant colonel, 2 captains, 4 lieutenants, 4 sergeants, 5 corporals, 1 bandsman, 36 privates, total 55 (*sic*). Grand total of killed, dead of wounds and wounded 95 " (*sic*).

the noble Col. Ferriar was especially distinguished even among such brave associates, and suffered severe losses among the officers.[1]

Páez says of the British Legion: " Those heroes, worthy compatriots of those who a few years before had fought with such firmness at Waterloo, were now suffering the hostile fire without yielding an inch until line of battle could be formed." [2]

In addition to the British Battalion, under command of Col. Thomas Ferriar, composed almost exclusively of English, Irish and Hanoverians, the records show the names of many other foreigners who took part in the battle. The Battalion of Rifles, which bravely threw itself between the Infante Battalion and the Valencey, to prevent the junction of those two forces, and was commanded by Lieut. Col. Arthur Sandes, numbered among its lieutenants Maurice O'Connell, and had Julien Taylor as a cornetist in the fifth company. The Battalion Vencedor en Boyacá was commanded by Col. John Uslar. Commanding the Boyacá Battalion was Lieut. Col. Ludwig Flegel, and second in command was Major William Smith. With the Tiradores who joined the charge of the British was Lieut. Col. Reinboldt. On the staff of Bolívar was Major Richard Murphy, a surgeon, and Capt. Daniel F. O'Leary, an aide-de-camp; attached to the General Staff was Capt. Eloy Demarquet; the adjutant general of the Second Brigade of the Guard was Lieut. Col. Philip M. Martin, who was wounded; Lieut. Col. George Woodberry was chief of the general staff of the third division. Capt. Carlos Castelli was with the Bravos of the Apure, and seven more foreigners, among whom was Lieut. Col. Miller Hallowes, were serving as field officers of the several corps of the army. In the list of various other officers

---

[1] O'Leary, *op. cit.*, XVIII, 338.

[2] Páez, *op. cit.*, I, 206.

engaged in the battle are found the names of forty-one more members of the foreign legion, of whom three were wounded.[1]

An anonymous account, supposed to have been related by a participant in the battle, was published in *All the Year Round* of March 28, 1868, under the caption " Carabobo ". This account states that the British Legion lost two-thirds of its number in killed and wounded, and that as the remains of the corps passed before the Liberator at double time he called them " Saviours of my country ".[2] The author of *Recollections of Service* states that Col. Mackintosh was in command of the British Legion; but the carefully documented and official account of the battle prepared by Col. Arturo Santana, under direction of the inspector general of the Venezuelan army in 1920, does not mention Col. Mackintosh in this connection. As a matter of fact, Col. Mackintosh was commanding the Albion Battalion in the campaign of the south at this time. The author of *Recollections of Service* says also that after the battle Bolívar embraced Col. Mackintosh and conferred upon him the rank of general of division, "and proceeding through the ranks of the Legion he (Bolívar) embraced every man, and bestowed upon the whole the order of Liberators. The two remnants of the British and Irish Legions were united by his Excellency's command, and were named on the field ' the Regiment of Carabobo '." [3] Duarte Level tells how the Regiment of Carabobo was formed from the detachments of English and Irish who had composed the British Battalion and says:

The value of their service was immense; the honors of victory

[1] Santana, *op. cit.*, 162-167; Archivo Nacional, Bogotá, Guerra y Marina Historia, DCCLXXVIII, 726; Florez Álvarez, *op. cit.*, 160-162, 247, 257.

[2] " Carabobo," in *All the Year Round*, March 28, 1868, no. 466, p. 388.

[3] *Recollections of Service*, II, 201; *Correo del Orinoco*, Sept. 29, 1821; O'Leary, *Documentos*, XVIII, 388; O'Connor, *op. cit.*, 56.

belonged to them; the debt of the nation to them was eternal. Carabobo was the British Battalion. The trophies of victory were bestowed on Páez. He monopolized the fame of this battle and our history does not adequately record the names of the foreigners who shed their blood there. To-day it is possible to search out only with great difficulty the names of a few of them. Ferriar, Davy, Scott, Minchin, and Brand; Lieuts. Samuel Collins, Otto Fritan (Trittan), James Patterson and John Hands, and sub-lieuts. Joseph Jervis, William Talbot and Pedro Brión.[1]

Baralt, the historian, says of the battle: " It was glorious for the republic, lent great honor to Páez, and won immortal renown for the British Legion which contributed powerfully to it, performing prodigies of valor." [2] The congress of Venezuela later commemorated the event by an appropriate inscription and monument.[3]

After the battle of Carabobo Bolívar instituted measures at once for mopping up the scattered detachments of the enemy who still remained in the coast departments of Venezuela and New Granada. He sent Heras to support Carillo's small detachment in the pursuit of Tello at San Felipe, and left Rangel to besiege Puerto Cabello.[4] Four days later the commander-in-chief arrived before Caracas, which the royalist general prepared to evacuate. A story is told that the city was actually taken by the unaided efforts of three young Irish lieutenants. These officers, without having asked or received any authority for their undertaking, had dressed

---

[1] Level, *op. cit.*, 432, 437. *Vide* Appendix H. for a complete roster of the officers and men still remaining in the Carabobo Battalion in November, 1823, who had taken part in the battle of Carabobo, from Archivo Nacibnal, Bogotá, Guerra y Marina, Historia, DCCLXXX, 519.

[2] Baralt, *op. cit.*, II, 48.

[3] Santana, *op. cit.*, 170.

[4] Archivo Nacional, Bogotá, Guerra y Marina, Historia, VI, 714; XXVI, 733; *View of South America*, 117.

themselves in the borrowed uniforms of insurgent generals and, under an ostensible flag of truce, had demanded, in the name of Bolívar, the surrender of the city. The Spanish governor was so badly frightened that he signed articles of capitulation, without realizing that these three were the sole representatives of the insurgent army. By this exploit the young Irish lieutenant who led it gained the sobriquet of the "Town-Taker".[1] Whether this story is true or not, Bolívar found the city almost deserted when he and his staff rode into it unopposed on June 29th. The next day he sent an aide to take possession of the neighboring port of La Guaira which also had been evacuated.[2]

In order to reap the fruits of victory, to prevent La Torre from exercising any further control in Venezuela, and to force the remnant of the royalist army to yield its last foothold on the soil of that province, the siege lines were drawn as tightly as possible about Puerto Cabello. The battalions of the Guard were selected for this duty and were stationed for the remainder of the year 1821 on the lines or in the neighboring cities of Valencia, Maracay or San Carlos. The headquarters of the Guard were established at Valencia with Gen. Manuel Manrique in command and Lieut. Col. George Woodberry as adjutant general.[3]

[1] *Recollections of Service*, II, 205.

[2] *Boletín de la Academia de Historia*, Caracas, IV, no. 16, p. 377.

[3] Of the several battalions of the First Brigade of the Guard the Anzoátegui contained 702 men; the Grenadiers, 998, the Vencedor at that time under Col. Uslar, 920; and the regiment of cavalry under Col. Rondon, 391. The Rifle Battalion, under Lieut. Col. Arthur Sandes, had suffered scandalous desertions and when it arrived at Barquisimeto, a month after the battle of Carabobo, it contained only 500 men. The vacancy in it caused by the death of Surgeon Michael O'Reilly was filled by the appointment of Stephen Macdavitt, who had been surgeon general of the Irish division under Montilla. Among other battalions on the lines before Puerto Cabello were the Bravos de Apure, 829 men; the Tiradores (strength not given); the Boyacá, under Lieut. Col. Flegel,

Unfortunately a close investment of Puerto Cabello was impossible because of the fact that it was open to the sea and could be freely visited and supplied by the Spanish fleet. La Torre took advantage of one such opportunity and on December 17, 1821, escaped with a portion of his troops to Coro while Morales raided the coast of that peninsula, threatened La Guaira and Caracas and recaptured Santa Marta. To remedy these disasters, operations were begun by the patriots to drive the royalists back into Puerto Cabello. In these campaigns known as those of Coro and of Zulia, the battalions of the Guard were engaged.[1] An incident which occurred in one of the actions in Coro is related to show the bravery of Col. Lyster, formerly of the Irish Legion. A patriot colonel had rashly charged the enemy's line of cavalry and had got around their rear. He became separated from his men and would have been killed had not Col. Lyster dashed through the same line after him. Together they then gallantly cut their way back again through the enemy and rejoined their own side in safety.[2]

It would be wearisome to the reader were an attempt made here to describe the numerous attacks, skirmishes and en-

1249 men; and the Carabobo Battalion under Lieut. Col. Brand who had recently received his promotion and been assigned to its command in place of the unpopular Col. Stopford. This battalion had also suffered severely from desertions. In the Carabobo Battalion lieutenants Charles Webster, David Steinson and John Hands were recommended for promotion to captains to fill vacancies caused by the death of Capt. Scott killed in action and the wounding of Captains Minchin and Smith. Lieut. Hands was particularly recommended as an attentive and efficient officer. Archivo Nacional, Bogotá, Guerra y Marina, Historia, VI, 54, 343, 363, 961; VII, 411; X, 227, 246, 265, 285, 352; LXXVI, 694; DCCLXXIX, 249; O'Leary, *Documentos*, XVIII, 514.

[1] *Iris de Venezuela*, April, 1822, *London Chronicle*, Dec. 21, 1821, March 15, 1822; *Gaceta de Colombia*, Sept. 8, 1822; *Annual Register*, 1821, "History," 263; 1822, "History," 281, 282; *Present State of Colombia*, 50; O'Leary, *Documentos*, XVIII, 391, XX, 69.

[2] Cochrane, *op. cit.*, I, 465.

gagements in which the Rifle and Carabobo Battalions and other organizations of the Guard, officered by foreigners, took part during these campaigns for the final liberation of Venezuela. These affairs were all very much alike and had no real military or other interest. The numbers of men engaged were small, probably about a hundred and seldom over five hundred on a side; so that few of the engagements would be considered of more importance than mere skirmishes. These operations may well be compared with those that took place during the Philippine insurrection of 1899-1901, when encounters between the hostile forces were of daily occurrence without any of them having a decisive result. To those who took part in these affairs they seemed at the time to be of considerable magnitude; yet they are so lacking in general interest or in importance of result, that history has not troubled to record them. In few of these engagements in the Philippine Islands did more than a battalion take part, and most of them were fought by a single company on the American side and a column of fifty men on that of the Filipinos.

Another point of similarity between this campaign in the Philippines and those of Coro and Zulia in Venezuela as well as that of the south of Colombia is, that all were fought in a tropical country of mountains and seacoast. The South American patriots were few in numbers, poorly equipped, badly armed and ill-disciplined like the Filipino insurgents, and the royalists may be compared with the American troops, except that they were not always acting on the offensive. In the Philippine campaign the Americans almost always did the attacking and the Filipinos remained on the defensive, seldom attacking except when they hoped to take the Americans at a disadvantage, as in an ambush in the mountains or in a night surprise on a village. In South America, on the other hand, the patriots pushed the campaign everywhere by vigorous attacks and acted quite as much on the offensive as did the royalists.

In these attacks the usual method was to occupy the main force of the defense by a concentration of fire on his center, while a company or platoon from the right or left, and sometimes from both wings at once, was sent around to make an attack on the flank or rear of the enemy. There was a great deal of noise and shooting, but not much slaughter, and the defensive force generally succeeded in making its escape, for the contestants seldom came to close quarters except when a bayonet charge was made. Consequently the majority of these affairs were inconclusive and amounted to nothing more than a driving back of the enemy from the position he occupied. Since he could then take up a new position further in the rear, the operation had to be repeated again in a day or two.

But campaigns are not successful unless the enemy is rendered incapable of further fighting. Decisive victories are not won by fire action alone, but must be pushed home by an attack in which the enemy's troops may be killed or captured.

In the British army, especially in the Peninsular War, great attention had been devoted to developing the bayonet attack, so that to an officer trained in that army the bayonet charge seemed the obvious means of ending a battle. When the British went into action they expected sooner or later to make a charge. Such was the case at Pántano de Vargas, Boyacá and Carabobo. When the British officers were distributed among other battalions they trained their men in British tactics and in this method of fighting which became more and more common throughout the patriot army.[1]

---

[1] The newspapers of the time contain many reports of skirmishes in which such tactics were employed. For some examples, see *Iris de Venezuela*, March 25, Aug. 5, 1822; *Anglo-Colombiano*, May 11, 1822; *Correo del Orinoco*, June 16, 1821; *Gaceta de Colombia*, May 26, Aug. 11, Sept. 15, 22, Oct. 13, 1822; *El Colombiano*, May 28, 1823; *London*

So enthusiastic was Bolívar over the charge of the British at Carabobo that he showed special favor to the newly formed Carabobo Battalion by directing that it should there-after always form the garrison of Caracas and receive full pay, without any deductions, for clothing or rations. This order was difficult to carry out, for the distinctions involved excited the jealousy of the native troops.[1] The records of the Vencedor Battalion, temporarily under Col. Uslar, show that for the last three months of 1821 and the first month of 1822 that battalion received only one quarter pay.[2] Col. Brand who, it will be remembered, had led the final charge and formed the square at Carabobo, and had succeeded Col. Ferriar in command of the Carabobo Battalion, soon volun-teered for more active service for his men. This battalion was then designated to take part in the campaign of Coro and in the subsequent operations in the department of Zulia and about Santa Marta, where many of its members fell victims to yellow fever.[3] The Carabobo Battalion in two months became a mere skeleton organization like the Rifle Battalion which was also serving at Santa Marta at that time. Likewise many of the Albions drifted down from the south without a cent of pay in their pockets, begging Col. O'Con-

Chronicle, July 18, Aug. 1, 1821, July 15, 1822, Jan. 15, March 25, April 22, 1823. In a letter to Bolívar Sucre himself wrote: "Your excellency knows that in the war in Pasto there is nothing to be done except either to attack or not to attack, and that in attacking you must seek the enemy with the bayonet, for otherwise there is no advantage in defeating him." Bingham Collection of Mss. Sucre Papers, No. 2025a, Sucre to Bolívar, Oct. 6, 1820. Gen. Level, *op. cit.*, 327, says that these flank attacks were the tactics of Napoleon, "inspired by the English officers who had learned them with Wellington."

[1] O'Leary, *Documentos*, XVIII, 408; *Present State of Colombia*, 99.

[2] Archivo Nacional, Bogotá, Guerra y Marina, Historia, X, 227, 246, 265, 285, 352.

[3] *Present State of Colombia*, 99.

nor, the chief-of-staff, to grant them passports to return to England.[1]

It will be remembered how Montilla had temporarily abandoned the siege of Cartagena to attack Santa Marta. After the capture of the latter city he resumed with increased vigor the siege of the former. He kept with him the Hussars and some dragoons,[2] for he was advised that active surprise attacks by flying corps were as effective in sieges as were great masses of immobile troops. If he should utilize cavalry to scout the principal areas near Cartagena and other detachments to prevent the royalists from gathering supplies, it was believed that the enemy would not dare to make sallies and that his own troops would be spared from the exhaustion caused by incessant guard duty. He therefore gave Col. Lara command of the lines of investment and Lieut. Col. Dunlop that of the scouting columns.[3] The royalist garrison was soon forced to abandon its strong position on the high hill of La Popa, a mile or two outside of the city, because the patriots among the inhabitants of Cartagena had cut off their supplies. The republican troops seized La Popa but could not utilize this hill to the best advantage, for they had no siege artillery. The energetic Col. Adlercreutz, however, reconnoitered the defenses until he discovered a carelessly-guarded 18-pounder which he captured one night and em-

---

[1] O'Connor, *op. cit.*, 56, 57.

[2] One of these cavalry officers was Sergt. Major Philipp (Felipe) Braun who belonged to the Hussars, but was later detached for duty in the south with the mounted Grenadiers of the Guard. Archivo Nacional, Bogotá, Guerra y Marina, Historia, XIII, 342, DCCLXXIX, 667, 696, 853; Carlos Cortés Vargas, *Participación de Colombia en la Libertad del Perú*, II, 131, III, 187. On Montilla's staff were serving Lieut. Col. Count Adlercreutz, Lieut. Col. Dunlop and Capt. William Ferguson. Archivo Nacional, Bogotá, Guerra y Marina, Historia, XVI, 730; DCCLXXVIII, 724; Archivo Montilla, III, Sucre to Montilla, Dec. 22, 1820.

[3] Archivo Montilla, III, Sucre to Montilla, Dec. 22, 1820.

placed on the top of La Popa. After that they were able to throw shells into the royalist fortress.[1] At the same time José Padilla with the republican fleet blockaded and bombarded the port from the sea side.

Conditions in the city due to starvation and bombardment steadily grew worse until Montilla, out of a feeling of humanity for the many innocent victims, wrote to the royalist commander suggesting negotiations for peace.[2] Finally at the end of September, 1821, after withstanding fourteen months of siege, Cartagena capitulated. Gen. Torres with his troops was sent to Santiago de Cuba and the port was thrown open to commerce.[3] Soon merchant ships began to arrive from all parts of the world, principally from the United States, loaded with cargoes of munitions for sale to the patriots. Among the military stores captured from the royalists were 3000 muskets, 3500 quintals of powder, 1300 quintals of lead and an extensive park of artillery. In his report Montilla especially recommended the conduct of the vanguard and its commanding officer, Lieut. Col. Adlercreutz.[4]

After the capitulation of Cartagena, and the surrender of Cumaná to Bermúdez at about the same time, there was nothing left to the royalists in northern South America except Puerto Cabello, Quito and the Isthmus of Panama.[5]

---

[1] O'Connor, *op. cit.*, 57, 58; *London Chronicle*, Nov. 28, 1821; Groot, *op. cit.*, III, 81, 82; *Boletín de historia y Antigüedades*, Bogotá, I, No. 6, p. 280; Archivo Nacional, Bogotá, Guerra y Marina, Historia, CCCLX, 183.

[2] Archivo Nacional, Bogotá, Guerra y Marina, Historia, III, 370.

[3] O'Connor, *op. cit.*, 57, 58; *Correo del Orinoco*, Dec. 15, 1821; *London Chronicle*, Jan. 6, 1822; *Present State of Colombia*, 48.

[4] O'Connor, *op. cit.*, 58; *Correo del Orinoco*, March 9, 1822; Archivo Nacional, Bogotá, Guerra y Marina, Historia, XV, 17, 23.

[5] Bingham Collection of Mss. *Bolívar letters*, no. 8, Bolívar to (no addressee), San Cristoval, May 26, 1820; Cochrane, *op. cit.*, I, 516.

To subdue the province of the Isthmus, Bolívar secretly prepared a picked expedition of 3,000 men, consisting of the Carabobo Battalion, the Grenadiers, Rifles, Tiradores, Vencedores en Boyacá and a squadron of Lancers of the Guard, for which transports were assembled to convey them from Santa Marta.[1] The expedition, however, was rendered unnecessary, for the inhabitants of the Isthmus, encouraged by the liberation of Cartagena, had taken advantage of the departure of the Spanish commander, Gen. Cruz Murgeon, to subdue a revolt in Guayaquil, and near the close of the year 1821 had declared their own independence at Porto Bello.[2]

Since there was no longer need of his attention on the Isthmus, Bolívar decided to carry out his other plan of clearing the Spaniards out of Quito and to aid Gen. Antonio José de Sucre, whom he had previously sent on to Guayaquil, to secure the adhesion of that province to the Republic of Colombia. Inasmuch as the campaign of the south under Valdés was not progressing satisfactorily, Bolívar felt that his own presence there with additional troops was essential.[3] Soublette was left as director general of the war in Colombia, with Lino de Clemente in charge of operations in the department of Zulia, Bermúdez in that of the Orinoco, and Páez in that of Venezuela. Bolívar then hastened south to Bogotá, leaving Gen. Bartholomé Salom to follow with the Guard.[4]

In the process of reorganizing the Guard the Battalions

[1] O'Leary, *Documentos*, XVIII, 421, 435, 447, 450, 464.

[2] *Iris de Venezuela*, March 11, 1822; *The Times*, March 14, 1822; *Niles Weekly Register*, XXII, 7, 102; Walker, *op. cit.*, II, 561; *View of South America*, 118; *Correo del Orinoco*, March 23, 1822.

[3] O'Leary, *Narración*, II, 119, 120; *Correo del Orinoco*, March 23, 1822; *London Chronicle*, Dec. 3, 1821.

[4] O'Connor, *op. cit.*, 56. Bingham Collection of Mss. Bolívar letters, no. 8; Archivo Nacional, Bogotá, Guerra y Marina, Historia, DCCLXXIX, 249.

Vencedor and Carabobo were sent by sea from Santa Marta to Rio Hacha, where they were disembarked and under the command of Gen. Lino de Clemente began their long march through the department of Zulia toward La Guaira. Gen. Clemente lamented the fact that he had only 228 effective men left in the Carabobo Battalion; for although it had started from Santa Marta with 339 men, twelve had died, sixty-nine were sick in hospital and thirty were musicians whom he did not count.[1] The Vencedor Battalion had been slated for the campaign of the south; but at the last moment it was relieved by the Battalion of Tiradores, in spite of the fact that this latter corps had suffered severely from fever while waiting in Santa Marta. The Rifles had been so reduced by sickness during this period that it had been found necessary to transfer their quarters to an Indian village about a league outside the city.[2] During this period, moreover, there was much confusion at Santa Marta, owing to the fact that many former royalist officers and a number of patriot officers as well who claimed to have lost their commissions were going around wearing the insignia of any rank which they chose to assume up to that of colonel.[3] Major William Smith, in requesting duplicates of his commissions, claimed that his servant had deserted, taking with him all the major's effects, his saber and his four commissions, including that of captain of cazadores, brevet major, major, and his citation for the star of the Liberators.[4]

Finally Gen. Salom's brigade, now consisting of the Rifle and Tiradores Battalions and the squadrons of Hussars and

---

[1] Archivo Nacional, Bogotá, Guerra y Marina, Historia, VI, 717, 732.

[2] O'Connor, *op. cit.*, 56, 57; O'Leary, *Documentos*, XIX, 193, XX, 40; Archivo Nacional, Bogotá, Guerra y Marina, Historia, VI, 736, 749.

[3] Archivo Nacional, Bogotá, Guerra y Marina, Historia, VI, 668, LXXVI, 713, 714.

[4] *Ibid.*, VII, 286.

Lancers of the Guard, set out in " bungas " up the Magdalena River. At Gamarra it disembarked, and crossing the Páramo of Cachiri followed the long trail through Bucaramanga, Socorro and Chiquinquirá toward the savannas of Bogotá. Again were many of the legionaries climbing the bleak and rugged mountains of New Granada, this time to do their share in the campaign of the south.[1]

[1] O'Leary, Narración, II, 123; *London Chronicle*, July 24, 1822.

CHAPTER X

Fighting on a Mountain-Side for Independence

General Salom's division reached Bogotá on January 23, 1822. Upon the arrival of these troops that city became the scene of reunions among the legionaries. As happens in every war, the capital and headquarters of the army was filled with officers and men of all kinds seeking under various pretexts escape from the hardships of the campaign. There were the sick and wounded cared for in the base hospitals and the convalescents discharged by the surgeons but in no hurry to rejoin their commands in the field. Likewise there were many assigned to duty in the performance of necessary staff activities. The headquarters of an army is a huge executive organization, the smooth and efficient functioning of which requires the constant attention of representatives of all departments of the staff. To enable an army in the field properly to carry on, there must be behind it at the capital of the country a skilfully-directed service of supply to keep it recruited, to furnish replacements for its casualties, to care for its sick and disabled and to send out a constantly increasing volume of supplies and munitions.

At the head of this organization was Gen. Santander, vice-president of Colombia, who was devoting all his time and energies to giving general supervision to the troops in New Granada and the south, to raising funds for carrying on the war, and to supplying the commanders of the armies both in the north and in the south with recruits, munitions, supplies, arms and money. His difficulties were enormous, but his skill as an organizer and financier and his persistence under discouragement overcame them all.[1]

Bogotá was a busy headquarters. Commissions met to decide weighty matters of policy. Inspectors came and went to conduct investigations and to make their reports. Sick and wounded were gathered into hospitals, restored to health and returned to duty.[2] Broken and worthless muskets were taken to pieces, repaired, put together again and reissued. New arms were purchased from foreign contractors, after having been subjected to rigid tests. Ingredients were gathered from distant points of the republic and compounded into powder. Lead was melted down and moulded into bullets. Beef cattle were driven in from the ranches. Taxes were collected. Farmer boys were drilled as militia.[3]

In addition to the officers performing important staff duties there were, of course, the usual numbers of hangers-on

---

[1] *Archivo Santander,* IV, 6, 8, 31, 33; *Gaceta de Colombia,* Feb. 3, 1822; Cochrane, *op. cit.,* II, 93; Archivo Nacional Bogotá, Guerra y Marina, Historia, DCCLXXIX, 47; *London Chronicle,* July 24, 1822; O'Connor, *op. cit.,* 57; Walker, *op. cit.,* II, 585.

[2] Among the sick in hospital and in the corps of invalids were Lieutenants William Sever and Anthony Kattz, First Sergeants Terence Nugent, Louis Danahie and Mark Procter, Corporal Michael Boyle and Privates John Maclean, Richard Brinkworth, Frederick Cross, Francis Maclean, John Doran, Lionel Boyle, James Smith, Michael Cousins and Mitchell Ferris. Archivo Nacional, Bogotá, Guerra y Marina, Historia, DCCLXXIX, 21, 22, 63, 89, 136, 608, 616, 702, 777, 778, 794, 804, 865.

[3] Among the foreign officers occupied with various important staff duties were Lieut. Col. Friedrich Adlercreutz and Capt. Ferdinand Sirakowski, inspecting and testing ordnance purchased under contract; Lieut. Col. Philip Viteri and Captains John Welsh and Narciso F. Martin, organizing militia units, Lieutenants Augustin Zinkernagel, John Murray, George M. McLean, Julian Kaugh and George Melian, drilling reserve companies and Doctors Henry G. Maine, Joseph F. Merisdale and Thomas Folson in charge of hospitals. Archivo Nacional, Bogotá, Guerra y Marina, Historia, XV, 24, XXVI, 805, 845; XXXV, 867, 925, 949; XLVII, 478; DCCLXXIX, 648, 683, 702, 822, 828, 855, 713; Hojas de Servicios, XXXI, 713.

who attach themselves to the army staff in the hope of securing some swivel-chair job; of utilizing personal friendship
or influence to obtain an undeserved reward or promotion;
or at any rate of finding some excuse for escaping the hardships and dangers of service in the field. Chief and foremost
among these was that prince of malingerers, Maj. Gen. John
D'Evereux, who with his aide, Capt. James Fraser, spent
his time at Bogotá, ostensibly in duties connected with the
general staff, but actually in trying to secure for himself reimbursement for his expenses in raising the Irish Legion.[1]

Several more foreign officers had been devoting their energies at the headquarters of the army to trying to obtain
their back pay. Some of these combined in writing to Bolívar a petition, dated Bogotá, Jan. 19, 1821, as follows:

We the English who find ourselves in this capital, although
we do not know your plans, rejoice infinitely if they are progressing favorably. Sir, we have been very sick since we came
to the city. The wounded are incurable. We find ourselves
without clothes, naked and bereft of money. We beg you for
charity, in God's name, and that you send us such alleviation as
you find convenient, that we may live more comfortably, by
your grace, Divine pity, and rewarded for glory. Excuse us for
the trouble, we are giving. May the life of our Liberator be
happy. (Signed) The English.[2]

A similar petition addressed to the Vice President on January 27 was endorsed by Santander, "Give them their full
pay every month and whatever clothing they need." [3]

[1] Archivo Nacional, Bogotá, Guerra y Marina, Historia, DCCLXXIX,
663, 811; Hojas de Servicios, XVI, 807. Likewise attached to the general staff were Lieutenant Colonels Peter Grant, Anthony M. Duran,
Augustine Freudenthal and John B. Minhuit as well as Lieut. Ramón
Clarque (Raymond Clark?).

[2] Archivo Nacional, Bogotá, Guerra y Marina, Historia, VI, 611.

[3] *Ibid.*, 612.

Lieut. Charles Minchin asked for his pay, but was told by the Minister of Finance that there was no money in the treasury. He then asked the government at least to refund seventy-four pesos to Mr. Thompson who had lent him that amount in order to enable him to go into the field.[1] Sublieutenant Karl Conratt, a German in the military hospital so badly wounded in the leg that he expected to lose it, if not his life, complained, " I have not a maravedí even to buy a cigar. Please send me my pay. In a few days I shall be without clothes." [2] Col. James Duff Patterson stated that he had not yet received any pay, except for one month when he entered Bogotá naked, and never any quarters except a straw shack during the campaign and subsequent occupation of Cartagena.[3]

[1] Archivo Nacional, Bogotá, *op. cit.*, III, 471.

[2] *Ibid.*, VI, 964. The national archives at Bogotá contain many other similar appeals, most of which were endorsed by Gen. París recommending or ordering payment, depending on whether his authority had jurisdiction in the case. Among these letters was one from Captain William Ravenscroft who, " finding himself sick and without money or resources," asked for payment of his back pay for ten months, so that he might retire to restore his health; *ibid.*, XXXV, 937, 939; one from Capt. Frederick Fulham who was then in Bogotá "in destitution, without money, clothing and resources"; *ibid.*, XXXV, 815; one from Lieut. Charles Trousdill who submitted his accounts and requested payment for the past ten months; *ibid.*, XXXV, 947; and one from Private Bryan Leacy who requested his pay from January to November, 1823. On Jan. 1st, he left for duty in the army of Boyacá under Col. Lyster. He had "received no pay in all that time." *Ibid.*, XXXV, 829, 900, 901.

[3] This claim dragged on until 1874 when, after the British legation had interested itself in behalf of Col. Patterson, an act of the congress of the United States of Colombia authorized payment to his attorney of the sum of 2400 pesos. Archivo Nacional, Bogotá, Guerra y Marina, Hojas de Servicios, XXXVI, 501, 504, 505, 506, 511, 526, 527, 528, 535, 537, 614; Registro general de jefes 1816 a 24, No. 709. Col. Patterson also received from Venezuela in 1877 a payment of $10,800 and a monthly pension of 18 venezolanos. In 1879 the amount of his pension was doubled. Archivo Nacional, Caracas, Ilustres Próceres, XXIV, 190.

An instance of allowing personal matters to interfere with the performance of official duty was that of Lieut. Augustin Zinkernagel, who requested leave to get married, stating that if this request were not granted he would die, for it was only this hope which kept him alive. A month later he wrote again complaining because his request had not been answered. In conclusion he stated that his fiancée was losing confidence in him. Evidently to regain this confidence he furnished his future father-in-law with copies of these requests. Although no documents showing the action of his commanding officer on his applications have been found, permission must have been granted, for five weeks later Lieut. Zinkernagel requested his discharge because he found it impossible to continue in service and at the same time support his wife properly. Perhaps feminine influence or his spirit of gallantry found the Minister of War complacent, for on December 12, 1821, he granted the request of Lieut. Zinkernagel to resign " on account of his young wife ".[1]

Not for long could the weary troops rest and enjoy the pleasures of the capital, for Bolívar's mind was working far ahead and his body must keep up with it. He was the kind of man who could not be satisfied with his past accomplishments, great though they were, but must always plan something greater and more magnificent. The liberation of New Granada and Venezuela was not enough. He must liberate Quito, and perhaps other provinces to the south. He must be on the march again.

Bolívar's first intention was to embark for Guayaquil at the port of Buenaventura with 2000 of the best troops of the Guards in transports which he had ordered Gen. Sucre to send, and personally to direct the campaign against Quito, leaving a force sufficient for the defense of the prov-

[1] Archivo Nacional, Bogotá, Guerra y Marina, Historia, VII, 261, 262, 265, 266.

ince of Popayán; but because of news which he received of the arrival at Guayaquil of the Spanish general Cruz Murgeon with reinforcements from Panamá and because of reports of Spanish cruisers off the coast, Bolívar was forced to entrust to Sucre alone the conduct of operations between Guayaquil and Quito while he himself marched the whole distance overland to attack the latter from the north.[1]

Bolívar had then set out from Bogotá on December 13, 1821, leaving orders for the Colombian Guards to follow him toward Cali.[2] Gen. Salom's division, in compliance with these orders, made its weary way through the torrid plain of Neiva and across the highest cordillera of the Andes via Guanacas to Popayán. On this march along the Andes the men suffered a repetition of the horrors of the campaign of 1819. Their feet were raw and torn because their hempen sandals were worn out and had not been replaced. During their advance up the Cauca valley to Popayán sickness was rampant among the troops. In a column of 1,000 men, thirty or forty fell sick daily. The climate and the hardships of the march were worse than the enemy's bullets.[3]

Bolívar had to hurry them on or else see his army waste away before his eyes. If he had waited for the junction of all his forces; if he had waited to discipline his troops; to mend their arms which were in bad repair; to receive the munitions which were reported to be on their way; to fatten his worn-out and emaciated horses and mules, all of which should have been done to put his army in shape for the cam-

[1] O'Leary, *Narración*, II, 121, 122; *London Chronicle*, May 6, 1822; Vicente Lecuna, *Campaña de Bombóná*, 9; Archivo Montilla, III, Sucre to Montilla, Dec. 22, 1820.

[2] O'Leary, *Narración*, 115, 120; *Iris de Venezuela*, Mar. 11, 1822; *Gaceta de Colombia*, Jan. 13, 1822.

[3] O'Leary, *Narración*, 123; *Archivo Santander*, VIII, 95; Lecuna, *Bombóná*, 10.

paign, he would have been no nearer his goal than at the beginning. " If," he wrote, " I wait until the expedition is complete, I shall have to wait to form another which in the end will be no better than the present one, because the majority of the troops will have gone to the hospital." [1]

He well knew the difficulties he would encounter when marching through the inhospitable region of Patía. He was aware that his baggage would be lost; that his cavalry would arrive without horses; that there would be no bread and very little meat; that the rains would not only cause much sickness, but would swell the rivers into raging torrents perilous to cross. Nevertheless the Liberator did not for a moment waver in his resolution, but wrote to Santander from Popayán: "Today I am going to leave for Pasto in spite of the difficulties piling up against me, as much on account of the news of Sucre's defeat as of the desertions, the sickness, the misery from which this army is suffering." [2]

At Cali, where was part of Col. Córdoba's division that had come by sea from Panamá to Buenaventura, Bolívar concentrated his army.[3] Gen. Pedro León Torres was ordered to march in advance with the first division, containing 1078 men, to Patía to observe the movements of the enemy, but not to risk a battle until the main body should arrive. He was also to forage for cattle and provisions for the whole army.[4] The second division came from Popayán to join the main body. This division contained only 975 men fit for duty and comprised the Rifles and the Squadrons of Hussars,

[1] O'Leary, *Documentos*, XIX, 213, 218; *Archivo Santander*, VIII, 95; Lecuna, *Bomboná*, 10.

[2] *Archivo Santander*, VIII, 138; Lecuna, *Bomboná*, 9-11. For Sucre's defeat at Guachi, see *infra*, p. 269.

[3] *Gaceta de Colombia*, March 24, May 5, 1822; Lecuna, *Bomboná*, 13.

[4] Bolívar to Pedro León Torres, Feb. 14, 1822 printed in Rafael Negret, *La Campaña del Sur y especialmente la Batalla de Bomboná*, 149, 151; *Correo del Orinoco*, April 8, 1820; Lecuna, *Bomboná*, 4.

Guides and mounted Cazadores of the Guard. The sick left in hospitals from both divisions amounted to 1200 men. In command of the second division and later of both divisions united was Gen. Valdés whom Bolívar had again restored to favor.[1]

At this point it will be remembered that after the reorganization following the battle of Boyacá Gen. Valdés had been sent south toward Popayán to clear the Cauca valley of royalists and to liberate the department of Pasto. He was to live off the country and not to rely on receiving any supplies from Bogotá. He was even expected to make his own powder.[2]

With the exception of the Albion Battalion, the troops of the division of Gen. Valdés were for the most part paper troops only and had to be organized as the campaign proceeded. The Neiva Battalion was raised in the south of Tolima by Lieut. Col. Pedro A. García. Major Joaquín París was compelled to utilize his Cazadores of the Vanguard

[1] J. Gabriel Pérez to Secretary of War, Feb. 26, 1822 in Negret, *op. cit.*, 152; Lecuna, *Bomboná*, 13. On Bolívar's staff at this time Gen. Bartolomé Salom was chief of staff and Col. Carlos Eloi Demarquet, adjutant. In the squadron of lancers was Major Philipp Braun. There were no foreign officers in the Bogotá, or Vargas Battalions. In the Vencedor en Boyacá Battalion was Capt. Miller Hallowes. In the cavalry of the second division serving with the Guides was Major Friedrich Rasch and with the Hussars, Major Francis Lecumberry. In the Rifles at this time were Col. Arthur Sandes, commanding; Sergt. Major Charles Rudd; in the first company Lieut. Felix Franco, commanding; in the second, Capt. Thomas Charles Wright; in the fourth, Captains Thomas Duxbury and James Whittle; and commanding the fifth was Capt. William Ferguson. Archivo Nacional, Bogotá, Guerra y Marina, Historia, VII, 301; X, 279, 301, 309, 314, 315, 319, 322, 323, 326, 327, 333, 344, 351; XXVII, 346; DCCLXXVIII, 888; DCCLXXIX, 41, 103, 179, 573, 594.

[2] *Vide* Chapter VIII; *Campaigns and Cruises*, 196-198; Bolívar to Valdés, March 27, 1820 in Negret, *op. cit.*, 117, 118; *Recuerdos históricos del Coronel Manuel Antonio López, ayudante del estado mayor general libertador*, 20.

as a base upon which to collect recruits from Cauca and Neiva, from which was organized the Battalion Bogotá of the Guard. It was, however, difficult to get recruits, inasmuch as the people avoided enrollment by every means in their power.[1]

The division meanwhile continued its march through the southern departments, and on April 28, 1820, encountered at La Plata three companies of the royalist advance guard. In this skirmish the royalists were entirely destroyed. Capt. Friedrich Rasch, of the first company of the Albions, with his own hands killed eleven of the enemy.[2] In leading the charge Col. Mackintosh rode over a steep bamboo bridge at full speed.[3]

After passing through Neiva the road leading over the cordillera became so difficult that mounted men were forced to dismount and walk, while the baggage and ammunition was transferred from the backs of the mules to those of Indian porters. In crossing the Páramo of Pitayó the sufferings experienced on the Páramo of Pisba were vividly recalled. Many men died of exposure. Great was the dejection of the exhausted troops when they learned upon arrival at the village of Pitayó that their hopes for a rest there were to be disappointed, since no provisions of any kind were to be found in the place.

Without having had a chance to refresh themselves, or even to clean their arms, the soldiers hurried along, hoping to

---

[1] O'Leary, *Documentos*, 155; López, *op. cit.*, 17, 19, 23; Archivo Nacional, Bogotá, Guerra y Marina, Historia, VII, 451, 668.

[2] Cochrane, *op. cit.*, I, 490, 491; this officer served in the subsequent campaign against Pasto as a major in the Squadron of Guides. *Cf.* p. 262, n. 1. Archivo Nacional, Bogotá, Guerra y Marina, Historia, VII, 301, López, *op. cit.*, 25.

[3] A traveller, who a few years later visited La Plata, wrote of Col. Mackintosh's exploit, "When you see this bridge, this seems incredible." Hamilton, *op. cit.*, I, 331.

reach a more hospitable country when, at the entrance to the village of Guambía they were suddenly attacked from the heights above the town. In spite of a heavy fire, they drove the Spaniards back again up the hill and into the woods that surrounded the town, leaving the road for about three leagues strewn with arms, accoutrements and baggage, as well as with the bodies of their killed and wounded. Lieut. Charles Smith, of the Albions, was promoted for bravery in this battle.[1] For saving the day at Pitayó much credit was due to Lieut. Col. Mackintosh and his two hundred Englishmen.[2] The Neiva Battalion also displayed great bravery and intrepidity in the action. As a reward for the latter's heroism it was enrolled in the Guard and given the name of the Vargas Battalion which was merged with it.[3]

The road to Popayán was now open, but the division was halted for some weeks at Quilichao and Cali to drill recruits. Gen. Valdés was blamed for spending the time in gambling and even for having looted the inhabitants in order to make good his losses. He neglected his troops and made no efforts to keep up their morale. Col. Mackintosh resented the treatment accorded his men, and when the general ordered the body of a captain of the Albions who had died of a fever in the hospital at Cali to be buried in the sand by the riverside, is said to have lost patience, threatening to march the Albions back to Bolívar. It was reported that Valdés, dreading Bolívar's displeasure, cringed and wept like a child, and by offering to give up the command to Gen. Mírez, succeeded in

---

[1] *Campaigns and Cruises*, I, 202-205; López, *op. cit.*, 25-28. Archivo Nacional, Bogotá, Guerra y Marina, Hojas de Servicios, XLII, 496.

[2] Gonzalo Búlnes, *Bolívar en el Perú*, II, 80; Baralt y Díaz, *op. cit.*, II, 13.

[3] Cortés Vargas, *Participación de Colombia*, I, 106, in which is quoted Bolívar's army order dated at Popayán, Feb. 8, 1822; *vide* also Blanco, *op. cit.*, VIII, 288; *Gaceta de Colombia*, March 3, 1822.

appeasing the resentment of the British officer.[1]   Valdés, however, was not actually relieved of command until he had lost more than half his men and utterly failed to accomplish his advance on Quito.

After leaving Popayán the difficulties of the march increased, owing to the roughness of the mountain trails and to the opposition of the enemy.   The worst natural difficulty was the crossing of the Juanambú, a mountain torrent which sweeps through precipitous gorges with such rapidity and depth as to be totally impassable in time of flood.   Taking advantage of this formidable obstacle, the warlike Pastusos had repeatedly shown their loyalty to the royalist cause by checking attempts of the patriot forces to pass.   On approaching this natural bulwark the grenadier company of the Albions was as usual marching in the advance guard, when it was suddenly fired upon from breastworks covering the only practicable pass both in front and on the left flank. While crossing the torrent the men were exposed to a galling fire which they could not return.   Many of the infantry became exhausted by their struggle through the swirling mass of waters and were carried across behind the cavalry. In spite of these difficulties, the patriots pressed on and drove the enemy from their defenses.[2]

The main royalist force under Calzada was entrenched in front of Pasto near Jenoi.   Here, on Feb. 2, 1821, it caught the patriots in a narrow defile where the latter were unable to advance more than two abreast.   The enemy were drawn up in a semicircle protected in front by a trench and breastwork and on the flank by an impenetrable thicket.   The patriot infantry were about to attack, when Valdéz ruined all chance of success by ordering the cavalry to charge the entrenchments.   This feat was not only impossible but fatal,

---

[1] *Campaigns and Cruises*, I, 210, 213, 214.

[2] *Campaigns and Cruises*, I, 226, 227; *Correo del Orinoco*, Jan. 20, 1821.

since the lancers became helplessly jammed in the narrow ravine without being able to return the enemy's fire, while the foot soldiers could neither make their way again to the front through the struggling mass of maddened horses nor escape from the stampede which ensued. A few royalists were taken prisoner but the rout of the patriot division was complete. Col. Mackintosh was wounded in the left hand. Only 400 escaped, while 700 remained in the hands of the enemy or fell killed or wounded in the " Guachibamba " or " Field of Blood ", as the Indians call this position. On this day the royalists had saved Pasto, the gateway to Quito from the north, and Valdés was in wild retreat back toward Popayán. It was later said that some English who were captured in this battle were executed in the plaza at Pasto.[1]

This failure of Valdés to take Pasto was his last chance for some time. Before he could reach Popayán he was met by Gen. Sucre who had been sent by Bolívar to relieve him of command.[2] Sucre also brought news of the armistice which had been declared between Bolívar and Morillo and of a raising of the flag of independence in Guayaquil. Sucre had orders to cooperate with the new republic against the royalists and determined to make the attack on Quito from the south, transporting his troops around to Guayaquil by sea.

The patriot troops were to be embarked from the two ports of Esmeraldas and San Buenaventura. To the latter was sent the newly organized Battalion of Santander, composed of black recruits, to discipline whom Col. Mackintosh and three of his English officers were assigned.[3] To the

[1] *Campaigns and Cruises*, I, 228; Cochrane, *op. cit.*, I, 491; Archivo Nacional, Bogotá, Guerra y Marina, Historia, VII, 473; O'Leary, *Documentos*, XIX, 247.

[2] *Campaigns and Cruises*, I, 229; Carlos A. Vivanco, "The Ecuadorian Campaign, 1821-1822 in *Inter-America* (Eng. Ed.), V, 219-221.

[3] *Ibid.*, 231; Walker, *op. cit.*, II, 499; Archivo Nacional, Bogotá, Guerra

port of Esmeraldas the Albion Battalion marched from Popayán. This body had suffered so severely from sickness and desertions and from inability to keep it filled with recruits that only one hundred men boarded the English brig "Ana" early in July for the voyage to Guayaquil. It seemed impossible to stop these desertions, especially from the Albion Battalion, when troops were on the march. On embarking at San Buenaventura, Sucre had with him only 600 men altogether.[1] " He began the campaign without money, without resources, almost without troops." [2]

On his arrival at Guayaquil, Sucre found many difficult tasks awaiting him. By Bolívar's orders, in addition to reorganizing his army for the new campaign against Quito, he was to perfect the formal incorporation of Quito with Colombia. He had to secure the cooperation of Gen. Santa Cruz and his Peruvian divisions, and persuade the junta of Guayaquil against allowing themselves to be annexed to Peru. He had to fight Spain openly and Peru secretly. Meanwhile, he must smooth factional disorders and put down revolts.[3] Hardly had he arrived in Guayaquil when the crews of six armed lighters which were in the harbor mutinied under the leadership of Col. Nicolás López, a former Spanish officer, who with Salgado and other republican chiefs proclaimed the king and carried off their own vessels as well as the corvette "Alejandro" and the brig "Ana". Sucre promptly manned two ships with members of the Albion Battalion and pursued

y Marina, Hojas de Servicios, XLII, 491. The three officers who marched with Col. Mackintosh were Lieut. Col. Augustin Freudenthal and Lieutenants David Shepherd and Donald Ross, Archivo Nacional, Bogotá, Guerra y Marina, Historia, VII, 500.

[1] O'Leary, *Documentos*, XIX, 61, 216; *Gaceta de Colombia*, March 24, 1822; Archivo Nacional, Bogotá, Guerra y Marina, Historia, VII, 431, 519, 522, 526, 550.

[2] *Archivo Santander*, VI, iii.

[3] O'Leary, *Narración*, II, 115; Vivanco, *op. cit.*, 314.

and captured the lighters before they could get out of the river. So energetic was Sucre's pursuit that only the "Alejandro" escaped.[1]

Meanwhile the Spanish army threatened Guayaquil. One column under Gen. Melchor de Aymerich was advancing from Quito to Babahoyo; the other under Col. Francisco González was marching from Cuenca via Yaguachi. Their junction at Babahoyo had to be prevented, so on Aug. 17th Sucre hastened toward Yaguachi to intercept González. Here, two days later, González suffered a complete disaster. Sucre captured 600 prisoners, 700 muskets and all the Spanish ammunition. The patriots lost twenty killed and twenty-one wounded.

In this engagement the Albion Battalion under Lieut. Col. Johnston took an active part; but the brunt of the battle was borne by the division of Gen. Mírez in which the Santander Battalion under Col. Mackintosh, who was again wounded in the hand, was serving.[2] Capt. Charles Smith, with twenty-five men of the Albion Battalion, destroyed the royalist rearguard while the Battalions Santander and Libertadores de Guayaquil pursued the enemy for more than three leagues as far as the Rio Nuevo. Sucre then marched toward Babahoyo, where Aymerich had arrived on his way to Yaguachi in the hope of effecting a junction with González. Though Aymerich refused to fight, he was so hotly pursued by the patriot cavalry that he lost 400 men, and his withdrawal became a rout.[3] The significance of the victory of Yaguachi was, that by preventing the junction of González with Ay-

[1] *Campaigns and Cruises*, I, 249-252; Vivanco, *op. cit.*, 224; Gen. Rafael Negret, "Batalla de Yaguachi" in *Memorial del estado mayor del ejército de Colombia*, XI, no. 110, p. 337.

[2] Negret, *Yaguachi*, 337, 338; Vivanco, *op. cit.*, 225; Cochrane, *op. cit.*, I, 491, 492.

[3] Negret, *Yaguachi*, 339; Archivo Nacional Bogotá, Guerra y Marina, Hojas de Servicios, XLII, 493.

merich, the Spanish commander-in-chief was forced to abandon his entire plan of campaign against Guayaquil.[1] Fortune seemed to smile on Sucre.

"How vain is hope and how fickle is victory," wrote Sucre only a month later to his chief, Bolívar, in a letter in which he mourned his failure to free Quito, the destruction of his division, and even the loss of his own reputation as a general. On Sept. 12, 1821, the impatience of his troops had forced him to risk a battle before he was fully prepared, attacking Aymerich in a position favorable to the latter, between Ambato and Guachi, on the road to Quito. Two separate charges were hurled against the royalist infantry who were driven from behind their breastworks; but the royalist cavalry forced back the attackers and the patriot army was completely routed with heavy loss. Most of the patriot officers were captured or killed. Both Lieut. Col. Johnston of the Albions and Lieut. Col. Mackintosh of the Santanders were wounded and captured. Capt. Charles Smith of the Albion Battalion also was captured, and Sucre himself wounded. Although forced to retreat, he had the satisfaction of having inflicted such heavy losses upon the royalists that they were unable to pursue him. About a thousand royalists in fact were killed and wounded in the battle of Guachi.[2]

In November an armistice for ninety days was agreed upon between Sucre and Aymerich, which enabled the patriot commander to recoup his losses and to await aid for which he had appealed to Gen. José de San Martín, who had become "Protector" of Peru after a successful campaign in

[1] O'Leary, *Narración*, II, 119; *Correo del Orinoco*, Jan. 5, 1822. Negret, *Yaguachi*, 337-339.

[2] O'Leary, *Cartas de Sucre al Libertador*, I, 29-31; Cochrane, *op. cit.*, I, 492; Vivanco, *op. cit.*, 227; Archivo Nacional, Bogotá, Guerra y Marina, Historia, VII, 502; XXXV, 886; XLII, 493; Hojas de Servicios, XXX, 916; López, *op. cit.*, 45.

La Plata (later Argentina) and Chile. Before, however, the Peruvian troops under Col. Santa Cruz could arrive, the armistice was broken by the royalists. Therefore, on Jan. 20, 1822, Sucre left Guayaquil and crossed the mountains to meet Santa Cruz. After their junction, the patriot army of the south was strong enough to effect the purpose of the campaign, and began its march on Quito. At Riobamba, April 21, an observation detachment of the royalist army was encountered and driven out of an advanced position which it had occupied for some time.

Since Capts. Bruix and Sowerby, Lieut. Latus and Cornet Olmost highly distinguished themselves in this engagement,[1] and Lieut. Col. Rasch was mentioned for calmness and courage, the unusual circumstances of the affair at Riobamba should be recorded. It seems that the officers of dragoons of the patriot army had been invited by the mounted officers of the royalist force to dine with them in Riobamba. Thinking that this invitation was in the nature of an extension of the truce, the patriot officers accepted. While the cavalry officers were in the midst of their conviviality, the royalist infantry treacherously attacked the patriot troops. Fortunately the republican Colonel Ibarra had maintained himself on the alert with the remainder of the cavalry and, at the first sound of firing, charged into Riobamba at the head of the grenadiers and dragoons. The dinner party was broken up and the royalists at once evacuated the town. Quite possibly this affair at Riobamba so depressed the morale of the Spanish as measurably to contribute to the later victory of Pichincha.[2]

---

[1] Gen. Miller says of these officers that Capt. Bruix was a very gallant Frenchman, son of Admiral Bruix. He had been a page to Napoleon. He met his death by an accident in Lima. Lieut. Latus, a young Englishman formerly of the rifle corps, died of his wounds at Lima. Miller, *op. cit.*, I, 353 n.

[2] Miller, *op. cit.*, I, 354; O'Leary, *Documentos*, XIX, 283, 285; Archivo

Aymerich, hoping for a repetition of his triumph at Gua-chi, had established himself in a strong position about twelve miles from Quito, and had converted the thick walls and farm buildings of some large " haciendas " into forts, be-hind which he kept his troops awaiting the arrival of re-enforcements from Pasto, while at the same time blocking the advance of Sucre upon the capital. The latter, finding that he could not persuade Aymerich to come out from be-hind his defenses and give fight, made a masterful march during the night of May 23 over the slopes of the volcano, Pichincha, in such a way as to interpose himself between the capital and any reenforcements which might come from Pasto.[1]

On the next day, May 24th, 1822, was fought the Battle of Pichincha. At eight o'clock in the morning the royalist commander saw the patriot columns marching along the heights of the volcano and realized that he was in danger of being cut off from his reenforcements. He hurriedly put his army in motion in pursuit of the patriots, and by nine-thirty had come into contact with them. Fire was first opened upon the Peruvian division of Santa Cruz. Gen. Mírez threw in his Colombian troops to support them and soon the engagement became general. Col. Córdoba with two com-panies of the Magdalena Battalion was sent around toward the royalist rear. The enemy detached three companies of the Battalion of Aragon with orders to make their way through the thick woods and attack the patriots' left flank. Success seemed to be about to crown their efforts to force themselves between the Magdalena and Yaguachi Battalions when, just in the nick of time, three companies of the Al-bions, who had been escorting the ammunition train some

Nacional, Bogotá, Guerra y Marina, Hojas de Servicios, XL, 975; *Gaceta de Colombia*, April 21, June 2, 1822. López, *op. cit.*, 49; Blanco, *op. cit.*, VIII, 361.

[1] López, *op. cit.*, 71, 73, 74; Vivanco, *op. cit.*, 321.

distance in the rear, arrived on the scene. The Albions charged with the usual British gallantry and put to flight the companies of Aragon. The Magdalena Battalion followed up the charge, and spread disorder to the main forces of the enemy. Then the whole royalist army broke and fled, pursued by Col. Córdoba with the Magdalenas, Yaguachis and Albions. The enemy reserves tried to renew the combat at the foot of the hill, but were overwhelmed by the patriot battalions and driven headlong from the field and even to the gates of Quito.

Col. O'Leary thereupon was sent into the city to demand the surrender of the Spanish commander, who agreed to capitulate with his entire force including a field marshal, fifteen colonels, 160 officers, 11,000 men, 14 guns, 1700 muskets, and all his military stores. The Spanish casualties during this battle were 400 killed and 190 wounded to 200 killed and 140 wounded of the patriots. Next day Aymerich in his capacity as viceroy formally surrendered the whole province of Quito, which eventually became part of the Republic of Colombia.[1]

Although Sucre had been in supreme command of the patriot army at the battle of Pichincha, he had not won the victory entirely without aid, for Aymerich was weakened by the non-arrival of the reenforcements which he expected Basilio García to send from Pasto. These reenforcements did not come because García was too busy defending himself and could not spare them. While Sucre kept Aymerich from sending aid to García, the latter was also prevented from supporting the viceroy. The plans for the campaign of the south, conceived by the genius of Bolívar, had worked out to perfection.[2]

[1] O'Leary, *Documentos*, XIX, 287, 289, 299; Vivanco, *op. cit.*, V, 321, 323, 324; Blanco, *op. cit.*, VIII, 406-412, 441, 447; Justin Winsor, *Narrative and Critical History of America*, VIII, 335. Andres García Camba, *Memorias*, II, 32; López, *op. cit.*, 74, 75.

[2] Negret, *Campaña del Sur*, 148; López, *op. cit.*, 62.

To understand the strategy of this campaign, it will be necessary to go back and recall the situation in Colombia. It will be remembered that Valdés had been sent south to capture Pasto and to advance even to Quito if he found it possible to do so. If he had accomplished this he might have shared with Sucre the laurels of Pichincha, but he had not captured Pasto, the back door to Quito, because García had been too strong and clever for him. When Bolívar heard of the disaster to Valdés at Jenoi he had temporarily relieved him from command of the vanguard of the army of the south, replacing him with Gen. Pedro León Torres. When his own hands were at last free in Venezuela and northern New Granada, Bolívar himself, as will likewise be remembered, had resolved to devote his personal attention to reinvigorating the campaign in the south and had repaired to Cali where he had concentrated a larger army and had resumed the advance on Pasto.[1]

Throughout the march southward the army was harassed by guerillas and local partisans who attacked the flanks and rear of the column and, because of their intimate knowledge of the country, always managed to escape. Moreover, they succeeded in capturing many of the republican soldiers, in tiring out the troops and in keeping their nightly bivouacs in constant alarm. Apparently all the inhabitants of Pasto and Patía, men, women and children, were hostile to the patriots and gave aid and information to the royalists. Fortunately, however, Bolívar by avoiding the direct road had succeeded in crossing the Juanambú at a less difficult place lower down, without encountering serious opposition.[2]

In order to accomplish the strategical objective of his cam-

[1] Negret, *Campaña del Sur*, 149; Lecuna, *Bomboná*, 4; López, *op. cit.*, 59-61; *Gaceta de Colombia*, March 17, 1822.

[2] *Ibid.*, May 5, 12, 1822; Lecuna, *Bomboná*, 14; 252; *Archivo Santander*, VIII, 259; López, *op. cit.*, 62; O'Leary, *Documentos*, XIX, 249.

paign, to intercept communication between the royalist troops in Colombia and those in Quito, the Liberator was endeavoring to thrust his army athwart the road somewhere south of Pasto between García's base at that point and Aymerich's at Quito. Bolívar had reached Consaca when he learned that García with 1800 men was occupying a position on the heights of Cariaco protecting the trails from Pasto.

On the morning of April 7, 1822, Bolívar began his advance and had gone as far as the " hacienda " of Bombaná when he received word from his scouts that the enemy occupied a strong position on the southern bank of the Cariaco brook. Not only was there a deep ravine, covered with dense woods along his front, but he had strengthened his lines with abbatis and stone parapets. The only way to cross the ravine was by a single narrow bridge, which was protected by the cross fire of infantry and artillery. Two guns enfilading the bridge and the ravine were posted at the left, and this flank was further protected by the impassable gorge of the Guaitara River. The right flank of the enemy's position rested on the steep slopes of the Pasto volcano which appeared to offer a prohibitive obstacle. This flank was guarded by four companies deployed in échelon behind stone parapets. It was indeed a formidable position.

In spite of the strength of the royalist defenses, Bolívar determined to break through them. He issued orders for Gen. Valdés with the Rifles Battalion to attack and turn the enemy's right flank; for Gen. Torres with the Bogotá and Vargas Battalions and the squadrons of Guides to charge the center and left of the position; and for the Vencedor Battalion and Hussars and Cazadores of the Guard to remain in reserve within range of the hostile artillery.

In compliance with these orders the two generals sent forward their troops. The battle began at half-past three in the afternoon. Gen. Valdés led his column in a long circuit

toward the left up the slopes of the volcano. In this advance
the Rifles were led by the first company under Capt. Ramírez
on the right and the second company under Capt. Thomas
Wright on the left, while the remainder of the battalion followed under Col. Sandes. There was no trail, and so steep
was the hillside that they had to dig in their bayonets for
use as hand-holds in climbing. The anxious eyes watching
their slow progress could not follow it far, for soon they
were lost in the haze and smoke of battle.

Meanwhile Gen. Torres deployed his division against the
center and left of the enemy's position. On the left they
were checked by the steepness of the gorge. In the center the
only way to cross was over the narrow bridge. There, in
spite of the fire poured upon it from rifles and guns, they
forced a passage. The Bogotá Battalion crossed first, followed by the Vargas. Both battalions fought gallantly to
capture the enemy's defenses, but could not break through
the abbatis. Every man who crossed the bridge was soon
stretched on the ground killed or wounded. Not an arm was
left to raise their fallen colors. Within half an hour Gen.
Torres and all the field officers were down. The remnant
of the battalions then reformed on the north side of the
ravine, unable to do anything except keep up a fire on the
enemy to distract his attention and to prevent him from sending reenforcements to his right flank.

It was a long and anxious wait until about five o'clock,
when the mist lifted momentarily to reveal the royalists fleeing from the defenses on their right hotly pursued by the
men of the Rifles. The battalion had struggled to reach a
crest above the royalist flank, whence they found that, exhausted as they were, they must descend about a thousand
feet to cross the Cariaco ravine, and then climb up again the
same distance on the other side. When they arrived before
the enemy's defenses they fixed bayonets and charged with-

out firing a shot. The royalists, having exhausted their ammunition, were compelled to abandon their defenses.

When Bolívar saw the enemy's right flank giving way he ordered the Vencedor Battalion to charge the center. This was joined by the remnants of the Bogotá and Vargas Battalions, all of whom pressed the assault so violently, until darkness stopped the battle, that the royalists were glad to be able to withdraw under cover of night. Owing not only to the darkness and the difficulties of the ground, but to their own exhaustion and severe losses, the patriots were unable to pursue. Although he barely escaped capture, García succeeded in withdrawing all his forces into the woods to another strong position on the road to Pasto.[1]

After the battle a suspension of hostilities for four days was agreed upon for the purpose of collecting the wounded and burying the dead. It is said that García generously sent back to Bolívar the colors of the Bogotá and Vargas Battalions which had been picked up from the ground at the foot of the parapet where they lay surrounded by the corpses of the color-bearers and those who accompanied them. With the colors was a message saying that he could not keep trophies which would dim the glory of two battalions which were so brave that although they could be destroyed, they could not be conquered.[2]

In the battle of Bomboná the royalist loss was 300 killed, wounded and captured, while the patriots lost 341 wounded

---

[1] This account of the battle of Bomboná is based on Gen. Negret's well-documented article, *La Campaña del Sur*, and on the documents contained therein, *q. v.*, 161-172, and on O'Leary, *Narración*, II, 134-138; *Documentos*, XIX, 237-240, 250. *Vide* also López, *op. cit.*, 65-69; Lecuna, *Bomboná*, 16-18.

[2] *Boletín de la Biblioteca Nacional del Ecuador*, 1921, nos. 6-7, p. 244; *Boletín de Historia y Antigüedades*, VII, nos. 75, 114. Gen. Negret says that Gen. López gives the words of García's message, but that he cannot find them in any other document. *Op. cit.*, 167.

and 116 killed, among whom were one general, one colonel, twenty-two other officers and 117 men wounded, and nine officers and 107 men killed. Of the Rifles, five officers and fifty men were killed. Capt. Featherstonhaugh fell transfixed by a bayonet, while he was slashing his way through the enemy with his sabre. Among promotions made on the field were those of Lieut. Col. Sandes to be colonel and Sergt. Primero Delgado of the Rifles to be sub-lieutenant. Captains Ramírez and Wright were mentioned for gallantry. O'Leary, aide-de-camp of Bolívar, attributed the victory of the patriots both to the military skill of Gen. Valdés and to the invincibility of the Rifles Battalion.[1]

The engagement at Bomboná was important because it and the campaign of which it was the culmination prevented García from sending the much-needed aid to Aymerich, and thus helped Sucre win the decisive battle of Pichincha. Another reason for the importance of Bomboná was, that it convinced the warlike inhabitants of Pasto that the royalist cause was a losing one. Together with the news of the fall of Quito, it persuaded García that he would do well to accept Bolívar's generous terms while he could. He therefore capitulated and Bolívar entered Pasto as victor on June 8, 1822.[2]

The road to Quito was now open and two weeks later Bolívar made a triumphant entry into that capital. He lost no time in recognizing the valuable results which had been

---

[1] O'Leary, *Narración*, II, 137; *Documentos*, XIX, 237-239, 244, 245; Blanco, *op. cit.*, VIII, 341-344. From muster rolls of the month after the battle it is possible to learn the names of the foreign officers who were on duty with the various organizations, and it is fair to assume that most of these officers took part in the battle. Their names are given on p. 262, n. 1, *supra*.

[2] O'Leary, *Documentos*, XIX, 264, 297; *Archivo Santander*, VIII, 259; Lecuna, *Bomboná*, 21; *Gaceta de Colombia*, June 30, 1822; *Annual Register*, 1822, " History," 282.

accomplished by Sucre. That officer was promoted general of division and appointed intendant general of the new Department of Quito. Lieut. Col. Mackintosh was promoted to full colonel and John Johnston, Charles Wright and Philip Brandsen became lieutenant colonels.[1]

Although the regular forces of the royalists had surrendered, the warlike Pastusos were not yet subdued, and under

[1] Blanco, *op. cit.*, VIII, 445, 597; *Gaceta de Colombia*, July 28, 1822, Vivanco, *op. cit.*, V, 326. Col. Johnston, who it will be remembered was wounded and captured at Guachi, had secured his exchange, and when he had recovered sufficiently from his wound, had returned to duty in time to take part in the battle of Pichincha. After several days rest in Quito, he was given permission to return to Bogotá to secure a settlement of his accounts with the government. Archivo Nacional Bogotá, Guerra y Marina, Historia, XXXV, 886, 887. Lieutenant Colonel "graduado" Friedrich Rasch was also promoted to lieutenant colonel "efectivo" and given command of the Dragoons. Archivo Nacional, Bogotá, Guerra y Marina, Historia, XVII, 7. It is impossible to give an exact translation of the words "graduado" and "efectivo," as they are not employed always with the same meaning. Both are honorary titles, the first designating a higher rank which carried with it neither additional pay nor command. The second conferred a promotion in title which might involve increase in pay or in command, or sometimes both, but did not necessarily do so. In the patriot army, where both troops and money were scarce, it was customary to find many captains commanding companies holding the honorary titles of lieutenant colonels "graduados," which had been conferred upon them as rewards for valor in action. This title corresponds to that of "brevet" in the U. S. Army and may ordinarily be so translated, but there is no title corresponding to that of "efectivo," which is therefore untranslatable. Bolívar apparently used it as a way of piling honor upon honor for repeatedly valorous conduct. Sometimes he even added still further honor by promoting to the rank of "vivo y efectivo." Sergeant major "Dionisio" (Dennis) Egan, who had joined Sucre's command only for the latter part of the campaign, including Pichincha, was mentioned by that general as "conducting himself with honor and exactitude proper in an officer of his rank." Archivo Nacional, Bogotá, Guerra y Marina, Historia, DCCLXXX, 860. The Battalion Vencedores en Pichincha was recommended for decoration for its conduct in the action of Pichincha. Archivo Nacional, Bogotá, Guerra y Marina, Historia, XVII, 45.

the leadership of Boves, revolted against Bolívar. Sucre, who was ordered to proceed against the malcontents with troops from the garrison of Quito, wisely chose to take the Rifles with him. On November 4, two hundred men of the cavalry left Quito to join him. After a forced march and a night attack, frustrated by heavy rain, at dawn of December 23, 1822 the second and fifth companies of Rifles succeeded in capturing the bridge of Guaítira under a heavy fire. On the 24th the enemy defending Pasto were encountered in an apparently impregnable position. Col. Sandes, having asked for and secured the honor of making the attack, sent the first and fifth companies of Rifles to capture the heights on the left, while he with the remainder of the battalions attacked the main position of the enemy above the church of Santiago. Gen. Salom led a charge of cavalry on the left and, after an hour and a half of fighting, the Pastusos fled in all directions, leaving Pasto in the hands of Sucre's men. Among those mentioned in orders for bravery and recommended for promotion to lieutenant colonels were Captain Wright of the second and Capt. Ferguson of the fifth company of the Rifles.[1]

Upon their return to Quito the Rifles were assigned to comfortable quarters in the convent of San Francisco but were subsequently transferred to the San Luís school buildings. So many troops were assembled in the city that there was a shortage of barracks for them and of stables for the horses. Among the organizations present were the Albion and Rifles Battalions, the Squadrons of Lancers, Hussars, Cazadores, Grenadiers, and Dragoons as well as medical corps units, the sick in hospital, the staff of the guard and the staffs of Bolívar, Sucre and the generals commanding

[1] O'Leary, *Documentos*, XIX, 405, 406, 486, 507; XX, 173; Blanco, *op. cit.*, VIII, 583; Archivo Nacional, Bogotá. Guerra y Marina, Historia, XVII, 161, 166, 167, 169.

divisions.[1] In command of the artillery and the arsenal at Quito was Capt. Adolf Klinger, who later lent invaluable services in keeping in repair the arms of the troops in the field and in supplying them with ammunition.[2]

Provisions were scarce and money was lacking for the proper pay of so many troops. It was necessary to reduce the pay of privates, drummers and corporals to a real and a half per day, and to give the other men and officers only half pay. In spite of the fact that the rations had been improved and then consisted of meat, salt, plantains and vegetable soup, the conduct of the troops was very bad. This was especially so in the cavalry, because these regiments were corrupted by the large numbers of former royalist cavalrymen who had been incorporated into them.[3] So much distressed by lack of adequate pay were the officers of the Guards that, in order to appear in public decently, they pledged their unpaid salaries to a merchant in the city in return for clothing. Before the end of the year, however, Sucre succeeded, by means of strenuous efforts, in securing sufficient supplies to re-clothe the troops with the exception of shirts and shoes, and managed to pay the officers of the Guard two-thirds of their salary.[4]

After the suppression of the outbreak in Pasto and the

[1] Archivo Nacional, Bogotá, Guerra y Marina, Historia, XVII, 73, 146; XXVI, 607, 619; *Gaceta de Colombia*, Aug. 25, 1822.

[2] Archivo Nacional, Bogotá, Guerra y Marina, Historia, XXVI, 723, 740, 837, 852; XLVII, 459; Bingham Collection of Mss., Sucre Papers, Nos. 1015-18, Adolfo Klinger to Sucre, reports from the commandant of the arsenal of the artillery park, March 10, 13, 14, 21, 1823.

[3] Archivo Nacional, Bogotá, Guerra y Marina, Historia, XVII, 57, 69; XXVI, 599; O'Leary, *Documentos*, XIX, 514. A "real" may be worth from five to twelve and a half cents, and the word may very properly be translated as a "bit" since it is a popular term for a monetary value rather than the official name of an actual coin. What the value of a real was at that time is not known.

[4] Archivo Nacional, Bogotá, Guerra y Marina, Historia, XVII, 77, 122, 142.

resumption of quiet, Bolívar, finding his resources nearly exhausted, determined to cut down expenses by reducing the number of troops in Quito. He therefore ordered that the two squadrons of dragoons be consolidated into one, the squadron of Grenadiers to be limited to 310, that of the Guides to 320 and their places to be supplied by militia. This consolidation of the cavalry and the muster-out of the Yaguachi Battalion resulted in many surplus officers, especially among the captains and lieutenants. The Liberator therefore was generous in allowing leaves to officers; and as this further reduced expenses, all soldiers from Quito, Guayaquil and nearby departments were sent home on furlough. Discharges also were freely granted.[1]

Accordingly, when some five or six officers and thirty men of the Albion Battalion signed a petition to be allowed to return to their homes, now that the liberation of the whole of Colombia had been completed, Bolívar ordered Col. Mackintosh to submit a roster of the foreign officers and men who were in his command, reporting whether they were in the old Albion Battalion or recently attached, in order that they might be sent to Bogotá to receive a settlement of their accounts.[2] On Aug. 2, 1822, Bolívar directed the captain of the brig "Ana" to transport Col. Mackintosh and fifty men of the Albion Battalion to San Buenaventura.[3] The battalion thence returned to Bogotá where it remained in garrison for the rest of the year 1822, pending the settlement of its accounts. This occasioned some delay, for many of the officers had lost their papers, either during service in the field or else because they had been captured.[4]

[1] Archivo Nacional, Bogotá, *op. cit.*, XVII, 8, 9, 16, 43; XXVI, 601, 603, 605, DCCLXXIX, 399-430.

[2] O'Leary, *Documentos*, XIX, 342; *Present State of Colombia,* 97; Cochrane, *op. ci.*. I, 492.

[3] O'Leary, *Documentos*, XIX, 357, 359.

[4] Archivo Nacional, Bogotá, Guerra y Marina, Historia, XXXV, 871; CCCLIX, 1002.

The Albion Battalion had no further active service, and was probably mustered out or disbanded about the middle of the year 1823, for no records of it subsequent to that time have yet been found. An account of an individual here and there has come to light, but it is certain that as an organization the Albion Battalion had ceased to exist.[1]

Most of its foreign members disappeared from South America, probably to return to their homes, although a few remained behind. However, other legionaries continued to serve in the various battalions to which they were assigned or to perform important duties on the staff. For Bolívar's work was not yet done. The last vestiges of the royal power had to be driven from Venezuela, and two more republics still were destined to be fashioned by the master mind and hand of the Liberator.

[1] A careful search of the documents in the national archives of Bogotá has brought to light the pay-rolls of the Albion Battalion for the months of October and November, 1822 and the muster rolls for October, November and December of the same year. Archivo Nacional, Bogotá, Guerra y Marina, Historia, DCCLXXIX, 680, 795, 838, 844, 861. *Vide* Appendix I for a copy of the muster roll for December 1822, which was the latest one found. The service record of Col. John Mackintosh shows that he was retired on June 23, 1823, with the enjoyment of his military exemptions, the right to wear the uniform of his rank, and a salary of 100 pesos per month, for wounds received in the service, incapacitating him for duty. Archivo Nacional, Bogotá, Guerra y Marina, Hojas de Servicios, XXX, 912. A letter has also been found from Col. Mackintosh to the Minister of War, dated at Bogotá, July 8, 1823, referring to the delay of the national property office in settling claims, and asking that orders be issued to expedite the settlement of the pay and allowances due Lieut. Col. John Johnston and other individuals of the Albion Battalion, in order that their accounts might be finally adjusted. Archivo Nacional, Bogotá, Guerra y Marina, Historia, XXXV, 98. It is possible that further documents may yet be found in the national archives at Bogotá or elsewhere which may throw light on the exact date at which the Albion Battalion was mustered out.

CHAPTER XI

Liberation Attained

After the victories of Bolívar and Sucre in the campaign of the south, the Republic of Great Colombia, composed of the three divisions, Venezuela, New Granada and Quito, showed promise of real advancement. There were, however, storm clouds still hanging over its northern and southern extremities which the Liberator could not afford to ignore. In the south the viceroy of Peru still held much territory for the Spanish crown, and with a powerful army threatened to crush the revolutionists in Lima. Gen. San Martín, fearing lest he might be unable alone to cope with the viceregal forces and with the jealousies and partisanships among the independents themselves, called on Bolívar for assistance. If this were not given and the revolution there were crushed, the next logical step for the viceroy would be to send his armies into Quito to overrun that division and restore it to its former condition as a colony. This was a very real danger, and Bolívar saw that the only way to assure the continued independence of the provinces which he had already liberated was to aid those further to the south, as yet unredeemed, to obtain their liberty likewise.[1]

In the north of Great Colombia too there was work to be done before Bolívar could feel that liberation was complete, for the royalists still held bases on the Caribbean coast of Venezuela at Puerto Cabello and Coro, from which there

[1] *Gaceta de Colombia*, Sept. 8, 1822; Cortés Vargas, *Participación de Colombia en la libertad del Perú*, I, 2, 3, 32, 34; *View of South America*, 8, 9.

was always danger of their issuing forth with renewed strength to reclaim parts of their lost provinces. As will be remembered, when Bolívar left for the south he had entrusted Páez with the duty of capturing these royalist strongholds and driving the invaders from the soil of the republic. In this campaign Páez kept with him in the division of operations of the province of Caracas several foreigners, among whom was more than one well-known name.[1]

[1] On the staff were Col. George Woodberry as adjutant general and chief of staff and Capt. Charles Wilthew, as field adjutant. In command of the Grenadiers of the Guard and sometimes of the Guard Brigade, in view of his rank as senior colonel, was Col. Johannes Uslar; in command of the Carabobo Battalion was Lieut. Col. Edward Brand; and in command of the Boyacá Battalion Lieut. Col. Ludwig Flegel. Col. Philip M. Martin commanded the Brigade of Cavalry. With the Tiradores of the Guard was Lieut. Col. Julius A. Reinboldt; with the Squadron of Hussars Lieut. Col. Friedrich Adlercreutz; with the National Artillery of the Isthmus, Lieut. Col. Francis Meyer; with the Bogotá Battalion, Sergt. Major William Smith; and with the Carabobo Battalion Capts. Charles Minchin and Charles Smith. Also serving in subordinate capacities were Lieut. Francis Manuit, Ensigns Alex. Marks and John Blanton, and 1st Sergt. Joseph Palmer, and Corporal James White. In the company of Cazadores of the Grenadier Battalion was sub-lieutenant Lorenzo Jones, and in the third company of the Anzoátegui Battalion was Lieut. Joseph Echartet. Lieut. Samuel Paramor, who had been promoted from a sergeant in the British Legion was transferred to the Orinoco Battalion for station at La Guaira. Besides those named there may have been others, for the records are not always complete and there is frequently the possibility of a foreign name, spelled as it sounds in Spanish, escaping the notice of the searcher. Furthermore the records often give only the names of commanding officers or of officers specially mentioned for some particular purpose. Therefore this list of foreigners must not be considered final. The most important records searched were those in the national archives at Bogotá and Caracas. Material was located in the following: Archivo Nacional, Bogotá, Guerra y Marina, Historia, VI, 210, 883; VII, 242; XVI, 714, 721, 730, 734, 735; DCCLXXX, 790, 807, 811, 813, 841; Hojas de Servicios, XXXI, 460; Archivo Nacional, Caracas, Ilustres Próceres, LXIV, 253; XCIX, 217; and in the National Academy of History at Caracas, Archivo Soublette, Documentos, II, III, for the year 1822. Information was also found in the following old newspapers: *El Colombiano*, July 2, Nov. 19, 1823; *Gaceta de Colombia*, Feb. 15, 1824.

The siege of Puerto Cabello, which began immediately after the battle of Carabobo, was a difficult operation to carry out; for to bring a siege to a successful conclusion implies the eventual starving out of the garrison, or at least the ability to infuse into it the fear of starvation. Such an outcome here was impossible, for Puerto Cabello was open to the sea and could be supplied by Spanish vessels at their pleasure. The Colombian squadron under Commodore Daniel Danells was too weak to prevent this, and the Spanish had at all times been able to hold command of the sea.[1]

Puerto Cabello also furnished a possible base to which reenforcements from Spain might be sent for the reconquest of Venezuela. For this reason La Torre realized the importance of his holding on as long as possible without risking his small force in any serious engagement. The patriots had various successes in outpost skirmishes, but all the time their forces were being steadily weakened by sickness and death due to garrison life under unhealthy conditions. Finally when the strength of his army had been reduced from 3279 to a few more than 1000, Páez resolved to abandon the siege as too costly and ineffectual, and marched his troops away.[2]

Taking advantage of this opportunity, Morales who had relieved La Torre in command of the royalist forces, on June 24, 1822, escaped from Puerto Cabello with 1200 men to Curaçao and thence to the peninsula of Goajira. Morales met and defeated Gen. Manrique, who was sent to oppose him, at Salina Rica. Morales then swung southward through the department of Zulia, hoping to establish a base on Lake Maracaibo, preliminary to further invasion of the interior of the country. In fear for the safety of Cúcuta, patriot

[1] Páez, *op. cit.*, I, 220; Cortés Vargas, *op. cit.*, I, 162; *London Chronicle*, April 22, 1823; Walker, *op. cit.*, II, 562.

[2] Páez, *op. cit.*, I, 221.

armies were hurried in around him from all sides, encircling the lake; Lieut. Col. Reyes González from Coro, Gen. Manrique from Gibraltar on the south shore of the lake, and Gen. Mariano Montilla with the army of the Magdalena from Santa Marta.[1]

Morales succeeded in occupying the city of Maracaibo, where he established his base, and for the rest of the year continued to threaten the valleys of Cúcuta. He also stirred up a revolt among the Goajira Indians near Santa Marta, the suppression of which necessitated strenuous measures on the part of the republicans. Gen. Manuel Manrique had to scatter his limited forces in small detachments to cover the immense territory involved. These detachments were sometimes too weak to resist, as was the case with that of Col. Reyes Vargas, whose tiny column was surprised at dawn,

[1] *Ibid.*, 223, 224; Archivo Soublette, Documentos, 1822, II, III; *Iris de Venezuela*, March 25, Aug. 5, 1822; *Gaceta de Colombia*, Feb. 17, 1822; *Present State of Colombia*, 85, 100; Archivo Nacional, Caracas, Ilustres Próceres, XL, 73; LX, 94; XCIX, 184, 217, 235; *El Colombiano*, July 2, 1823; Cortés Vargas, *op. cit.*, I, 162, 163. Archivo Nacional, Bogotá, Guerra y Marina, Historia, XXXV, 853; Hojas de Servicios, XXXI, 460; Dávila, *Diccionario Biográfico*, 228, 229; Scarpetia y Vergara, *op. cit.*, 702. In this connection should be mentioned Henry Weir and Thomas Charles James Wright, since both of them later became generals. At that time Weir was only a captain, but was given command of three companies and sent to head off a part of the royalist advance. He took by assault trenches on the east shore of Lake Maracaibo and surprised a royalist garrison, capturing one hundred and fifty prisoners. Among the Englishmen taking part in the Campaign of Zulia, as this rally against Morales was called, were Lieut. Col. Charles James Minchin, who was chief of staff of Gen. Zarda's division operating in Goajira and Capt. Rupert Hand, who commanded a company of flankers, was seriously disabled in an accident and had to retire from service. In the Carabobo Battalion were Lieut. Jacob Harrison, 2nd Sergt. John Norton and 1st Corporal James White. Sub-lieutenant John Brown, who came down from the capital to take part in this campaign received in all only twenty-nine " pesos " pay and returned to Bogotá in a state of destitution, without money or clothing.

dispersed and captured by the enemy. The nearest garrison consisted of only fifty men and could do nothing to help.[1] Gen. Montilla set out from Rio Hacha to attack Maracaibo, but, having been delayed by the rains, imprudently allowed his advance guard of only a thousand men to proceed eight days' march ahead of his main body. Morales, taking advantage of this mistake, sallied forth to encounter Montilla and defeated him on November 13, 1822.[2]

Morales, however, had committed an equally serious error by leaving too weak a garrison in Maracaibo, so that, during his absence, Manrique had sent two hundred men of the Orinoco Battalion and a platoon of thirty dismounted dragoons into the city to occupy it without encountering effective opposition. They captured a considerable quantity of munitions, clothing and provisions belonging to the royalists, but were not strong enough to attack the forts guarding the entrance to the lake. Upon his return, therefore, Morales was able to retire safely into one of these, Fort San Carlos.[3]

Then Gen. José Padilla, admiral of the patriot fleet which had been assembled for the siege of Cartagena, but which had been released for other operations after the capitulation of that stronghold, swept down from the north in search of the Spanish admiral, Angel Laborde. Under the command of this officer the royalist squadron in Lake Maracaibo consisted of three brigantines, twelve schooners and seventeen "flecheras" and other small vessels.[4] In the patriot squad-

[1] Archivo Soublette, Documentos, 1822, II (folios not numbered).

[2] Archivo Nacional, Bogotá, Guerra y Marina, Historia, XXXV, 853; Hojas de Servicios, XXXI, 460; Archivo Nacional, Caracas, Ilustres Próceres, XCIX, 217; L. Florez Álvarez, "Acción de la Marina Colombiana en la Guerra de Independencia," in *Memorial del Estado Mayor del Ejército de Colombia*, no. 89, p. 134.

[3] Florez Álvarez, "Acción de la Marina," 149, 150; *Gaceta de Colombia*, Jan. 4, 1824.

[4] Florez Álvarez, "Acción de la Marina," 139-141.

ron were the same number of brigantines, but only seven schooners and thirteen light craft including " flecheras ".[1]

In order to come to blows with the enemy squadron it was necessary for Padilla to lead his own through the narrow entrance to the lake. This was protected by islands on which were strong forts under the guns of which it was necessary to pass at short range. Making the mouth more difficult were sand-bars extending almost across it and leaving only a narrow channel which could be navigated by none but light-draught vessels under the guidance of skilled pilots.

A council of war aboard the flagship decided in accordance with Padilla's wishes to come to grips with the enemy. Therefore, after sounding the channel and placing buoys to mark it, the patriot squadron began to force the bar at half-past two on the afternoon of May 8, 1823. The " Gran Bolívar " and " Independiente " ran aground. The latter soon succeeded in floating itself again, but the former remained hard and fast in spite of all efforts to release it. Meanwhile with the guns of Fort San Carlos firing upon it at point-blank range, the " Gran Bolívar " was soon a total wreck. The " Espartana " too ran aground, but not until it had passed the islands and was beyond the range of the forts. It was eventually refloated. To bring the other vessels through, it was necessary first to lighten them by removing their guns and ballast. This operation was tedious and time-consuming, so that it was half-past four o'clock in the morning of the 9th before the remainder of the squadron was safely over the bar and at anchor inside the lake.[2]

[1] Florez Álvarez, "Acción de la Marina," 141; *Gaceta de Colombia,* Feb. 29, 1824; Archivo Soublette, Documentos, 1822, III. Among the commanders of the patriot ships were Captains Renato (René) Beluche, Joseph de Bellegarde, Nicolás Joly and Walter Davis Chitty; also Lieutenant Clement Castell. Of these the first three were Frenchmen and the last was an American, Capt. Chitty was an Englishman.

[2] Florez Álvarez, 143, 144.

The Spanish admiral seemed loath to trust his squadron in a decisive action with the patriots, so managed to elude his pursuers for many weeks. There were, it is true, several fights between individual vessels, and on June 25th a fierce battle took place between the flotillas of "flecheras" and light craft, in which the republican vessels proved themselves superior; but it was not until the 24th of July that the main fleet was caught in a position from which it could not escape without giving battle. The entire royalist fleet was anchored in line near the shore before the city of Maracaibo, while the Colombian fleet was maneuvering to windward on the open waters of the lake.[1]

The patriot brigantines and schooners were sailing southward in single column, followed by the lighter vessels, when at about two-thirty the signal was hoisted on the flagship to form line abreast and attack. Owing to the difference in sailing qualities of the vessels, this order could not be executed in unison. The patriot line was thrown into confusion, yet each ship picked out an antagonist of approximately its own size. In half an hour the signal to board the enemy was hoisted and left flying at the masthead of the "Independiente".

The foe opened with guns and musketry until the fire became incessant. The Colombian ships undaunted held to their course, without firing even a pistol, until their yard-arms touched those of the anchored enemy. Then from their sides burst a roar of shot and over their bulwarks dashed a mob of seamen. The battle became a hand-to-hand fight between the crews. It was a series of duels between ships. The "Independiente" bore down on and subdued the "San Carlos". The "Confianza" ran foul of a royalist schooner and overwhelmed its crew. The three-master "Emprenda-

[1] Florez Álvarez, "Acción de la Marina," 146, 147, 164; Blanco, *op. cit.*, IX, 20-22.

dora" made the brigantine "Esperanza" strike its red and yellow flag. The "Marte" battered to kindling several of the enemy. All the patriot ships fulfilled their duty, but in the smoke which hung about their sides and decks, it was hard to see just what was happening. The sea was covered with pieces of wreckage, broken spars, ropes and blocks, hatch-covers, corpses and men swimming. Some of the enemy ships tried to save themselves by slipping their cables and sailing out of the melée, but in vain. The patriot ships clung to their sides like hounds to a wounded deer. Eleven of the larger vessels were captured and the "Esperanza" blew up. The felucca "Relámpago" was captured by the light flotilla. In pursuing the fleeing Spanish ships this light flotilla under Capt. Walter D. Chitty performed its duty like efficient cavalry ashore.[1]

At half-past five in the afternoon firing ceased and both fleets, the victors and the vanquished, were anchored together. Padilla demanded of Laborde the surrender of his squadron, and the latter was compelled to admit that this had already been accomplished, for what he had had was utterly annihilated. On August 3rd Gen. Morales signed a capitulation surrendering to the patriots the city of Maracaibo, the fortress of San Carlos and all territory occupied by the royalist troops. Many of the royalists took oath to abandon forever the territory of Colombia; those who were Colombians entered the service of the patriots; and Morales and the Spanish troops were permitted to withdraw to Cuba.[2]

To Padilla and to the widows and orphans of those who were killed in this battle the congress of Colombia granted rewards in money, a gold medal to the admiral and chevrons

[1] Florez Álvarez, "Acción de la Marina," 161, 162, 166.

[2] Florez Álvarez, "Acción de la Marina," 165, 166, 170; *El Colombiano*, Aug. 13, 20, Sept. 17, 1823; *Annual Register*, 1822, "History," 244, 245; Blanco, *op. cit.*, IX, 23-25.

of honor to the other officers. All in fact who took part in this memorable naval battle of July 24th were declared to be members of the Order of Liberators of Venezuela, and many were promoted for valor.[1] In order to celebrate the victory, furthermore, the chanter of the cathedral at Bogotá composed a pæan, "To the Victors".[2] On the hundredth anniversary of the battle a Colombian historical journal declared: " The Battle of Carabobo did not secure the independence of Venezuela. It was the battle of Maracaibo which sealed the independence, not only of Venezuela, but of all of Great Colombia." [3]

The decisive result of the battle of Maracaibo was, that it destroyed for the remainder of the war the naval power of Spain on the north coast of South America. Now that there was no fleet to protect their landing, there was no longer fear of the arrival of reenforcements from Spain. Of like importance was the fact that at last the siege of Puerto Cabello could be renewed with some hope of success. Since provisions could no longer be brought to them by sea, the royalist troops shut up in that fortress could be threatened with starvation.

Páez therefore promptly reestablished the siege of Puerto Cabello and shut off access to the fortress, meanwhile calling upon Calzada, the royalist commander, to surrender in order to prevent useless effusion of blood.[4] On October 29, the

---

[1] Florez Álvarez, "Acción de la Marina," 167, 168; Blanco, *op. cit.,* IX, 25, 26; *Gaceta de Colombia,* Feb. 29, 1824; *El Colombiano,* Apr. 28, 1824. Among the citations appear the names of Capt. Walter D. Chitty promoted from frigate captain to ship captain; Marine guards F. Estunard, Carlos Hueck and Juan Mackan to frigate ensigns; and Samuel Piliot, Marcos Mankin, and José Carminaty to commissions in the navy, as a reward for services rendered to the squadron.

[2] José E. Machado, *Cantón Lírico,* 72, 73.

[3] *Repertorio Boyacense,* July 24, 1923, no. 65, p. 835.

[4] Páez, *op. cit.,* I, 230. The chief of staff of Páez's division since

fort of Mirador de Solano, an advanced observation post, was captured; thereafter Páez was able to reconnoiter the interior of the town and to prepare his plans for the assault. He notified Calzada that, unless he agreed to surrender within twenty-four hours, the patriots would capture the city and put all its defenders to the sword. Waiting until the end of the period, Calzada replied that the place was defended by old soldiers who knew how to do their duty and, if worst came to the worst, they were resolved to follow the glorious example of Sagunto and Numancia. At the same time the royalist soldiers gathered on the walls and shouted defiance to the patriots, urging that they come and put them to the sword.[1]

Páez ordered the attack to take place on the night of November 7th. Every gun of the patriot artillery was to fire without rest throughout that entire day and night. A continuous fire, moreover, was to be kept up on the city from all sides, so that the defense would be worn out and unable to anticipate from what direction the attack was to come. At ten o'clock at night 400 men of the Anzoátegui Battalion and a hundred lancers, naked and carrying nothing but their arms and ammunition, began the attack by advancing through the mangrove swamps. Other companies attacked the batteries, while a flotilla of launches swept into the inner port, driving the defenders from the wharves. At

August 11, 1820, was Col. George Woodberry, whose signature is found on most of the reports and bulletins concerning the siege. The lists of promotions in this division granted on recommendation of the commanding general, army of Venezuela, do not appear to contain the names of any foreigners. Archivo Nacional, Bogotá, Guerra y Marina, Historia, DCCLXXX, 813, 841; *Gaceta de Colombia*, Feb. 15, May 30, 1824; Blanco, *op. cit.*, VIII, 437; *Iris de Venezuela*, June 24, 1822; *El Colombiano*, Nov. 26, 1823.

[1] Páez, *op. cit.*, I, 230, 232, 233; *El Colombiano*, Nov. 4, 1823; Walker, *op. cit.*, II, 564.

dawn the patriots were in possession of most of the city and
Calzada sent an offer of surrender. This was accepted, and
Páez gained possession not only of the city and its garrison,
but of sixty guns, 620 muskets, six launches, and munitions
of all kinds. The royalists lost 156 killed, fifty-six wounded
and fifty-six officers and 539 men captured, while the patriots
lost only twelve killed and thirty-five wounded.[1]

On Nov. 10, 1823 the articles of capitulation were ratified,
by which the royalist troops were allowed to march out with
drums beating and colors flying. After having been received
with all the honors of war, they were transported to Cuba.
On December 20, the inhabitants of Puerto Cabello assembled in the plaza and amid great rejoicing took the oath to
the constitution of the republic.[2]

The royalists had thus been entirely driven out of Venezuela and New Granada and the north was free. Bolívar
could now call upon Colombia to furnish more troops and
supplies to aid him in completing his plans for liberating
Peru. Two battalions of infantry and a regiment of cavalry
were organized in Puerto Cabello for service as auxiliaries.
Fifteen hundred troops boarded six warships of Commodore
Beluche's squadron at Maracaibo and Cartagena and were
transported to Porto Bello, whence they crossed the Isthmus
to Panamá and sailed on other transports for Callao.[3]

While these events had been going on in the north Bolívar
had not deemed it advisable to answer in person the appeals
from Peru for help. Political as well as military conditions

[1] Páez, *op. cit.*, I, 234-236; *El Colombiano*, Nov. 11, 19, 1823; *Repertorio Boyacense*, Nov. 7, 1923, no. 56, p. 889.

[2] Páez, *op. cit.*, I, 237, 238, 242; *Gaceta de Colombia*, June 27, 1824; *Present State of Colombia*, 51; *View of South America*, 120, 121.

[3] *El Colombiano*, July 7, Sept. 1, 1824; *Gaceta de Colombia*, Dec. 19, 1824. *Present State of Colombia*, 149, Appendix A; F. O. 18/1, J. P. Hamilton to Foreign Office, Dec. 19, 1823; O'Leary, *Narración*, II, 127; *Documentos*, XX, 250, 426.

in that province were such that the prestige of his own presence there would have been highly desirable; yet he had felt
that he must remain to watch the north and to keep Páez
supplied with men, money and munitions. Furthermore he
could not leave Colombia without the consent of the congress. He had therefore decided to send Sucre to Lima in
the dual capacity of commander of the Colombian forces in
aid of Peru and as the diplomatic representative of Bolívar
to Torre Tagle, the leader of one of the Peruvian factions.[1]

Before leaving for his new post there was much to be
done by Sucre. He had to reorganize his army by consolidating veteran squadrons and battalions, by recruiting to full
strength other battalions, and by training recruits. He had
to gather supplies and munitions, to secure vessels, to equip
and provision them as transports, and to assemble them and
all his troops at Guayaquil. These activities were not un-
accompanied with trying difficulties. Objection was made to
the forcible enlistment of recruits and to the taking of farmer boys out of their homes. The crowd of recruits soon
rendered the regular barracks inadequate. Reimbursement
was demanded for damages done to the convent in which
some of the Rifles were quartered. Even churches were
used to care for the overflow, until an order was issued by
the government forbidding the quartering of troops in them.
The commandant of the Vencedor Battalion was relieved
from command for too severe treatment of his men and
charges were brought against three officers of the Bogotá
Battalion.[2] Most of the troops were marched to Guayaquil
and only 354 in all were left in Quito. These consisted of
the Rifles Battalion, to which were attached all unassigned
officers, a company of artillery under Capt. Adolf Klinger,

[1] Cortés Vargas, *Participación de Colombia*, I, 2, 109-111, 165.

[2] Archivo Nacional, Bogotá, Guerra y Marina, Historia, XXVII, 278;
O'Leary, *Documentos*, XIX, 388, 392, 436.

and four squadrons of Lancers, Hussars, Cazadores and Grenadiers.[1] About this time the inhabitants of the province of Pasto again broke out in a revolt, for the control of which it was necessary to detach the Bogotá Battalion and other troops from Guayaquil under the command of Col. Juan José Flores.[2]

At length, about the middle of March, 1823, the first division of the Colombian army in aid of Peru was fully organized under the command of Gen. Manuel Valdés. The first brigade under Gen. Jacinto Lara comprised the Battalions Vencedor en Boyacá, Voltígero and Pichincha; while in the second brigade under Gen. José M. Mírez were the Rifles and Bogotá Battalions and the Regiments of Hussars and Grenadiers.[3] The first brigade was the earliest to sail, leaving Guayaquil, March 18, on eleven ships. A month later the Rifles Battalion sailed on the transports " Perla ", " Rosa ", " Mirla " and " Dolores ".[4] When the Rifles Battalion arrived in Peru it contained 1,200 Indians and only ten British officers.[5] It had the reputation then of being one

[1] Archivo Nacional, Bogotá, Guerra y Marina, Historia, XIII, 279, 360, 363; XVII, 43, 73; XXVI, 748; XXVII, 225, 512; O'Leary, *Documentos*, XIX, 410, 519; Bingham Collection of Mss., Sucre Papers No. 1258. Arturo Sandes to Sucre, Feb. 1, 1823.

[2] Archivo Nacional, Bogotá, Guerra y Marina, Historia, XXVI, 643; O'Leary, *Documentos*, XX, 180, 193. It was not until July 10, 1824 that Col. Flores was able to report that he had suppressed this revolt and that Pasto was completely restored to tranquillity. *El Colombiano*, Oct. 8, 1823; *Gaceta de Colombia*, May 9, June 27, July 11, Sept. 12, 1824.

[3] Archivo Nacional, Bogotá, Guerra y Marina, Historia, XIII, 279, 360, 363; XVII, 73; XXVII, 290, 349, 366, 371; Cortés Vargas, *Participación de Colombia*, I, 98-100; O'Leary, *Documentos*, XIX, 478, 481; *Gaceta de Colombia*, Aug. 25, 1822.

[4] O'Leary, *Documentos*, XIX, 484, 513; XX, 7.

[5] Miller, *op. cit.*, II, 159; Blanco, *op. cit.*, VIII, 608; O'Leary, *Documentos*, XIX, 513. Although Miller mentions ten British officers, the names of only seven can be identified. These were Col. Arthur Sandes,

of the worst-behaved organizations in the army. Since it was too indulgently treated by its officers, it was likely to commit any kind of excess or breach of discipline. To prevent desertion on the march, its recruits had to be lashed together. Sucre believed that a good creole major was needed for this battalion and asked that one be sent.[1]

On May 12 the majority of the Bogotá Battalion sailed on the " Balcarcel ", "Armonia " and " Brown ",[2] while a detachment of Hussars boarded the transport "Chimborazo". The rest of the cavalry did not leave until three months later.[3] As it was impossible to outfit all these organizations fully before they sailed, an officer was supplied with cash which he was to expend in buying whatever clothing was needed for the officers and men of the Rifles and Bogotá Battalions. He was ordered immediately upon arrival in Lima to uniform the band of the Rifles with all the elegance possible. The red cloth for the cuffs and collars of the uniforms of the Bogotá Battalion failed to arrive in time, so green was substituted.[4]

commanding, with Charles Richard Rudd as Sergeant Major; in the second company were Capt. Thomas Charles James Wright and Lieut. Charles Church; commanding the fourth company was Capt. Thomas Duxbury; and with the fifth company were Capt. William Ferguson and 1st Sergt. Richard Wilson. The last named was of course not a commissioned officer; but in the patriot army a sergeant major appears to have been an extra commissioned grade between a major and a lieutenant colonel. Archivo Nacional, Bogotá, Guerra y Marina, Historia, XIII, 328, 332, 334, 336; XXVI, 938.

[1] O'Leary, *Documentos*, XIX, 513; XX, 8; *Cartas de Sucre al Libertador*, I, 81.

[2] Archivo Nacional, Bogotá, Guerra y Marina, Historia, XXVI, 643; *El Colombiano*, Aug. 27, 1823. One company of this battalion had been retained in Pasto to assist in subduing the uprising.

[3] *El Colombiano*, Aug. 27, 1823; O'Leary, *Documentos*, XX, 15, 29; Archivo Nacional, Bogotá, Guerra y Marina, Historia, XXVII, 290, 349, 366, 371.

[4] O'Leary, *Documentos*, XIX, 388, 466; XX, 29.

The transports had been badly provisioned and the troops suffered for lack of sufficient food during the voyage. Some of the supplies put aboard for the officers' messes were of inferior quality and soon spoiled. The wine turned to vinegar and was so bad that not even the sailors would drink it. There were no tablecloths, knives, forks, spoons or plates. Beef on the hoof and plantains needed to complete the rations were left behind because of the failure of the contractors to deliver them on time. Since the voyage lasted from thirty to sixty days, the privations and sufferings of the troops were severely felt. The " Venganza " was nearly shipwrecked, and as it had no pumps the Vencedor Battalion, divided into reliefs of two officers and forty men each, had to work night and day bailing to keep it afloat.[1]

Toward the end of May Sucre himself arrived at Lima to take command of the whole Colombian auxiliary army in Peru, and presented his credentials to the Peruvian congress.[2] He found conditions discouraging, owing to hostility between the political parties in the city of Lima. Because of this internal discord he believed it impossible to defend the capital against the approach of the Spanish commander, Gen. José de Cantérac, with superior forces. He therefore evacuated Lima and withdrew his troops to Callao with the intention of holding that port as his base.[3]

The Bogotá Battalion was kept for the defense of Callao, but the Rifles took the field and pursued the enemy after they

[1] Archivo Nacional, Bogotá, Guerra y Marina, Historia, XVI, 940; XLVI, 948; Cortés Vargas, *Participación de Colombia*, I, 69, 100.

[2] O'Leary, *Documentos*, XX, 43; Manuel Antonio López, *Campaña del Peru por el ejército unido libertador*, 4; Archivo Nacional, Bogotá, Guerra y Marina, Historia, XVII, 128; Carlos A. Villanueva, *Fernando VII y los nuevos estados*, 227, 230.

[3] O'Leary, *Documentos*, XX, 115, 200; *Annual Register*, 1822; " History," 282, 283.

had been driven from Lima. Meanwhile a Peruvian division under Gen. Andrés de Santa Cruz had been sent to southern Peru, to distract the enemy's attention from the capital and to seize and hold as a base of operations Quilca, Ita, Arica and the other so-called " intermediate " ports. With the intention of cooperating with Santa Cruz, Sucre also went south and arrived at Arequipa, which he occupied without opposition on September 1. He took with him the Pichincha, Vencedor and Voltígero Battalions and some fifty Peruvian cavalry under Col. John Miller.[1]

This " campaign of the intermediate ports " accomplished nothing except the destruction of the division under Santa Cruz and the serious crippling of that under Sucre. The cause of this failure was primarily due to lack of cooperation between the allies and to serious blunders on the part of Santa Cruz. The Peruvian general, failing to keep Sucre informed as to his plans or destination, divided his own force in the face of the enemy, so that he did not feel strong enough to risk an engagement.[2] Without the support that he expected from the Colombians, which did not come because of his own failure to tell Sucre where to send it, Santa Cruz abandoned the campaign and retreated toward the coast. On this retreat he was constantly harassed by the royalists and lost many men, and all his baggage in spite of Col. Frederick Brandsen's efforts to cover the retreat with his cavalry.[3]

Sucre had tried to join his ally and, in order to do so, had marched his men across fifty leagues of desert. In spite of

[1] O'Leary, *Cartas de Sucre al Libertador*, I, 86, 87; *Documentos*, XX, 24, 200; Miller, *op. cit.*, II, 69, 167.

[2] O'Leary, *Documentos*, XX, 448; O'Connor, *op. cit.*, 108, 109; Cortés Vargas, *Participación de Colombia*, I, 202-204, 207, 208.

[3] For the subsequent treason and dismissal of Col. Brandsen, *vide* Chapter XIII.

the fact that they traveled only at night, they suffered so from heat and thirst that 300 of his men died from exhaustion. Sucre remained at Arequipa awaiting definite instructions from Santa Cruz until he learned of the latter's retreat. Finding himself deserted by his ally and attacked by the enemy in an unfavorable position, Sucre on October 8 began his withdrawal from Arequipa, with Col. Miller and his cavalry acting as rear-guard to protect the infantry. After a rapid march of three days, Sucre arrived at Quilca and, having embarked his infantry with great difficulty through the surf, sailed for Callao. The cavalry was sent back overland under Col. Miller to Ica.[1]

Sucre's heart was not in this campaign. He feared to risk in it the lives of any of his precious Colombians. He was glad that he had only 2,000 of them with him, and when any of them died, grieved like a father over the loss of a son.[2]

On his return to Callao and Lima, Sucre found that affairs had been going from bad to worse. The struggle for leadership between José Bernardo Torre Tagle and José de la Riva Agüero had resulted in the setting up of two governments, both claiming to represent the revolution, and in the establishment of Riva Agüero's capital at Trujillo.[3] Factional bitterness was rife; everyone suspected his neighbor; one party of patriots hated the other and the royalists hated them both; the nobility and clergy, rendered bitter by the

---

[1] Miller, *op. cit.*, II, 76, 77; Cortés Vargas, *Participación de Colombia*, I, 193, 211-213; Bingham Collection of Mss., Sucre Papers, No. 1535, Guillermo Miller to Sucre, Aug. 20, 1823; *El Colombiano*, Jan. 7, 1824; Thomas Sutcliff, *Sixteen years in Chile and Peru from 1822 to 1839 by the retired governor of Juan Fernández*, 77.

[2] O'Leary, *Cartas de Sucre al Libertador*, I, 81; Simon B. O'Leary, " Bolívar en el Perú " in *Repertorio Caraqueño*, I, Oct. 28, 1879, p. 85.

[3] Villanueva, *Fernando VII*, 229, 230; Enrique D. Tovar y R., " Bolívar en Carás " in *Cultura Venezolana*, III, 158; Sebastián Llorente, *Historia del Perú desde la proclamación de la independencia*, 146.

suppression of titles of nobility, favored the royalists; the wealthy had been reduced to indigence because their mines and estates had ceased to yield any income; those who had money deemed it prudent to live as though they had none; social life and amusements were suspended; business was at a standstill; the wharves were encumbered with foreign goods which supercargoes of ships were unable to dispose of; English importing firms were on the verge of bankruptcy; the common people were in direst want; and swarms of desperate peasants and bands of banditti infested the roads leading to Lima.[1]

These conditions reacted on the troops. Soldiers in disguise turned to highway robbery. Such scandalous reports of the conduct of the Rifles, Voltígero and Pichincha Battalions came to his ears that Bolívar sent inspectors to make secret investigations.[2] The money that the Peruvian delegates had promised for the support of the Colombian troops was not forthcoming. Their clothes were worn out, yet there was no cloth with which to repair them. The ration was reduced to six ounces of rice and eight ounces of salt meat per day. One ounce of salt was made to go among four men. The Rifles, who for a time were encamped near a large cane-field, were allowed sugar as part of their ration. No tobacco was obtainable, and even the higher officers were obliged to solace themselves with coca.[3] Sometimes their

[1] Gilbert Farquhar Mathison, *Narrative of a Visit to Brazil, Chile, Peru and the Sandwich Islands during the years 1821 and 1822*, 256, 258, 259, 264, 284; *London Chronicle*, Jän. 25, 1822.

[2] Mathison, *op. cit.*, 264; Tovar, *op. cit.*, 179.

[3] O'Leary, *Documentos*, XXI, 10, 13; O'Connor, *op. cit.*, 126. Coca is the dried leaf of a large bush which flourishes in the Andean region. The leaves are chewed by the Indians for their narcotic effect. While coca does not take the place of food, it is said to lessen the cravings of hunger, so that when under its influence, the Indians are able to go several days without eating. It is also believed to diminish the fatigue of mountain-climbing.

rations were so scanty that the men became too weak to perform their duties or even to stand through a drill. Some stole clothing from their barracks in order to buy food, others gave up in despair and deserted.[1]

Meanwhile more Colombian troops were sent to Callao. During September the Vargas Battalion had come in the corvette " Pinchincha ". Early in November, 1823, the brigantine "Chimborazo" arrived with the transport " Helena " after a voyage of seventy days from Panamá. On these ships came Lieut. Col. Francis B. O'Connor with four companies which he had raised on the Isthmus. The rest of this battalion had been disembarked in the province of Guayaquil for the purpose of assisting in suppressing the insurrection at Pasto. O'Connor had refused to obey this order as it was a verbal one and in contravention of the written order which directed him to proceed to Peru. He was supported in this attitude by Capt. Ramsey, an Englishman in command of the " Chimborazo " and by Capt. Simpson, an Irishman who commanded the " Helena ".[2] O'Connor subsequently was transferred to the command of the Vargas Battalion, and later was assigned to the position of chief of staff of the United Army of Liberation.[3]

[1] O'Leary, *Documentos*, XIX, 216, 437; XXI, 13, 22.

[2] O'Connor, *op. cit.*, 61, 72, 76-81; O'Leary, *Documentos*, XX, 30; *Gaceta de Colombia*, Dec. 19, 1824; Archivo Nacional, Bogotá, Guerra y Marina, Historia, XLVII, 948.

[3] O'Connor, *op. cit.*, 63, 81-92, 93, 95. In his capacity as chief of staff, O'Connor became very intimate with Sucre, of whom he relates some interesting anecdotes. Among other incidents he tells how Gen. Sucre and Col. Sandes both fell in love with the same girl (the daughter of the Marquis of Solando at Quito). Sucre suggested tossing a coin to determine which should marry her. Sandes agreed and O'Connor was chosen to act as umpire. The coin was tossed and gave the victory to Sucre. To celebrate the event, O'Connor opened two bottles of Irish whiskey which he had been keeping for St. Patrick's Day, and assembled an informal party consisting of Sucre, O'Connor, Sandes, Capt. Belford

After repeated requests from the republican leaders in Peru to come to their aid, Bolívar had at last been able to secure the consent of the Colombian congress, and feeling that affairs in the north were in a satisfactory state, had boarded the " Chimborazo " and sailed from Guayaquil on August 7. Before doing so, however, he had given orders for more Colombian troops to follow him to Peru. In accordance with these orders, battalions and squadrons continued to arrive at Callao for the rest of the year and well on into 1824.[1]

The voyage of the troops from Panamá to Guayaquil and from Guayaquil to Callao or from Panamá to Callao direct was, in those days of sailing vessels, an extremely long and difficult undertaking; for the opposition of the north-flowing Humboldt current and the prevailing head-winds or calms near the coast often made it necessary for a ship to sail many days to the westward in order to encounter conditions favorable to make any progress southward. Such navigation required that masters of vessels possess the utmost skill in seamanship. During the war there was at first the additional danger of being overhauled, and captured or sunk by a Spanish man-of-war or privateer. At this time, however, the seas had been fairly well cleared of such pests by the

Hinton Wilson (aide to Bolívar), Capt. William Ferguson, and some other Irish officers who were in the Rifles Battalion. O'Connor also tells the pathetic story of his orderly trumpeter, Patrick, who had accompanied his colonel to the Peruvian campaign. This poor lad was the the sole survivor of the regiment of Lancers. Patrick had cheerfully withstood the severest hardships but at the little village of Recuay became so ill that he could no longer keep up. He lingered on through St. Patrick's Day, but when his Saint's day had passed, this last soldier of the Irish Legion was dead. O'Connor, *op. cit.*, 91, 102.

[1] *Gaceta de Colombia*, Sept. 19, Dec. 19, 1824; Archivo Nacional, Bogotá, Guerra y Marina, Historia, XXVII, 366; Cortés Vargas, *Participación de Colombia*, I, 165, 169, 216; O'Leary, *Documentos*, XX, 29, 283, 324, 606; XXI, 10.

energy of Admiral Cochrane and his ships of the Chilean navy.[1] In addition to overcoming these dangers, the mere assemblage of enough transports to carry all the Colombian troops was in itself a gigantic task that could only be accomplished through the cooperation of sea captains and ship owners of British and other foreign nationalities.[2]

[1] *Campaigns and Cruises*, I, 253-278, 403; Sutcliffe, *op. cit.*, 24, 25, 27; *Journal written on board H. M. S. Cambridge*, 31-33; William Bennett Stevenson, *Historical and descriptive narrative of twenty years residence in South America*, III, 271, 274, 279, 400, 415; Camilo Destruge, *Biografía del General Don Juan Illingworth*, 11-30 and *passim*; Thomas Cochrane, Lord Dundonald, *Narrative of services in the liberation of Chile,, Peru and Brazil from Spanish and Portuguese domination*, I, xii, xiii, 23 and *passim*. Thomas Cochrane, Earl of Dundonald, had been a high officer in the British navy. Having been disgraced from his rank, he accepted a commission from Bernardo O'Higgins, Supreme Director of Chile, to organize a navy for that new republic. The first duty of the infant fleet was to transport the La Plata-Chilean army of San Martín to attack the royalists in Peru. During San Martín's operations in Peru the fleet had kept open communications with Chile and had destroyed Spain's naval power in that part of the Pacific. With Cochrane, as captains of his ships, had come a number of Englishmen and Americans. Among these were Captains Robert Foster, W. Wilkinson, James Ramsey, and Spry, Crosby, Wooster, Morris, Carter and Charles. Lieutenants Vowell and Noyes of the Albion Battalion were transferred to the Chilean navy and joined Cochrane at Guayaquil. Other companions of Cochrane were Admirals Guise and Illingworth who later became prominent in organizing navies for Peru and Guayaquil.

[2] Mention has already been made of Capt. Ramsey of the " Chimborazo " and Capt. Simpson of the "Helena", as well as of Capt. Thomas Charles James Wright who had taken part in the naval battle of Maracaibo and was subsequently doing transport duty with his schooner "Guayaquileña." Besides these, Capt. Harris brought 300 men from the garrison of Panama on the brigantine "Zodiac"; Capt. John Spry helped to transport troops; Capt. Jean S. Mothon, a Frenchman, commanded the armed brigantine "Colombia"; Robert Bell, a resident of Buenaventura offered the services of his corvette "Alexandro", and the intendente of Guayaquil secured the lease of the merchant ships " Monteagudo" and "Mirrow"; William Henderson signed a contract whereby he gave Bolívar the use of the brig "Ana," and it must not be forgotten that Thompson and Mackintosh had furnished the " Prince " and

On his arrival in Peru, Bolívar, who had been invested with supreme military and political authority, took hold of matters with a firm hand. He had first to overcome the opposition of Riva Agüero and then to meet that of Torre Tagle, who turned against him. He raised funds for the support of his troops, collected horses and mules for transport purposes, ordered that the troops be trained by long and frequent practice marches in order to harden them for mountain climbing; and with the loyal assistance of Sucre, generally brought order out of chaos. He accepted the offer of the royalist Battalion of Numancia to desert to the flag of independence, reorganized it as the Voltígero Battalion, and caused it to be so trained that it soon was one of the best in the army; and its captains eventually all became generals.[1]

Just as affairs had not been moving smoothly for the revolutionists in Peru, so all was not well with the royalist army. Gen. Pedro Antonio Olañeta claimed that the king had nominated him to be viceroy of Peru, refused to serve under the *de facto* viceroy La Serna, and withdrew with his command to Upper Peru (now Bolivia) whither Gen. Gerónimo Valdéz (royalist) was sent to counteract his designs. This exhibition of jealousy and insubordination influenced the normally slow and vacillating commander-in-chief of the royalist army toward even more caution. He kept himself in his

"Britannia" for transporting the first contingents from England in 1817. Archivo Nacional, Bogotá, Guerra y Marina, Historia, VI, 887: XVI. 940; Hojas de Servicios, XLVIII, 733; *Gaceta de Colombia*, March 7, Sept. 19, 1824; Cortés Vargas, *Participación de Colombia*, II, 6, 8, 10, 12.

[1] O'Connor, *op. cit.*, 103, 106, 108, 125; O'Leary, *Documentos*, XX, 430, 446, 453, 454, 464; XXII, 185, 195, 218; *Narración*, II, 252, 255, 256; López, *op. cit.*, 107; Cortés Vargas, *Participación de Colombia*, II, 37-40, 55-57; *El Colombiano*, Dec. 1, 1824; Bingham Collection of Mss., Sucre Papers, No. 865, Tomás de Heres to Sucre, Sept. 25, 1821; Robert Procter, *Narrative of a journey across the cordillera of the Andes and of a residence in Lima and other parts of Peru in the years 1823 and 1824*, 279, 284-286.

headquarters at Cuzco, allowing Bolívar to assemble his army in the valley of the Huaráz unopposed.[1] Fortunately for the royalists, the spirit of their soldiers was good. Each regiment had an Indian " cacique " as colonel, with a Spaniard as lieutenant colonel to advise him. This system was popular with the Indians and kept the ranks filled with recruits. The men were well drilled and disciplined, for all the non-commissioned officers were Spaniards. There were fifteen battalions assembled into five regiments in which all the privates were Indians, and every Spanish soldier was either a sergeant or a corporal. All Spaniards who could read were first sergeants.[2]

The royalist army of the north, under the command of Gen. Cantérac, consisted of two divisions of infantry each of 3500 men under Brig. Gens. Morato and Monet respectively, a division of cavalry of 1300 men under Gen. Bedoya, and an artillery unit of nine guns. This whole army thus contained 8300 men. The United Army of Liberators of Peru totaled 8080 combatants, of whom 5123 were the infantry and 589 were the cavalry of the Colombian contingent, and 1702 of the infantry, 519 of the cavalry and 25 of the artillery belonged to the Peruvian forces.[3]

[1] Miller, *op. cit.*, II, 86; Cortés Vargas, *Participación de Colombia*, II, 50, 51; *El Colombiano*, Aug. 11, Sept. 29, 1824.

[2] *El Colombiano*, March 2, 1825.

[3] Cortés Vargas, *Participación de Colombia*, II, 129, 130; III, 106-107. A roster, dated Patavilca Feb. 7, 1824, found in Archivo Nacional, Bogotá, Guerra y Marina, Historia, XLVII, 826 enumerates the Colombian contingent as follows:

Divisions	Corps	Totals
1st Div. Infantry Army of Colombia	Rifles	947
	Vencedor	970
	Vargas	769
2nd Div. Inf. of Colombia	Bogotá	778
	Voltígeros	798
	Pichincha	739
	Total infantry	5001
Cavalry of Colombia	Grenadiers and Hussars	498

The figures in the text, while approximately the same as those given by

At Huamachuco, Bolívar assembled a council of his generals. O'Connor, Sucre's chief of staff, attended with his general and was the only colonel present. As the junior in rank he was called upon first to give his opinion, and advocated opening the campaign against the royalist army at once. Bolívar then, without calling upon any of the generals, rolled up his maps and remarked, " There is nothing more to say. This young man has given us a correct lesson on the art of war. To-morrow the army will begin its march." [1]

In accordance with this decision, the patriot army started early in June, 1824 in the direction of Cerro de Pasco and Huanuco. Each division followed a different valley in the mountains. That of Gen. Córdoba, at the time comprising the Voltígero, Pichincha and Vargas Battalions, ascended the valley of Huaráz southward to its head. This division formed the vanguard of the army and was followed by the Peruvian infantry. The main body was composed of Gen. Lara's division with the Rifles, Vencedor and Bogotá Battalions, the cavalry, and the baggage train, and was accompanied by the Peruvian cavalry. This division marched to the eastward of the central cordillera, but in order to reach the point of concentration near Huánuco both divisions had eventually to leave their valleys and climb the lofty cordillera.[2] Gen. Miller, commanding the cavalry, worked inces-

Cortés Vargas do not quite agree with his, undoubtedly owing to the fact that they were taken from a report of an earlier date. It is believed that both these sets of figures were correct for the dates at which they were reported. The strength of organizations of an army in the field is apt to fluctuate considerably from day to day, due to losses from transfers, discharges, desertions and death, and to gains from recruits and transfers.

[1] Referring to this anecdote, which O'Connor has related in pages 104 and 105 of his memoirs, Tovar says that he has verified it and can affirm that it is more or less exact in spite of its egotism. " Bolívar en Carás," 171, n.

[2] O'Leary, *Documentos*, XXII, 339, 343; Cortés Vargas, *Participación de Colombia*, II, 111, 112, 114, 115.

santly in sending out patrols to scout and obtain information
of the enemy while at the same time screening the movements
of his own army. His description of the crossing of the
cordillera gives a vivid picture of the difficulties encountered, especially by the horsemen.[1]

In order to save their horses for contacts with the enemy,
mules were ridden on the march and each man led his own
horse. The mountain trails were so narrow that it was impossible to march other than in single file. Often the ascent
was so steep that even the mules could not carry them and
the men had to dismount. At such times sabres and lances
became encumbrances which caused the men to lose their intervals. Narrow shelving ledges, which formed the only
foothold along the perpendicular cliffs, deep gullies, projecting rocks, and numerous waterfalls presented obstacles, the
passing of which necessitated the expenditure of great caution and much time. The combination of all these difficulties often strung out the column so that its end was lost to
view in the bottom-most ravines, while its head was scaling
the crest of a ridge. Sometimes night fell before the entire
column could reach the halting-place. Then it was necessary
to post trumpeters at difficult points along the trail, to prevent those who had fallen behind from going astray in the
darkness. In case part of the column did lose the proper
trail, it must somehow keep on climbing until it joined the
trail higher up; for it was impossible to turn the horses and
make them retrace their way along those narrow ledges or
in the slippery cleft of a mountain torrent. To make these
difficulties harder, was added the fact that the climbing was
done at such altitudes that the thermometer seldom stood
above zero, and the desert mountain-tops furnished no shelter against the winds and snows. The difficulty of breathing
often became so intense that whole battalions suddenly gave

[1] Miller, *op. cit.*, II, 121, 123, 125, 128, 129, 217-219.

up the struggle and dropped limply down. Then it was necessary to kill some of the men as examples to make the rest of the battalion get up and resume the march. To have allowed them to lie there until they fell asleep would have been fatal. Sometimes the only way to save the life of a sufferer was to bleed him at his temple. On bright days the reflected sunlight was so intense that many suffered the agonies of snow blindness.

A drove of 6,000 head of cattle, under charge of a commissary, followed the army; as did a train of 300 mules carrying the reserve ammunition. Each division, however, was responsible for its own cartridges in sufficient quantity to last through an ordinary engagement. Stores of clothing, equipment and armament for the army were under charge of the supreme command. In addition, the beef and rations of rice, tobacco, salt and coca were carried and issued by the commissary at general headquarters.

After a month of such marching, all divisions had crossed the cordillera and had arrived at their objective. Gen. Miller's cavalry scouts were in contact with the royalist cavalry screening Cantérac's army. The latter had at last moved from his cantonments; but he had started too late, for he found that Bolívar had already completed the concentration of his forces.[1]

In the campaign of Peru in 1824 there took place three engagements which are of sufficient interest for description here: the battle of Junín, the rear-guard action at Matará, and the battle of Ayacucho. The battle of Junín, which was fought near Cerro de Pasco, on Aug. 6, 1824, was unique in the military annals of the nineteenth century, for in it not

---

[1] O'Leary, *Narración*, II, 265-267; *Documentos*, XXII, 357, 378; O'Connor, *op. cit.*, III; Cortés Vargas, *Participación de Colombia*, II, 117-123; Bingham Collection of Mss., Sucre Papers, No. 831, F. B. O'Connor to Sucre, Feb. 9, 1824.

a shot was fired. It was strictly a cavalry engagement fought with sabre and lance alone. The infantry were present, but only as spectators, while the opposing squadrons charged each other back and forth on the narrow plain between the rock escarpment of the hills and the swampy borders of the Lake of Reyes. In three-quarters of an hour " the boasted cavalry of the Spaniards were in a state of total and disgraceful flight." Colonels Carvajal, Silva and Bruix and Major Brown cut their way through the hostile cavalry, and led a handful of troopers after the retreating royalist infantry. Lieut. Col. Charles Sowerby[1] also distinguished himself. He received two lance wounds and died on the field of battle in the arms of his friend, Gen. Miller. After the patriot Gen. Necochea was wounded, the supreme command of all the cavalry in Bolívar's army was awarded to Gen. Miller, the hero of the day. Although the results of this victory were rather moral than physical, it was important nevertheless in determining the outcome of the campaign; for it destroyed the morale of the royalist cavalry that no longer was able to carry out efficient scouting or to bring back to Cantérac information as to the movements of the patriot generals.[2]

Bolívar remained with the army until he reached Cuzco when, learning that his presence in Lima was essential, he

[1] Charles Sowerby was born in Bremen of British parents in 1795. As a young man he joined Napoleon for the Russian campaign. Later he offered his sword to the patriots of La Plata and Chile and fought at the battle of Maipo. When San Martín's army went to Peru he was assigned to the Peruvian contingent which fought under Sucre at Riobamba and Pichincha. He was with the second squadron of Hussars of this contingent when he met his death at Junín. Azpúrua, *op. cit.*, III, 457; Scarpetta y Vergara, *op. cit.*, 603.

[2] Miller, *op. cit.*, II, 130-136; O'Connor, *op. cit.*, 116; O'Leary, *Documentos*, XXII, 420, 421; Rafael Negret, " Junín, primer centenairo," in *Memorial del Estado Mayor del Ejército de Colombia*, Nos. 145-146, pp. 310, 311; German G. Yáñez, *Junín y Ayacucho*, 18, 19, 23.

entrusted the command to Sucre and returned to the capital. The instructions to use his own discretion in carrying out the objects of the campaign were interpreted by Sucre to mean that he was to continue the pursuit of Cantérac, force him to give battle and defeat him.[1]

Near Matará on Dec. 3, 1824, while Sucre's army was crossing the difficult ravine through which flowed the brook called Corpaguayco, it was briskly attacked from the rear by the Spanish general, Valdéz. The rear-guard under Gen. Lara was ordered to hold back the royalist attack until patriot cavalry, artillery and train could cross the stream. The Rifles Battalion, under Col. Sandes, formed the extreme rear element of Gen. Lara's division and bore the brunt of the action. While the main body of the patriots was fording the stream, the Rifles deployed along the bank of the ravine and stubbornly held back the attacks of the enemy. But a single battalion could not permanently withstand a whole division and at last the gallant Rifles were overpowered and dispersed. The Vargas and Vencedor Battalions, which also formed part of the rear guard, rallied and resisted the shock until they too were scattered, but not until the cavalry and remainder of the army had escaped. The engagement lasted all afternoon and was extremely costly to the rear guard, which was sacrificed to save the army. Major Thomas Duxbury of the Rifles and 200 men from the three battalions engaged, were killed. The field train, spare horses, and one of the two field guns fell into the hands of the enemy. The Rifles Battalion, having lost 502 men missing in addition to those killed, was reduced to a mere skeleton.[2]

In making up his report to Bolívar, Sucre ordered O'Con-

[1] O'Leary, *Narración*, II, 287; *Documentos*, XXII, 508; O'Connor, *op. cit.*, 125, 126.

[2] O'Connor, *op. cit.*, 135; Miller, *op. cit.*, II, 159; López, *op. cit.*, 48, 125; *The Times*, April 15, 1825.

nor to carry as present those who were missing since Matará, " because Bolívar will be distressed to see so many missing, since the greater part are from the Rifles, which is his favorite corps."[1] This engagement at Matará may be compared with that at Pántano de Várgas, for while it was not decisive in itself, it set the stage for the great triumph which was to be enacted a few days later. At both Pántano de Vargas and Matará the steadfastness and valor of British officers helped to save the patriot army and made possible the decisive victories of Boyacá and Ayacucho.

The battle of Ayacucho was fought on Dec. 9, 1824 on the plains of Ayacucho, high up in the Andes, 11,600 feet above the sea. Sucre's army, with both flanks protected by ravines, was drawn up on the plain facing the heights of Condorcanqui on which Cantérac's army was established. The battle was opened by the Spanish viceroy José de La Serna, who led down from the heights four columns from the royalist center and left. He was at once charged by Córdoba's Colombian division and Miller's Peruvian cavalry. The royalist divisions wavered, broke and were driven back in disorder before Gen. Valdéz, who commanded the royalist right, had been able to accomplish a turning movement which he had begun against the left flank of the patriots. Miller, seeing this attack coming, withdrew his cavalry and threw it against Valdéz, while Gen. Lara supported him with his division which was in reserve. Due to the prompt action of Gen. Miller, the threatened attack against the patriots' left flank resulted in a failure. Valdéz, realizing that his attack was checked, and seeing the main body of the viceroy's army already in flight, and the tricolor flag of Colombia waving above the heights of Concorcanqui, withdrew precipitately from the field.

[1] O'Connor, *op. cit.*, 156.

The defeat of the royalists was due to the fact that their movements were not properly coordinated. The order for battle had directed that the center and left were to wait until Valdéz had outflanked Sucre's position and then to fall upon him in front and right flank; but this plan was spoiled because of the impatience of the troops who advanced too soon, thus bringing on the battle before the other divisions could properly support each other or the artillery prepare for action. La Serna himself was wounded and captured. Fourteen hundred royalists were killed, 700 were wounded, and 11 guns were lost. The patriots lost 370 killed and 609 wounded. Cantérac, who became viceroy when La Serna was captured, was forced to sue for terms, and agreed to capitulate with 16 colonels, 68 lieutenant colonels, 484 officers and 3200 men.[1]

The part taken by the English in this battle cannot be considered especially important.[2] The Bogotá Battalion was

[1] O'Connor, *op. cit.*, 148, 149; Miller, *op. cit.*, II, 165, 170, 175; Yáñez, *op. cit.*, 43, 44; *El Colombiano*, April 6, 1825.

[2] Among the foreigners participating in this battle were in the staff Cols. O'Connor, Althaus and Bruix and Dr. Blair; in the Rifles Battalion, Col. Arthur Sandes, commanding, First Sergeant Hugo Kiguel in the first company, Lieut. Col. James Whittle, commanding the second company, Musician John Benak, in the third company, and Lieut. Col. William Ferguson, commanding the fifth company; in the Vencedor Battalion, Capt. Miller Hallowes of the grenadier company; in the Vargas Battalion, First Sergeant Patrick Jay of the company of Cazadores, and probably Henry Leoper (who does not appear listed, but was promoted to the rank of lieutenant colonel in that organization after the battle); in the Bogotá Battalion, Sergeant Major Peter Anthony May, Capt. Gilmore Gregg (promoted to lieutenant colonel) of the first company, Lieut. Anastasio Ronchs and drummer Francis Coy of the fourth company, and sublieut. Charles Lee (who was promoted to lieutenant "graduado" in the grenadier company); in the Voltígeros, Lieut. Richard Reed and Sub-Lieut. Ignatius Ferrer of the fifth company; in the Hussars, Capt. Ignatius Lecumberry attached to the Third Squadron (who was recommended for promotion to lieutenant colonel and adjutant major); and in the Pichincha Battalion, Private John Blake of the fourth company. All these names

one of the four Colombian battalions in Córdoba's division which made the first charge, but the three battalions of Lara's Division, the Rifles, Várgas, and Vencedores, were held in reserve and took little part in the fight. Sucre reported that the Várgas Battalion led by its capable commander, Moran, worked wonders, but the Rifles were held in reserve and did not take part in the fighting. He, however, recommended Col. Sandes for promotion to brigadier general. He also mentioned for valor Capt. George Brown of the grenadier company of the Pichincha Battalion, who was wounded while raising the flag of Colombia on the crest of Condorcanqui. The chief of staff felt that his commander should have been more liberal in his recommendations, for Col. O'Connor says of this report: " The only foreigners mentioned by Sucre were Col. Sandes of the Rifles and Capt. Brown. He did not mention the brave and meritorious captains of the Rifles

are quoted in Cortés Vargas, *Participación de Colombia*, III, 36, 37, 38, 39, 40, 48, 56, 58, 59, 67, 70, 71, 119, 150, 161, 174, 175, 178, 186, 187, 188, 189, 191, 194, 203 from the muster rolls of their respective organizations or from lists of citations, all of which are filed in the national archives of Bogotá, Sección República, Guerra y Marina. O'Connor, *op. cit.*, 149 corroborates the report that it was Capt. George Brown of the Pichincha Battalion who raised the Colombian flag on the summit of Condorcanqui. The losses suffered by these battalions in the battle of Ayacucho are given in *El Colombiano*, March 9, 1825, as follows:

Battalion	Killed		Wounded	
	Officers	Men	Officers	Men
Rifles	4	122	1	88
Vencedor	1	30	3	121
Vargas	0	40	1	48
Bogotá	1	31	2	65
Voltígeros	0	19	8	55
Pichincha	0	12	8	51
Caracas	0	30	9	124
Cavalry	3	16	7	28
	9	300	39	580

Battalion, Wright, Ferguson, Harris, Hallowes, or the brave Lieut. Gilmore Gregg who had been in the lancers regiment of the Irish Legion, or the intrepid Lieut. Col. Philipp Braun of the squadron of Grenadiers of the Guard, nor his own chief of staff who had selected the site where the battle was to be fought." [1]

On the field of battle at Ayacucho the royalists had 9310 men to the patriots, 5780, and eleven guns to the patriots' one; [2] yet in one short hour the smaller force had decisively defeated the larger; the Spanish army of Peru was destroyed; the viceroy was a prisoner in the hands of the patriots; the war was at an end. The results of the battle of Ayacucho were momentous. In his capitulation the viceroy agreed to withdraw all Spanish troops from the former viceroyalty of Peru. Cantérac himself graciously congratulated Bolívar on this victory and saluted him in the name of the other Spanish generals. [3]

The only royalist forces left in Peru after the battle of Ayacucho were those under Gens. Olañeta and Rodil who refused to acknowledge that Cantérac's capitulation included them. Olañeta who, it will be remembered, had set up for himself in Upper Peru, now continued to assert that he represented the royal authority in that department. In March, 1825, his example of insubordination and disloyalty to his immediate superior was followed by one of his own subordinates, Col. Carlos Medinaceli, who turned against him and proclaimed, the independence of Chibcha. On April 1, Medinaceli met Olañeta in battle, wounded and defeated

---

[1] O'Connor, *op. cit.*, 149; Benjamin Vicuña Mackenna, *El Wáshington del Sur*, 217.

[2] Cortés Vargas, *op. cit.*, II, 241-250; Torrente, *op. cit.*, III, 489; Francisco García Calderón, *Latin America; its rise and progress*, 71; *The Times*, April 15, 1825; O'Leary, *Documentos*, XXII, 574.

[3] *El Colombiano*, April 6, 1825.

him. Olañeta's wound proved mortal, Medinaceli threw in his lot with the patriots, and on April 3, 1825, Sucre declared the war in Upper Peru at an end.[1]

Having refused to accept the terms of capitulation for the troops under his command, Gen. José Ramón Rodil shut himself up with them in the castle of Callao, where he was besieged by the patriot army under Gen. Bartolomé Salom, assisted by the combined Colombian and Peruvian squadrons under Admiral John Illingworth. For more than a year the garrison held out against every bombardment and attack, although the starving troops were reduced to eating horses, dogs, cats, and even rats, and scores of them were dying from typhoid fever. Rodil stubbornly refused to surrender; but at last when his own officers deserted him and aided the republicans to gain an entrance into the fortress the brave general grimly asked for a parley. On the 23rd of January, 1826, the flag of Peru was hoisted over the main fort and was saluted with salvos of artillery and the music of the Peruvian national hymn.[2] The last stronghold of royalty had fallen. Two new republics, Peru and Bolivia, had gained their independence and the liberation of Spanish South America was attained.[3]

[1] O'Connor, *op. cit.*, 160, 167, 168; *View of South America*, 166; Vicente Lecuna, *Documentos referentes a la creación de Bolivia*, I, 143, 144; O'Leary, *Narración*, II, 375; *The Times*, May 6, 1825.

[2] *El Colombiano*, Aug. 9, 1826; *View of South America*, 148; *Journal of H. M. S. Cambridge*, 68, 72; Eleazar López Contreras, *El Callao Histórico*, 126, 143, 144, 147, 161-166; F. O. 18/37, Consul Wood to Foreign Office, Feb. 8, 1826; *Campaigns and Cruises*, I, 407.

[3] The liberation of southern South America had been effected without the aid of Bolívar or of the Colombian troops. La Plata, Chile, Uruguay and Paraguay had won their independence through the efforts of San Martín or of their own local leaders, without help from the Liberator; but all movements for independence reacted upon one another, because they were nearly simultaneous and necessitated the dissipation of Spain's resisting power over a wide area. As a result of the weaken-

ing of the mother country, all such movements came to a successful conclusion at about the same time.

The last stand of the royalists in southern South America was that of a small force under Governor Quintanilla which had been holding out on the island of Chiloé near the southern coast of Chile, but this too had been captured only a week before the fall of Callao, on Jan. 18, 1826 by the Chilean general, Ramón Freire.

In the capture of Chiloé Major William de Vic Tupper sustained an important part. He led the final charge of the grenadier companies and was brevetted a lieutenant colonel for his gallantry on that occasion. With the return of peace, life in the army became irksome to him and he tried to secure a position with a mining company, for as he wrote, " Military officers are here no longer required, and foreign officers are therefore looked upon as a burden which sooner or later must be shaken off." Sutcliffe, *op. cit.*, 255, 257-259; *Campaigns and Cruises*, I, 362, 412, 436; F. O. 18/37, Consul Wood to Foreign Office, Feb. 24, 1826.

CHAPTER XII

Some of the Legionaries and Their Later Fortunes

AFTER Ayacucho, or more strictly speaking, after the disbandment of the Albion Battalion, the history of the several legions became the history of individuals. Although the majority had returned to their homes or gone elsewhere in search of adventure or of a livelihood, there were many legionaries who still remained in South America, either as officers in the armies or navies of Colombia, Venezuela, Ecuador and Peru, or as private citizens to build up fortunes or raise families in the lands of their adoption.

In the old days of the standard three-volume novel it used to be the custom for novelists to devote the final chapters of the last volume to relating the subsequent careers of the various characters that had not been brought to an end earlier in the story. Everyone was neatly disposed of. The wicked were given their deserts, and the good were made to live happily ever after. In history, however, such a distribution of rewards and punishments is not possible; even ex-presidents often pass their declining years in monotony. It would therefore not be profitable, even if it were possible, to follow the careers of all or even most of the legionaries,[1] but there is obtainable enough data to throw considerable light on the careers of several of the representative members who are

[1] Angel María Galán in his *Las Legiones Británica e Irlandesa*, 19-33, has given a list of one hundred and seventy-one foreigners serving in the British and Irish Legions. This list is valuable for reference, in spite of numerous inaccuracies in the spelling of proper names and of such serious omissions as those of Generals O'Leary and Manby. To supplement this list, brief statements are given in Appendix J of the records of Englishmen and Irishmen whose names were omitted by Galán or whose services were incompletely stated by him.

interesting as links with the history of later epochs leading down even to the present day.

After the war most of the Colombian troops were sent home for demobilization, but the Vencedor, Vargas and Rifles Battalions were kept with him by Sucre who remained to establish a government for the newly-born republic of Bolivia.[1] With the Rifles Col. Sandes continued as commandant until he was promoted to brigadier general and moved first to Arequipa and then to Guayaquil.[2] After about a year's stay at La Paz, these Colombian battalions were sent back to Guayaquil, where on Jan. 26, 1827, they broke into a mutiny headed by a Col. Bustamente. On investigation it proved that the officers and soldiers were not disloyal, but merely wanted to be paid and sent home. So on July 28, 1830 the Rifles Battalion was ordered disbanded. This event took place at San Carlos where, rather than to allow their colors to be sullied by ignoble hands, the officers of the battalion solemnly burned them in the principal plaza.[3] In referring to the Rifles and to its long-time commander, Bolívar had once at a banquet stated that the utmost intrepidity could always be expected from Col. Sandes and his men in every engagement in which they took part. There are not enough records to make it possible to follow the history of Col. Sandes much beyond this period, but some of his descendants were said to have been living in Venezuela as recently as 1911.[4]

[1] Lecuna, *Documentos referentes a Bolivia*, I, 497; Bingham Collection of Mss., Sucre Papers, Nos. 1260, 1263; F. O. 18/16, Henderson to Canning, June 9, 1825.

[2] Archivo Nacional, Bogotá, Guerra y Marina, Historia, VI, 394; Hojas de Servicios, VII, 84; Bingham Collection of Mss., Sucre Papers, Nos. 1259, 1261; O'Leary, *Correspondencia*, XII, 408, 410.

[3] Florez Álvarez, *Campaña libertadora*, 247; Level, *op. cit.*, 401.

[4] *Un Rasgo de Bolívar en Campaña*, 58; *El Universal* (Caracas), June 12, 1911.

On the night of October 10, 1831 the Vargas Battalion likewise mutinied under the lead of one of its first sergeants, because it had received no pay and was without rations or clothing. Its former commander, Gen. James Whittle, was ambushed and killed, but the mutineers were pursued by a squadron of militia and nearly all were captured and executed.[1]

In addition to Gens. Sandes and Whittle, there were five more officers of the British and Irish Legions who became generals of the line. These were Thomas Charles James Wright, Thomas Manby, John De Sola, Henry Weir, and Miller Hallowes.

Gen. Miller Hallowes, although born in England, came with the Irish Legion and with it made the charge at Carabobo. He also served in the Second Hussars, Grenadiers of the Guard, and in the Vencedor and Rifles Battalions. He fought through the campaigns of the south and of Peru. With the Rifles at Matará he was the hero of that noble rear-guard stand. He served at the first siege of Callao and in the expedition to the intermediate ports under Sucre. In 1829 he took part in the campaign of Pasto and Popayán and against Guayaquil until its surrender. He was decorated with the Star of the Order of Liberators both of Venezuela and of Quito, with the chevrons of Carabobo and Junín and with the medal of Ayacucho. Gen. Tomás C. Mosquera, later president of Colombia, said of him: "This general is active, careful, and brave. Every place the defense of which he is in charge of is in the best of order and never requires any attention from me."[2]

[1] Scarpetta y Vergara, *op. cit.*, 704; Manuel de Jesús Andrade, *Ecuador, Próceres de la independencia*, 405, 408, Pedro Fermín Cevallos, *Resumen de la historia del Ecuador desde su origen hasta 1845*, V, 55.

[2] Archivo Nacional, Bogotá, Guerra y Marina, Hojas de Servicios, XXIII, 415, 418; Scarpetta y Vergara, *op. cit.*, 215.

Gen. Henry Weir came as a lieutenant in one of the early contingents and soon rose to the rank of major. He served with the Albion Battalion in the campaign of New Granada in 1819, in the campaign of the Apure under Páez in 1820, in Venezuela under Bolívar in 1821 and at Carabobo. In the final siege of Puerto Cabello he took part in all actions. It will be remembered that as a captain in command of three companies he led a bayonet charge against the hostile trenches on the east shore of Lake Maracaibo, driving Morales back tc Alta Gracia. In 1823 with two companies of the Carabobo Battalion he frustrated an attempt of the garrison of Puerto Cabello to make its escape by means of a night sally. After independence was established he was commissioned a general in the army of Colombia, and served on the general staff of the first division and as commanding general of the second division of the Army of the North. In 1856 he left active service but four years later was recalled to become chief of operations in the State of Santander. He was commanding general of both the first and second divisions of the Second Army in 1862, until he was wounded at the defense of the fortified barrack of San Agustin and he finally left the service. In the civil war of Colombia he gave noteworthy proofs of fidelity to his adopted country and was distinguished for his knowledge of the art of war. He remained in Colombia until his death on Oct. 7, 1871.[1]

Gen. John de Sola came with the British Legion in 1819 and fought as a lieutenant at the battle of Carabobo. Subsequently he had resigned from the army to live by manual labor, but in 1852 he asked for retirement for disability.

[1] Archivo Nacional, Bogotá, Guerra y Marina, Hojas de Servicios, XLVIII, 747; Archivo Nacional, Caracas, Ilustres Próceres, XCIX, 184; Scarpetta y Vergara, *op. cit.*, 702; José María Baraya, *op. cit.*, II, 93, 94; Archivo Nacional Caracas, *Despachos de retiros, de licencias, de premios, de inválidos*, 718; *cf.* p. 286, n. 1.

This was granted with the rank of colonel in the army of Venezuela. In 1854 he served as chief of staff to Gen. José Laurencio Silva and in 1857 was reinstated as colonel on the active list. The following year he was promoted to be brigadier general.[1]

Gen. Thomas Manby, it will be remembered, had come to Angostura on the corvette " Tartar " as a captain with one hundred and fifty English and Germans and had helped in the organization of the British Legion. He fought at Boyacá, Carabobo and Pichincha. In the last battle he acted as adjutant general for Sucre. After the scattering of the British Legion, he remained in Colombia and kept up a correspondence with many of its former field officers. In 1823 he became a naturalized citizen of Colombia and was appointed military chief of the province of Tunja and Neiva, where he served under Gens. Urdaneta and Pedro Fortoul. The Liberator called him an excellent, brave and honorable man, and decorated him with the stars of the Liberators of Venezuela and Cundinamarca, with the cross of Boyacá, and with the medal of Pichincha. After the death of Bolívar, he retired to private life and made his home in Bogotá in the enjoyment of a pension granted for his services. He there married Josefa, daughter of Gen. Pedro Fortoul. In 1880 he was promoted brigadier general in the Colombian army but did not long enjoy this distinction, for on Feb. 11, 1881 he died at Bogotá, and was buried with high public honors. With him passed away the last field officer of the British Legion.[2]

Gen. Thomas Charles James Wright had an interesting and unusual career both on land and sea. He came in the second contingent with Gen. English and served under Urda-

[1] Archivo Nacional, Caracas, Ilustres Próceres, XXIII, 297.

[2] Scarpetta y Vergara, *op. cit.*, 287; *Boletín de Historia y Antigüedades*, XII, 545, 547.

neta, Bermúdez, Monagas and Mariño in Oriente, and in the campaigns of Coro and Maracaibo. Having had experience as a cadet in the English coast guard, he was assigned to duty as an officer of marine infantry. As such he was present at the naval action of Lake Maracaibo and at the siege of Puerto Cabello, for which he was awarded the chevron of " valor and constancy ". He commanded a flotilla of small armed boats and while on this duty was several times wounded. In the action of Moján he was commended for leading his flotilla in an attack on the left wing of the enemy's squadron and for maintaining the fight until he had fired his last cartridge. Later, having landed with an assaulting party under Gen. Manrique he distinguished himself by capturing a Spanish flag. In 1824 he was promoted captain of marine infantry, and having been transferred to the south, was awarded the Peruvian medal of honor. In 1829 he was promoted lieutenant colonel and appointed adjutant general of the general staff at Bogotá. Meanwhile Ecuador had separated from Colombia and under Flores had set itself up as an independent republic. Wright followed Flores and became a colonel in the army of Ecuador. In 1832 he was appointed commanding general of the department of Quito, and subsequently went to London, first as confidential agent of Ecuador to supervise the division of the Colombian loan, and later as consul general and secretary of legation. In the latter capacity he assisted in drawing up a treaty of peace, friendship and commerce between Ecuador and Spain. In 1845 he returned to Ecuador and was promoted brigadier general by Flores. In 1869 he was granted a pension by Venezuela with the salary of colonel, but did not live to enjoy it as he died that same year at Weston.[1]

[1] Archivo Nacional, Bogotá, Guerra y Marina, Historia, XIII, 332; Hojas de Servicios, XLVIII, 733; Archivo Nacional, Caracas, Ilustres Próceres, XCIX, 229; Bingham Collection of Mss., Sucre Papers, No. 506; O'Connor, *op. cit.*, 186; Andrade, *op. cit.*, 405.

Gen. William Miller, another Englishman, did not come with either the British or the Irish Legions, nor was he, under a strict interpretation of the term, one of the legionaries. Yet inasmuch as he fought side by side with the troops in the campaign for the liberation of Peru and since his services were so essential for the successful outcome of that campaign, it would be unfair to omit mention of him when discussing the careers of those Englishmen who became generals in the armies of the new republics. William Miller was born in Wingham, Kent, in 1795, and began his career as an officer in the British army, with which he served in the Napoleonic wars and also in the United States in the War of 1812. He landed in South America in 1817 and placed his sword at the disposal of Gen. San Martín, who appointed him a captain in the Army of the Andes which was being formed for the invasion of Chile. For saving his guns from capture at the disastrous rout of Cancha Rayada, Chile, Miller was promoted major. His advancement to colonel followed after he had been thrice wounded at Pisco, Peru, whither he had come as a member of the army which San Martín led from Chile for the protection of the Peruvian patriots.

When Bolívar arrived in Peru and organized his United Army of Liberators by consolidating his own Colombian battalions with San Martín's former La Plata-Chilean contingents and the local Peruvian troops, Miller received his appointment to the grade of brigadier general. How Gen. Miller helped to win the battle of Junín has already been described, as well as how he drove back the flanking movement of Valdéz at Ayacucho. After the war Gen. Miller was appointed governor of Potosí and grand marshal of Peru. He asked Sucre for a commission in Holland, Russia, or some other part of Europe, but declined to go as consul, as that was a purely commercial position the duties of which could be performed by a mere captain in the army. At a dinner given at Cuzco in honor of the Peruvian generals, a toast was proposed to Gen. Miller in which he was praised for having fulfilled the ancient prophecy that the Incas of Peru would be restored to their independent throne by strangers from England. In 1826 Miller returned to London where, as payment for his services to Peru, he was allowed to draw upon the Peruvian agents there the sum of $20,000. He had been away from England for so long that he wrote to a friend that he felt like a stranger and was filled with astonishment at the size of London and its wealth and civilization. In 1834 Miller was back again in Peru where he became commanding general of the army. He died at Callao in 1861.[1]

Gen. Wright was not the only amphibious officer, for the career of Admiral Illingworth was even more remarkable. John Illingworth had been a lieutenant in the British navy and after the Dutch and Danish campaigns had returned to England with his health shattered. In 1817 he had been selected by the Chilean agent in London to command the ship which brought Admiral Cochrane to Valparaiso. It was but natural therefore that when the latter began his organization of the Chilean navy he should choose Illingworth to be one of his captains. Thus Capt. Illingworth (or " Illingrot " as his name became translated into Spanish and as even he eventually was accustomed to sign it), in command of the " Rosa de los Andes " of the Chilean navy, executed many missions for his admiral, cruising along the Pacific coast as far north as the Bay of Panamá, and made a survey of the

---

[1] Miller, *op. cit.*, II, 53, 59, 184 n., 273. Bingham Collection of Mss., Sucre Papers, Nos. 1027, 1243, 1244, Guillermo Miller to Sucre, July 26, Sept. 12, 1825, July 19, Aug. 17, 1826. Capt. Andrews, *Journey from Buenos Aires to Potosi and Arica in the years 1825-26*, II, 272; V. Constancio Franco, *Reseñas Biográficas de los Próceres y Mártires de la Independencia de Colombia*, 23.

Atrato River as a possible route for an interoceanic canal. While at Panamá he tried to negotiate with the royalist Gen. Horé for the release of McGregor's men who, as will be remembered, were held there as prisoners of war, but failed to accomplish this purpose. On May 12, 1820 in an action off Punta Galera the little corvette " " Rosa de los Andes " of only 36 guns defeated the Spanish ship of war "Prueba" armed with 52 guns and manned by a crew of 550 men. After further successes Illingworth sailed for Guayaquil, where his ship was wrecked.[1] He then joined the army of Colombia, in which Bolívar appointed him a colonel.

On arrival of the Guides and the Albion Battalion at Guayaquil, Col. Illingworth aided Sucre in reorganizing his army for the campaign of Pichincha. After his victory at Yaguachi, Sucre ordered Col. Illingworth to march with a flanking column of 300 recruits directly on Quito by the shortest route, to cut off the retreat of the royalists, while he himself with his main force of 3,000 moved via Babahoyo and Guaranda. So promptly and rapidly was Illingworth's march conducted that he was almost at the gates of Quito when Sucre was defeated at Guachi. It seemed as though Col. Illingworth might have captured Quito and destroyed the royalist base had not Sucre suffered this defeat. Col. Illingworth, however, left with his small force unsupported, was obliged to abandon his advance on the capital and, after leading the royalists a chase in the mountains, had succeeded in bringing his detachment back to Guayaquil in September, 1821, without having suffered the usual desertions or any serious sickness, except among the officers.[2]

---

[1] Destruge, *Illingworth*, 1-55, *passim*; Weatherhead, *op. cit.*, 101.

[2] Destruge, *Illingworth*, 60-65; O'Leary, *Documentos*, XIX, 64; Archivo Nacional, Bogotá, Guerra y Marina, Historia, VII, 613; XXVII, 232-239; Bingham Collection of Mss., Sucre Papers, No. 691, 695, 710, 714, Juan Illingrot to Sucre, April 17, June 5, Nov. 6, 15, 1821, López, *op. cit.*, 44, 45, 49.

After the incorporation of Guayaquil into the Republic of Great Colombia, Illingworth was appointed commanding general of this maritime department, where he established a nautical school and thus became the real founder of the navy of Ecuador. In 1823 he became a citizen of the republic and married Mercedes de Decimavilla. He yearned to give up the cares of office and to return to private life, so, at his own request, was granted retirement from active service. It seemed that his services could not long be spared, for within two years he was back in harness again. He had been forced to accept the post of vice-admiral in command of the united fleets of Colombia and Peru, to take the place of Admiral Guisse who had been tried and dismissed for too much political activity and attempted extortion. In the course of this new duty Admiral Illingworth with his fleet had blockaded the castle of Callao and had shared with Gen. Salom the honor of receiving the surrender of Rodil and the last royalist troops to remain in Peru. In 1826, while commanding the navy of Colombia, he conducted operations against the Spanish fleet in the Antilles and organized an expedition for the liberation of Cuba, in accordance with plans of Bolívar which were never put into execution. The following year he returned to Guayaquil, where he was at last permitted to enjoy a well-earned rest.[1]

Charles James Minchin also lent his aid in building up the navy. He first appeared as aide-de-camp to Admiral Brión, but desiring more active service secured his transfer to the Apure where he joined Páez and did duty with the Hussars,

[1] Destruge, *op. cit.*, 73-76, 101, 108-110, 115; Archivo Nacional, Bogotá, Guerra y Marina, Historia, XVII, 149, DCCLXXIX, 898; López, *op. cit.*, 131; José Hipólito Herrera, *El Album de Ayacucho; colección de los principales documentos de la guerra de la independencia del Perú*, 172. For the records of some other British and Irish legionaries who were assigned to duty with the republican navies, see Appendix K.

and later in command of the first company of British Chasseurs. At Carabobo, although wounded in the thigh, he took command after Ferriar and Davy had fallen and, as will be remembered, ordered the British to form square to resist the charge of the royalist cavalry. Wounded again in the right shoulder, he kept on fighting until at last, weakened by loss of blood, he could no longer stand. After he had recovered from his wounds he joined the Carabobo Battalion, but was soon assigned to staff duty under Soublette. As chief of staff of one of the divisions operating in the north of Venezuela and New Granada, he continued in the army with intervals of duty aboard ship until the end of the war. In 1827 he retired with pension and honors, married and settled down in Coro. In 1855 he was again recalled to active service and assigned to duty as " comandante de armas " at Caracas and minister of the supreme court martial. He was promoted to major general and eventually became minister of war and marine. In 1866 he was still living in Caracas, surrounded by his family.[1]

It will be remembered that upon the muster out of the Albion Battalion, Cols. Mackintosh and Johnston ended their active service in the army. Both of them were awarded pensions because of their wounds. Col. Johnston tried to return to England but died while en route at Bocas del Toro, on the Isthmus of Panamá.[2] Col. Mackintosh lost the use of his hand. After having married Elizabeth Archer in London, he retired to Bogotá where he was associated with the half-pay officers, Col. Brand and Capt. Hugo Hughes, both of whom had become deaf and never recovered their

[1] Archivo Nacional, Bogotá, Guerra y Marina, Hojas de Servicios, XXXI, 460; Azpúrua, op. cit., III, 427-430.

[2] Cochrane, op. cit., II, 132; Hamilton, op. cit., I, 57; Boletín de historia y antigüedades, XII, Nos. 140-141, p. 547.

[3] Archivo Nacional, Bogotá, Guerra y Marina, Historia, MCCCXVIII,

hearing.[3]　In 1836 during a flurry of diplomatic trouble when war with England seemed to threaten, Cols. Brand and Mackintosh were called upon, as half-pay officers of the army, to swear that they were ready and willing to serve in defense of New Granada against England. Fortunately, however, the war clouds blew over, and the aged colonels were not required to turn against the land of their birth.[1]

In contrast to these records of honor stands the discreditable conduct of one of the foreign officers. Rupert Hand, a native of Dublin, came to Venezuela in the British Legion of Gen. English, with which he made the campaign under Urdaneta and Páez and took part in the battle of Carobobo. He was promoted captain in 1819 and lieutenant colonel four years later. He was engaged in the siege of Puerto Cabello and suffered a hernia during the campaign of Coro. On Sept. 4, 1824 he was retired and left for Mérida to regain his health. Shortly after his arrival there he was arrested for burglarizing the post-office. Although the evidence against him was strong, he was acquitted before the supreme court martial at Bogotá, partly because of influence used in his behalf and partly because he was a hero of Carabobo and belonged to the Order of Liberators. After Gen. José M. Córdoba's revolt against Bolívar in Chocó and his defeat at Santuario in 1829, the wounded rebel general was attacked and murdered in his own house. Hand was accused of being the murderer, but claimed that he had com-

127; Hojas de Servicios, XXIII, 378, XXX, 916; Hamilton, *op. cit.*, I, 82, El Secretario de la Guerra y Marina, *Exposición que dirige al Congreso de Venezuela en 1855*, p. 37; 1860, p. 3; J. Stewart, *Bogotá in 1836-7*, 259; Dávila, *Diccionario biográfico*, I, 47.

[1] Archivo Nacional, Bogotá, Guerra y Marina, Hojas de Servicios, XXX, 912; Archivo Nacional, Caracas, Ilustres Próceres, XII, 23; Stewart, *op. cit.*, 259; Scarpetta y Vergara, *op. cit.*, 57, 285. It is said that the great grandsons of Colonels Mackintosh and Johnston are still living in South America; the latter, Dundas Johnston, is a carpenter in Bogotá and the former, a mining engineer in Coro.

mitted the deed in obedience to orders from his superiors. During Hand's confinement on these charges, strong influence, including that of an English commodore, was brought to bear to save him. Nevertheless, Hand was tried, found guilty, and sentenced to death, but when notification of this sentence arrived at the prison it was found that he had escaped. According to one author, nothing more was heard of him after this, but according to another, Hand was still living in Caracas in 1846 as a lieutenant colonel on the retired list.[1]

While the officers of the line performed important functions in training and leading troops, it is probably true that those on the staff exerted a more far-reaching influence, not only upon Bolívar himself and the other generals, but upon the whole policy of equipping and training the army. Among the staff officers frequent reference has already been made to Col. George Woodberry and Col. Francis Hall. Of the career of the former after the capitulation of Puerto Cabello, for which he was largely responsible, little is known beyond the fact that he was granted retirement in 1825.[2] Col. Francis Hall came to Santa Marta with D'Evereux as one of his aides. He was originally an officer of infantry, but his suggestions and recommendations for the organization of a corps of engineers caused him to be commissioned a colonel of engineers in command of it. After the war Col. Hall settled in Quito, intending to live the life of a philosopher and disciple of Jeremy Bentham. He devoted himself to literature, science and the arts, and in 1827 published *The Present State of Colombia* which has so often been quoted

[1] Archivo Nacional, Caracas, Despachos de retiros, de licencias, de inválidos, 718; Eduardo Posada, "Ruperto Hand" in *Boletín de Historia y Antigüedades*, No. 62, VI, 97-105; Dávila, *Diccionario biográfico*, I, 228.

[2] *El Argos* (Caracas), Sept. 6, 1825.

in these pages. Also he founded among young men of distinguished families a radical club called the " Society of Free Citizens of Quito " and was the organizer of the "Partido Nacional" (National Party). By this activity he incurred the enmity of Gen. Flores. In 1833 Col. Hall took part in a conspiracy against Flores, and on October 19 was killed while attempting to put his plot into execution.[1]

Of the foreign medical officers Dr. James H. Robinson was one of the first to offer his skill to the cause of the insurgents. Shortly after his arrival at Angostura, on October 22, 1818, he received a commission from Bolívar designating him as director general of the hospitals of the Free Provinces of New Granada. The doctor died from the effects of the climate, but not until after he had written a rather unflattering account of his experiences, published under the title of a *Journal of an Expedition 1400 Miles up the Orinoco and 300 Miles up the Arauca; with an account of the country, the manners of the people, military operations, etc.*[2]

Dr. Thomas Foley, an inspector general of hospitals, likewise failed to keep faith with the republican cause; for on his return to London he warned English companies that they would inevitably be ruined if they invested in Colombia since that republic had only $300,000 in its treasury. This statement he made in spite of the fact that before leaving Bogotá he had been given $240,000 with instructions to pay $40,000 to the troops in Cartagena and to keep $200,000 for himself until further orders.[3]

---

[1] Archivo Nacional, Bogotá, Guerra y Marina, Historia, XXXV, 881; Hojas de Servicios, XXIII, 406; Registro general de jefes, No. 713; O'Connor, *op. cit.*, 55; Pedro Moncayo, *El Ecuador de 1825 a 1875, sus hombres, sus instituciones y sus leyes,* 68; Camilo Destruge, *Album biográfico ecuatoriano,* II, 138-142.

[2] Robinson, *op. cit.*, vi, vii, 98, and *passim.*

[3] Archivo Nacional, Bogotá, Guerra y Marina, Historia, VI, 289; *Archivo Santander,* X, 342; O'Leary, *Documentos,* XIX, 235.

Doctors Mallery and Merrick became surgeons in the patriot army, the latter with the rank of sergeant major.[1] Dr. Thomas Alexander who was a surgeon and sergeant major in 1817 died of an epidemic at Old Guayana and left his widow, Soledad Pérez, without means of support.[2] Dr. Blair was surgeon of the Rifles Battalion during the campaign in Peru.[3] Dr. Small on arrival at Guayaquil was encouraged to open a pharmacy there.[4]

Dr. William P. Smith was originally surgeon of the Irish Legion, but later was appointed surgeon major of the Department of the Magdalena. He married a lady in Santa Marta where he was on duty in charge of the hospital. After having lived there for twenty-five years he asked for six months' leave on full pay and retirement with pension. He based his appeal on the grounds that he lacked pecuniary resources and that his sons were of an age at which they needed an education.[5]

Dr. Henry George Maine began as surgeon major in charge of the inspection of hospitals on Margarita Island. He went with the Irish Legion to Rio Hacha in 1820. While there he was active in obtaining medicines from Jamaica, Grenada and other West Indian islands. He also took the sick and wounded to Jamaica where they could more rapidly be restored to health. After his transfer to Cúcuta his conduct won the good will of the inhabitants, and the excellent state of his hospital gained the admiration of the commanding general of the division. On his arrival at Bogotá, pleading ill health he asked to be relieved from accompanying the

---

[1] O'Leary, *Documentos*, XIX, 408; Bache, *op. cit.*, 150.

[2] Dávila, *Diccionario biográfico*, I, 8.

[3] O'Connor, *op. cit.*, 122.

[4] O'Leary, *Documentos*, XX, 346.

[5] Archivo Nacional, Bogotá, Guerra y Marina, Hojas de Servicios, XLIII, 653, 656, 659; F. O. 18/37, Fauche to Canning, Oct. 9, 1826.

troops further on their march to Popayán.   Like many
others, he also found it desirable to press the government for
a settlement of his accounts.[1]

In 1818 Dr. Charles Moore of London became a surgeon
first class and sergeant major in the patriot army; in 1830
he was promoted to colonel and in 1834 retired.   From 1818
to 1822 he was on duty in military hospitals in the campaigns
of Venezuela and of the south; from 1823 to 1828 he acted
as surgeon on the personal staff of the Liberator.[2]   Although
Bolívar kept Dr. Moore with him for five years, he is reported to have said of his surgeon that he was a good man
but a trifle timid.   In order not to hurt Dr. Moore's pride,
Bolívar pretended to have faith in his medical advice and to
take his prescriptions.   Another staff officer quotes Bolívar
as saying, " my physician is a luxury, not a necessity—the
same as my chaplain whom I discharged ".[3]

In addition to his physician, Bolívar always kept at least
one or two English officers on his staff; for he seemed to
enjoy their society as well as to profit by his conversation
with them in improving his ability to speak English.[4]   Probably the earliest of these was Capt. Chamberlayne, who came
to Venezuela in 1816 before the arrival of the first contingents.   This officer had resigned his commission in one of the
British West India regiments to accept the post of aide-de-
camp to Bolívar with the rank of lieutenant colonel.   When
the latter was obliged to abandon Cumaná, he ordered Col.
Chamberlayne to remain with a small force and defend the

[1] Archivo Nacional, Bogotá, Guerra y Marina, Historia, X, 518, 740;
XXXV, 923, 924; Hojas de Servicios, XXX, 708, XXXI, 712, 713.

[2] Archivo Nacional, Bogotá, Guerra y Marina, Historia, XIII, 265;
Hojas de Servicios, XXXI, 75; Miller, *op. cit.*, II, 293; O'Leary, *Documentos*, XX, 380; Roberto Andrade, *Campaña de 20 días*, 266.

[3] Louis Perú de Lacroix, *Diario de Bucaramanga*, 99, 100.

[4] Hamilton, *op. cit.*, I, 235.

citadel until he received aid. Unfortunately the Liberator's affairs at that time were at so low an ebb that he was unable to send the promised relief. Sickness, wounds and death reduced Col. Chamberlayne's garrison to only a few men, yet he held out against the attacks of the royalists until all hope of doing so any longer was gone. He then ordered his handful of survivors to prepare to surrender and to open the gates to the enemy. When the Spanish officers rushed in, they found that Col. Chamberlayne had killed his wife, who had remained with him throughout the siege, and had committed suicide over her body.[1]

It is possible that this superb heroism and devotion on the part of Col. Chamberlayne helped to determine Bolívar's decision to secure the services of more Englishmen like him. That the Liberator did well in trusting to the loyalty and valor of Englishmen is amply proved by many instances, and especially by the fact that he later owed his life to another member of his staff, Col. William Ferguson. On the night of September 25, 1828, a band of conspirators forced an entrance into the president's palace in Bogotá, with the intention of killing Bolívar. In the excitement the Liberator succeeded in escaping from a window of his bedroom, but Ferguson, who had rushed to the door to protect his chief, fell shot and stabbed to death by the assassins.[2]

As a young man, Ferguson had left a minor position with a firm in Demerara to enlist as a drummer-boy in the British Battalion on the lower Apure. After his capture by the

[1] *Recollections of Service*, I, 110-114; Hippisley, *op. cit.*, 466; Bolívar to Maxwell Hyslop, June 10, 1816 in *Boletín de Historia y Antigüedades,* Academia Nacional de Historia, Bogotá, IX, No. 101.

[2] O'Leary, *op. cit., Apéndice*, XXIX, 372, 375; Posada, *op. cit.*, 227; Azpúrua, *op. cit.*, III, 345; Scarpetta y Vergara, *op. cit.*, 150. A window marked with a tablet in the Ministry of Foreign Relations (formerly the presidential palace) at Bogotá is still shown as the one through which Bolívar jumped to the street

royalists and confinement as a prisoner of war for fourteen months at Puerto Cabello, he managed to escape and make his way to Margarita Island where he joined the Irish Legion. Chosen as an aide by Montilla, he made the campaigns of Rio Hacha, Magdalena and Cartagena. During the years 1819 and 1820 he was twice wounded. Having been promoted to captain in the Rifles, he fought at Bombóna, Junín and Ayacucho, remaining in the campaigns of Peru and Upper Peru until after the collapse of Olañeta's revolt. On one occasion he was tried for some breach of discipline and sentenced to be shot, but on the appeal of the captain of a British man-of-war was restored to the command of his company. In 1826 he received a colonelcy, and from 1824 to the time of his death was on the personal staff of the Liberator. One of the most important missions entrusted to him by Bolívar was that of carrying into Upper Peru the new constitution for the Republic of Bolivia for delivery into the hands of Sucre, then at Chuquisaca. The ride from Lima, which led across the higher Andes, was most exhausting, yet the distance of 1,800 miles was accomplished by Ferguson and his companion, Capt. Belford Hinton Wilson, in nineteen days.[1]

This companion, the son of Gen. Sir Robert Wilson of the British Army, received his education at Westminster and Sandhurst. He was then sent by his father to Colombia with a letter offering his services and asking that Bolívar might appoint him his aide. Young Wilson joined just in time to be present at the battle of Junín, was accepted by Bolívar as his aide and given the rank of captain. In August, 1824, he was granted leave on account of his health. He improved the time by spending it aboard the vessels of the

[1] Archivo Nacional, Bogotá, Guerra y Marina, Historia, XIII, 336; Hojas de Servicios, XVI, 648; Azpúrua, *op. cit.*, III, 344; O'Connor, *op. cit.*, 93, 94.

Peruvian squadron and on the American warship " United States ", where he was kindly received by Admiral Guisse and Commodore Hull. For his remarkable ride in carrying the Bolivian constitution to Sucre, the latter promoted him to the rank of colonel. Fearing, however, the jealousy of other officers over whom he was jumped, Wilson at first refused this promotion, and only accepted it when ordered to do so by Bolívar.[1] Gen. Miller described him as an excellent young man, very well educated, who had come with the noble ambition of meriting honor and glory in the cause of liberty.[2] Wilson indeed was devoted to his chief, and wrote to his father that he regretted that his absence at the time had prevented his sharing the fate of Ferguson in saving the life of the Liberator.[3] He remained with Bolívar until the latter's death in 1830. In 1832 Wilson was appointed British consul general in Peru, and in 1849 given a similar post in Venezuela.[4] In his will dated Santa Marta, Dec. 10, 1830, the Liberator directed that his executors transmit his thanks to Gen. Sir Robert Wilson for the excellent conduct of his son, Col. Belford Hinton Wilson, " who has accompanied me so faithfully until the last moments of my life ".[5]

The best known of the foreign officers who remained after the other legionaries had completed their service were Generals Daniel Florence O'Leary and Francis Burdett O'Connor, for the reason that these staff officers published memoirs de-

---

[1] O'Connor, *op. cit.*, 72, 117; Miller, *op. cit.*, II, 293-296; O'Leary, *Correspondencia de extranjeros notables*, I, 96.

[2] Bingham Collection of Mss., Sucre Papers, No. 1820, Guillermo Miller to Sucre, Nov. 23, 1823.

[3] O'Leary, *Correspondencia de extranjeros notables*, I, 156.

[4] Grover Cleveland, *Presidential Problems*, 187; *Simón Bolívar, Libertador de la América del sur, por los más grandes escritores americanos*, 451.

[5] Bolívar's will published in *El Centenario de Simón Bolívar en la República Argentina*.

scribing their experiences in South America. The writings of O'Leary in particular are so extensive and contain so many valuable documents that since their publication they have formed the basis of most of the biographies and histories of Bolívar. As chief aide-de-camp to Bolívar, O'Leary had unusual opportunities of observing the conduct and character of the Liberator, and with the instincts of an historian he took pains to collect the originals or copies of much of the correspondence which passed through his hands. O'Leary's memoirs are published in twenty-nine volumes, comprising twelve volumes of correspondence, fourteen of documents, and two of narration (with, in some later editions, an appendix volume containing additional narration and documents). The two of narration were originally written by O'Leary in English, but before publication were translated into Spanish by his son, Simón Bolívar O'Leary.

The recollections of Francis Burdett O'Connor constitute another valuable source of information concerning the wars of independence, and give many interesting and intimate details about the lives of the patriot leaders, especially of Sucre and Bolívar. Francis Burdett O'Connor was born in Cork on Jan. 19, 1781. He was the brother of Fergus O'Connor. In 1798 their father, Roger O'Connor, was banished from Ireland and his estates were confiscated as punishment for leading a rebellion against England. Francis tried to cross the channel to offer his services to Napoleon but failed in the attempt. Later, through the assistance of Col. Aylmer, he succeeded in purchasing from D'Evereux a commission in the 10th Lancers, a regiment in the Irish Legion.[1] It will be recalled also that O'Connor was one of the few officers of the Irish Legion who remained faithful during the mutiny at Rio Hacha. He was promoted to lieutenant colonel and

[1] O'Connor, *op. cit.*, 16; *Boletín de Historia y Antigüedades*, VIII, 258.

served through the Magdalena campaign on the staff of Montilla, until he was ordered to go to Panamá and organize the Isthmian Battalion. This body he was able to recruit largely from ex-officers and sergeants of the royalist army. One of his first and most prized recruits was " a magnificent drum major ".[1] No sooner than mustered in, the Isthmian Battalion was ordered to Callao to take part in the campaign in Peru.

The activities of O'Connor in this campaign, his transfer to Sucre's staff and his efficient conduct at the battle of Ayacucho have already been narrated. He then followed Sucre into Upper Peru, where he was entrusted with the direction of the final operations,[2] receiving after the death of his chief the rank of general in the army of the new republic of Bolivia. He was highly thought of by President Santa Cruz who conferred upon him the star of a commander of the Legion of Honor of Bolivia, and entrusted him with various important missions.[3]

With the pay which he had received for his services in the Colombian army,[4] O'Connor bought a farm in Tarija whither he retired in 1839 to enjoy domestic repose and bring up his family far from the turmoils and disturbances into which the revolt of Gen. Ballivian had thrown Bolivian politics.[5] When Gen. Braun urged him to invest his savings in some English house as a precaution against the reverses

[1] O'Connor, *op. cit.*, 63.

[2] *Ibid.*, 70, 95, 160; F. O. 18/16, Henderson to Canning, June 9, 1825.

[3] O'Connor, *op. cit.*, 290, 358, 365.

[4] For his military services O'Connor received in government notes of the Republic of Colombia a total of 27,800 " pesos." Of this sum 9,000 was for his salary as lieutenant colonel, 8,800 as a bonus for his part in the victory at Ayacucho, and 10,000 for his salary as colonel since Pichincha. O'Connor, *op. cit.*, 254.

[5] *Ibid.*, 171, 416.

of political fortunes, O'Connor replied that his father's family had become the victims of the English government and that he himself had given up his English citizenship and had become a Bolivian.[1] On Oct. 5, 1871, O'Connor died, leaving his unfinished memoirs to be assembled and published by his grandson, Francisco O'Connor D'Arlach.[2]

More important than O'Connor as a staff officer in influencing the policies and decisions of the leaders of the revolution was Gen. O'Leary. Like O'Connor, Daniel Florence O'Leary was born at Cork, but nine years later. As will be remembered, he came to Venezuela as a cornet in Wilson's Red Hussars, but soon transferred to the staff of Gen. Anzoátegui. During the campaign in New Granada in 1819 he took part in all important engagements and was slightly wounded at Pántano de Vargas. At Carabobo he was attached as aide-de-camp to the staff of Bolívar, on whose staff he remained throughout most of his subsequent career.[3]

O'Leary's writings above mentioned show such loyal devotion to his chief that it is impossible to believe the story that when a raiding party of royalists set fire to the town of Garaza where Bolívar was spending the night, O'Leary, who was sleeping in another room in the same house, ran out without warning the Liberator of his danger of capture.[4] Another story of probably no great authenticity is to the effect that once when Bolívar told Ferguson that he was surprised that he did not get on well with O'Leary since they

[1] O'Connor, *op. cit.,* 393.

[2] *Ibid.,* 416 (n. by editor).

[3] O'Leary, *Narración,* I, 484; Archivo Nacional, Caracas, Ilustres Próceres, LX, 321; Archivo Nacional, Bogotá, Guerra y Marina, Historia, XIII, 310; Perú de Lacroix, *op. cit.,* 73; Andrade, *Próceres de la independencia,* 287; Franco, *op. cit.,* 28.

[4] *Recollections of Service,* II, 12.

were fellow countrymen, Ferguson replied, " Nor he with me. I believe that my character is too frank for his." [1] Bolívar nevertheless reposed great confidence in O'Leary, steadily promoted him to higher rank and repeatedly entrusted him with important duties, as for example in 1823, when he was sent on a mission to Chile to obtain troops and money for the Peruvian campaign. The highest rank reached by O'Leary was that of brigadier general, although he was offered a further promotion to major general, which he declined in order that he might not become involved in a civil war.[2]

In 1830 Gen. O'Leary was sent to the United States as envoy extraordinary and minister plenipotentiary from the Republic of Colombia. Two years later he retired from the army and went to Jamaica to write his memoirs. He then was sent as minister plenipotentiary from Venezuela to Spain, where he was also made British minister. From about 1840 to his death he represented Great Britain as charge d'affaires and minister at Bogotá. He died there on February 24, 1854.[3]

Gen. O'Leary married Soledad Soublette, the sister of Gen. Soublette and had five sons, Simón Bolívar, Carlos, Arturo, Daniel and Oscar, and four daughters, Soledad, Bolivia, Ana and Carolina. It was Simón Bolívar O'Leary who prepared his father's memoirs for publication. Carolina was the mother of the present representative in Bogotá and

[1] Perú de Lacroix, *op. cit.*, 122.

[2] O'Leary, *Documentos*, XX, 495, 521; O'Connor, *op. cit.*, 64; Perú de Lacroix, *op. cit.*, 52, 53, 79.

[3] Archivo Nacional, Bogotá, Guerra y Marina, Historia, MCCCXVIII, 118; O'Leary, *Ultimos años de la vida pública de Bolívar*, Introduction, 21; Lecuna, *Papeles de Bolívar*, 218; *Memorial del Estado Mayor del Ejército de Colombia*, No. 122 contains photographic copies of O'Leary's commissions, the originals of which are in the possession of his grandson, Dr. Julio Portocarrero at Bogotá.

head of this distinguished family, Dr. Julio Portocarrero O'Leary.[1]

The reader cannot fail to have observed that a goodly proportion of the English-speaking leaders of the legionaries were Irishmen. Obviously such important members as O'Leary and O'Connor were. As to their associates, it has not always been possible to determine positively whether they were English or Irish; but there appears to be sufficient evidence to warrant the statement that, of the others mentioned in this chapter, Doctors Foley and William P. Smith, Rupert Hand, Col. Ferguson, and Generals Sandes, Minchin and Wright were Irishmen.

[1] *Memorial del Estado Mayor del Ejército de Colombia*, No. 122, p. 404.

CHAPTER XIII

Soldiers from Many Nations in a Common Cause

From what has so far been said the impression may have been given that the foreign legionaries were Englishmen and Irishmen exclusively. Unless further information were supplied, this would be a fair assumption, because of the fact that recruitment was carried on so largely in England and Ireland, that most of the individuals sailed from English and Irish ports, and that the foreign contingents bore throughout their service such names as the " English Legion ", the " Irish Legion ", the " British Legion " and the " Albion Battalion ". The assumption, however, is not sound, for there were many men of other nationalities among the legionaries.

Col. Uslar's and Col. Needham's contingents were almost entirely composed of Germans, especially Hanoverians, and at the outset were occasionally called the " Hanoverian Legion "; but they soon became merged in the larger organizations of foreigners and lost their identity. Even so they continued throughout the war to provide within the British Legion a group of officers whose careers and services were of the utmost importance.

As a matter of fact, the first foreigners to come to Venezuela and lend their services to the cause of independence in numbers large enough to constitute an important factor, even before the arrival of the British and Irish Legions, were Americans and Frenchmen. When Miranda gave up in discouragement his efforts to secure aid from England to revolutionize his native land he transferred his efforts to the

341

United States, and there raised a following that in 1806 sailed with him from New York in the ship " Leander ". Most of them were captured and executed by the Spanish authorities. The description of their adventures and sufferings is graphically told by one of their number, James Biggs, in his *History of Don Francisco de Miranda's attempt to effect a revolution in South America; in a series of letters by a gentleman who was an officer under that general, to his friend in the United States* and is too well known to require further mention. Suffice it to record that in this expedition some fifty citizens of the United States were captured and eight paid the penalty of death.[1]

Shortly thereafter a number of Frenchmen engaged in an effort to foment a spirit of independence in the Spanish colonies. One of them, named Demolard, with fifty other French emigrés arrived in Baltimore about the middle of November, 1809, in the frigate " Tilsit " from Bayonne. There they gathered about them a number of Spanish-American malcontents and plotted to send emissaries into the colonies in South America. The Frenchmen took charge of four different parties that were to organize revolutionary units on the coasts of New Granada and Venezuela. The details of their conspiracy reached the ears of Antonio Amar, the Spanish viceroy, who sent instructions to the governors of Panamá, Porto Bello, Cartagena, Santa Marta and Rio Hacha to

---

[1] Biggs, *op. cit.*, 77, 78, 242; also *cf.* J. H. Sherman, *A general account of Miranda's expedition, including the trial and execution of ten of his officers, and an account of the imprisonment and sufferings of the remainder of his officers and men who were taken prisoners*, 119, 120. Of the ten who were executed, Gustavus A. Burgudd was a native of Poland and Paulo Theodore George was a Portuguese. The remaining eight were either from New York or Philadelphia. Another interesting account is the *History of the adventures and sufferings of Moses Smith during five years of his life from the beginning of the year 1806 when he was betrayed into the Miranda expedition until June, 1811.*

search all vessels, especially American, to prevent the smuggling in of these emissaries disguised as crew, cooks or servants. So apprehensive was he of the possible results from this conspiracy, that he expressed great satisfaction upon learning that he was to be relieved by a new viceroy, Francisco Vanegas.[1]

While it is not possible to trace the activities of all the Frenchmen, it is probable that several of them remained in America and continued to give their support to the spirit of revolt which they had aroused. Moreover, it is certain that a number of names of Frenchmen appear in the early annals of the revolution.[2] Among these may be mentioned Pierre Labatut,[3] who in 1813 was in command of a patriot division in Cartagena and under whom Bolívar was serving when he first crossed the mountains of New Granada into Venezuela; and Gen. Manuel de Serviez, who came to Cartagena in 1812 and fought for two years in the Cauca valley under the orders of Nariño. In 1816, at the head of the second line of defense Serviez saved the patriot army from destruction and led what was left of it to safety at Bogotá. In October of the same year he met his death at the hands of an assassin at Achaguas whither he had gone to cooperate with Páez.[4]

Before joining Serviez in 1813 at Popayán, Charles Louis Castelli had seen service under Napoleon. He was subsequently attached to the British Legion, directed the fortifi-

---

[1] He wrote also in this connection to the naval commander at Cartagena and to Luís de Onís, the Spanish minister at Washington. The several letters are all dated July 4, 1810. The historian, Gen. J. D. Monsalve, of Bogotá, has in his private archives transcripts of them said to have been made from copies of official correspondence found in the desk of Viceroy Amar.

[2] *The Times,* April 18, 1817; *The Morning Chronicle,* Nov. 25, 1818; *The British Monitor,* Feb. 21, 1819.

[3] *La Nación* (Caracas), Nov. 23, 1910; Galán, *op. cit.,* 10.

[4] Galán, *op. cit.,* 9.

cations in San Fernando, and was under fire at Carabobo and Puerto Cabello. He was appointed civil and military chief of San Felipe and governor of Mérida. He assisted O'Leary also in suppressing the defection of Gen. Córdoba at Santuario. In 1830 Castelli became a brigadier general, but two years later was retired as a colonel. In 1849 he was promoted major general and again retired on account of his various wounds. In 1851 he became minister of war and marine, dying at Caracas in 1860. His widow was granted a pension.[1]

Gen. H. L. V. Ducoudray-Holstein attached himself to Bolívar, whose chief of staff he became, during the assembly of the expedition at Aux Cayes and its subsequent arrival on the coast of Venezuela. Judging from his own account,[2] he could not get along with the Liberator and prematurely abandoned the army of independence. At any rate his accusations against Bolívar show him to have been shamefully disloyal to his chief, and hence quite unworthy of confidence.

Another Frenchman, often called a Mexican, who was present with Bolívar at the momentous meeting at Aux Cayes, when the forces for the final attempt at liberation of Venezuela were assembled and organized, was Louis Aury,[3] who sided with Montilla and Bermúdez in their opposition to the Liberator as commander of the expedition. Aury's part in

---

[1] Archivo Nacional, Bogotá, Guerra y Marina, Historia, X, 400, 701; Registro general de jefes, No. 707; Dávila, *Diccionario biográfico*, I, 78; Scarpetta y Vergara, *op. cit.*, 97.

[2] Ducoudray-Holstein, *op. cit., passim; London Chronicle*, Nov. 19, 1822.

[3] Louis Aury, who claimed the rank of brigadier general of the armies of Mexico had, with a fleet of privateers, assisted McGregor in the seizure and occupation of Amelia Island. He had then captured the islands of Santa Catalina, Old Providence, and San Andrés, the last of which McGregor used as his base in his expedition against Porto Bello. Eduardo Posada, "Luís Aury" in *Boletín de Historia y Antigüedades*, Bogotá, Año VII, No. 78, pp. 337, 352, 359; F. O. 72/216, Letter from the Captain of the Spanish brig "Perinón," Feb. 11, 1818.

the subsequent operations consisted in blockading the port of Cartagena with his squadron and in conducting a war of privateers against Spanish merchantmen in the Caribbean Sea. In 1821 he asked to be incorporated in the regular navy, but Bolívar declined to grant the request on the ground that he had no more use for privateers which disgraced the flag of Colombia, and ordered Aury to leave the country. The latter, however, was eventually granted the rank of captain in the navy of Venezuela and given indefinite leave with one-third the pay of his rank.[1] It was a French naval officer named Nicolas Joli, moreover, who commanded the brigantine " Gran Bolívar " in the squadron of Admiral Brión, and was with Padilla in his cruise against the coasts of Cartagena, Santa Marta, Puerto Cabello, and Maracaibo.[2]

With Aury came as his secretary a young Frenchman named Louis Perú de Lacroix, who afterwards attained the rank of general in the Colombian army. For some time he was attached to the staff of Bolívar, whose confidence he abused by publishing in a much-criticized work supposedly detailed reports of statements made by the Liberator in intimate conversation with members of his staff.[3]

Among other Frenchmen who joined the armies of Colombia during the height of the revolution the best known were Charles Eloi Demarquet, who was adjutant general to Gen. Salom during 1821 and in his campaign of the south in 1822, until he was appointed secretary general to Bolívar in

---

[1] Posada, " Luís Aury," 342, 345, 349, 350, 354, 365; *Correo del Orinoco*, March 31, 1821; Archivo Nacional, Bogotá, Guerra y Marina, Historia, VI, 403-439; *Gaceta de Colombia*, Dec. 8, 1822.

[2] Archivo Nacional, Bogotá, Guerra y Marina, Historia, XV, 55; *Exposición que dirige al Congreso Constitucional de los EE. UU. de Venezuela el Ministro de Guerra y Marina, 1833*, 75, 76; Archivo Soublette, Documentos, III, 1822 (folio not numbered).

[3] Posada, " Luís Aury," 351; Perú de Lacroix, *Diario de Bucaramanga*, 6-8, 25, *passim*.

1823,[1] and Baron Bruix, whose heroism has already been
recounted in connection with the description of the battle of
Junín, when he with Miller and Sowerby charged with a few
hussars and mounted grenadiers until they had turned defeat
into victory.[2]

After the early efforts of those who stirred up the spirit
of revolt, it is probable that the most important services lent
by Frenchmen were on the sea. Prominent officers in the
republican navy who had come from France were Commodore René Beluche, who was second in command to Padilla,
and Major Jean B. Destruge, who was surgeon in the squadron blockading Maracaibo; Capt. Souflen, who commanded
the "Americana" at the siege of Cartagena in 1815, and
Capt. Bellegarde Bastigue, who was killed at the battle of

[1] Archivo Nacional, Bogotá, Guerra y Marina, Historia, X, 228;
DCCLXXIX, 567, 568.

[2] Report of Gen. Andrés García of the royalist army on the battle of
Junín in *Repertorio Boyacense*, Sept. 1, 1924, p. 1087; *La Nación*
(Caracas), Nov. 23, 30, Dec. 19, 1910 also mentions the following French-
men as joining the patriot army: in 1814 came Col. Louis Bernard
Chatillon, who was killed while commanding a force of patriots at Pam-
pares; in 1816 Capt. Duchemin and Lieut. Duflis, both of whom followed
McGregor in the retreat from Ocumare; in 1818 Sergeant Major Antonio
Sasmajus, or Chasmaillon, who was captured near Casanare and executed
by the royalists in 1819; and in 1820 Col. Garcin, who served under
Sarda in the Magdalena campaign. Besides these the records show that
Lieut. Col. Pierre Gullion was appointed governor of Veraguas on the
Isthmus of Panama (Archivo Nacional, Bogotá, Guerra y Marina, Historia, XXXV, 878); and that Lieut. François Manuit was in the first
company of Dragoons of the Guard during the assault and capture of
Puerto Cabello, in 1823 (*ibid.*, DCCLXXX, 790). Manuit continued in
the army of Venezuela and in 1863 was retired with the rank and one-
third salary of colonel. *Exposición que dirige al Congreso Constitucional de los EE. UU. de Venezuela el Ministro de Guerra y Marina,*
1855, pp 31-34, 1866, p. 69. At the end of the war Major François
Giraud was granted indefinite leave with pay and Private Joseph Betan-
court sick leave on half-pay. *Ibid.*, 1850, Archivo Nacional, Bogotá,
Guerra y Marina, Historia, XXVI, 835.

Lake Maracaibo, while commanding the "Antonia Manuela", In this same battle Capt. Henri Bertmon and Julian Joupat, pilot of the "Leona", were wounded.[1]

It is likewise true that the most valuable assistance furnished by Americans was that due to the valor, energy and ability of seamen. Preëminent among them was John Daniel Danells,[2] who arrived at Margarita in 1818 and joined the squadron of Admiral Brión with his brig, the "Inestimable", and the "Mérida" which he had captured from the royalists. He took part in the operations of this squadron off the coast of Cumaná, at La Guaira, and finally in the blockade of Puerto Cabello. For some technical error in his conduct at the battle of Lake Maracaibo, he was tried by court martial, but was asquitted. In 1822 he was sent to the United States

[1] Louis Voigt, who later became a lieutenant colonel of infantry, was in the navy for four years as an aide to Admiral Brión and took part in the operations against Barcelona and Cumaná and on the Magdalena River. Archivo Nacional, Bogotá, Hojas de Servicios, XLVII, 215. In addition to the foregoing *La Nación* (Caracas), Nov. 23, Dec. 1, 8, 9, 1910 also mentions the following less important French naval officers: Capt. Lomine, who came in 1814 and continued in the Colombian navy commanding the Piñeres; Ensign Trillon Trillet, who was wounded at the naval battle of Maracaibo; Ensign Jean M. Au, who also fought under Padilla at that battle and in the siege of Puerto Cabello; and a marine named Curtois who was in the Colombian navy in 1823. *Cf.* also *Gaceta de Colombia*, Oct. 17, 1824. Dr. Alexandre Prospero Reverend also lent important service to the patriot government. After Waterloo he was exiled from France and determined to join the cause of liberty in the new world. On arrival at Santa Marta in 1824 he was appointed by Montilla to the post of medical head of the board of health of that city. When in 1830 Bolívar came there suffering from his last illness, Dr. Reverend was called in to attend him and was present at his deathbed. Scarpetta y Vergara, op. cit., 507; Alejandro Prospero Reverend, *La última enfermedad de Simón Bolívar, passim.*

[2] John Daniel Danells was born in Baltimore in 1786. He began his services to the cause of Spanish-American independence in the navy of the Banda Oriental (at present the Republic of Uruguay), where Artigas gave him the grade of captain of armada in 1817. Archivo Nacional, Caracas, *Ilustres Próceres*, XXIII, 69.

to buy a corvette of war. This ship, which was rechristened the "Bolívar", he presented as a gift to the Republic of Colombia. He also remitted the cost of two brigantines and three schooners furnished by him to the Colombian navy during the blockade of Puerto Cabello, and cancelled the debt due him for munitions which he had supplied for the revolutionists in Margarita in 1818. As a reward for his services he was retired in 1844 with one-third of the salary of a captain in the navy and a bonus of 4,000 " pesos ". He returned to Baltimore, where he died in 1856. His son, Simón Bolívar Daniel Danells, for many years held the post of Venezuelan consul in Baltimore.[1]

It is natural that other Americans should have sought service under their compatriot. Among them were Capt. Joseph C. Swain, who entered the navy in 1822 and was a lieutenant under Capt. Danells at Maracaibo in the last blockade and capture of Puerto Cabello, and under Capt. Beluche in the cruise of the corvette " Bolívar " in 1824, the ship which he himself commanded as a captain in the operations of 1825 and 1826;[2] and Clement " Castell " (Calthell) who came from the United States in 1819 to become captain of a frigate in the Colombian navy, and as commander of the "Aventura Picot " took part in the operations against Cumaná, in the Magdalena campaign and in the battle of Lake Maracaibo.[3] Thomas Severs entered the service as a marine guard on the brig " Vencedor " in the operations against Cumaná.

---

[1] *Ibid.*; Dávila, *Diccionario Biográfico*, I, 110; Azpúrua, *op. cit.*, III, 273-275; Archivo Soublette, Documentos, II, 1822 (folio not numbered); *London Chronicle*, Feb. 1, May 31, Sept. 6, 1822; *Gaceta de Colombia*, Sept. 5, 1824; *Annual Register*, 1823, " History," 244; New York Public Library, MSS. Division, Miscellaneous Papers, William Dawkins, Captain in the British Navy to Commodore Daniel (*sic.*) April 4, 1823.

[2] Archivo Nacional, Bogotá, Guerra y Marina, Hojas de Servicios, XLII, 727.

[3] Galán, *op. cit.*, 21; Scarpetta y Vergara, *op. cit.*, 78.

As an ensign he participated in the blockade of Puerto Cabello and the attack on Rio Hacha. After his promotion to
lieutenant and while in command of the ship " Padilla " he
committed some offense for which he was sentenced to dismissal. This sentence, however, was not executed, and in
1844 he was allowed to retire with one-third of his salary.
He married Antonia Gonisac at Angostura, and six years
later died in the United States. Shortly thereafter his widow
married again, and in 1854 his pension was transferred to
his son.[1]

Following in the footsteps of these earlier sailors from the
United States came some who remained for only a few years
during the war for independence. James Williams joined in
1822 and held the rank of ensign for about six years and a
half, performing his duty in the battle of Lake Maracaibo
and the siege of Puerto Cabello.[2] John M. Doyle in 1825
received his contract and salary as ensign from the consul
general of Colombia in New York. He experienced too
much difficulty in learning to speak Spanish, so left the navy
after two years.[3] In 1824, Lieut. Francis X. Curtis was
assigned to command of the warship "Libertador" stationed
at the port of Angostura, but his record shows no other
duties.[4]

Except for those in the navy [5] and the unfortunates of the

[1] Archivo Nacional, Caracas, Ilustres Próceres, LXXXVI, 202.

[2] Archivo Nacional, Bogotá, Guerra y Marina, Hojas de Servicios,
XLVIII, 728.

[3] Ibid., XII, 802.

[4] *Ibid.*, Historia, CCCLX, 362.

[5] *La Nación*, Oct. 26, Nov. 25, Dec. 9, 1910, notes the following additional names: Capt. Peter Storm, who commanded the schooner " Peacock" at the battle of Lake Maracaibo; Lieut. Marcus Mankin, who
entered the navy at Juan Griego in 1821, and was promoted for gallantry
in action at Lake Maracaibo; and Lieut. James Batle (*sic.*) who was
killed in that same engagement while serving aboard the schooner
" Peacock."

" Leander " expedition, very few Americans shared in the
work of the legionaries. Of those who fought in the
army, data appears to be obtainable only about Alexander
Macaulay and Felix Jastran. The latter began his long
military career in 1813, received a commission as colonel,
and saw hard fighting in the early engagements as well as at
both battles of Carabobo and at Ayacucho.[1] Col. Alexander
Macaulay joined Nariño in New Granada in 1810 and held
the important post of adjutant and inspector general of the
army of the province of Popayán until in 1813 he was taken
prisoner at Pasto and shot by order of viceroy Sámano in
conformity with the normal treatment accorded by both sides
to prisoners taken during the brutal period of " war to the
death ".[2]

In connection with assistance from American sailors and
soldiers, aid in supplies furnished by merchants and contractors of the United States must not be overlooked.
O'Connor relates how " after the capitulation of Cartagena
there soon arrived merchant ships from all parts, principally
from the United States.[3] It will be remembered that among
them was a cargo of arms, clothing and equipment belonging to William Robinson, an American, from whom, after
having them inspected by Col. Adlercreutz, Montilla bought
supplies worth 5,000 " pesos ". In an official test of French
and English muskets supplied by Robinson, thirty-one French
muskets burst and 225 passed the test, whereas twenty-six

[1] *La Nación*, Dec. 8, 1910, Galán, *op. cit.*, 28; Scarpetta y Vergara,
op. cit., 238.

[2] O'Leary, *Correspondencia*, XII, 373, 374; Azpúrua, *op. cit.*, I, 403-
405; Reports by Col. Alexander Macaulay in *Documentos históricos en
Pasto, Publicación oficial*, República de Colombia, Departmento de Nariño,
87-89, 91, 95, 97, 99. Henry M. Brackenridge, *Voyage to Buenos Aires
performed in the year 1817 and 1818 by order of the American government*, 115, n.

[3] O'Connor, *op. cit.*, 58.

of the English muskets burst and 403 passed the test. All the powder proved to be of good quality, and was recommended for acceptance as suitable for service. 500,000 ball cartridges also were furnished under his contract by Robinson.[1]

Three Canadians, moreover, deserve mention. These were John Glenn, John Robertson and James Loedel. The first of the three, born in Montreal, was a merchant in Caracas at the time of the revolution in 1810. After the earthquake he removed to Cartagena, where he became a personal friend of Bolívar and contributed funds to the patriot cause. He was rewarded with a commission as lieutenant colonel and placed in command of the militia of Soledad and Barranquilla. In 1831 he retired from the army and politics and died in 1853.[2] John Robertson entered the British army and rose to the rank of lieutenant colonel. While secretary to the government of Curaçao he was sent as commissioner to Caracas. There he joined the revolution of 1810 and performed duty on the staff of Miranda. After the arrest of his chief, he emigrated to Cartagena and was promoted to the rank of general and " comandante de armas " of that province. In 1815 he returned to Jamaica, where he died at Kingston in 1817 of fever brought on by exposure during the war. In 1845 his widow was granted a pension because her husband had given up an annual salary of £3,000 to serve the Republic of Venezuela. With this pension, however, was attached the condition that she should reside in that country.[3]

Col. James Loedel began his career in Mexico in 1816 as a lieutenant in the first battalion of Cazadores of America in

[1] Archivo Nacional, Bogotá, Guerra y Marina, Historia, XV, 19, 21, 25, 43; Hamilton, *op. cit.*, I, 137.

[2] *Boletín de Historia y Antigüedades*, año VI, No. 70, pp. 640, 641.

[3] Archivo Nacional, Caracas, Ilustres Próceres, LXXV, 311.

the congressional guard of honor. There he took part in various actions under Gen. Mina, was captured by the royalists and confined for three months in the castle of San Juan de Ulúa. In 1820 he managed to reach Colombia and was there commissioned a captain in the Girardot Battalion. That year he took part in the capture of Santa Marta and next year won special distinction in the siege of Cartagena.[1]

Of all the Germans among the legionaries the Hanoverians were the most important, and of the Hanoverians Col. Johannes Uslar was the best known. Since so much has already been said about him, it remains only to relate his career after 1823, when he retired from active service to marry Dolores Hernández of Valencia. In 1830 he was granted retired pay at one-third the salary of his rank, and two years later became a naturalized citizen of Venezuela. He began farming near the field of Carabobo, and was so successful that his sugar-plantation " Alto Uslar " became known throughout all Venezuela. From time to time he was recalled to active service to perform the duties of military commander of the neighboring city of Valencia. In 1853 he was promoted brigadier general, the next year major general and in 1863 general-in-chief. On April 1, 1866, Gen. Uslar died at Valencia at the age of eighty-seven. His widow received a pension. In spite of his long residence in Venezuela, Gen. Uslar never learned to speak Spanish fluently.[2] It will be recalled also that when Uslar was recruiting in Hamburg he was assisted by von Clauditz. This officer came to Venezuela as a captain, was assigned to the

[1] Archivo Nacional, Bogotá, Guerra y Marina, Historia, XXVII, 485; Hojas de Servicios, XXV, 742.

[2] Archivo Nacional, Caracas, Ilustres Próceres, XCIV, 306; *Exposición al Congreso de Venezuela que dirige el Secretario de Guerra y Marina*, 1833, pp. 62-63; Carlos Schoffer, " Los Alemanes en Venezuela " in *Süd-u-Mittel Amerika* (Berlin), translated and reprinted in *El Universal* (Caracas), June 12, 1911; *El Luchador* (Caracas), May 10, 1912.

Albion Battalion, and on May 31, 1820, was promoted to sergeant major of that organization.[1]

Next to Gen. Uslar the most important Hanoverian was Baron Friedrich von Eben who contracted with López Méndez for a Venezuelan commission and sailed from Hamburg Feb. 26, 1820. Arrived at Angostura, he placed himself under the protection of the Liberator who received him as a volunteer staff officer. In spite of its previous declaration that it would not admit to the army any more foreign officers except in the lowest grades, the Venezuelan congress passed a special act authorizing the admission of Baron von Eben at whatever rank Bolívar might be pleased to give him. In 1825 his appointment as brigadier general was confirmed by the congress, and in the following year he took command of a brigade operating before Popayán.[2] A fellow countryman, Karl Richard, also experienced difficulty in obtaining confirmation of his rank, but on the recommendation of Sucre was made a major.[3]

Gen. J. A. von Reinboldt, a Hanoverian by birth, had formerly been in the British service. He joined the patriot army as a major and was highly valued for his efficiency as an officer. In 1823 he was stationed at Cartagena as a colonel in command of a battalion of sharpshooters with which he had several times distinguished himself in action against the Goajira Indians near Santa Marta. Eventually he attained the rank of brigadier general. In 1824 he was naturalized as a citizen of Colombia.[4]

[1] Archivo Nacional, Bogotá, Guerra y Marina, Historia, I, 657-659; Registro General de Jefes, No. 251; *El Luchador*, May 10, 1912.

[2] Archivo Nacional, Bogotá, Guerra y Marina, Historia, VI, 380, 384, 386, 387, 388; XVI, 911; XXV, 862.

[3] Richard, *op. cit.*, 196, 201, 268, 269; Bingham Collection of Mss., Sucre Letters, No. 1848, William White to Sucre, May 5, 1820.

[4] Archivo Nacional, Bogotá, Guerra y Marina, Hojas de Servicios, XXXVI, 510; *El Colombiano*, Jan. 12, 1825; *Recollections of Service*, I, 183; Hamilton, *op. cit.*, I, 25.

Thomas Boysen, another Hanoverian, joined the Colombian navy in 1819 and held the rank of lieutenant for nine years and eight months, during which time he was captured by a Spanish ship and held as a prisoner of war for a few weeks.[1] Capt. Otto Trittan (Fritan) came from Hamburg and served for eight years and a half in the Rifles and Carabobo Battalions, taking part in the battle of Carabobo, the expedition of Santa Marta, the defense of Maracaibo, the campaign of Coro and the siege of Puerto Cabello.[2] Still living in Panamá in 1869 was Karl Wilhelm who landed at Angostura in March, 1818 as an officer of Wilson's Red Hussars. Wilhelm passed practically all his military career under Páez, whose aide-de-camp he was until after the capture of Puerto Cabello, when he was sent to Bogotá with the official report of the victory. There Vice-President Santander took a fancy to him and appointed Wilhelm his aide-de-camp.[3]

Another German who did not come with Uslar was Capt. Philip Sibel (or Seybold) who was in Hippisley's Hussars in 1818. He fought under Páez on the Apure in 1819 and under Bolívar in the campaign into New Granada. He was then transferred to the squadron of dragoons of the south.[4] Normally Col. Friedrich Rasch was likewise a cavalryman, but he became an infantryman for a while in 1822 when he was transferred to the Albion Battalion. His commanding officer, Col. Thomas Manby, certified to his gallantry in saving the life of Sucre at Guachi and to his promotion for bravery in the action of La Plata. After Ayacucho Col.

---

[1] Archivo Nacional, Bogotá, Guerra y Marina, Hojas de Servicios, IV, 920.

[2] *Ibid.*, XLIV, 365.

[3] *Ibid.*, XLVII, 742.

[4] Archivo Nacional, Caracas, Ilustres Próceres (not yet filed or numbered), Carlos Schoffer, *op. cit.*, in *El Universal*, June 12, 1911.

Rasch took part in the siege of Callao and in 1838 became military commandant at Cartagena. His total period of military service to Sept. 17, 1831, was nineteen years, four months and eighteen days.[1] In the artillery was found Capt. Adolf Klinger, who it will be remembered, commanded the arsenal as well as the artillery depot at Quito, and performed the prosaic but essential duty of keeping in repair the arms of the troops in campaign in the south.[2]

Gen. Philipp Braun was one of those who drifted to South America independently from the West Indies. Andrade[3] calls him English, but O'Connor[4] says he was a native of Germany. The spelling of the surname and the fact that O'Connor knew Braun personally lend weight to the latter statement. Wherever he came from, Braun as a young man settled in Santo Domingo whence he joined the Colombian patriots. He became a sergeant major of the Voltígero Battalion in which were incorporated some of the officers and men of the Isthmian Battalion raised by O'Connor. During the march to Quito, it was only through the urgent interposition of O'Connor with Sucre that Braun was saved from being shot as punishment for some disobedience, or as it was proved later, some serious misunderstanding of orders. This incident was soon forgotten by his superiors, and for his valor at Junín Braun was rewarded by promotion to the rank of lieutenant colonel and given command of the mounted grenadiers. After the founding of the new Re-

[1] Archivo Nacional, Bogotá, Guerra y Marina, Historia, XIII, 303; XXVII, 537; Hojas de Servicios, XL, 975, 978; O'Leary, *Documentos,* XIX, 198.

[2] Archivo Nacional, Bogotá, Guerra y Marina, Historia, XLVII, 459, 478, 723, 740; XXVI, 805, 837, 845, 852; Bingham Collection of Mss.; *Sucre Papers,* Nos. 1015-18. *Cf.* p. 280, n. 2.

[3] *Próceres de la independencia,* 63.

[4] *Op. cit.,* 121.

public of Bolivia he was commissioned colonel and later general in the army of that nation. Such was the influence which he still retained over his battalion of Voltígeros that when it revolted under the leadership of Sergeant José Guerra on Christmas night, 1827, Col. Braun was able, single-handed, to arrest the ringleader and to persuade the men to return to their duty. At the battle of Socabaya he contributed so much to the victory that President Santa Cruz issued a bulletin in which he declared that Gen. Braun had comported himself in a manner worthy of his lifelong reputation. In 1839 Gen. Braun was assassinated by a compatriot at La Paz.[1]

The reader will recall how Major Freudenthal commanded the assault on Fort Agua Santa and later marched with the Rifles Battalion to the port of Buenaventura to board ship for the campaign of Peru. The name of Lieut. Karl Conrad, also of that battalion, is not so well known; for apparently the only record which he has left behind to transmit his history is a letter complaining that he had not received any salary since he left Bogotá under the command of Major Freudenthal six months before.[2]

[1] O'Connor, *op. cit.*, 43, 96, 97, 99, 132, 285, 325, 352, 405; Andrade, *op. cit.*, 63; Bingham Collection of Mss., Sucre Papers, Nos. 1242, 1526, Felipe Braun to Sucre, Jan. 30, March 16, 1824; Josè Domingo Cortés, *Galería de hombres célebres de Bolivia*, 74, 75, 109; Moderate Omiste, *Historia de Bolivia*, 31; Scarpetta y Vergara, *op. cit.*, 57.

[2] Archivo Nacional, Bogotá, Guerra y Marina, Historia, XVI, 942; XXXV, 856. Also in the Rifles Battalion were seven Germans who in 1819 received commissions as sub-lieutenants. These were Wilhelm Franklin, Johannes Meyers, Moritz Rietzen, Mons Larson (*sic*), August Zinkernagle, Wilhelm Schzacks (*sic*) and Karl Minnecke. *Ibid.*, Registro General de Jefes, No. 255. In the Boyacá Battalion at Valencia in 1821 as adjutant to Col. Flegel was Sub-lieutenant Gregor Schmeider. *Ibid.*, Historia, VII, 56. *La Nación*, Dec. 1, 8, 1910, mentions likewise that there were two German captains, Henrich Meyer and Otto Joithan, a Hamburger, who took part in the campaigns of the east of Venezuela in 1819, of Carabobo in 1821 and of Coro in 1822 to 1823; and that in

Noteworthy among the Germans who had come from La Plata and Chile with San Martín's army to cooperate in the liberation of Peru were two colonels who ended their careers with tragedy. These men were Clement Althaus and Friedrich Bransen. Of the former O'Connor speaks highly, calling him " one of the most distinguished and meritorious generals of Peru ",[1] and of the latter San Martín said " he was brave, intelligent, well educated, a gentleman in every sense and well known in danger ".[2] Col. Althaus was chief of engineers in the army of Peru but was captured near Cuzco by the royalists; so witnessed the battle of Ayacucho from the heights of Condorcanqui as a prisoner of war in Cantérac's army. This victory secured his own release, but later, while in command of the ship "Asia" he assisted Gen. Castilla, a prisoner of war to escape to Arequipa. For this President Santa Cruz imprisoned Col. Althaus, who fell ill, pined away and died within a few days.[3] Col. Brandsen espoused the faction of Riva Agüero, the rebel ex-president of Peru, after having given his word of honor not to do so.

the navy was Jacob Kreidlein, who joined in the early days of the expedition from Aux Cayes, served under Admiral Brión and until the end of the war, performing important duties at Puerto Cabello and in cruises to Porto Rico and to North America. For Kreidlein's record of service see also Archivo Nacional, Bogotá, Guerra y Marina, Hojas des Servicios, XXIV, 413. On December 31, 1831, Thomas Reber, another German, was a first lieutenant and adjutant in the Sixth Battalion of Militia. At that date he had already had a total service of twelve years, eleven months and twenty-three days. He had disembarked at Angostura in the detachment under Col. Elsam. After that he had served in the Albion and Santander Battalions and in the first battalion of reserves. He had taken part in the campaigns of the Apure, New Granada, and the south. He had fought also at Pántano de Vargas, Boyacá, la Plata, Pitayó and Jenoi. Hojas de Servicios, XXXVIII, 137.

[1] *Op. cit.*, 95.

[2] O'Leary, *Documentos*, XX, 249.

[3] O'Connor, *op. cit.*, 128, 337; Miller, *op. cit.*, II, 178.

He was tried by court martial, found guilty and sentenced to dismissal and to exclusion from ever holding any other public office in the country.[1]

With Uslar in the Hanoverian Legion came Ludwig Flegel, a Pole who, it will be remembered, later distinguished himself at Carabobo and became lieutenant colonel in command of the Boyacá Battalion. In 1822 he married Ursula de Liendo at Caracas, and retired to devote himself to the cultivation of his two haciendas, " Cabeza de Tigre " on the Petare and " La Vega " at Ocumare. Eleven years later he died at Caracas but his widow received no pension.[2] Another Pole who was generally regarded as a German was Gen. Philip Maurice Martin, whose birthplace is sometimes attributed to Warsaw and sometimes even to Scotland. He had served as a naval sub-lieutenant with Nelson on the " Victory " at Trafalgar. He had then joined Miranda's expedition in 1806, had won a reputation for valor in the early campaign, and had continued serving under Bolívar until he retired in 1823. He was generously treated by the Liberator, who gave him a farm. He prospered financially and settled in Colombia, but never took part in any of the subsequent civil wars for, he said, he came to serve the cause of independence, not the hatred of brother agianst brother.[3]

Two other Poles were Ferdinand Sirakowski and John de Brigard. The former, as a captain, commanded the second company of Hussars of the Guard at Bogotá in 1822 and

[1] O'Leary, *Documentos*, XXIII, 27; *Correspondencia de extranjeros notables*, II, 164; Federico de Brandsen, *Escritos del coronel don Federico de Brandsen*, 15.

[2] Archivo Nacional, Bogotá, Guerra y Marina, Historia, VI, 883; VII, 52, XVI, 721, 735; *Archivo Soublette, Documentos*, 1822, III (folio not numbered); Dávila, *Diccionario biográfico*, I, 152; Schoffer, *op. cit.*, *El Universal*, June 12, 1911.

[3] Archivo Nacional, Bogotá, Guerra y Marina, Historia, VII, 242; Hippisley, *op. cit.*, 468; Baraya, *op. cit.*, II, 71; Franco, *op. cit.*, 25.

later in the south, but after his promotion to lieutenant colonel he was recommended for detached service in purchasing munitions in the West Indies. While stationed at Bogotá he had asked permission to marry, since he " had pledged himself publicly to María Infanta Rusiano ". As to whether he was permitted to keep his pledge, the records appear to contain no further information.[1] John de Brigard came in 1818, served through the campaigns of Venezuela, Magdalena and the south, and in 1824 retired because of poor health. He settled in Colombia and founded a family which is still living in Bogotá. The present representative of this family is Emilio de Brigard Órtiz who is a priest in the capital.[2]

The only Swedish member was an officer whose technical knowledge was of immense importance to the independent army in the branches of both engineering and ordnance. This was Count Frederick de Adlercreutz, who belonged to a wealthy and distinguished family. It is not clear exactly when he came to South America; but in 1821 he was present at the siege of Cartagena under Montilla, who was so favorably impressed with his knowledge of engineering that he entrusted to him the duty of planning the land operations. It was he also who supervised the tests of the muskets furnished under contract by the American merchant, Robinson. He then commanded a column in the attack on Santa Marta and later, as military commander of Mompox, performed notable services for the government. For part of the time he held the rank of lieutenant colonel in the cavalry and for the remainder was an officer of engineers. After the break-up of the Republic of Great Colombia, Count

[1] Archivo Nacional, Bogotá, Guerra y Marina, Historia, X, 723; XXXV, 909; DCCLXXIX, 739, 822, 855.

[2] Archivo Nacional, Bogotá, Guerra y Marina, Hojas de Servicios, V, 628; Scarpetta y Vergara, *op. cit.*, 64.

de Adlercreutz remained loyal to Bolívar, as did most of the foreign officers who had continued in the army after the end of the war, and like them suffered from the misfortunes which befell the followers of the Liberator. So impoverished did he become that on his return to London he was compelled to appeal for help to the Swedish minister in that city.[1]

Three Hollanders furthermore may be mentioned. George Henriquez arrived in 1820 and saw service as a lieutenant in the campaigns of the Magdalena and of the south, taking part in the battles of Ciénaga de Santa Marta, Yaguachi and Pichincha.[2] Henry Samuel (or perhaps the name should be Samuel Henriquez as O'Leary writes it) joined in 1817, was appointed captain and adjutant, and continued in the army until 1822 when he retired for disability.[3] Charles Ludovico, arriving in 1812, became a sergeant major and fought in most of the early battles as well as in those of the campaign of the south.[4]

Two officers came from Curaçao at such an early date

[1] Archivo Nacional, Bogotá, Guerra y Marina, Historia, XV, 17, 23; *Boletín de Historia y Antigüedades*, año I, No. 6, p. 280; O'Connor, *op. cit.*, 45, 46, 57.

[2] Galán, *op. cit.*, 28.

[3] *La Nación* (Caracas), Dec. 8, 1910; O'Leary, *Documentos*, XIX, 382.

[4] *La Nación*, Oct. 26, 1910. Scarpetta y Vergara, *op. cit.*, 277, states that Charles Ludovico was born on the island of Curaçao. Some lists contain the names of two Russians, about whom however little information seems to be available. *La Nación*, Dec. 8, 1910 states that one of them, named John Mayer, entered the army as an ensign in 1818 and saw action in Venezuela as well as at Gameza, Pántano de Vargas, Boyacá, Pitayó and Jenoi in New Granada. *Cf.* also Scarpetta y Vergara, *op. cit.*, 305. Andrade, *op. cit.*, 241 records that the other Russian, Lt. Col. Juan Teópilo Minuth made the campaign of 1822; *cf.* also Scarpetta y Vergara, *op. cit.*, 330, which credits Minuth likewise with presence at the siege of Cartagena, the occupation of the Isthmus of Panama in 1822-23, the campaign of Maracaibo and the campaign of the south.

and played such an important role in the revolution that they were generally considered Venezuelans. It is true that this Dutch island lay so close to the coast that the commercial interests of its inhabitants had become almost identical with those of the Venezuelans, yet as the islanders were born under a flag other than that of Spain they were actually foreigners and cannot be omitted from consideration as legionaries even if they were not looked upon as such by the foreigners from Europe. One of these natives of Curaçao was Manuel Piar, who joined Miranda in 1810, and as a general led the armies of Venezuela on many a hard-fought field during the early days of discouragement. The credit of the capture of Angostura and the expulsion of the royalists from Guayana is largely his. In spite, however, of the importance of his services, he was accused of treason, convicted and sentenced to death. The circumstances of the case were such that Bolívar evidently felt it his duty to resist all appeals for clemency and ordered the sentence to be carried into execution.[1]

Probably the man from Curaçao on whom Bolívar placed the greatest confidence and whose services he valued the most highly was the other resident, Pedro Luís Brión. Born in 1782, he studied at Amsterdam, and at the early age of seventeen distinguished himself for bravery in the defense of northern Holland against the English and Russians. His father died leaving him a fortune which necessitated his return to Curaçao. He was then sent by his brother-in-law to New York, where he was engaged in the study of nautical science until he reached the age of twenty-one. In 1804 and 1805 he gained distinction in the defense of his native island against the English, and for several years prospered as a merchant.[2]

[1] Robinson, *op. cit.*, 99; O'Leary, *Narración*, I, 427; *Documentos*, XV, 421-423.

[2] Henry de Sola, *Biografía del Almirante Brión*, 9, 10, 11.

In 1815 Brión joined the Venezuelan revolutionists who were gathering at Aux Cayes. It was he who nominated Bolívar as general-in-chief of the proposed expedition, supporting him against the other candidates, Mariño, Piar and Bermúdez. Brión's word had considerable weight in the conference, for in addition to his personal services he offered guns, munitions and money to support the revolution, and at his own expense fitted out a ship for the patriots. On March 30, 1816, when the expedition sailed from Haiti to Margarita with 250 men and muskets for 6,000 more, he accompanied it as admiral of the fleet. In the operations culminating in the capture of Angostura, Admiral Brión commanded a squadron of five brigs and two schooners. During the same year he scouted the Antilles for war-supplies and recruits, bringing them to Angostura to enrich the patriot cause. In pursuance of these operations he attacked Spanish merchantmen wherever he found them on the high seas and carried so many of them as prizes into Juan Griego on the island of Margarita, that twelve and a half per cent of their value was said to have been enough to defray the expenses of keeping the British and Irish Legions on the island and of outfitting them for their campaigns against Barcelona and Rio Hacha. If this was the case, Brión was evidently the chief supporter of these legions during their first two years of suffering. That his liberality was not appreciated by the recipients is evident from the fact that few if any of them have been able to write anything but evil of him.[1]

During the expedition to Rio Hacha Montilla quarrelled with Brión and deprived him of his title of admiral. Two years later Brión went to Bogotá and tried in vain to secure reimbursement for the sums he had advanced from his own

[1] *Cf.* the works by Hippisley, Brown, Hackett, Adam and Chesterton frequently cited, *supra*.

private purse for the support of the revolution. He then returned to Curaçao where he died on Sept. 27, 1821.[1] Brión's liberality indeed in devoting himself and his fortune to assist foreigners in gaining their liberty recalls the help furnished by Lafayette to the American colonists during their revolution.

From Haiti came Marceline Guillot, who accompanied McGregor in his expedition of 1817 against Amelia Island. In 1822 he took service in the Republic of Colombia for the operations about Maracaibo. He was appointed military commander of Ciénaga by the governor of Santa Marta, and two years later was sent to organize and discipline the militia of Neiva, where he remained until after the end of the war. His total service in the army was over thirteen years, a time during which he attained the rank of lieutenant colonel.[2]

Italy also sent a group of its sons to aid the spread of liberty. Unfortunately the careers of two of them were far from creditable. Mention has already been made of Capt. Jenaro Montbrune who was chief of staff of the division in Guayana, whom Hippisley characterized as a " consummate rascal ", and who was dismissed from the army. Later,

[1] de Sola, *op. cit.*, 12, 13, 16, 21, 25, 26; *Boletín de la Academia Nacional de Historia*, Caracas, Apr. 30, 1917, IV, 204, 205; *The Times*, Sept. 12, 1820; New York Public Library, Mss. Division, Miscellaneous Papers, Luís Brión to Peter Wirgman, March 3, 1819.

[2] Archivo Nacional, Bogotá, Guerra y Marina, Hojas de Servicios, XIX, 977. Among other inhabitants of the West Indies, *La Nación*, Nov. 30, Dec. 1, 8, 9, 1910 lists three Dominicans and three Cubans. The former were Lieut. Bernardo Bocanegra, who fought in the campaigns of Magdalena and Maracaibo; Capt. Sarmiento Raimundo Rendón, who served in Venezuela from 1810 to the fall of Puerto Cabello; and José Ramón Cabral, who was chief of staff to Gen. Bermúdez. The Cubans were Col. Miguel Troncoso, who came in 1810 to New Granada and followed Bolívar in his march over the mountains into Venezuela; Sergt. Major José Ignacio Grau, who fought at Carabobo and Puerto Cabello; and Col. José Rafael Heras, who died heroically at the taking of Maracaibo.

however, he rejoined as a volunteer in the division of Monagas and remained until after the capture of Maracaibo in which he took part. He was mentioned for distinguished conduct at the battle of Centaura in 1819 and at the naval action off the port of Notre, Margarita Island in 1816.[1]

In the early days of the revolution, when Bolívar was defending Puerto Cabello, he appointed an Italian named Bignoni to command the castle which was the key to the position. Bignoni betrayed his trust and opened the castle to the royalist troops under Monteverde whom he joined. After the battle of Boyacá, when the prisoners of war were brought before him, Bolívar recognized among them his former subordinate, and ordered the traitor to be hanged.[2]

It is more pleasant to turn to the careers of three Italian naval officers, Giuseppe Russián (*sic*), Giuseppe Raffetti, and Babastro. The last named commanded a division of large ships blockading Cartagena when Montilla was besieging that city from the land side.[3] Raffetti was recommissioned as a frigate lieutenant in the navy, after having lost his original commission when he was wounded in the hand in which he was carrying it. He was then ordered to scour the seas as a privateer with the schooner " Buytre ".[4] Russián entered the republican navy in 1816 and held the rank of frigate lieutenant in the squadron under Joli. He was put ashore on Margarita Island to recover from illness and while there married Ana Flex. In 1832 he was naturalized as a citizen and in 1848 was recalled to service, but took sick and died at Carúpano. His widow was granted a pension in 1864.[5]

---

[1] Archivo Nacional, Caracas, Gobernación de Guayana, VII, 86; Hippisley, *op. cit.*, 437, 446; Archivo Nacional, Bogotá, Hojas de Servicios, XXX, 247, 248.

[2] López, *op. cit.*, 16; O'Leary, *Narración*, I, 575.

[3] Baralt y Díaz, *op. cit.*, II, 12.

[4] Archivo Nacional, Bogotá, Guerra y Marina, Historia, VI, 48, 49.

[5] Archivo Nacional, Caracas, Ilustres Próceres, LXXII, 119.

In the army Custodio Ripoll became a sub-lieutenant of infantry in 1821 and was still in service with that rank in 1830.[1] Lieut. Col. Manfredo Bertolazzi (or Berzolari) was chief of staff of the patriot army at Rincón de los Toros in 1818, when he was taken prisoner and shot by the royalists.[2] Lieut. Col. Pasini (Passoni or Pasioni) held the post of adjutant general during the campaign of Venezuela in 1817-1818. He was highly respected and esteemed for his valor. Unfortunately his services were lost to the patriots when he was killed at the battle of Sombrero.[3] Capt. Carlos Caballi joined Miranda in 1812, but within a year was wounded in the hand at Victoria, again three times wounded at Cerrito Blanco and finally captured at Barquisimeto. He managed to escape the fate usually meted out to prisoners of war during the period of " war to the death ", and to obtain his release in time to rejoin the patriot army after the battle of Jenoi.[4]

Preëminent among all the Italians, both for his abilities and for the value of his services, was Agostino Codazzi.[3]

[1] Archivo Nacional, Bogotá, Guerra y Marina, Historia, VII, 66.

[2] *La Nación* (Caracas), Nov. 30, 1910.

[3] O'Leary, *Narración*, I, 449, 450. In his report on the battle of Sombrero, Lieut. Col. Bertolazzi said of his compatriot, "Adjutant General Passoni was well thought of throughout the army. Wherever there was danger he was there at the head of his guerrillas, mounted on his horse and conspicuous with all the decorations of his rank. He made himself a target for the enemy. Pierced by a bullet, he met the death of a brave man." O'Leary, *Documentos*, XV, 612.

[4] Scarpetta y Vergara, *op. cit.*, 72.

[5] Agostino (Giovanni Batista) Codazzi was born at Lugo, Italy, studied in the military school founded at Bologna by the French, and continued his military education in the Academy of Pavia. He was admitted to the Regiment of Horse Artillery of Bologna, and as an officer took part in the battles of Lützen, Bautzen, Culm, Dresden and Leipzig in 1813. At the battle of Mantua he was on the staff of Armandi. In 1814, because of the dissolution of the French army he joined the Italian Legion in the army of Beauharnais, as a lieutenant of artillery. Herman Albert Shumacher, *Biografía del Gral. Agostino Codazzi*, 5, 6.

In 1817 Codazzi and Constantino Ferrari, who were in Baltimore at the time, joined Gen. Villaret who was there seeking recruits for the Venezuelan navy. The two young Italians were shipped on the " América Libre " under Capt. Charles Barnard with orders to report to Admiral Brión's fleet in the West Indies. Instead of obeying orders, Capt. Barnard joined Commodore Aury in besieging Amelia Island, and Codazzi, who had been entrusted with the direction of the attack, was thereupon appointed a lieutenant in Aury's squadron. The ship " Mercury ", on which Codazzi was an officer, was detached by Aury to join the squadron of Admiral Brión, which was at that time scouting the Antilles and protecting the disembarkation of the foreign legionaries. While on this duty, Codazzi found himself at Angostura and at other places along the Orinoco where he met many of the British officers. In 1818, he was promoted to captain and next year to sergeant major for his skill in directing attacks on Forts Santa Catalina on the island of Old Providence and San Felipe at the entrance to the Gulf of Dulce in the Captaincy General of Guatemala.

After the battle of Boyacá, Aury took his squadron to the Gulf of Darien and sent Codazzi, who had become his aide-de-camp to offer his support to Bolívar. Major Codazzi with great perseverance made his way up the Atrato and Quibdó Rivers in a canoe and finally reached Bogotá, after having overcome the almost insuperable obstacles of the journey. Bolívar, as will be remembered, refused to accept the services of Aury because he did not approve of his privateering operations and because of the latter's hostility to Brión. Codazzi, however, was recognized and in 1820 was promoted to lieutenant colonel " for his great and good services and devotion to the cause of independence ". In spite of the prospects of advancement, he soon became homesick and returned to Italy, where in 1823 he bought a farm and settled down apparently to a life of " peace and oblivion ".[1]

Codazzi, however, could not stand the inactivity for more than three years; hence in 1826 he returned to Colombia, where he was reinstated in the army with the rank of colonel of artillery. Bolívar admitted him to the Order of Liberators, treating his services as continuous since 1818 and his absence in Italy as leave. Assigned to duty as chief of artillery at Maracaibo, he began there his valuable work as a geographer by surveying the shores of the lake and the mountainous regions of Trujillo and Merida. The value of accurate maps for fostering agriculture was recognized by Páez, then president of Venezuela, who showed his appreciation of this work by appointing Codazzi chief of the general staff of the army. In a similar manner was completed the survey of the province of Coro. In 1849 by a decree of the congress of New Granada, Codazzi was appointed a lieutenant colonel of the corps of engineers in the army of that republic, for the purpose of preparing plans for a trans-isthmian railway, and for a national military college. The latter was successfully founded with Codazzi as its first director, the plans for the railway were completed with his usual skill, and then he turned his efforts toward a topographical survey of New Granada. In 1854 his completed work was presented to the secretary of state.[2]

This survey covered the eight provinces of Ocaña, Pamplona, Santander, Socorro, Soto, Tundamo, Tunja and Vélez, including 187 rivers and almost continuous mountain chains. It comprised four volumes of description, with a set of maps of each of the provinces named. This monumental work was

[1] Shumacher, *op. cit.*, 3, 7, 8, 11, 17-19, 21, 22-28; Archivo Nacional, Bogotá, Guerra y Marina, Historia, VI, 430-439.

[2] Shumacher, *op. cit.*, 30, 31, 33, 38, 42-45, 51, 119; Dávila, *Diccionario Biográfico*, I, 92.

considered of such value that the congress awarded its author a new contract with an annual salary of 4800 " pesos ". In addition to this geography of New Granada, other works of Codazzi were his *Resúmen de la Geografía de Venezuela,* his *Atlas Físico y Político de la República de Venezuela,* both published at Paris in 1841, his *Projecto de poblar con las razas teutónicas los terrenos altos y hasta ahora incultos de Venezuela,* brought out at Caracas in 1842, and his *Esposición que dirige a la H. Diputación Provincial en su reunión ordinaria de 1846 el Gobernador de Barinas, Coronel Augustin Codazzi,* issued also at Caracas in 1846.[1]

Codazzi reported against the feasibility of the Atrato River route and in favor of the Panamá-Colón Canal route. In 1852 he was promoted colonel of engineers, and two years later a general on the general staff in the army of New Granada. On February 7, 1859, while engaged in a surveying expedition in the Valle de Upar he died at the age of seventy-seven.[2] Codazzi's military career during the war for independence was not particularly noteworthy; but his subsequent services in exploring and mapping Venezuela and New Granada have been of outstanding importance, not only to those two republics but to the whole world as well.

[1] Shumacher, *op. cit.,* 125, 147, 161; Manuel Segundo Sánchez, *Bibliografía Venezolanista,* 58. The map in this book is based largely on Codazzi's *Atlas Físico y Político de la República de Venezuela.*

[2] Shumacher, *op. cit.,* 165, 189, 225, 243.

CHAPTER XIV

What the Legionaries Signified

OPINIONS as to the significance of the foreign legionaries for the liberation of Spanish South America vary somewhat with the nationality of the writers. In general histories of the South American countries, written in English, a wrong impression is frequently produced by saying too little about the Legion, and by introducing this little in such a way as to convey the idea that much more could have been said, but that the exploits of the Foreign Legion are too well known to require further elucidation. As a matter of fact, they are so little known that the reader receives only a vague and exaggerated conception. British writers, on the other hand, like Koebel and Mulhall, who have dealt at all specifically with the subject extol at length the achievements of their countrymen.[1] Books and articles by Englishmen also, which treat of the wars for Spanish-American independence, lay much the same stress. Temperley, for example, writes: "The English Legion was a veritable Old Guard of Bolívar's motley forces."[2] Petre in his preface assigns the credit for the victories of Boyacá and Carabobo mainly to the valor of the British, and continues: " even in Ayacucho English officers played a leading part ".[3] The few officers of that nationality present at Ayacucho undoubtedly did their duty;

[1] *Cf.* William Henry Koebel, *British Exploits in South America*; Michael George Mulhall, *The English in South America*.

[2] H. W. V. Temperley, *Life of Canning*, 175.

[3] Petre, *op. cit.*, vii.

but in point of fact no one other than Miller and O'Connor (an Irishman) played a leading part.

The accounts by contemporary English travelers in South America would naturally be tinged with pride in the exploits of their countrymen; hence it is not surprising to find Stewart writing that during the administration of Bolívar, the English were in high favor;[1] Edmund Temple, that "Great Britain is the only nation in Europe whose principles and friendship have produced in South America an uninterrupted predilection in its favor";[2] and in one of the anonymous works, the statement that a number of experienced English and Irish officers who accompanied or followed the troops were an invaluable acquisition to the patriots.[3] The *London Chronicle* declared that the arrival of the English troops had " created a much greater and more general confidence in the result of the contest than could possibly have existed previously ",[4] and the *Annual Register* announced that Bolívar made his plans for the campaign into New Granada only after he had received a very important accession of force principally from the arrival of English troops.[5] Even O'Leary could not refrain from rejoicing that " the valor of these troops (Gen. English's British Legion) often turned the balance in favor of victory ".[6]

Naturally Spanish-American historians prefer to assign most of the glory to their own leaders; yet they have almost without exception gone out of their way to express their gratitude for the help which came from abroad. These

[1] Stewart, *op. cit.*, 95.

[2] Edmund Temple, *Travels in various parts of Peru; including a year's residence in Lima*, 237.

[3] *View of South America*, 99.

[4] *July 5, 1819.*

[5] 1819, " General History," 242.

[6] *Narración*, I, 522.

writers have been remarkably fair in the matter and have generously given to the foreigners all the credit that they could possibly deserve.[1]

In attempting to weigh the importance of the services of the legionaries it will become at once apparent that the careers of the various individuals were of unequal value. Some of them were mere adventurers who acted entirely for their own interests and did more harm than good to the South American revolutionists. McGregor and D'Evereux were such, and Henry Wilson was even worse, for he was also a traitor. McDonald was not as bad as the others, for he had less ability and was therefore less dangerous, and English was not as bad because he died early enough to prevent his committing more serious blunders.

Many of those who came with the contingents of 1817 and 1819 were triflers, who by their incessant quarrels and complaints injured themselves and the nation from which they had come more than the cause which they had pledged themselves to serve. Forgetting this pledge, men of that stamp abandoned their commands and returned home to spread their calumnies against Bolívar and the patriot officers and men, who for a short time had been their brothers in arms. Chief among these will be recognized the Hippisleys (father and son), Hackett, Brown, Chesterton and Ducoudray-Holstein.

On the other hand, there were many who remained to the end of the war and did splendid work in organizing and commanding battalions of natives as well as of their fellow Europeans. Arthur Sandes, brave but easy-going comman-

---

[1] *Cf.* Lecuna, *op. cit.*; Level, *op. cit.*; Restrepo, *op. cit.*, Santana, *op. cit.*; Cortés Vargas, *op. cit.*; Negret, *op. cit.*, Posada, *op. cit.*, Galán, *op. cit.* Bolívar was reported to have said that Restrepo in his *Historia de Colombia* was too unjust to certain foreigners, especially to Serviez and McGregor, who certainly should not be reproached with lack of valor. Perú de Lacroix, *op. cit.*, 199.

der of the Rifles, was one of these. Johannes Uslar, who imparted such superb discipline to the Grenadiers, was another. John Mackintosh, the last leader of the Albions, was a third, and in the navy there were John Illingworth and John Daniel Danells, the latter of whom did much to convert the privateering fleets of Brión and Aury into a real navy. James Rooke and Thomas Ferriar are two heroes whose laurels will never fade, and whose names were honored above the rest because they gave their lives so gallantly in battle. The engineering knowledge of Adlercreutz and Hall was of inestimable value in an army where such skill was scarce. As aides to Bolívar and Sucre, O'Leary and O'Connor exerted a happy influence; and on the staff of Páez, Woodberry performed duties of almost equal importance. As examples of heroic devotion and self-sacrificing loyalty to their chief, the characters of William Ferguson and Belford Hinton Wilson shine resplendent. Then too, after independence had been won, Generals Weir, Wright, Manby and Codazzi devoted the remainder of their lives to the service of their adopted country.

Having such a variety of individuals to deal with, some mode of classification must be adopted before the true significance of the legionaries can be estimated. A prominent Venezuelan historian[1] groups the foreigners as follows:

---

[1] For this classification the writer is indebted to Dr. Vicente Lecuna of Caracas, who gave it to him in the course of conversation about the importance of the Foreign Legion. As far as the present writer is aware, it has never been published in the form given, but the conclusion which Dr. Lecuna intended to convey is stated in that historian's *Papeles de Bolívar*, 12, n.: "The best troops in the world can accomplish nothing, unless they are well led. With Bolívar at Pántano de Vargas and Carabobo the English were invincible; but they broke shamefully on other occasions, even when they were led by their own officers, as at Barcelona, Cumaná, the province of Santa Marta and Porto Bello. Also it may be observed that those English officers who held high rank in the wars of independence and later civil wars, did not accomplish any notable results."

first, various expeditions that came to Angostura and the Apure, from which the Albion Battalion went to fight at Boyacá, the British Legion at Carabobo and the Rifles at Bomboná and Ayacucho, all these serving directly under the command of Bolívar; second, the sailors, American, French, Italian and Dutch; third, the men who accompanied Urdaneta from Margarita to Barcelona, Cumaná and Maturín; and fourth, those in the train of Montilla from Margarita to Santa Marta and Cartagena. The services of the third and fourth of these groups he considers futile.

While this classification is valuable as showing the point of view of one of the most accurate and profound of present-day Venezuelan historians, it is, like all generalizations, susceptible of criticism for omitting some important factors. Thus the British Legion which made the famous charge at Carabobo was composed not only of those who came to Angostura in the first group, but of practically all those who remained in the third group after its transfer from Maturín to the Apure and likewise of the few who were left in the fourth group after the revolt of the Irish Legion. The point, however, which the Venezuelan historian intended to make was, that when the foreigners fought under Bolívar (or Sucre) their services were of immense value, but when they were under the orders of less skillful generals, their efforts resulted in futility.

Since, however, the character and importance of the legionaries varied with the length of time during which they remained in South America and with the increase in skill and efficiency which they acquired as they became better adapted to conditions and as they learned more readily to understand and appreciate those with whom they associated, it seems to the present writer that a better system of classification would be to divide the service of the foreigners into three periods, not strictly according to dates, but rather according to the prevailing moral characteristics exhibited.

Thus the first period is that of the arrival of organizations recruited in England, Ireland or Germany; a period of disillusionment and discontent; of faulty adjustment, and of weeding-out of weak and unsuitable individuals. The second period is that of hard campaigning by battalions of foreigners which had been organized after their arrival in America, but which possessed the *esprit de corps* of a common nationality. This was the period of decisive battles, of Boyacá, of Carabobo, of Bomboná and of Pichincha. The third period is that of the breaking-up of battalions and the scattering of the foreign officers throughout the army to instruct organizations of natives in European discipline and tactics and to aid the commanders by furnishing them expert staff assistance. This was the period of the disbandment of the Albion Battalion; the strict disciplining of the Grenadiers by Uslar and of the Isthmian Battalion by O'Connor; the intrepid attack by the light squadron under Chitty at Lake Maracaibo; and the stubborn defense of the Rifles under Sandes at Matará.

In the first period the contingents of 1817 and 1819 suffered greatly while adjusting themselves to unfamiliar conditions of food and climate, because the men were inexperienced and the officers incompetent for the high rank which they had suddenly acquired. During this period the weaklings dropped out, the British Legion degenerated into an undisciplined mob on the march to Maturín, and the Irish Legion mutinied and deserted almost en masse at Rio Hacha. It is probable that at this time the presence of foreigners in the independent army was a source of more evil than good. As has been shown in an earlier chapter, their complaints had a certain basis of truth in conditions which could not be remedied at the time because of lack of resources, but were so exaggerated as to give an entirely wrong impression and were published to excuse their authors' premature abandonment of the cause which they had sworn to serve.

In any war waged by colonists to secure their independence from the mother country there are inherent in the nature of the struggle many hardships to be suffered by the patriot troops which may be avoided by both contestants in a war between wealthy and powerful nations. In the latter both sides send into the field standing armies seasoned to endure hardships or volunteers led by trained officers and supplied by a staff which has every storehouse of the nation at its command; while in the former the weakness and poverty of a thinly-populated colony are matched against the wealth and resources of a powerful country. It will, therefore, be interesting to make a few comparisons between this war for the liberation of the northern and northwestern portions of Spanish South America and that struggle which was more nearly like it than probably any other, namely, the revolution of the Thirteen American Colonies.

In the American Revolution the fighting was limited mainly to the comparatively small area of the Atlantic seaboard of the New England colonies, and of New York, Pennsylvania, New Jersey, Delaware, Maryland and the south Atlantic colonies down to Georgia. In South America it spread throughout the vast extent of the present republics of Venezuela, Colombia, Ecuador, and Peru. The entire battle-ground of the Thirteen Colonies, and much more beside, could be put into the present Colombia alone.

In the American Revolution Washington's longest march occurred during the concentration of his troops for the Yorktown campaign. It extended from near West Point on the Hudson River across New Jersey and the narrowest part of Delaware to Chesapeake Bay, where transports were boarded to take the troops to the peninsula between the York and the James Rivers in Virginia, a distance of about four hundred miles.¹ In the campaign of the south, Bolívar's troops marched from Bogotá across half the length of Colombia and one-third of what is now Ecuador to Guayaquil, more than seven hundred miles, to say nothing of the preliminary march of concentration by the Guards Division under Salom of five hundred miles from Santa Marta to Bogotá and the subsequent thousand miles across the full length of Peru during the campaign of Ayacucho to the capitulation of Olañeta on the borders of Upper Peru. This entire march was carried out along the loftiest mountain range in the New World, while Washington's march was over gently-rolling country along a coastal plain.

During the campaign of the south, Bolívar had to fight almost every step of his way through a hostile population, while Washington never encountered opposition from the enemy at any time during his march and was often aided by patriotic and sympathetic inhabitants. It will be remembered also that Bolívar's other great march from Mantecal to Boyacá led him across vast areas of submerged tropical plains during the hottest and most unhealthy season of the year and then up over mountains 12,000 feet high through the bitter cold due to the rarefied atmosphere. The other long march of the American Revolution, which was made by Gen. Greene when he drove Cornwallis from South Carolina into Virginia, was carried out during the delightful season of early spring in the foothills of central North Carolina, where the Continental Army never had to climb more than 2,000 feet above sea level.² It is true that Arnold's march to Quebec through the wilderness of the Maine forests was beset with unforeseen difficulties and resulted in excessive losses, yet this march was short when compared with those of Bolívar.

¹ Matthew Forney Steele, *American Campaigns*, I, 51, 52.
² *Ibid.*, 48-50.

In the Continental Army the nadir of suffering was reached during the winter of 1777-78 at Valley Forge, when the poverty-stricken American troops were only half clad and half fed and officers thought so little of their commissions that they resigned them in disgust or allowed themselves to be cashiered for peculation of funds or neglect of duty. In his despair at these results of the parsimony of the Congress, Washington feared lest his army would become too weak to resume operations in the spring.[1]

The poverty of the Venezuelan and Colombian treasuries has already been referred to and the suffering of the troops from poor and scanty food and from lack of clothing described, but the fact that these conditions were much worse than those befalling the American troops and continued, not only for a season, but throughout all the long years of the war, must be emphasized. In 1819 the commanding general of the province of Guayana reported that he had to institute a system of fines for breaches of discipline to get enough money to buy a drum on which to sound the assembly for drill.[2] Even as late as 1825 Sucre continued to complain that his horses were so weak and worn out they were not worth the alfalfa which they ate, his officers lacked sufficient clothing to appear with decency in company, and that his men were actually naked.[3]

It will be remembered that the chief cause of complaint among the foreigners was the failure to receive the pay which they believed to be due them. Whether or not these complaints were justified, may now be learned from the official records. What can be said as to the truth of the

[1] Sparks' *Writings of Washington*, V, 313, 321, 322, quoted in Emory Upton, *The Military Policy of the United States*, 37.

[2] Archivo Nacional, Caracas, Gobernación de Guayana, VII, 131.

[3] Bingham Collection of Mss., Sucre Papers, Nos. 161, 831, 833, William Miller and F. B. O'Connor to Sucre; O'Leary, *Documentos*, XX, 47, 142; Archivo Nacional, Bogotá, Guerra y Marina, Historia, VI, 980; XVII, 126.

statement that no pay was received, when the actual pay-rolls signed by the men themselves show payments even as early as September, 1818, and January, 1820?[1] Of course the salaries paid were small, but they were the most that could be afforded from the limited resources of a people struggling for their independence; and it must be remembered that citizens of the country were at that time expected to give their services in the army without pay of any kind.

The statements of those foreigners who remained in the patriot army to the end of the war revealed the truth that Bolívar was anxious to treat them fairly, although at first he was unable to satisfy their demands; and that as soon as the resources of the nation were sufficient, he saw to it that its obligations were rigorously met. Until Bolívar's successful campaign into New Granada in 1819, the independents had only a precarious hold on the plains of the Orinoco and had no resources from which to fill their empty treasury. Yet, after the occupation of Bogotá, Bolívar gave orders that the English were to receive full pay, although the natives were to receive only half as much.[2] In spite of this apparent injustice to his compatriots, the Liberator was unable to satisfy the importunities of the foreigners. It was said that Bolívar understood English, but that he refrained from speaking it for a long time, for fear that the English might take advantage of this additional facility of making more frequent demands upon him for more pay.[3] It seems that

---

[1] Archivo Nacional, Caracas, Gobernación de Guayana, XIV, 137 and pay-roll for Sept. 30, 1818 (folio not numbered); also for pay-rolls of 1821 and 1822; cf. Archivo Nacional, Bogotá, Guerra y Marina, Historia, XIII, 258; XVII, 35, 79; XXVII, 542; DCCLXXVIII, 748, 766, 839, 865, 895, 906, 907, 986, 987; DCCLXXIX, 154, 155, 444, 589, 661, 844. One of the earliest of these, that of the English under Lieut. Col. Harrison in Bogotá, April 11, 1821, has been copied as a sample and is given in full in Appendix L.

[2] O'Leary, *Documentos*, XVI, 503, 508, 509.

[3] Brown, *op. cit.*, 84.

the British found it hard to live like the natives on laurels decreed to soldiers returning from victorious campaigns. To be authorized to wear a red chevron two inches in diameter on the arm and a silver medal on the breast may have been satisfying to a Venezuelan's pride,[1] but it was hardly so to a Britisher's appetite.

The favoritism shown to the foreigners in the matter of pay was an added cause of jealousy on the part of the creoles. Notwithstanding his inability to find enough money to pay all, Bolívar was doing his best to pay the foreigners. In a proclamation addressed to the "brave soldiers of the Irish Legion", dated Dec. 14, 1819, he stated: "Venezuela has not enough resources to repay you as your services deserve, but all the promises which Gen. D'Evereux has made will be complied with by the government of Venezuela."[2] The assertions of returned adventurers were uttered too early and with too much bitterness to be trusted. Those made by O'Connor, O'Leary, Miller and Walker after the war had ended seem more reliable and are found to be corroborated by the official records.

As soon as the treasury at Angostura had been replenished with the booty taken at Bogotá, salaries began to be paid with some degree of regularity. By a decree of 1821 regular monthly pay was established for the various grades in the army.[3] Subsequent modifications in laws and regulations

[1] Decrees of Santander, Nov. 29, 1821, Dec 7, 1823 in *Colección de Decretos dados por el poder ejecutivo de Colombia en los años de 1821 a 1826*, 212, 239; Dávila, *Diccionario Biográfico*, I, vi.

[2] *Proclamas de Bolívar, Sucre, Santander y Padilla*, 41.

[3] Blanco, *op. cit.*, VIII, 110. The pay-rolls for 1821 to 1823 show regular payments each month to the troops engaged in the field as well as to those stationed at Bogotá. In a single month amounts as high as 11,057 "pesos" were paid to the Rifles Battalion and 1,220 to the Hussars of the Guard. On Dec. 4, 1822 the Albion Battalion received 1,013 "pesos" and on Jan. 27, of the same year four captains of the Vencedor Battalion were paid 120. Archivo Nacional, Bogotá. Guerra y Marina Historia, XVII, 146; DCCLXXIX, 585, 701, 844, 845; *cf.* also p. 378, n. 1.

changed the rate of pay from time to time, but the average salaries seem to have been about 100 " pesos " a month for a colonel, thirty for a captain, twenty for a lieutenant, ten for a first sergeant, and from three to eight for a private.[1] These amounts were very little, it is true, but such small pay was not unusual in the armies of that time, especially on the American continents. Even in the royalist army, Spanish officers received only one quarter pay and that for only one month during the year.[2] In the reorganization of the United States Army in 1792, the schedules established therein showed the monthly pay of a captain to be but $40.00 and that of a private no more than $3.00.[3] In the force raised by Gen. St. Clair for his campaign against the Indians in the Northwest Territory in 1791, the rates of pay were even less, for a colonel received only $60.00 and privates only $2.10 per month.[4]

In order to pay even these small salaries in South America, strenuous means were adopted to replenish the exhausted treasuries. In Venezuela, in 1817, a decree was published sequestering all real estate belonging to royalists who should emigrate from the republic. The funds so secured were to be devoted to the payment of officers and soldiers according to rank.[5] In his efforts to satisfy the foreigners, Bolívar secured the passage of another decree in 1819 which promised to the British the same rights and privileges as the natives who served in the army. The amounts promised by

[1] Archivo Nacional, Bogotá, Guerra y Marina, Historia, DCCLXXVIII, 766, 839; DCCLXXIX, 154, 155; *El Colombiano*, Oct. 29, 1823.

[2] *Gaceta de Colombia*, March 3, 1822, quoting Morillo to Barreiro, October, 1818.

[3] Upton, *op. cit.*, 81.

[4] Theodore Roosevelt, *The Winning of the West*, III, Part I, 150-151.

[5] Bolívar's decree of Oct. 10, 1817, published in *London Chronicle*, Jan. 12, 1818; *El Colombiano*, Dec. 17, 1823.

the Venezuelan agent in London were to be paid in full and arrears of rations were to be made up in money.[1] By the law of Sept. 29, 1821, for the partitioning of the national domain, lands sequestered from emigrés were to be sold, and from the proceeds the promised bonuses were to be paid at the rate of 500 " pesos " to privates, 4,000 to lieutenants, 8,000 to majors, and so on up to 15,000 to brigadier generals.[2] In December, 1824, Bolívar issued a decree directing that the victorious army of Ayacucho should be paid at once and that this payment should take precedence over all other indebtedness of the state.[3]

English observers, writing at this later date, admitted that Colombia had honorably redeemed the pledges which had been given to its foreign defenders, and some even charged the new nation with extravagance.[4] In subsequent years, when the treasuries of the republics of Colombia and Venezuela had been established on firm foundations, installments of retired pay or ample pensions were annually paid to many of the foreign officers and enlisted men who had remained in the army or who had suffered wounds or other physical disabilities during the war.[5] It is evident that care had to be used to prevent unscrupulous officers from taking advan-

---

[1] Walker, *op. cit.*, II, 437, 438; *Gaceta de Colombia*, Oct. 10, 1824.

[2] Walker, *op. cit.*, II, 544; *Iris de Venezuela*, Feb. 4, 1822. The reports of the *Comisión central de repartimientos de bienes nacionales de Venezuela* for 1827, 1829, Archivo Nacional, Caracas, show allotments of property confiscated from royalist emigrés to numerous foreign officers. For a partial list see Appendix M.

[3] O'Connor, *op. cit.*, 153.

[4] Hamilton, *op. cit.*, I, 253; *Present State of Colombia*, 115; *Correo del Orinoco*, Nov. 27, 1819, June 3, 1820; *El Voto de Venezuela*, 34-36, 184; Archivo Soublette, Documentos, I.

[5] For records of some of these pensions to foreign officers see Appendix M. These lists must not be considered as complete or exhaustive, but only as examples.

tage of this liberality; for in 1823 orders were issued that foreign officers, or such as were naturalized citizens, who had been granted leave to return to Europe, must in order to receive their pay prove that they were not being paid by any other nation as officers in its service.[1]

Arrangements were likewise made for the payment of foreigners serving in the navy. This was to be done through contractors. In 1823 Lemon and Forsyth, navy agents, were paid a lump sum of $1,371, and Commodore Danells was paid two installments, one of $3,150 directly to himself, and the other of $4,000 through the commodore of the corvette " Carabobo ".[2] In 1824 contracts were authorized to be made with foreigners for service in the navy for not less than two years at a rate of pay of not more than ten "pesos" a month and a bonus of not more than eighteen.[3]

Because of his efforts to treat the foreigners with liberality, Bolívar must have been forced to a realization that they were hardly worth what they cost. Not only the favoritism shown to them in the matter of pay aroused the jealousy of the creoles, but the insistent complaints of many of the British officers could not have been other than subverting to the discipline of the latter. Moreover, the conduct of the foreigners on more than one occasion was certainly not such as to merit reward over that of the native-born patriots. The treason of Col. Wilson nearly alienated the loyalty of one of Bolívar's most valuable generals, the disorders committed by the British Legion under Gen. English and Col. Blossett tried the patience of another of his generals beyond endurance; and the mutiny of the Irish Legion at Rio Hacha made even Bolívar himself glad to be rid of them.

The disgraceful conduct of these men cannot be glossed

[1] *El Colombiano*, Dec. 10, 1823.

[2] *Ibid.*, May 21, 1823.

[3] Decree of Santander, July 7, 1824 in *Colección de Decretos*, 182.

over or excused; but it may not seem quite so black when it is compared with that of other troops of laxly-disciplined and poorly-paid armies. Of the men who took part in St. Clair's campaign against the Indians in 1791, "the six months' levies wanted to go home and tried to, while the militia deserted in squads and bands. Those that remained were very disorderly".[1] On January 1, 1781, the men of the Pennsylvania line regiments, discontented over the shortage of pay, clothing and rations, rose in revolt and marched toward Philadelphia with the intention of demanding redress from the government.[2] In June, 1783, the troops in Lancaster and Philadelphia mutinied and surrounded the state house, threatening the Congress with violence in case their grievances were not righted within twenty minutes.[3] Gen. Van Rensselaer's attack on Queenstown, July 13, 1812, failed miserably because of the desertion of a large part of his force, under the very fire of the enemy.[4]

Bolívar would not have been human had he always kept his patience when the foreigners acted as they did, and when so many of them pestered him with demands for more pay and higher rank. An interesting parallel in the American Revolution is revealed in a letter written by Washington, in which he mentions the annoyance caused by the " swarms " of French officers applying to enter the American army, few or none of whom " look lower than field officers' commissions ".[5] Bolívar even had cause to lose faith in the honesty of British merchants; for one of them insisted that he pay for a lot of useless equipment in order that he might

[1] Roosevelt, *op. cit.*, III, part I, 153.

[2] Upton, *op. cit.*, 55.

[3] *Ibid.*, 64.

[4] *Ibid.*, 102, 103, quoting Van Rensselaer's *Affair of Queenstown*, Appendix, p. 62 (p. 66 in edition of New York, 1836).

[5] *Ibid.*, 29 quoting Sparks' *Writings of Washington*, IV, 328.

select such articles as he really needed, whereas others furnished under contract at from two to five pounds sterling firearms such as it was said any gun manufacturer would have been glad to supply at a guinea apiece. In all cases the prices paid were high.[1]

In the second period the cadres of officers which López Méndez had assembled in England were broken up and the officers were subjected to a thorough weeding-out process. Many had died of disease or dissipation, and the weaker ones had gone home of their own accord. A traitor had been imprisoned and the boasters and blowhards had been sidetracked to posts where they could do no harm. The great trouble during the first period was, as has been said, that so many junior officers had been jumped rapidly into places of high rank and so many incompetents had been given commands which they were incapable of exercising. During the second period it was the survival of the fittest, and the best men were coming to the top. Such pompous inefficients as Hippisley, Blossett, English and D'Evereux had been replaced by Sandes, Mackintosh, Rooke and Ferriar. Almost at once the change was manifest in the improved tone of the men. Under these competent commanders the reorganized British Battalion, Albions and Rifles soon acquired pride, enthusiasm and *esprit de corps*. They were anxious to get to grips with the enemy and to show their mettle. Once they

[1] Temple, *op. cit.*, II, 82, 85, 86; Rodríguez Villa, *op. cit.*, IV, 51; O'Leary, *Documentos* XVIII, 407, 482; Archivo Nacional, Bogotá, Guerra y Marina, Historia, XXXV, 913, 918; Archivo Soublette, Documentos y Copiadores, I, III (folios not yet numbered) in Academia Nacional de Historia, Caracas; Archivo Nacional, Caracas, Gobernación de Guayana, II, 226, 229, 230. The aid in munitions furnished to the patriot armies by British merchants is considered by some writers as of almost equal importance to the reenforcements of men who joined the foreign legions. *Cf.* Walker, *op. cit.*, II, 607; F. O. 72/228; San Carlos to Castlereagh, Jan. 4, 1819; Jerónimo Becker, *La independencia de América*, 47; *London Chronicle*, Sept. 16, 1820; Ducoudray-Holstein, *op. cit.*, II, 105.

had taken the field in 1819 they were kept constantly marching and frequently fighting, so that they were so busy suffering real hardships that they no longer had time to complain
over imaginary ones. It is a well-known fact that troops
are healthier while undergoing the rigors of active service
than while they are subjected to the enervating and often
demoralizing idleness of camp or garrison; so these battalions rapidly improved in endurance and became better fitted
to withstand the climate. It has been shown that they gave
good accounts of themselves in battle. There is no question
that the success at Carabobo was largely due to the steadfastness of the British Battalion; and it is generally admitted that they made possible the victory of Boyacá by
charging the heights and saving the patriot army at Pántano
de Vargas. The Albions took a not unimportant part also in
the battle of Pichincha, but the actual winning of victories
does not constitute the only significance of the foreign
legionaries during this period.

Up to 1818 the operations of the patriot divisions in
Venezuela had been limited to little more than raids and
skirmishes in which the enemy was thoroughly harassed,
but no permanent acquisitions of territory could be made.
Caracas had been repeatedly occupied and abandoned again,
because the patriot army was too small to afford the detachment of a garrison sufficiently strong to hold it. The cow-
boy guerrillas under Páez were so active and efficient that
they kept the royalists in constant terror from their raids,
but they were not steady enough in organized warfare to
make Angostura a safe capital for the insurgent government.

Such operations were well enough in a war in which extermination of one's opponent was the object; but even in
this kind of warfare the royalists were getting the better, for
since 1810 the population of Venezuela had suffered a loss
either directly or indirectly due to the war, of 316,336, or

one-third of its whole number.[1]   It was evident that in order
to win the war Bolívar must drive the royalist armies out of
Venezuela and New Granada; he must maintain the offensive and consolidate his victories.   This he could not do unless he had a force of disciplined infantry to hold the advantage won by Páez and his light horsemen of the plains.
The Liberator wanted to invade New Granada in order to
help the weak and struggling patriots there to win their independence and to keep it, but he knew that the cavalry of
Páez would be useless in the mountains, and he could not
spare any infantry from Venezuela.   Bolívar was not the
man ever to lose hope, even if his hopes then looked extremely dim.   Just at this juncture the foreign contingents
began to arrive, and by 1819 enough of them had come to
assure Bolívar that the period for the execution of his plans
was at hand.   At last he had an army which was relatively
strong enough to keep his opponents so busy in Venezuela
that they could not fall upon his rear while he was crossing
the mountains.   He could now carry out his cherished plan
of invading New Granada.[2]

The arrival of the foreign contingents increased not only
the strength of the patriot army but its mobility as well.   Detachments sent to reenforce Urdaneta, Bermúdez and Nariño
enabled those generals to push operations against Morillo so
actively in the north that the royalist commander-in-chief
was unable, until too late, to spare a single division to support Barreiro in his defense of New Granada.

It is difficult to obtain data as to the total independent
forces during those early years; for they were so scattered in

---

[1] O'Leary, *Bolívar y las repúblicas del Sur: Argentina, Chile, Brazil,
Uruguay, Paraguay, Bolivia,* 196; *London Chronicle,* March 17, 1820.

[2] Bingham Collection of Mss., Bolívar Letters, 5, 6, 7, Bolívar to
Guillermo White, Oct. 22, 1818; Feb. 9, April 4, 1819. Bartolomé Mitre,
The Emancipation of South America, condensed translation of the
History of San Martín by William Pilling, 390.

small detachments and the staff organization was so inadequate that any estimate based upon the reports of strength and rosters which have thus far come to light, must necessarily be incomplete. A few extracts taken from the records of the Gobernación de Guayana in the national archives at Caracas will be interesting as showing the smallness of the detachments of patriots under arms in the province of Guayana. A report, dated Oct. 22, 1817, reveals that only 821 men were recruited from the towns of the interior during the preceding eight months.[1] Another dated Feb. 27, 1819, shows the total strength in the department of detachments from the national artillery, the Battalion of Angostura and the cavalry to be only 183 officers and men.[2] The roster of the First Civic Company of Angostura for March 30, 1819 enumerates three officers, three sergeants, four corporals, thirty-one privates—a total of forty-one.[3] Other rosters dated Old Guayana, Sept. 26, 1819, give a total of twenty-five in the corps of national artillery and of 124 in the First Battalion of the Orinoco, of whom two officers and seventeen men were on the sick list, two officers and ten men were on detached service, one officer and twenty-five men were on leave, and only six officers and sixty-one men were fit for duty.[4]

By comparing the sizes of the battalions composed exclusively or largely of foreigners with those filled entirely with natives, it will readily be seen how large a proportion of foreigners there was in the patriot army, even though the actual number of such officers and men was small. Thus in the

[1] Archivo Nacional, Caracas, Gobernación de Guayana, II, 251.

[2] *Ibid.*, II, 94.

[3] *Ibid.*, VII, 127.

[4] *Ibid.*, VII, 198, 199. For similar data *cf.* also *Ibid.*, VII, 210; XIV, 146, 158, 165, 238, 262; Archivo Soublette, Documentos, 1822, II; Archivo Nacional, Bogotá, Guerra y Marina, Historia, VI, 340, 341; XXVII, 446.

column of operations against Caricure in the army of the
east on August 29, 1821, the Rifles, consisting of only
seventy-seven men was the largest battalion, next to which
came the Tiradores of Mompox with seventy, while the company of artillery was a mere handful of eighteen.   The entire column comprised six different organizations with a total
of 306.[1]   On January 31, 1822, the garrison of Caracas consisted of 430 men, of whom eighty-two belonged to the
Carabobo Battalion.[2]   In the Division of the South under
Gen. Salom on June 13, 1822 the second brigade of the
Guards contained the Rifles, Vencedor, Bogotá and Vargas
Battalions with respective strengths of 852, 495, 457, and
305.[3]   Although the number of foreigners in Bolívar's army
has been stated as high as 6,000, it is probable that not more
than 150 survived to the end of the war and that the actual
number present in any campaign did not exceed 1,200.[4]

[1] Archivo Nacional, Bogotá, Guerra y Marina, Historia, VI, 21.

[2] Archivo Soublette, 1822, *Documentos*, II (folio not numbered).

[3] Archivo Nacional, Bogotá, Guerra y Marina, Historia, X, 219.   For
similar data, *cf.* also *ibid.*, XVI, 730; XVII, 189, XXVII, 412; Archivo
Soublette, Documentos, 1822, II, III.

[4] Navarro y Lamarca, *op. cit.*, II, 744 n. gives the following table of
English (sic) auxiliaries brought to Venezuela in 1817-1819:

Col. Wilson	cavalry	60	1817
" Hippisley	"	120	"
" Campbell	rifles	130	"
" Gilmore	artillery—6 guns	90	"
" MacDonald and other officers		20	"
Contingent of Col. Elsom		572	1819
" " " English		1200	"
Germans (Hessians) of Elsom		300	"
Contingent of McGregor		900	"
Irish brigade of D'Evereux		1729	"
Irish contingents of Col. Gore		387	"
	Total	5508	

Torrente, *op. cit.,* II, 462 says that no fewer than 9000 foreigners came
at different times to Venezuela and New Granada to reenforce the rebel
armies, but that perhaps not 100 were surviving in 1830.   Cochrane, *op.
cit.,* I, 464, says that the "total of foreign legions and corps cannot be
estimated at less than 4,000 to 4,500."

The royalist commander-in-chief likewise was unable to concentrate his full force at the point of attack; for whenever he reconquered any territory from the insurgents he had to leave behind a division or detachment strong enough to hold it. Thus although the entire royalist army in the whole of Venezuela and New Granada was probably somewhat larger than was that of the republicans, nevertheless the size of the forces which could be brought into opposition at any particular time or place was approximately equal.

In the campaign of 1818 no battles were fought in which more than 3,500 were engaged on either side. At Calabozo on February 12, 3,500 independents were opposed to 1,900 royalists and at Cojedes on May 2, 3,500 royalists fought 1,500 independents; but in other engagements seldom did the strength of either side exceed more than a few hundred. The largest force which Bolívar commanded in any engagement was at the second and most famous battle of Carabobo, when his strength amounted to 6,000. In this battle, as has been shown, only one of the three divisions of the army (the division in which was the British Battalion) was actually engaged until the enemy began its retreat. Up to 1818 Bolívar had fought thirty actions in Venezuela, in only ten of which more than 900 men took part.[1] In these days of millions of men facing each other on lines hundreds of miles long, a few thousand men fighting on a battlefield all parts of which can be seen at one glance through a pair of field-glasses, seem trivial and unimportant; yet such was the normal size of armies in the days of the wars for independence on both continents of America. When the actual number of men in the field was so small, the addition of a few hundred more would often tip the balance and win the victory, or at least would enable a commander to embark on undertakings hitherto impossible.

[1] Nicolás González Chávez, *Cuadros sinópticos de la guerra de la independencia de los Estados Unidos de Colombia,* 5, 6, 8.

Reverting again to the American Revolution for an analogy, the similarity of the conditions existing at Yorktown in 1781 cannot fail to be observed. There Cornwallis with an army of 7,247 men was cooped up at the end of a narrow peninsula from which he had hoped to be able to embark and escape his pursuers. Unfortunately for him, the English fleet on which he had relied had been driven off by the presence in Chesapeake Bay of the French fleet under De Grasse, so he had either to starve or else to break his way through the cordon of 16,000 Continental and French troops which blocked his retreat up the peninsula. The numerical superiority of his foes being too great for him, Cornwallis was forced to abandon hope of escape and to ask for terms of surrender. In the besieging force at this time there were only 8,000 Continentals. Had these been the only troops opposed to him, Cornwallis might well have dared a combat on equal terms; but the American army had been given a strength double his own by the cooperation of 8,000 Frenchmen under Rochambeau and Lafayette. With these combined armies the superiority of Washington's force was irresistible. The actual number of the 8,000 Frenchmen at Yorktown was not so important as the relative size of the contending armies. Without the French, the American and British forces were about equal; but the timely arrival of the French aid, small as it was, made the surrender of Cornwallis a foregone conclusion.[1]

Likewise in the liberation of Spanish South America the actual number of legionaries was not so important as the fact that the arrival of these foreigners gave Bolívar's strength relative preponderance for the time being over that of the royalists. In a campaign between evenly-matched armies as small as were those led by Bolívar and Morillo, a few hundred men more or less on one side or the other might

---

[1] Steele, *op. cit.*, I, 51-53.

be the deciding factor. In operations such as took place in Venezuela and New Granada the mere presence of a single battalion of foreigners was relatively as important as was that of the Second Division of the American Expeditionary Force at Château Thierry.

The coming of the foreigners made possible the invasion of New Granada in 1819; the success of this campaign opened the way for the consolidation of Venezuela and Colombia into one republic; and the support lent by the Republic of Great Colombia facilitated the liberation of Ecuador and Peru and the founding of Bolivia. Thus it was the timeliness of the arrival of the foreign legionaries which constituted another important phase of their significance during this period.

By the time the third period had developed, many more of the foreigners had died off or had gone home, and those who remained had become accustomed to conditions of living in South America. They had, moreover, become familiar with the language, and as they were able to express themselves in Spanish they became better friends with the South American officers and their value as instructors was enhanced. Since there were scarcely enough enlisted men to maintain the distinctive organizations of foreigners intact, many of these men were commissioned and assigned the duty of assisting in the training of battalions of creoles. The result of this training and disciplining as exhibited in improved morale and intrepidity of attack became apparent throughout the remainder of the war and was especially evident at Bombona and Matará and in the naval action of Lake Maracaibo. In the attacks on Puerto Cabello, too, the strict discipline of the Grenadiers, imparted by Col. Uslar, must not be overlooked. Perhaps more important than the additional weight thrown into the campaign of 1819 by the foreign troops was this reinvigoration of the whole army by the infusion of foreign ideas and knowledge of European tactics in the campaigns which brought the war to an end.

As the foreigners became better acquainted with their allies they learned to appreciate their good qualities and to enjoy their friendship. They soon found that Bolívar was uniformly kind to them and that he gave them no just cause to complain of him or of his government. It began to dawn upon them that the supposedly unfair treatment which they had at first experienced was entirely limited to subordinate commanders and that most of their early sufferings were due to the inexperience and indifference of their own officers.[1]

That more favorable reports of Bolívar and his cause were reaching home was evident from the number of prominent men who wished to lend their aid or spoke in praise. Lord Byron, ever the friend of liberty, expressed a longing to live in the land of Bolívar. One of the Ypsilantis and Sobieski, the nephew of Kosciuszko, wished to become Bolívar's aides. Wellington spoke of him as an extraordinary commander.[2] Daniel O'Connell, the Irish patriot, it will be recalled, wrote to Bolívar, asking him to accept the services of his son, Capt. Morgan O'Connell, who was sailing as a member of the Irish Legion. Sir Robert Wilson pronounced a eulogy on Bolívar in Parliament, and, as will be remembered, sent his third son, Belford Hinton Wilson, to serve on his staff.[3]

As the first period merged into the second and the second into the third a gradual change was being wrought in the

[1] O'Leary, *Narración*, I, 486; Blanco, *op. cit.*, VIII, 551; *London Chronicle,* Feb. 6, 1818; Hamilton, *op. cit.,* I, 143; *Present State of Colombia,* 114; *Recollections of Service,* II, 192, 193, 227, Adam, *op. cit.,* 138; Perú de Lacroix, *op. cit.,* 199.

[2] Blanco, *op. cit.,* VIII, 423; *London Chronicle,* Feb. 1, 1822; *The Times,* Aug. 8, 1883; C. Parra-Pérez, " Bolívar y sus amigos del extrangero ", in *Cultura Venezolana,* III, 306.

[3] O'Connor, *op. cit.,* 55; Azpúrua, *op. cit.,* III, 286; O'Leary, *Correspondencia de extranjeros notables,* I, 184; II, 36, 37; Lecuna, *Papeles de Bolívar,* 45; Parra Pérez, *op. cit.,* 261. *Cf. supra,* Chapters VII and XII.

minds of the South American generals, and they too were modifying their opinions of their foreign allies. At first the patriot chiefs objected to the presence of so many inexperienced officers and tried to get rid of them by threats and starvation, although they were willing to keep the privates who could be useful. In order to encourage the importation of the latter, ship-owners were offered a bonus of $175 per man.[1] Brión was quoted as having said that " he wished the British Legion had been in Hell before he saw them ", to which an officer of rank in the British Legion spiritedly replied, " he did not believe there was one in that corps who did not entertain the same wish with regard to their admiral ". Yet on the occasion of one of his victories, Brión had invited some of these same British volunteers to help him celebrate.[2]

Early in the war it was reported by Major Perkins, aide to Gen. Bermúdez, that his general was jealous of having British officers in the service and that he wanted the men and not the officers.[3] At first Gen. Soublette complained that the greatest trouble was, that all the foreign officers wanted to begin as colonels, if not as generals, so there were colonels by the million. Yet he believed that the English were valuable in the field.[4] When after the battle of Boyacá many soldiers from the Albion Battalion were drifting down to Santa Marta in their efforts to return home, Col. Carreño told O'Connor, his chief of staff, not to bother him for instructions in each case but to give all of them their passports, saying, " Let them go, we don't need them any longer." [5]

---

[1] Hackett, *op. cit.*, viii; *London Chronicle*, Jan. 21, 1820 quoting *Dublin Journal,* Jan. 15, 1820.

[2] Chesterton, *op. cit.*, 54; *Morning Chronicle*, July 25, 1818.

[3] Hippisley, *op. cit.*, 254; Brown, *op. cit.*, 189.

[4] Gil Fortoul, *op. cit.*, I, 282 n.; O'Leary, *Correspondencia*, VIII, 12.

[5] O'Connor, *op. cit.*, 53, 54.

Later, however, it was admitted that the British cavalry officers, who acted as instructors to the " llaneros " of Páez, had effected a vast improvement in the training of these men, and those who at first had been looked upon merely as heretics were now valued as liberal and useful friends.[1] Páez himself, recalling in his autobiography the experiences of the war for independence, said that the English did not come to gratify their ambition but for the sake of adventure and excitement. He added that Sir Robert Wilson and others deserved a vote of thanks from the Venezuelan congress.[2] Such a vote was passed by the Colombian congress at Cúcuta for the efforts of Sir Robert Wilson in promoting the cause of independence.[3]

After the battle of Pántano de Vargas, Anzoátegui in conversation with Dr. Foley admitted that the British whom he had considered not worth their rations were now " worth their weight in gold ".[4] Even Urdaneta conceded that the British displayed in their attack on Fort Agua Santa an audacity and intrepidity worthy of great praise and in little accord with their lack of subordination and discipline.[5]

The sentiments of Bolívar, as judged by his published expressions of them, must often have been dictated by policy, yet these show that the foreigners were advancing in his esteem in steady accord with the progress of events. At first he had high hopes from the arrival of so many of them; then he became disgusted with their complaints and the trouble they were causing; often he was overwhelmed with admiration at their bravery, and finally he gave them more than their share of credit for what he himself had accomplished.

[1] *Morning Chronicle*, Dec. 25, 1818.
[2] Páez, *Autobiografía*, I, 246, 247.
[3] *London Chronicle*, Feb. 4, 1822.
[4] Cochrane, *op. cit.*, I, 488, 489.
[5] Urdaneta, *op. cit.*, 164.

In acknowledging the receipt from Col. Hippisley of the report of his arrival, Bolívar thanked the colonel for the generous services " you so gratuitously offer to my country ".[1] At a banquet at Angostura, Bolívar toasted D'Evereux and the officers and soldiers of the Irish Legion with the words: " England has its legion, and Ireland has raised its army; with such powerful and voluntary aid, there is nothing to fear and everything to hope." [2] At another time he said he esteemed Gen. D'Evereux most highly and expressed his surprise at the defection that had taken place among such of his troops as had landed at Margarita. He looked with hope for the arrival of the rest of the Irish Legion.[3]

On the other hand, his growing disgust at the conduct of these troops is revealed in what he wrote to Montilla regarding their revolt at Rio Hacha.[4] Moreover, angered at the incessant complaints of the foreigners, he is said to have ordered the execution of a British sergeant who had acted as spokesman for the soldiers in their protest against being made to march without shoes.[5] Then in 1820, realizing that the cost of transportation of the foreign mercenaries was excessive and that they were frequently incapacitated because they were unable to stand the climate, he had ordered in disgust that no more foreign officers should be admitted into the service, and that such as had already arrived but had not yet received confirmations of their commissions, should not be granted rank higher than that of lieutenant colonel.[6]

[1] Hippisley, *op. cit.*, 560.

[2] Adam, *op. cit.*, 128.

[3] *Ibid.*, 137.

[4] *Cf.* Chapter VII, also Richard, *op. cit.*, 188.

[5] Chesterton, *op. cit.*, 133.

[6] *Correo del Orinoco*, Dec. 2, 1820; Richard, *op. cit.*, 196, 201, 268, 269; Hackett, *op. cit.*, 64; Level, *op. cit.*, 395.

However, after his return from the campaign to New Granada, at a dinner in Angostura, Bolívar thanked the British officers for their services, and in toasting the memory of Col. Rooke, he said: "To him I owe all my good fortune in New Granada, and to him Venezuela is indebted for the preservation of her president and will hereafter have mainly to attribute her liberty." [1]   In a speech to the Granadans at Paya he said: " From remote climes a British Legion has left its glorious fatherland to acquire the renown of being the saviours of America." [2]   At a dinner aboard H.M.S. "Cambridge" on November 7, 1824, he expatiated in glowing terms upon the power of Great Britain and the readiness with which it lent its aid to nations which were struggling for freedom and independence.[3]   Finally, when Bolívar was able to look back upon his work as successfully accomplished, he several times said to members of his staff that the real liberator of Colombia was López Méndez; for he himself was sure that he would not have been able to bring to a successful conclusion the celebrated campaign of 1819, if it had not been for the opportune and efficacious aid of all kinds which that efficient agent sent from London.[4]

During the period of the reorganization of his army, moreover, Bolívar expressed himself as glad to have at last so many Europeans who could discipline his troops and help the inexperienced officers with their example.[5]   It was said that whenever he feared trouble from his own men, he

[1] *Recollections of Service*, II, 31.

[2] O'Leary, *Narración*, I, 563.

[3] *Journal written on board H. M. S. Cambridge*, 62.

[4] Restrepo, *op. cit.*, II, 595, n. 39a to p. 473.   This is good primary evidence, because in this note Restrepo says that he himself several times heard Bolívar make the quoted statement.

[5] Bingham Collection of Mss., *Bolívar Letters*, No. 5, Bolívar to Guillermo White, Feb. 9, 1819. *Campaigns and Cruises*, 78.

selected his personal guard from among the English troops,[1] and it is certain that he was fond of having foreign officers about him. On this point it will be remembered that he kept on his personal staff Ferguson, Belford Hinton Wilson, Perú de Lacroix and, above all, O'Leary.[2] The familiar presence of these officers and their daily conversation must have done much to mold the ideas of the Liberator. The influence of the body physician is well known, so the mere mention of the names of Dr. Moore and Dr. Foley as being in constant attendance on Bolívar is enough. Then, too, Sucre appointed O'Connor his chief of staff, and Páez kept Col. Woodberry in a similar post through the two active years between Carabobo and the fall of Puerto Cabello. It will also be recollected that Urdaneta, Montilla, Salom, Santander, and other generals in the patriot army frequently assigned foreign officers to positions on their staffs. Influence over the tone of the whole army must undoubtedly have been exerted to a marked extent by the foreigners who occupied such positions.

O'Leary is the one foreigner above all others whom South Americans whose ancestors knew and valued his services love to cherish in memory to this day, just as Americans delight in honoring Lafayette; but the Irish soldier had only himself to give, for he lacked the wealth and family prestige which were of so much importance among the contributions of the French nobleman. It is possible also to find a parallel with von Steuben, whose great usefulness lay in his ability to drill and whip into shape the untrained and undisciplined levies of Washington's army. In Uslar, another German, Bolívar had a similar drill-master and disciplinarian, but Uslar's influence was chiefly limited to his own brigade, whereas that of von Steuben extended throughout the army.

[1] Robinson, *op. cit.*, 156.

[2] Miller, *op. cit.*, II, 293; Hippisley, *op. cit.*, 381.

At the risk of seeming to repeat, it may be well here to summarize somewhat the foregoing estimate of the significance of the foreign legionaries and in doing so to venture a rough approximation of dates. Thus the first period in their career would fall between the years 1817 and 1819. In this period, though the services of the legionaries were futile, the years themselves were of value for assembling, training, weeding-out and hardening the individuals who remained to perform the work of a later time. During the second period, comprising the years 1819 to 1821, the decisive battles of Boyacá and Carabobo occurred. It was then that the opportune reenforcements by foreigners enabled Bolívar to inaugurate the plans which proved to be the turning-point in his career, and that the valor of the legionaries in battle did so much to make those plans succeed. During the third period, from 1821 to 1824, the chief service of the foreigners consisted in the influence they exerted in training troops and in guiding the operations of the staff.

A fourth period might properly be added; for the years from 1824 onward to the present day are undoubtedly of importance as a time of fraternization, of naturalization and of memories. It has already been shown how, after the battle of Ayacucho, Wright, Weir, Manby and Illingworth remained in the armies of the South American republics until they became generals, and how Uslar, O'Leary and O'Connor retired with laurels to settle down as citizens and to infuse their blood into the peoples of the new nations. Others who became naturalized or who established themselves in the several countries helped to extend the feeling of fraternity and good will between Colombia and other nations, especially Great Britain whose sons had helped in the winning of independence.[1]

[1] Among these was Col. Edward Stopford who founded in 1823 and edited *El Colombiano*. This newspaper was printed partly in Spanish

As time went on the ordinary people throughout the Republic of Colombia learned to appreciate the value of the services which the foreigners had rendered them. At the town of Guativita, when a detachment of the Albions passed through, the Indians greeted them with " Viva la nación inglesa, amigos de la República de Colombia " [1] (Long live

and partly in English and was believed to be one of the most influential journals in Caracas. F. O. 18/37, Henry Bold Hurry to Foreign Office, July 28, 1826. Illingworth joined the firm of Jones, Powles, Hurry & Co. in Bogotá, the name of which was then changed to Powles, Illingworth & Co. *El Constitucional,* Bogotá, Jan. 19, 1826. The firm of Herring, Powles & Co., owned various gold mines in Antioquía and a silver mine in Margarita. Other English mining companies were Reid, Irwin & Co., Cockburn, Goldsmith & Co., which contracted for valuable mines in Antioquía, and the Colombian & Peruvian Mining Association which had eight gold and silver mines in Antioquía, Popayán and Chocó. F. O. 18/37, Consul Wood to Foreign Office, Jan. 30, 1826. The governments of both Colombia and Venezuela, moreover encouraged the naturalization of foreigners, fostered immigration by conferring on settlers the same rights as citizens and by donating grants of lands to colonization societies, and favored the business interests of foreigners by giving them valuable concessions, such as the exclusive privilege of navigating the rivers in steamboats on the Orinoco above Angostura to Col. James Hamilton for the term of ten years, and on the Magdalena to John B. Elbers for twenty-one years. Elbers had formerly held a contract to furnish vessels to the Colombian navy. To Charles Stuart Cochrane was given for eight years the exclusive right to erect factories in northern Venezuela for working sheet copper, and to Edward Hall Campbell of Newcastle-on-Tyne the concession to manufacture powder without competition for twelve years. Archivo Nacional, Bogotá, Guerra y Marina, Historia, XXVII, 401; XXXV, 919, 920, 921; *El Colombiano,* July 16, Aug. 27, Oct. 15, 22, Nov. 4, 1823; *Gaceta de Colombia,* May 2, 1824; *London Chronicle* July 14, 1819; *The Times,* March 9, 1925; Decree of Santander, Feb. 9, 1826 in *Colección de Decretos,* 194; F. O. 18/16, Henderson to Canning, April 28, 1825. For further reports as to the good feeling toward England and the liberal treatment of foreigners, *cf.* also F. O. 18/1, 18/16, Consul General James Henderson to Foreign Office, Dec. 22, 1823, March 4, 1825; F. O. 18/37, Consul Wood to Foreign Office, Jan. 30, 1826; Temple, *op. cit.,* 84; Andrews, *op. cit.,* v; British Museum, Additional Mss., 38300, Liverpool Papers, CLXXXII; folio 98, 38371 folio 43; *London Champion and Sunday Review,* Aug. 3, 1817; *London Chronicle,* April 26, 1822.

[1] Hamilton, *op. cit.,* I, 189.

the English nation, friends of the Republic of Colombia).
As one traveler there in 1824 says, "In fact to be an Englishman in a *passe par tout* through the republic."[1]   A later
traveler in Peru and Bolivia, writing of the attitude of the
better-class citizens toward the foreign officers who had remained, cites as an instance a certain "Don Manuel of La
Paz who had some large transactions with British merchants
and personal acquaintance with Gen. Miller, Col. O'Connor
and Dr. Nicol, and was much prepossessed in their favor, so
that his house should (*sic*) at all times be at the disposal of
the English."[2]   Dr. Barreiro, of Cúcuta, was especially fond
of the English and kept open house for the British officers
in the patriot army.[3]

In his message to the congress in 1823 the minister of
foreign relations of Colombia, referring to the necessity
for prompt payment of the foreign debt, said: "Colombia
owes an immense debt of gratitude to numerous British subjects and earnestly desires to give them positive proof of it,
if not with reprehensible profusion, at least with the utmost
liberality."[4]   That same year and again in 1826, Santander
called the attention of the congress to the great services rendered to Colombia by England.[5]   In 1822 at a dinner in
London to Francisco Antonio Zea, minister plenipotentiary
from the Republic of Colombia, at which the Duke of Somer-
set presided, Zea in responding to a toast stated: "It was
in Great Britain that at the time of its utmost need Colombia
found firm and faithful friends to come to its support. The
injuries of Spain will soon be forgotten—the friendship of

[1] Cochrane, *op. cit.*, II, 283; *cf.* also Capt. W. H. Smyth, *The Life and
Services of Captain Philip Beaver, late of his Majesty's Ship Nisus,* 336.

[2] Temple, *op. cit.*, II, 80.

[3] Hamilton, *op. cit.*, I, 303.

[4] *El Colombiano*, Aug. 20, 1823.

[5] *Ibid.*, June 4, 1823; F. O. 18/25, Patrick Campbell to George Canning,
Jan. 4, 1826.

Great Britain will be cherished warm in our hearts as long as life shall beat in them." [1] As late as 1864 this feeling was expressed by the acting President of Venezuela in his toast, " I drink to the English government which has always been the protector of Venezuela and has set the best example for free states to follow." [2]

It is true that such official expressions of gratitude were directed to the English government, but South Americans themselves have not been unmindful of the individual services of the foreigners who came to the aid of their patriotic forebears when they were weak and inexperienced. The portraits of many of these men from overseas hang in the historical museums among those of the native forefathers of independence, and their bodies rest in the national pantheons beside the tombs of Bolívar and Sucre. The Republics of Venezuela and Colombia have been generous to a fault in rewarding those foreigners who fought for their independence, and the national archives at Caracas and Bogotá are filled with records of pensions and rewards granted to men who lent even the most trivial assistance to their cause. Long years after they had ceased to serve Spanish South America and had returned to Europe to exploit the knowledge they had gained, McGregor and D'Evereux received rewards from the young republics far exceeding in munificence the value of what they actually did.

The memory of the legionaries accordingly is kept ever fresh in the minds of each new generation of Spanish Americans. Historians and the people generally in Venezuela and Colombia seldom fail on proper occasions to mention the debt they owe to those foreigners and to speak of the importance of their services. When on February 11, 1881 Gen. Thomas Manby died at Bogotá public honors, as will

---

[1] *London Chronicle*, July 11, 1822.

[2] Edward B. Eastwick, *Venezuela. or Sketches of life in a South American Republic*, 75.

be remembered, were decreed to his memory as the last chief to survive from the glorious British Legion;[1] and upon the eightieth anniversary of her birth the army of Colombia published a special number of the memorial of its general staff in honor of Doña Carolina O'Leary Soublette de Portocarrero, the daughter of Gen. O'Leary, which began with these words of dedication: "And you, noble lady, daughter of O'Leary, niece of Soublette, relative of Bolívar; you of aristocratic English (*sic*) lineage and of the stock of our American forefathers, you are a link—a link of gold—between the to-day and the yesterday of the Republic."[2]   When she died a year or two ago, so great was the gratitude to the memory of her father that the president and congress decreed to her the pomp of a military funeral and the honor of burial from the cathedral (an honor, so far as is known, never before conferred upon a woman).   Referring to the war of independence, the Colombian statesman and historian, Antonio Maria Galán, wrote:

The heroic efforts which men born in America made to win the right to govern themselves are no more to be admired than are the deeds of those generous strangers who, abandoning their fatherlands, their families, their interests and all their worldly wealth in Europe, came to a region unknown to them to help break the chains of a people groaning under a foreign yoke.[3]

On the front of the beautiful capitol building at Bogotá, the first thing which strikes the eye of him who enters is a bronze wreath of laurel leaves framing a marble tablet.   On this tablet the gratitude of a nation is inscribed, in words impressive through their simplicity: " Colombia to the forefathers of Venezuela and to the British Legion."

[1] *Boletín de Historia y Antigüedades*, XII, Nos. 140, 141, pp. 545-547.

[2] *Memorial del Estado Mayor del Ejército de Colombia*, No. 122, p. 3, quoting speech by Dr. Fabio Lozano T., Aug. 10, 1919.

[3] Galán, *op. cit.*, 7.

APPENDIX A

Translation from Archivo Nacional, Bogotá, Guerra y Marina, Historia, I, 668: Geo. Elsam, Col. Angostura, Aug. 13, 1819 to Col. Uslar; submits a return of officers of the 2nd Rifles under the command of Uslar—

Col. Uslar			Sept. 1, 1818
Major Manby			Aug. 7, 1818
Major Freudenthal			Aug. 8, 1818
Capt. Johnston			Dec. 1, 1818
"	Clauditz		Dec. 15, 1818
"	Smith		Feb. 2, 1819
"	Floyd		Feb. 5, 1819
"	Cockett (Lockett?)		May 26, 1819
"	Bothmer		May 29, 1819
"	Bidwell		June 1, 1819
"	Weir		June 4, 1819
"	Heaver		June 6, 1819
"	Brown		June 10, 1819
1st Lieut. Dunkin			Jan. 1, 1819
"	"	Casely	Jan. 5, 1819
"	"	Bendle	Jan. 7, 1819
"	"	Weaver	Jan. 9, 1819
"	"	Jonson	Jan. 11, 1819
"	"	Fulton	Feb. 7, 1819
"	"	Weston	Feb. 5, 1819
"	"	Hands	Feb. 7, 1819
"	"	Ashdown	April 10, 1819
2nd Lieut. Shipart (Gifart?)			Jan. 1, 1819
"	"	MacGuire	Jan. 4, 1819
"	"	Aukinstale	Jan. 7, 1819
"	"	Sheppard	Jan. 9, 1819
"	"	Atkinson	June 16, 1819
"	"	Seman	June 19, 1819
"	"	de la Hunte(?)	June 21, 1819
"	"	Rich	June 23, 1819
"	"	Becker	June 25, 1819
"	"	Daley	June 27, 1819
"	"	Solas	Aug. 24(?), 1819

APPENDIX B

From Archivo Nacional, Caracas, Gobernación de Guayana: "Lista de los oficiales y Tropa Extranjera que existe en esta plaza bajo el mando accidental del Mayor Ferrier, con inclusión de las mujeres inglesas cuyos maridos se hallan en el Ejército."

Sargent, Mayor	Ferrier	P.		Jacobs	P.
Otro id	Filly	P.		Christian	P.
Otro id	Mahony	P.		Murphy	P.
Capitán	Elanditz	P.		Rice	P.
Otro id	Palmer	P.		Lemor	P.
Otro	Sutherland	P.		Pearce	P.
Otro	Burk	P.		Cardy	P.
Otro	Hippesley	P.		Balsann	P.
Teniente	Triton	P.		Wells	P.
Otro	Tomás	P.	Soldados	Pascal	P.
Otro	Alexander	P.		Broun	P.
Otro	M. Muchin	P.		Brollen	P.
Doctor	Henry	P.		McGargan	P.
				Hinds	P.
	Nexter	P.		Flinn	P.
	Wrightt	P.		Heikt	P.
	Claver	P.		Fettman	P.
	Tribuler	P.		Reimer	P.
	Atchinson	P.		Hatterman	P.
Sargentos	Deris	P.		Hircek	P.
	Deleny	P.			
	Flium	P.		Neiter	P.
	Harrison	P.		Capbell	P.
	Rice	P.		Flinn	P.
	Price	P.		Pilse	P.
	Schrarder	P.	Mujeres	Flinn	P,
				Furry	P.
				Garnuy	P.
				Price	P.
				Furry	P.

Angostura, Junio 16 de 1819.
El Coronel Jefe: Francisco Conde.

APPENDIX C

From Archivo Nacional, Caracas, Gobernación de Guayana (not dated, but probably in 1820) : " Lista de las mujeres y niños irlandeses en Angostura."

Mujeres

Power
Cloide
Pollock
Crampsey
Iland
Yames
M. Keon
English
Tymmons

Niños

James
Ocallagan
Carrol
Carrol
Carrol

M. Coello.

APPENDIX D

From Archivo Nacional, Caracas, Gobernación de Guayana:
"30 de Setiembre 1818.

Lista de los Oficiales, Sarjentos & Británicos bajo la manda (sic) del Coronel Rooke, haciendo fatigue (sic) hora en Guarnición de Angostura por sus sueldos del 1er día mes de Setiembre, hasta el ultimo 30 mo con sus proporciones, 1818."

Rango	Nombre	Regimientos	Pesos	Reparar
Coronel	Jayme Rooke	1 Husrs.	10	
Capitán	Juan Denis	"	10	Pagador
"	Philip. Seybold	"	10	
"	R. Bracken	"	..	Ausente con permisión en servicio
"	Tomas Palmer	"	10	
Teniente	Carlos Smith	"	8	
"	Juan Dodson	"	8	
"	Tomas Simpson	"	8	
Capitán	Robto. Vowell	"	10	
Tentiente	J. R. Tomas	"	8	
Corneta	J. Brown	"	6	
"	Juan Paumier	"	6	
"	Samuel Lamb	"	6	
"	Tomás Heyliger	"	6	
Cirujano	Guillermo Murphy	"	8	Ayudante de Cirujano.
Sarjento	Roberto Dodson	"	3	
"	Enrique Lloyd	"	3	
"	Juan Hoyatt	"	3	
"	Hugo W. Intires	"	3	
"	Juan Clark	..	3	
"	Tomás Harrison	"	3	En servicio
"	Abraham Woodward	"	3	
"	Alexandro Denning	"	3	Ordenanza General Montillo
"	Henrique Alton	"	3	Maestro Sastre
"	Alexandro Munroe	"	3	
"	Roberto Bennet	"	3	
"	Juan Gray	"	3	En servicio

Cabo	Guillermo Larkin		"	2	
"	Jorge Hinds		"	2	
"	Juan Taylor		"	2	
"	Mateo Egan		"	2	en el Hospital
"	Juan Cooley		"	2	
"	David Bartlett		"	2	
"	Jorge Whitesides		"	2	
"	Guillermo Amofs		"	..	Guayana
"	Roberto Marlton		"	2	
"	Juan Purcell		"	2	
Capitán	Jorge Cook	2	"	10	Ayudante
Teniente	Juan Burke		"	8	
Sarjento	Terance Nugent		"	3	
"	Jaime Sutherland		"	3	
"	Pedro Donehigh		"	3	
"	Juan Iribolet		"	3	Prisionero
"	Guillermo Dyos		"	3	

Sumario

```
 1 Coronel .......................................  10
 5 Capitanes a 10 qualer ....................... 50
 5 Tenientes a  8  "  .......................... 40
 4 Cornetas  a  6  "  .......................... 24
 1 Ayudante Cirujano ...........................  8
16 Sarjentos a 3 qualer ........................ 48
 9 Cabos a 2 ................................... 18
```
                                            ———
                                    198 Pesos

Jayme Rooke Col: Commandante
Juan Denis Capitán Pagador 1er Hùsares.

APPENDIX E

From Archivo Nacional, Bogotá, Guerra y Marina, historia, 11, 504:
" Lista de los S. S. Gefes y Oficiales de la Legión Británica en Achaguas."

Clases	Nombres	Fecha de despacho	Si tiene o no despacho	por quien dado
Teniente Coro-				
nel	Tomás Ferrier	30 Abril 1818	tiene	S. E. el Libertador
id	Tomás Harrison	26 Sbre. "	id	id
Mayr. Com. grº.				
de Tte. Cor.	Guillerme Davy	id	id Mr.	id
Mayor	Carlos Carver	id	id	id
id	José Deighton	id	id	id
id	Eduardo Brand	25 Junio, 1820	no tiene	Gral. Páez.
id	Juan Ferrier	26 " "	tiene	S. E. el Libertador
id	Brooke Young		no tiene	Gral. Páez.
id	De Reinboldt		id	id
id	Dennis Egan		id	id
id	Charles Sechen		id	id
Cap. comg'de				
Tte. Cor.	Noble McMulin	24 Dbre. 1817	de capitán	id
id	Juan Trainor	26 Spbre, 1818	" "	S. E. Libertador
Capitan	James Scott	10 Fbro., 1819	tiene	id
id	Robt. Gordon	id	id	"
id	Henri Weir	4 Junio, 1819	id	S. E. el V. P. Zea.
id	Carlos Minchin	1º Spbre, 1819	id	Gral. Páez.
id	John Lanagan	6 id 1820	no tiene	id "
id	Wm. Rabenscroft	" " "	id	" "
id	Juan Forbes	8 " "	id	id "
id	Juan Gill	29 Obre, 1820	id	" "
id	Charles Smith	21 Julio, 1819	id	Gral. Devereux
id	J. Brown	26 " "	id	" "
id	J. Schaw	28 " "	id	" "
id	Paterson	30 " "	id	" "
id	John M'Carty	23 " "	id	" "
Teniente	Charles Webster	28 Enero 1818	tiene	S. E. el Libertador
id	Pedro Obrien	26 Spbre, 1818	id	id id
id	Tomas Ridgeway	"	id	" "
id	James Fox	26 Spbre, 1818	id	" "
id	D. Steinson	" " "	id	" "
id	Carlos Church	15 Enero, 1819	"	" "
id	" Ashdown	" " "	"	" "

408

id	Henry Gobbons	" " "	"	" "
id	John Hubble	12 April, 1819	"	" "
id	John Hands	12 April, 1819	"	S. E. el Libertador
id	J de Sola	24 Mayo, 1819	tiene	S. E. el V. P. Zea.
id	Lynch	31 Julio, 1819	no "	Gral. Devereux
id	Jacob Harrison	3 Spbre "	"	" "
id	Saml Paramor	9 Abril, 1820	"	Gral Paez
id	Tomás Underwood	7 Junio, 1819	"	
id	Tomás Lloyd	19 Julio, "	"	
id	A. Houston		"	
Sub teniente	John Brown		"	

N. Dicky
N. Mortimar
J. Stewart
Mathews
Laurence } no tienen   Gral. Devereux
Talbot
Walter O'Callagan
Edº O'Callagan
Keough
James Nervill

Cirujano Mayor	Ricardo Murphy	26 Sbre, 1818	tiene	S. E. Libertador
id	Robert Fry	25 Enero, 1818	id	" "
Cirujanos	Eduardo Brown		no tiene	S. E. V. P. Zea
id	John Stanton			
id	Shaw			
id	Smith			
id	A. Ackinson			

Achaguas a 23 de Obre de 1820
Judas Piñango

APPENDIX F

From Archivo Montilla III, C No. 3:
"Exercito Libertador de Colombia.

División Irlandesa.

Estado de fuerza de que se compone le dicha división en el dia de la fecha."

Cuerpos:	Enfermos			Fuerza disponible							
	Gefes y Ofic⁹	Tropa	Total	Gefes	Capitanes	Oficiales	Tamb y Mus	Sargentos	Cab⁹ y Sold⁹	Cirujanos	Total
Regimiento Lanzeros	12	35	47	4	10	24	1	28	203	4	274
" Cundinamarca...	5	36	41	2	5	30	3	25	165	2	232
" Tiradores.......	4	38	42	1	6	14	3	18	100	2	144
Artilleria	..	..	..	..	1	2	..	6	19	..	28
Total	21	109	130	7	22	70	7	77	487	8	678

Notas: que tambien en los buques van 33 mujeres y 6 ninos de los oficiales y tropa a quienes se pasan raciones.

Estado Mayor de la División

El comandante en Gefe de la División el Sor Cor.¹ Mariano Montilla;
Gefe del E. M. el Sor Coronel Eduardo Stopford.

Adjuntos del E. M. { el Ten.ᵗᵉ Coro.¹ Juan Minuth / el Ten.ᵗᵉ Diego Jugo / el id Diego Lister

Ayudantes del Sor. Comd.ᵗᵉ en Gefe { el Capitán Guillermo Ferguson / id In. Edo⁰ Byrne.

El Cirujano Mayor de la Divisⁿ Guillermo Fitzgibon.
Agregado al E. M. el Coronel Ramón Ayala.
Juan Griego Marzo 4 de 1820. 10⁰

E. Stopford
Gefe de E. M.

APPENDIX G

From Archivo Nacional, Caracas, Gobernación de Guayana:
" Lista de los Oficiales y soldados Ingleses Presentes."

Angostura 22 de Junio 1820.

Ten.^{te} Coronel	1 Pedro Grant	
Mayor	1 Manbey R de A——	Ejecutivo
Capitan	1 W. P. Titythomeas	ditto
"	2 Dodoron R. de A	ditto
"	3 Stacey	
"	4 W. G. Carelpied	
Teniente	1 Guillermo Boyle	en Hospital
Sargentos	1 Campbell R de A.	Ejecutivo
"	2 Francisco Smith	Prisoner
"	3 Madden	Ejecutivo
Cabo	1 Thos M. Connell	ditto
Soldados	1 Guillermo Harris	ditto
"	2 Daniel Callaghan	ditto
"	3 Thomas Talnragar	Prisoner
"	4 Juan Roberts	Efectivo
"	5 Ricardo Evans	Desertor
"	6 William Alg	ditto
"	7 Samuel Batio	Efectivo
"	8 Juan Nott R. de A	ditto
"	9 Clayd L. J.	Prisoner
"	10 Horan S. J.	ditto
"	11 Merchant L. J.	ditto
"	12 William Ikaldham	en Hospital
"	13 Carlos Ykampeton	ditto
"	14 Timothio Crawley	ditto
"	15 Juan Mullazan	ditto

Total

Efectivo 60 Husares 2 sargentos 76 soldados;

Prisioneros 1 Sargento y 4 soldados ;

Desertores 2 soldados;

en Hospital 1 Oficial y 4 soldados.

W. Fitz Thomas
Capitan I. B.

411

APPENDIX H

Translation from Archivo Nacional, Bogotá, Guerra y Marina, Historia, DCCLXXX, 519:

Republic of Colombia   Carabobo Battalion

List of field officers, officers and men who took part in the battle of Carabobo on June 24, 1821, with statement of the rank held by them on that date.

Rank	Name	Rank held on the day of the battle
Lt. Col. Comd't	Edward Brand	in action as major
Lt. Col. grad.	John Ferriar	" " " "
Capt.	Robert Gordon	" " " captain
"	Rupert Hand	" " " "
"	Henry Weir	" " " "
"	Charles D. Minchin	" " " "
"	Charles I. Smith	" " " "
"	John Lannigan	" " " "
"	William Gill	" " " "
"	John Steinson	" " " lieutenant
"	John Hands	" " " "
"	Charles Webster	" " " "
" grad.	James Mathews	" " " "
" "	Charles William Ashdown	" " " "
Lieut.	John Benj. Hubble	" " " "
"	Otto Trittan	" " " "
"	Jacob Harrison	" " " "
"	William Talbot	" " " sub. lieut.
"	Walter O'Callaghan	" " " " "
"	Acheson Woolsey	" " " " "
Sub-lieut.	Joseph Jarvis	" " " 1st Sergt.
Brigade Sergt.	Michael Dunn	" " " "
1st Sergt.	John McCoormick	" " " private
"	John Dunaven	" " " 2nd Sergt.
"	John Ross	" " " 1st Sergt.
"	John Stewart	" " " Private
"	William Walker	" " " 2nd Sergt.
"	William Silvester	" " " "
2nd Sergt.	Henry Comer	" " " "
"	James Hawkins	" " " Private
"	John McCann	" " " "
"	Thomas Gibbons	" " " 1st Corporal
"	Patrick Harris	" " " "
"	James Jordan	" " " Private
"	William Wilmot	" " " 2nd Sergt.

412

1st Corporal	William Fincham	"	"	"	Private
"	John Milton	"	"	"	"
"	James Gilbert	"	"	"	"
"	John Walsh	"	"	"	"
"	Charles Varney	"	"	"	"
"	William Ashford	"	"	"	1st Corporal
"	Thomas Conway	"	"	"	Private
"	Richard McDonald	"	"	"	"
"	William Gordon	"	"	"	"
"	John McCoy	"	"	"	"
"	Henry Ellis	"	"	"	"
"	John McKay	"	"	"	"
"	Thomas Callan	"	"	"	"
"	Robert Mullens	"	"	"	1st Corporal
"	William Mitchell	"	"	"	Private
"	Thomas Stark	"	"	"	"
"	James Seabright	"	"	"	"
"	John Ward	"	"	"	"
"	Robert Coles	"	"	"	"
"	Francis McDermot	"	"	"	"
"	Thomas Simpson	"	"	"	"
"	John Jaffe	"	"	"	"
"	Samuel Wooley	"	"	"	"
Musician	James Clark	"	"	"	Musician
"	Charles Watkins	"	"	"	"
"	Henry Hill	"	"	"	"
"	Thomas Dyram	"	"	"	"
"	John Hubert	"	"	"	"
"	Charles Croney	"	"	"	"
"	John Williams	"	"	"	"
"	Joseph Olive	"	"	"	"
"	Edward Murphy	'	"	"	"
"	Charles Brown	"	"	"	Private
Private	William Hill	"	"	"	Cornetist
"	John Harold	"	"	"	"
"	Solomon Reilly	"	"	"	"
"	Joseph Spears	"	"	"	"
"	William Barry	'.	"	"	Private
"	John Bradley	"	"	"	"
"	Gabriel Burges	"	"	"	"
"	Mataldo Campbell	"	"	"	"
"	William Davis	"	"	"	"
"	James Dailey	"	"	"	"
"	Michael Egan	"	"	"	"
"	James Farrell	"	"	"	"
"	William Field	"	"	"	"
"	John Gardiner	"	"	"	"
"	John Gedney	"	"	"	"
"	John Graham	"	"	"	"
"	Michael Jones	"	"	"	"
"	Thomas Kemp	"	"	"	"
"	John McDermot	"	"	"	"
"	Gregory Meats	"	"	"	"
"	John Naughton	"	"	"	"
"	Michael Niel	"	"	"	"
"	Jarvis Oldfield	"	"	"	"
"	John Boyle	"	"	"	"

"	William Byford	"	"	"	"
"	Lewis Lloyd	"	"	"	"
"	Hugh Dailey	"	"	"	"
"	Edward Goodright	"	"	"	"
"	John Kelly	"	"	"	"
"	James Langley	"	"	"	"
"	Daniel Lynch	"	"	"	"
"	Madin McCarthy	"	"	"	"
"	Philip Mellon	"	"	"	"
"	James Murray	"	"	"	"
"	Joseph Nauger	"	"	"	"
"	James Oldham	"	"	"	"
"	Joseph Pinner	"	"	"	"
"	William Ryan	"	"	"	"
"	Edward Reilly	"	"	"	"
"	Samuel Shipman	"	"	"	"
"	Peter Slaine	"	"	"	1st Corporal
"	Richard Hodges	"	"	"	Private
"	Thomas Bidwell	"	"	"	"
"	George Ashenhurst	"	"	"	2nd Sergt.
"	John Kayne	"	"	"	Private
"	John Charles	"	"	"	"
"	John Gregory	"	"	"	"
"	William Hutt	"	"	"	"
"	Walter Hardy	"	"	"	"
"	Patrick Mullaly	"	"	"	"
"	James Thomas	"	"	"	"
"	Mathew McAllister	"	"	"	"
"	John Hurst	"	"	"	"
"	Daniel Dowd	"	"	"	"
"	John Dougherty	"	"	"	"
"	Joseph Masia	"	"	"	"
"	James English	"	"	"	1st Sergt.
"	William Baxter	"	"	"	Private
"	John Grice	"	"	"	"
"	James Hurley	"	"	"	"
"	Edward Madden	"	"	"	"
"	James Muggleton	"	"	"	"
"	Patrick McDonald	"	"	"	"
"	William Owens	"	"	"	"
"	William Thompson	"	"	"	"
"	William Merido	"	"	"	1st Corporal
"	Samuel Mills	"	"	"	Private
"	John Hefferon	"	"	"	"
"	Henry Stymire	"	"	"	"
"	Nicholas Tracy	"	"	"	"
"	John Pea	"	"	"	2nd Sergt.
"	John Solomento	"	"	"	Private
"	James Blake	"	"	"	1st Corporal
"	James Conollon	"	"	"	Private
"	Rufino Finn	"	"	"	"
"	Henry Kane	"	"	"	"
"	Benjamin Keller	"	"	"	"
"	William Lawrence	"	"	"	"
"	Christopher Lawrence	"	"	"	2nd Sergt.
"	William McCauley	"	"	"	Private
"	Thomas Mannon	"	"	"	"

"	James Niel	"	"	"	"
"	Charles Spencer	"	"	"	"
"	William Turner	"	"	"	"
"	James Thompson	"	"	"	"
"	Michael Walsh	"	"	"	"
"	Stephen Wilson	"	"	"	"
"	Thomas Blair	"	"	"	1st Corporal
"	John Bruce	"	"	"	Private
"	John Haverling	"	"	"	"
"	Peter Murphy	"	"	"	"
"	Thomas Langoff	"	"	"	"
"	Charles Plum	"	"	"	"
"	Thomas Stoors	"	"	"	"
"	James Smith	"	"	"	"
"	John Scott	"	"	"	1st Corporal
"	James Taylor	"	"	"	Private
"	Philip Woods	"	"	"	"
"	John Williams	"	"	"	1st Corporal

Valencia, Nov. 15, 1823.

(Sgd.)   Robert Gordon

Major, temporarily in command.

Approved.

(Sgd.)   Edward Brand

Commanding.

APPENDIX I

From Archivo Nacional, Bogotá, Guerra y Marina, Historia, DCCLXXIX, 861:

" Battallón Albión   República de Colombia

Lista de revista del Comisario que pasa del expresado en el dia de la fecha."

Clases	Nombres	Destino
Coronel	Juan Mackintosh	enfermo
Teniente coronel	Juan Johnston	
Sargento Major	Tomás Manby	
Teniente coronel graduado, Capitán	Juan Bendle	enfermo
Capitán	Carlos Smith	
id.	Tomás Palmer	enfermo
id.	Guillermo Brown	
id.	Archibald Dunlop	
id.	Julian Ravenscroft	
Teniente 1°	Federico Fulham	
id.	Hugo Macmanus	
Teniente	Donald Ross	enfermo
id.	Pedro Obrine	
id.	Carlos Trousdale	
id.	Julian Linch	
id.	Julian Kain	
id.	Eduardo Cave	
id.	Juan Brown	hospital
id.	Eduardo Duke	
id.	Tomás Mara	
Sargento 1°	Tomás Raber	
id.	Tomás Bates	hospital
id.	Jorge Walder	
id.	Andrew Burgess	
id.	Garrat Noland	
id.	Victorio Obitzer	guardia
id.	Andreas Shoecroft	
Sargento 2°	Tomás Jacobs	
id.	Alexandria (sic) Monroe	
id.	Juan Davis	
id.	Carlos West	
id.	Jorge Liebie	
id.	Julian Shirley	
Cabo 1°	Herman Shrider	
id.	José Davey	guardia
id.	Tomás Williams	id.
id.	Jorge Eldridge	
id.	Juan Suttcliff	

416

id.	Jacob Teison	
id.	Jacob Betcherman	
Corneta	Pedro Hutchinson	
Soldado	Juan Shenton	
id.	Enrique Bates	
id.	Julian Mason	
id.	Jacob Getts	
id.	Diego Roso (Ross?) (Roe?)	
id.	Pedro Gannon	
id.	Tomás Jones	
id.	Miguel Cunningham	
id.	Juan Ledger	
id.	Tomás Francis	
id.	Miguel Flinn	
id.	Dionicio Downey	
id.	Francisco Frisby	
id.	Juan Butcher	
id.	Julian Larkin	hospital
id,	Francisco Fuge	id.
id.	Samuel Dolloway	id.
id.	Brion Lacey	id.
id.	Julian Lobley	id.
id.	Carlos Brown	id.
id.	Juan Smith	id.

Cuartel General, Bogotá, 3 de diciembre
de 1822

El Comandante
(Sgd.) Juan Johnston.

APPENDIX J

Below are given records of service of additional British and Irish legionaries whose names were found principally in the national archives at Bogotá and Caraças. Where the information is already in print, only the name, rank and nationality are mentioned, together with the page number of Scarpetta y Vergara where all necessary data about the individual may be found.

Beggs, Francis, colonel, commissioned by D'Evereux, March 20, 1820 in the Regiment of Tiradores, Irish Legion. Archivo Nacional, Bogotá, Guerra y Marina, Historia, XXXV, 847; *cf*. also *supra,* Chap. VI.

Birgo, J., (English) colonel. Sarpetta y Vergara, 50.

Boyd, Charles (Irish) sergeant major, enlisted at Margarita; 1819; campaigns of 1820-21; commanding platoon of foreigners in New Guayana; in charge of ammunition train on march to New Granada; total service, two years nine months. Archivo Nacional, Caracas, Ilustres Próceres (not yet filed or numbered).

Brion, Peter (English) lieutenant. S. & V. 65.

Collins, Samuel (English) lieutenant colonel. S. & V. 109.

D'Cros, Frederick (Irish) sergeant-major. S. & V. 125, 126.

Dunlop, Archibald, captain, began service under Col. Elsam, Sept., 1818 campaigns on the north coast and in the south; captured at Esmeraldas, applied for retired pay as captain, since he forfeited his half pay in England. Archivo Nacional, Bogotá, Guerra y Marina, Historia, XXXV, 869, 870.

Duncan, James (Irish), captain, in squadron of militia cavalry; total service, six years twenty-two days. Hojas de Servicios, XIII, 203.

Duran, Antonio Maria, lieutenant colonel " vivo y efectivo ", commanded a squadron of " Dragones de la Unión " in which was serving a company of the Irish Legion. H. de S. XIII, 768.

Egan, Dennis (Irish), sergeant major with rank of lieutenant colonel attached to the general staff of Zulia; campaigns and battles of Pichincha, Cartagena, Santa Marta, artillery brigade of Maracaybo. G. & M., Hist., DCCLXXX, 859.

Flynn, Michael (Irish), first sergeant, in actions of Cojeda, Gameza, Pántano de Vargas, Boyacá, Pasto, campaigns of Venezuela and the south, served in Albion, Cauca and Vargas Battalions and half brigade of artillery; total service, twelve years, eighteen days, from 1818 to 1830. H. de S. XV, 305.

Fraser, James (Scotch), lieutenant colonel, gave his services to Colombia for thirty-two years and three months. He was aide to Gen. D'Evereux until 1822, was then for two years in command of the Boyacá Battalion, and from 1825 to 1827 was holding the post of military commandant of the province of Mérida, where his principal duty was that of organizing reserve troops. He was then given indefinite leave, although he continued to interest himself in the militia of Pamplona. He died at Bogotá June 9, 1878. G. & M., Hist. X, 690; H. de S. XVI, 807; Franco, *op. cit.*, 15.

Grant, Peter, lieutenant colonel, was aide to General Pedro León Torres at Achaguas in 1820. G. & M., Hist., II, 506.

Harrison, Jacob, captain, while very young came with the detachment of the Irish Legion, under Lieut. Col. Julius Reinboldt, which was attached to the British Legion for the campaign of the Apure. In the Carabobo Battalion he went through the campaigns of Coro and Maracaibo and took part in the siege of Puerto Cabello. In 1826 he fought at La Guaira and two years later was promoted captain. He continued in the army until 1836, when he obtained an indefinite leave on one-third salary. Archivo Nacional, Caracas, Ilustres Próceres, XL, 73; Despachos militares, 47; Dávila, *Dic. Biog.*, I, 229.

Hogan, Maurice (Irish) sergeant major. S. & V., 225.

Hubble, John B. (English). S. & V., 229.

Keogh, William (Scotch), lieutenant. S. & V., 248.

Laiton, Stephen, ensign promoted from 1st sergeant in the Neiva Battalion. In the examination for promotion he especially distinguished himself "answering satisfactorily all questions, showing good intelligence, application for study, knowledge of the cavalry arm, skill in reading and writing." H. de S., XVII, 513, 514.

Lawless, Thomas (Irish). S. & V., 255.

Lecumberry, Ignatius, Colonel. While still a lieutenant he was captured by the royalists near Quito, but was exchanged during the armistice of 1821 and assigned to duty with the Squadron of Dragoons. For bravery at the battle of Ayacucho he was recommended for promotion to captain. In 1834 he was, in accordance with the law of February 12, 1833, incorporated in the army of Venezuela as a colonel. O'Leary, *Docs.* XIX, 478; *Report Min. War Venez.* 1834.

Lee, Charles, captain. Enlisted as private, June 1, 1811. Total service fourteen years, one month. Campaigns of the north, south, Pasto and Peru; battles of Chituga, Cachiri, Popayán, Junín, Matará, Callao; captured at Cachiri and forced to serve in the royalist army until 1816 when he deserted; taken prisoner again at Popayán; wounded at Matará. H. de S. XXV, 480.

Lee, Robert, sergeant major. S. & V., 256.

Lyster, William (Irish), colonel, in Irish Legion, served for four years under Páez and Soublette. Sept. 19, 1823 asked for retirement with salary and military privileges pertaining to his rank. G. & M. hist. XXXV, 905; Arch. Soublette, Docs. III.

MacGuire, Lorenzo (Irish), captain. S. & V., 284.

MacMunup (full name not known. Possibly Hugo MacManus, of the Albion Battalion is meant), sub-lieutenant, served in campaign of Apure, in action at Gameza and Pántano de Vargas, where he was wounded. *La Nación* (Caracas), Nov. 8, 1910.

MacPherson, John (Scotch), captain, campaigns of Oriente de Venezuela, Cúcuta, Zulia; wounded in naval battle of Maracaibo. *Ibid.*

Maguire, James (Irish) lieutenant, campaign of the coast in 1819; in action at Molino, Riohacha, Turbaco, Monteclaro; executed by the royalists. *Ibid.*

Matwell (full name not known) captain, campaign of Venezuela; siege of Puerto Cabello, 1823. *Ibid.*

Miller, John D., sub-lieutenant, entered army of the Apure Nov. 1816, as a first sergeant; sub-lieutenant, March 1, 1819; ensign in a cavalry regiment of the Guides in 1823. *Boletín Hist. y Antig.* VIII, 292.

Moran (full name not known) captain, campaigns of Apure, New Granada, 1819, south, 1822; engagements Bonza, Pántano de Vargas, Boyacá, Riobamba, Pichincha. *La Nación,* Oct. 26, 1910.

Munro, George, lieutenant, entered the service in 1818; campaigns of the " llanos ", Carabobo, Coro, Zulia, where he suffered disability from fever. G. & M. hist., XXXV, 927.

Murray, Thomas, general, entered the service in 1818; campaigns of Magdalena, 1820-21, Zulia, 1822-23, Maracaibo, 1823. *La Nación,* Oct. 26, 1910. *Cf.* also S. & V. 380.

Neeham, John (Irish), colonel; arrived in 1817, campaigns and engagements of Apure, Oriente, Semen, Bocachica, Órtiz, Calabozo, Peru and Callao. *La Nación,* Oct. 26, 1910.

Norton, John, sergeant, took part in all campaigns of the British Legion and of the Carabobo Battalion in the campaign of Zulia. Served in Peru in Vencedor Battalion. In 1829 on account of the loss of his sight, he retired with pay of five " pesos " per month and the right to use his uniform; in 1830 his pension was increased; in 1842 he was granted permission to return to Ireland with his passage paid by the government of Venezuela, but he remained in Valencia where he died in 1847. Ilustres Próceres, LX, 94.

O'Brien, Peter, lieutenant, campaign of Boyacá; came to Bogotá Jan. 19, 1823, to secure settlement of his accounts; ordered paid Oct. 31, same year. G. & M., Hist. XXXV, 933.

O'Dogherty, William, lieutenant, came to Margarita in 1819 in British Legion; campaign of Cumaná; returned to England on sick leave. G. & M., Hist. XXXV, 932.

Peaten (full name not known), captain of Rifles, wounded at the capture of Ciénaga of Santa Marta in 1820. *La Nación,* Nov. 23, 1910.

Philean, F. (Irish) captain of Rifles, wounded at the capture of Ciénaga of Santa Marta in 1820. *Ibid.*

Powell, John, a British half-pay officer, received a commission from Col. Maceroni and was sent to join McGregor. While at Havana he was arrested on suspicion and confined in the Morro, but was later released through the intercession of the commander of a British ship of war. In 1820 he offered his services to Colombia in any capacity and asked if his commission would be considered valid. The result of his application is not known. G. & M., Hist., I, 662, 663.

Russell, John (Irish) had ten years service with the patriots in Buenos Aires. He then fled to Colombia and remained hidden for three years in Antioquía and Cali. In 1821 he asked Bolívar to attach him to a corps in which he might die in defense of the fatherland. There is no record of his having done any service for Colombia, but on Nov. 26, 1824 he asked for a pension. G. & M., Hist., VII, 19, 198.

Sadleir, Nathaniel, gave up his half pay in the 69th Regiment of Infantry in the English army to join the British Legion. He was killed in the attack on Cumaná. In 1823 his brother applied for his back pay, commutation of rations, and bounty. G. &. M., Hist., XXXV, 943.

Samper, Joseph A., sub-lieutenant, entered the army on July 14, 1821; he had a total service of six years three months and four days in the Rifles, Tunja and Boyacá, Battalions, and was engaged at Gámeza, Pántano de Vargas, Boyacá and Carabobo. G. & M., Hist., VII, 54.

Scott, James, sergeant major, and a lieutenant of the same name were present at Carabobo in the English lancers. Another Scott, first name not known (Irish), captain and adjutant of the Albion Battalion, was also at this battle and was killed there. G. & M., Hist., XXXV, 944; *La Nación,* Nov. 23, 1910.

Smith, Charles (Irish) captain, made the campaigns of the Apure and of the South and was engaged at Gamarra, Cañafístolo, Pitayó, Jenoi, Yaguachi, and Pichincha. *La Nación,* Nov. 23, 1910.

Smith, William (Scotch), colonel, came to Angostura with Uslar; campaign of the Apure under Páez; at Carabobo as ser-geant major of Boyacá Battalion, commissary of the army of the centre of Venezuela until 1826, when he refused to follow Páez in separating from Colombia. Bolívar then granted him retirement as colonel. From 1828 to 1830 he was commissary general and auditor of the national treasury; in 1837 minister of war and marine and in charge of the departments of treasury and foreign relations; in 1841 he was director of the national bank; in 1824 while commanding the congressional guard he was wounded in the defense of the congress; in 1857 he died at Caracas, and two years later his widow received a pension. Ilustres Próceres, LXXXVIII, 101.

Talbot, George (Irish), captain, appointed lieutenant in 1822, captain in 1827, total service to the end of October, 1827, five years, nine months and twenty days. Served in the Boyacá Battalion in campaigns of Coro and in the East; severely wounded at siege of Puerto Cabello; adjutant of the garrison of Caracas until transferred to the corps of Maracaibo. H. de S., XXIV, 118.

Talbot, William (Irish), captain. S. & V., 612.

Terrion, John (English), lieutenant colonel. S. & V., 618.

Thompson, Thomas (English), civilian contractor. S. & V., 618.

Vernau, George, captain, came with the British Legion with which he took part in the campaign of the east in 1819. In 1822 he was retired for severe wounds received, August 11, in the victory of Sábana de la Guardia, where he fought " with extraordinary valor, commanding a company of infantry ". In 1827 he was reappointed to the army as a lieutenant, but in 1830 was again retired with one-third of his salary for dis-ability due to the loss of his left leg from wounds. Ilustres Próceres, XCVIII, 82.

Watts, Henry John, lieutenant of the Caracas Battalion, joined in 1818; wounded at Maracaibo in 1823; commissioned as 1st lieutenant of infantry, Oct. 25, 1828. *La Nación,* Nov. 25, 1910; Despachos militares No. 2, p. 56.

Weston, Richard (Irish), lieutenant, enlisted as private after Boyacá; promoted corporal, sergeant and ensign in 1819; entire service in Carabobo Battalion in campaigns of Barinas, Maracaibo, and Puerto Cabello. *La Nación,* Nov. 25, 1910; H. de S., XLVIII, 730, 731.

White, Richard, colonel, in action at Apure, Bonza, Pántano de Vargas, Boyacá, Carabobo, Junín, Ayacucho, commanding Vargas Battalion. S. & V., 704.

White, William, civilian, was an Englishman by birth but before the first revolution of 1810 he became a Venezuelan by adoption, and enthusiastically used his influence in trying to secure from the English government aid for the Venezuelan patriots. He had long been a friend of Bolívar with whom he kept up an active correspondence from his home in Trinidad. The important services which William White rendered by transmitting to England information received from Bolívar have already been referred to (*supra,* Chapter VI, p. 140, n.). After independence had been gained, White left Trinidad with all his family to devote himself to the welfare of the new republic. He was appointed collector of internal revenue at the capital of Colombia and member of the council of government of Venezuela. Later he held the office of auditor general of the tobacco tax. His services and character were so highly appreciated that it was even suggested by a leading newspaper of Caracas that the citizens of Venezuela go into public mourning at his death which occurred sometime in November, 1834. *Gaceta de Venezuela,* Nov. 22, 1834, quoted in Azpúrua, *op. cit.,* II, 407, 408; S. & V., 704.

Wilthew, Charles, colonel, arrived at Angostura in March, 1818, as an officer in the Red Hussars under Col. Wilson; made all the campaigns of the lower Apure under Páez; sent on a mission to Bogotá where he was taken sick; returned to Venezuela in 1822; took part in campaigns of Coro, Maracaibo and Puerto Cabello. Páez sent him to Bogotá with his official report of the capture of Puerto Cabello. While at Bogotá Col. Wilthew was appointed aide-de-camp to Vice-President Santander. H. de S., XLVIII, 741; Hamilton, *op. cit.,* I, 270.

APPENDIX K

Here follow records of various Birtish and Irish officers who were assigned to duty in the navies of Colombia and Venezuela. Most of these records are taken from the national archives at Bogotá or Caracas, but where they are already in print as in Scarpetta y Vergara, page references to that work are noted, and no data other than the name, nationality and rank are given.

Brown, Thomas (Scotch), captain of frigate, total service eleven years, eleven months, three days, from November 1, 1816 to Oct. 25, 1828; first commissioned by Admiral Brión as a lieutenant commanding the schooner " Coneja " cruising off Cuba and Haiti; transferred to brig of war " Indio Libre " at Margarita island; action at Barcelona, capture of Angostura, blockade of Puerto Cabello; 1822-24, transporting troops between Guayaquil and Peru; 1826-28, routine naval cruises and transporting troops along north coast. Archivo Nacional, Bogotá, Guerra y Marina, Hojas de Servicios, V, 942.

Brun, James, ship-captain, began service November 1, 1819 as a captain in the Vencedor Battalion at Cúcuta; transferred to squadron of cavalry of the Guard as adjutant to Col. Rondón; commissioned to construct thirty boats on the river Julia; in action at Carabobo; then assigned to command brig-of-war cruising off the coast of Venezuela as a privateer; subsequently appointed captain of the port at Cartagena; retired from active service in 1843. He sent his son Richard to the nautical school in order to fit him to become an officer in the navy. *Ibid.*, IV, 879; V, 688, 696.

Buch, Richard John (English), lieutenant of frigate. S. & V., 68.

Clarke, William Somers, lieutenant of marine infantry, began service as a lieutenant in the British Legion, Jan. 18, 1819; then in the cavalry of the division of operations on the coast; transferred to the marine infantry, Jan. 6, 1823. Participated in capture of Barcelona, attack on Cumaná, taking of Rio Hacha, siege of Cartagena, engagement at Ciénaga, blockade of Puerto Cabello, fight with Spanish frigate " Constitución " in 1823; squadron of operations 1825-26; campaign against factions of Cumanacoa, 1827-28. H. de S., XLII, 130.

Cock, Richard John, lieutenant of frigate, assigned to duty abroard brig-of-war " Victoria," by order of Admiral Brión; in actions of Barcelona and Cumaná; second in command of brig-of-war " Restaurador " at the blockade of Cumaná; engaged at blockade of Puerto Cabello; at San Juan de Nicaragua 1825-26; on indefinite leave with one-third salary after March, 1828. *Ibid.*, VIII, 119.

Finley, George, naval ensign, served on corvette " Carabobo " in cruise off Porto Rico 1822-23; capture of corvette " María Francisca," 1822; final blockade and capture of Puerto Cabello in 1823; cruise in brig " Pichincha " to the coast of Spain in 1826-27. Captured and imprisoned in Algeciras until August 28, 1827, when he was discharged and sent with despatches to Gibraltar. At the last date he was only nineteen years old. *Ibid.*, XV, 505.

Gram (full name and rank unknown), who was reported by Morillo in 1818 to have formed a corps of marines under Brión, but who was believed to be so disgusted with the service that he was ready to betray his admiral. Rodríguez Villa, *op. cit.*, III, 699.

Henderson (full name unknown), commander of brigantine " Cauca " in 1822, was operating against the coast of Esmeraldas and Barbacoas. He captured the island of Tinoco and the Spanish commandant Lieut. Col. Vicente Parra, two officers, twenty-five men and fifty rifles with ammunition. *Gaceta de Colombia,* June 16, 1822.

Hughes, Hugo (English), lieutenant colonel. S. & V., 228.

Innes, David B. (Scotch), captain of frigate, took service in London Dec. 1, 1816, with López Méndez; arrived at Margarita March, 1817; assigned to duty on brig-of-war "Gen. Arismendi", cruising off Puerto Cabello and to Porto Rico; took aboard the munitions which arrived on the " Dowson " and " Britannia " and transported them to the Orinoco; transferred to the brig-of-war " Colombia " under Capt. Hill; in action at Guiria and Rio Hacha; took Montilla with staff, artillery and munitions from Rio Hacha to Santa Marta; transported troops from Cartagena to the south; in 1828 appointed captain of the port of the province of Margarita, H. de S., XLVIII, 832.

Jeffrey, William H. (Irish), lieutenant of frigate, began service nuder Capt. Nicolas Joli at San Bartolomé, Feb. 1, 1819; engaged at Barcelona and Cumaná same year; carried ammunition and supplies from the island of St. Thomas to Montilla at Rio Hacha; cruising about West Indies; Jan. 17, 1821 captured by Spanish brig " San Antonio "; returned to the service of the republic Sept. 13, 1824; cruising in West Indies; transporting the Vargas and Callao Battalions from Chagres on the Isthmus of Panama to Santa Marta. *Ibid.*, XXIV, 117.

Locke, George W., sub-lieutenant of frigate, began service Jan. 9, 1823, as naval ensign on brig-of-war " Independiente "; in battle of Lake Maracaibo and siege of Puerto Cabello. *Ibid.*, XXIV, 844.

Murray, Thomas, general, came with the British Legion; made campaigns of Magdalena and Zulia. Appointed first adjutant on the staff of Padilla; engaged at battle of Lake Maracaibo; took part in more than twenty actions; died at Bogotá in 1823. Franco, *op. cit.*, 26.

Richards, Thomas (rank unknown) arrived at Cartagena in 1815; offered his services in the army at Cartagena, Bogotá and elsewhere; after the defeat of the patriots in Cartagena by Morillo, crossed the mountains and " llanos," arriving at Angostura in 1817; joined the navy under Brión with whom he served until 1821; retired to Curaçao and then to Caracas where he married Maria Vergara, and had thirteen children. He died in poverty at Caracas on Sept. 6, 1840. Azpúrua, *op. cit.*, III, 144.

Speed, William, ensign of frigate, total service in national navy four years, twenty-three months and sixteen days; began as a marine guard Nov. 6, 1822; in that year cruised to Porto

Rico and blockaded Puerto Cabello; 1826-27 cruised to the coasts of Spain and Africa. H. de S., XLI, 826.

Stagg, Leonard, general, began service as a naval lieutenant under Brión, May 15, 1822; took part in blockades of Puerto Cabello and battle of Lake Maracaibo; in 1825, was sent on a mission to the United States in a brig under Nicolas Joli; on December 15, 1830 he signed a "manifesto of the fleet" in Guayaquil as a faithful adherent of Bolívar and of the integrity of Colombia. *Ibid.,* XLII, 128; Andrade, *op. cit.,* 369.

Stuart, William (born in New York), naval ensign, entered the service of the republic June, 1822; served on the corvette "Bolívar" at the capture of the "María Francisca" and in the first blockade of Puerto Cabello. His commanding officer reported that he was not a navigator and that he knew only how to read and write English. *Ibid.,* XLII, 103.

Taylor (full name and rank not known), while in command of the schooner of war "Pichincha" was sent to Guayaquil under Col. Thomas Charles Wright to demand explanations from the Peruvian corvette "Libertad" for blockading Guayaquil; took part in the naval action off Point Malpedo, Aug. 31, 1828; killed in an ambuscade in the mountains in 1833. Andrade, *op. cit.,* 384.

Unsworth, John, naval lieutenant, was wounded in the action between the Peruvian corvette "Libertad" and the schooner "Guayaquileña" off Point Malpedo, Aug. 31, 1818. *Ibid.,* 388.

On March 15, 1828, certain naval officers stationed at Puerto Cabello signed a vote of confidence in Bolívar. Among the names were those of Cadet William Woodrow, Ensign George Finlay, Surgeon B. L. Miller, Lieut. A. B. Smith, Lieut. William H. Jeffrey, First Commandant of Marine Infantry George Woolsey and Capt. Joseph C. Swain. *El Voto de Venezuela* 184.

The Report of the Minister of War and Marine of Venezuela for 1834 gives the following list of naval officers who received one-third salary during the years 1832-33:

	Rank	Name	Amount "Pesos"	"Reales"
Captain	of ship	Nicolas Joli	639	89
"	" "	Sebastian Boguies	159	99
"	" "	W. D. Chitty *	106	66
"	" frigate	John Clarck (sic)	460	
"	" "	James Bluck	460	
"	" "	Joseph Swain	460	
First	lieutenant	Francis Curtis	220	
Second	"	Thomas Sever	79	93
"	"	William Seward	160	

* In 1818 Chitty commanded the brig of war "Libertador" which brought to Margarita the muskets, powder, lead, and other munitions sent from England by López Méndez. *Morning Chronicle*, Dec. 4, 1818.

APPENDIX L

From Archivo Nacional, Bogotá, Guerra y Marina, historia, DCCLXXVIII, 895:
Lista de Revista, Comisaria y siguientes para los nombrados ingleses.

Teniente Coronel	Tomás Harrison	$140	pesos
Sargento Mayor	Carlos Carver	100	ps
id id	Dionisio Egan	100	ps
Cp. Tt. Crl. Agregado	Noble M'Mullin	$ 60	ps
Capitan	Archibaldo Dunlop	60	ps
id	Guillermo Ravenscroft	60	ps
id	Diego D. Patterson	60	ps
id	Jorge Brown	60	ps
id	Juan Shaw	60	ps
id	D. McCarthy	60	ps
id	Guillermo Brown	60	ps
id	Diego Whittle	60	ps
id	N. Duxbury	60	ps
Teniente	Pedro O'Brian	$ 40	ps
id	Tomás Ridgway	40	ps
id	Federico Fox	40	ps
id	Tomás Dickey	40	ps
id	Tomás Lloyd	40	ps
id	Diego Brown	40	ps
id	G. M. Mortimer	40	ps
id	Timotheo Keogh	40	ps
id	Guillermo Lynch	40	ps
Soldados	Guillermo Brum	$ 10	ps
id	Antonio Peña	10	ps
id	José Rowe	10	ps
id	Manuel Zapata	10	ps

$1,340

Bogotá 11 de Abril
de 1821—11

F. Harrison
Teniente Coronel
L. B.

APPENDIX M

Excerpts from the records of pensions, bonuses and retired pay of foreign officers and soldiers in the armies of Venezuela and Colombia, in *Exposición que presenta al Congreso de Venezuela el Secretario de Guerra y Marina sobre los negocios de su cargo en 1832,* pp. 8, 9, 41:

Under the law of Sept. 17, 1830 indefinite leave with one-third salary was granted to four generals, ten colonels, sixteen commandants, twenty-two captains, three lieutenants and four sublieutenants. Those with certificates of disability were to continue to receive full pay.

Report of expenses	" Pesos " per year
Permanent army	334,272
Retired on one-third pay	80,256
Invalid pensions	30,348

(Signed) Carlos Soublette
Caracas, Jan. 20, 1832.

Ibid. for 1833, pp. 68–71. List of those granted disability pensions:

Name	Rank	" Pesos " per year
James Hurle	1st sergeant	96
John Macormack	2nd sergeant	60
Timothy Conolly	1st Corporal	72
Thomas Cullen	" "	48
Hugo Dale	" "	72
William Fincher	" "	48
Paul Hoteman	" "	48
Joseph Donovan	Private	60
Thomas Gray	"	60
Charles Hams	"	39
Thomas Holwood	"	60
Edward Reilly	"	40
Maria Flute	Englishwoman	67
Juliana Pat	"	67
Maria Flute	English child	67
George Flute	" "	67
Julian Flute	" "	67

431

Ibid., for 1834, pp. 62–69. Officers to whom have been granted invalid pensions for the years 1832–33:

	"Pesos"	"Reales"
Captain Dennis O'Reilly	230	50
" Pedro Montesino	360	
1st Sergeant Richard Ryan (in the mines)	8	
1st Corporal Timothy Conolly	66	
" " William Tinechin	48	
" " Paul Holterman	48	
" " Hugo Daley	72	
" " Thomas Callan	4	
Private Thomas Green	60	
" Nicholas Connell	60	
" Joseph Donovan	60	
" John Gardner	48	
" Charles Hunt died	30	33
" Edward Reilly	37	
" Thomas Howard	60	
Women, Catalina Prat	68	24
" Maria Flute	68	24
Children, George Flute	68	24
" Julian Flute	68	24
" Maria Flute	68	24

Ibid., for 1834, p. 51. List of officers who have taken one-third salary for the years 1832–33:

	"pesos"	"reales"
Col. Ignatius Lecumberry	139	98
" Charles Castelli	139	98
" George Woodberry	559	92
" Johanes Uslar	559	92
1st Commandant Thomas Richard	399	96
" " Lem Ferrer	233	31
" " Henry Weir	399	89
2nd " Daniel Maclaughlin	279	96
Capt. Francis Manuit	180	00
" Jacob Harrison	90	39
" Pedro Montesino	165	00
" William Ashdown	180	00
" John B. Grisell	180	00
" Philip Sibol	180	00

Ibid. for 1855, p. 41. The name of 2nd Commandant John Macpherson was dropped from the invalid pension list because of his death.

From Archivo Nacional, Caracas, Despachos de retiros, de licencias, de premios, de inválidos, folio 718 — commissions carrying retired pay and invalid pensions issued to:

William Gill, captain " efectivo " of infantry as of Oct. 29, 1820.

Rupert Hand, captain of infantry as of April 3, 1819.

Robert Gordon, captain of infantry as of Feb. 10, 1819.

Nathaniel Whitman, captain of infantry, promoted to lieutenant colonel of infantry.

Henry Weir, captain of infantry as of June 4, 1819.

John Lanigan, captain of infantry, Sept. 6, 1820.

Lieut. Samuel Paramor of infantry declared of rank as of Dec. 2, 1819.

Thomas Underwood, lieutenant of infantry, July 7, 1819.

From Archivo Nacional, Caracas, Ilustres Próceres, XLIV, 245. First sergeant John Kelly was retired in 1843 for disability caused by fourteen wounds. He claimed to have been wounded at Boyacá and in the attack on Fort Agua Santa, but it would have been impossible for him to have been at both these places at the same time.

In Dávila, *Diccionario Biográfico,* the following additional names of foreigners who were awarded pensions by Venezuela are noted:

Private John Gardner, granted certificate of disability by Great Colombia; promoted corporal and granted pension by Venezuela in 1842; died at Caracas in 1856; *op. cit.,* I, 182.

Capt. John Hands pensioned in 1855; at his death his daughter received his pension. *Ibid.* I, 229.

Major John Irwin died in 1842 at Maracaibo, where he was surgeon in the military hospital. His daughter, Margarita, received his pension. *Ibid.* I, 260.

Sergeant Major Daniel MacLaughlin retired at Bogotá in 1824; with rank and pay of lieutenant colonel and the right to wear uniform; died at Caracas in 1844. *Ibid.,* I, 314.

Private Thomas Plumard retired for disability in 1823, with salary and right to wear uniform. *Ibid.,* II, 114.

Lieut. Col. Thomas Richards died at Caracas in 1840; his widow received his pension. *Ibid.*, II, 160.

From the report of the "Comisión central de repartimientos de bienes nacionales de Venezuela " for 1829:

Folio	Rank and Name	Date of Allotment	Amount "Pesos"	"reales"
15	Private George Dillon	June 20	250	
15	Capt. Joseph Howard	July 3	901	
15	Col. Edward Stopford	July 11	21,377	7
20	Col. Juan Landa	Nov. 10	4,738	7
13	Col. Charles Smith	April 28	6,000	
13	Lieut. Col. Daniel Macklauquin (sic)	April 28	2,891	7
13	Lieut. Col. John Sherwood	May 1	1,500	
10	Capt. Dennis O'Reilly	Jan. 17	4,000	
2	Col. Joseph Florence McLeanen	Oct. 11, 1827	3,532	6 4/8
14	Capt. of frigate José Raffeci (sic)	May 25	5,960	2
3	Capt. of frigate David B. Innes	Nov. 9, 1827	6,000	
24	Dr. Samuel Forsyth	June 8, 1830	14,000	
24	Col. Philip Maurice Martin	July 5, 1830	7,000	

From Archivo Nacional, Bogotá, Guerra y Marina, Historia. Disability pay for soldiers of all classes was increased by decree of Aug. 11, 1822. XXVII, 571.

Commutation of rations for seven years unpaid since October, 1817 was recommended for Anna Tucker Rooke, widow of Lieut. Col. James Rooke, XXXV, 936.

Pension Bureau, Feb. 11, 1847, grants pension to Isabel Archer, widow of Col. John Mackintosh, 320 "reals" per month for eight years, counting from May 31, 1846 (the day after her husband died) and extending it to his two minor children, Jorge Juan Tomás and Mariana (Maria Ana). MCCCXVIII, 115.

BIBLIOGRAPHY

I. Sources

1. MANUSCRIPT MATERIAL

"Archivo del Libertador," containing numerous copies of documents from official and private sources, in possession of Dr. Vicente Lecuna of Caracas.

Archivo del Gral. Mariano Montilla, ordenado y clasificado bajo la dirección del Señor Vicente Lecuna, in the possession of the Misses Uztáriz Montilla at Caracas. (Not all the folios are as yet numbered.)

Archivo del General Carlos Soublette in the Academia Nacional de Historia at Caracas. (Not all the folios are as yet numbered.)

Archivo Miranda, in the Academia Nacional de Historia at Caracas. (Not all the folios are as yet numbered.)

Archivo Nacional, Bogotá, sección República, Guerra y Marina:
> Historia;
> Hojas de servicios;
> Registro de Jefes 1816 a 24, Nombramientos y ascensos militares del 8 de febrero de 1816 al 18 de agosto 1924.

Archivo Nacional, Caracas, Revolucíon y Gran Colombia:
> Comisión Central de repartimientos de bienes nacionales de Venezuela;
> Despachos de retiros, de licencias, de premios, de inválidos;
> Gobernación de Guayana;
> Próceres y servidores. Ilustres Próceres, 1810 a 1824.

Bingham collection in Yale University Library:
> Bolívar Papers;
> Sucre Papers;
> Prieto Villate, Elías, note-book containing a description of the battles of Pántano de Vargas and Boyacá written from accounts told by his father, Javier Luís Villate and Francisco Marino Soler, who were eye-witnesses and participants in the events.

British Museum, London. Manuscript Division.
> Additional Manuscripts:
>> Liverpool Papers;
>> Ravenga " Memoir on the Republic of Colombia ";
>> Wellesley Papers.

435

Egerton Manuscripts.
　Army General Order, April 25, 1815;
　Army General Orders, British Army in Belgium.
Información genealógica Jurado-López Méndez. This is a beautifully
　illuminated manuscript album in the possession of Col. Santos Jurado
　y López Méndez, of Caracas.
New York Public Library, Manuscript Division, Miscellaneous Papers:
　William Dawkins, captain in the British navy, to Commodore
　Daniel, April 4, 1823.
　Luís Brión to Peter Wirgman, March 3, 1819.
Public Record Office, London.
　Foreign Office Records (referred to as F. O.)
　War Office Records (referred to as W. O.)
Transcripts of copies of official correspondence found in the desk of
　Viceroy Antonio Amar, now in the possession of Gen. J. D. Monsalve
　at Bogotá.

2. BOOKS

Adam, William Jackson, *Journal of voyages to Marguaritta, Trinidad
　and Maturín; with the author's travels across the plains of the
　llaneros to Angostura, and subsequent descent of the Orinoco in the
　years 1819-1820; comprising several interviews with Bolívar.
　Sketches of the various native and European generals.* Dublin, 1824.
American State Papers. Foreign Affairs, IV, Washington, 1834.
Andrews, Capt., *Journey from Buenos Aires through the Provinces of
　Cordova, Tucuman, and Salta to Potosi, thence by the deserts of
　Carauja to Arica, and subsequently on behalf of the Chilean and
　Peruvian Mining Association in the years 1825-26.* London, 1827.
Antepara, José Maria, *South American emancipation; documents his-
　torical and explanatory.* London, 1810.
Archivo Santander, 20 vols., Bogotá, 1913-1925.
Bache, Richard (Lieut.), *Notes on Colombia taken in the years 1822-23;
　with an itinerary of the route from Caracas to Bogotá, and an
　appendix; by an officer of the U. S. Army.* Philadelphia, 1827.
Biggs, James, *The history of Don Francisco de Miranda's attempt to
　effect a revolution in South America; in a series of letters by a
　gentleman who was an officer under that general, to his friend in
　the U. S.*, Boston, 1808.
Bingham, Hiram, *The journal of an expedition across Venezuela and
　Colombia in 1906-07; an exploration of the route of Bolívar's cele-
　brated march of 1819 and of the battlefields of Boyacá and Carabobo,*
　New Haven, 1909.
Blanco, José Félix, *Documentos para la historia de la vida pública del
　libertador de Colombia, Perú y Bolivia.* Caracas, 1875-78.

Brackenridge, Henry Marie, *Voyage to Buenos Aires performed in the years 1817 and 1818 by order of the American government.* London, 1820.

Brandsen, Federico de, *Escritos del coronel don Federico de Brandsen,* Buenos Aires, 1910.

British and Foreign State Papers, vols. IV, V, VI, London, 1838, 1837, 1835.

Brown, Capt. C., *Narrative of the Expedition to South America which sailed from England in 1817, for the service of the Spanish patriots,* London, 1819.

Burke, William, *Additional reasons for our immediately emancipating Spanish America,* London, 1808.

Cabrera de Nevares, Miguel, *Memoria sobre el estado actual de las Américas y medio de pacificarlas,* Madrid, 1821.

Campaigns and Cruises in Venezuela and New Granada, and in the Pacific Ocean, 1817 to 1830; also Tales of Venezuela, illustrative of revolutionary men, manners, and incidents, 3 v. in 2, London, 1831.

Cartas de Bolívar, 1799 a 1822, prologo de José Enrique Rodó y Notas de R. Blanco-Fombona, Paris and Buenos Ayres, 1912.

Chesterton, George Laval, *An Autobiografical Memoir,* 2 vols., London, 1853.

——, *Peace, War and Adventure. A narrative of proceedings in Venezuela in South America in the years 1819 and 1820; with general observations on the country and people; the character of the republican government; and its leading members,* etc., London, 1820.

Cochrane, Charles Stuart, *Journal of a residence and travels in Colombia during the years 1823 and 1824,* 2 v., London, 1825.

Codazzi, Giovanni Battista Agostino, *Atlas físico y político de la República de Venezuela,* Caracas, 1840.

——, *Atlas geográfico e histórico de la República de Colombia,* Paris, 1889.

Colección de Decretos, dados por el poder ejecutivo de Colombia en los años de 1821 a 1826, Bogotá, 1833.

Duane, Col., William, *A visit to Colombia in the years 1822 and 1823 by la Guayra and Caracas, over the cordillera to Bogotá and thence by the Magdalena to Cartagena,* Philadelphia, 1826.

Ducoudray-Holstein, Gen. H. L. V., *Memoirs of Simón Bolívar, President Liberator of the Republic of Colombia; and of his principal generals; comprising a secret history of the revolution, and the events which preceded it, from 1807 to the present time,* 2 v., London, 1830.

Dundonald, Thomas Cochrane, *Narrative of services in the liberation of Chile, Peru and Brazil from Spanish and Portuguese domination.* London, 1859.

Eastwick, Edward B., *Venezuela; or sketches of life in a South American Republic*, London, 1868.

Exposición que dirige al Congreso Constitutional del los E E. U U. de Venezuela el Ministro de Guerra y Marina en 1855; 1860; 1866. Caracas, 1855, 1860, 1866.

Flinter, George Dawson, *A history of the revolution of Caracas, comprising an impartial narrative of the atrocities committed by the contending parties, illustrating the real state of the contest,* London, 1819.

García Camba, Andrés, *Memórias del general García Camba para la historia de las armas españolas en el Perú,* 2 v., Madrid, 1916.

Hackett, James, *Narrative of the Expedition which sailed from England in 1817 to join the South American patriots,* London, 1818.

Hall, Col. Francis, *Colombia: Its present state, in respect of climate, soil, productions, population, government, commerce, revenue, manufactures, arts, literature, manners, education and inducements to immigration, with Itineraries partly from Spanish surveys, partly from actual observation,* London, 1825.

Hamilton, Col. John Potter, *Travels through the interior provinces of Colombia,* 2 v., London, 1827.

Hansard's Parliamentary Debates, vols. XXXV, XXXVI, XXXVIII, XL and I (N. S.), London, 1817, 1818, 1819, 1820.

Herrera, José Hipólito, *El Album de Ayacucho; colección de los principales documentos de la guerra de la independencia del Perú.*

Hippisley (G)., *A narrative of tthe expedition to the rivers Orinoco and Apure in South America which sailed from England in November, 1817, and joined the patriotic forces in Venezuela and Caracas,* London, 1819.

Lieut. Col. Hippisley's Writings collected from his magazine articles and bound in book form but never published. In the possession of Dr. Manuel Segundo Sánchez of Caracas.

Journal written on board His Majesty's Ship " Cambridge," from January 1824 to May 1827, by the Rev. H. S., Chaplain, Newcastle, 1829.

Lecuna, Vicente, *Documentos referentes a la creación de Bolivia,* 2 vols., Caracas, 1925.

——, *Papeles de Bolívar,* Caracas, 1917.

A List of Officers of the Army and Royal Marines on full and half-pay, with an Index (British Army List), London, 1815, 16, 17, 25.

López, Manuel Antonio, *Recuerdos históricos del colonel Manuel Antonio López Ayudante del estado mayor general libertador, de la guerra de la independencia, Colombia i el Perú,* 1819-1826, Bogotá, 1889.

Maceroni, Francis, *An Appeal to the British Nation on the affairs of South America; particularly as regards those of New Granada,* London, 1825.

——, *Memoirs of the Life and Adventures of Colonel Maceroni*, 2 vols., London, 1838.

MacGregor, Gregor, *Exposición documentada que el General Gregorio MacGregor dirigio al Gobierno de Venezuela y resolución que a ella recayó*, Caracas, 1839.

Mathison, Gilbert Farquhar, *Narrative of a Visit to Brazil, Chile, Peru and the Sandwich Islands during the years 1821 and 1822*, London, 1825.

Miller, John, *Memoirs of Gen. Miller in the service of the Republic of Peru*, 2 v., 1 port. maps, Lima, 1828.

Morillo y Morillo, Pablo, *Manifiesto que hace a la nación española el teniente general D. Pablo Morillo, conde de Cartagena, Marqués de la Puerta, y general en jefe del ejército expeditionario de Costa Firme*, Caracas, 1820.

Narrative of a voyage to the Spanish Main in the Ship " Two Friends," London, 1819.

Narrative of the Expeditions under General MacGregor against Porto Bello, including an account of the voyage, and of the causes which led to its final overthrow, by an officer who miraculously escaped, London, 1820.

O'Connor, Francisco Burdett, *Independéncia Americana. Recuerdos de Francisco Burdett O'Connor, coronel del ejército libertador de Colombia y general de división de los del Perú y Bolivia*, Madrid, Biblioteca Ayacucho (not dated).

O'Leary, Daniel Florencio, *Memorias del general O'Leary*, 29 vols., Caracas, 1879-88.

——, *Bolívar y la emancipación de Sur América*, Madrid, 1915.

——, *Bolívar y las repúblicas del sur, Argentina, Chile, Brasil, Uruguay, Paraguay, Bolivia*, Madrid, 1919.

——, *Cartas de Sucre al Libertador*, Madrid, 1919.

——, *Correspondencia de extranjeros notables con el Libertador*, 2 v. in 1, Madrid, 1920. These four items are reprints from *Memorias del general O'Leary*.

——, *Ultimos años de la vida pública de Bolívar*. This is a reprint of the "Apéndice" (Volume 29) of the *Memorias*, Madrid (no date).

Páez, José Antonio, *Autobiografía del General José Antonio Páez*, 2 vols., New York, 1878.

Palacio Fajardo, Manuel, *Outline of the revolution in Spanish America, or an account of the origin, progress and actual state of the war carried on between Spain and Spanish America; containing the principal facts which have marked the struggle. By a South American in London*, London, 1817.

Persat, (Maurice), *Mémoirs du Commandant Persat, 1806 a 1844*, Paris, 1910.

Perú de Lacroix, Louis, *Diario de Bucaramanga; o Vida publica y privada del Libertador, Simón Bolívar*, Paris, 1912.

Present State of Colombia, by an officer late in the Colombian service, London, 1827.

Proclamas de Bolívar, Sucre, Santander y Padilla, Bogotá, 1878.

Procter, Robert, *Narrative of a journey across the cordillera of the Andes and of a residence in Lima and other parts of Peru in the years 1823 and 1824*, London, 1825.

Pradt, Dominique de Fourt de, *Des colonies et de la révolution actuelle de l'Amérique*, 2 v., Paris, 1817.

Rafter, M., *Memoirs of Gregor M'Gregor; comprising a sketch of the revolution in New Granada and Venezuela, with biographical notices of Generals Miranda, Bolívar, Morillo and Horé and a narrative of the expeditions to Amelia Island, Porto Bello and Rio de la Hacha, interspersed with revolutionary anecdotes*, London, 1820.

Recollections of a service of three years during the war of extermination in the Republics of Venezuela and Colombia, by an officer of the Colombian navy, London, 1828.

Reverend, Alejandro Próspero, *La ultima enfermedad de Simón Bolívar*, Paris, 1866.

Richard, Karl, *Die Republick Colombia; Briefe an seine Freunde von einem hanoverischen Officier geschrieben in dem yahre 1820*, Leipzig, 1822.

Richardson, James D., *A Compilation of the Messages and Papers of the Presidents, 1789-1897*, 10 vols., Washington, 1896-1899.

Robinson, J. H., *Journal of an expedition 1400 miles up the Orinoco and 300 miles up the Arauca; with an account of the country, the manners of the people, military operations, etc.*, London, 1822.

Semple, Robert, *Sketch of the present state of Caracas; including a journey from Caracas through la Victoria and Valencia to Puerto Cabello*, London, 1812.

Sevilla, Rafael, *Memorias de un oficial del ejército espanol; campañas contra Bolívar y los separatistas de América*, Madrid, 1916.

Sherman, John H., *A general account of Miranda's expedition; including the trial and execution of ten of his officers, and an account of the imprisonment and sufferings of the remainder of his officers and men who were taken prisoners*, New York, 1808.

Rodríguez Villa, Antonio, *El teniente general Don Pablo Morillo, primer conde de Cartagena, Marqués de la Puerta*, 3 vols., Madrid, 1908-10.

Smith (Moses), *History of the Adventures and sufferings of Moses Smith during five years of his life from the beginning of the year 1806 when he was betrayed into the Miranda expedition until June, 1811*, Brooklyn, 1812.

Smyth, William Henry, Capt., *The Life and services of Captain Philip Beaver, late of his Majesty's Ship " Nisus,"* London, 1829.
Sparks, Jared, *The Writings of George Washington*, 12 vols., Boston, 1855.
Stevenson, William Bennett, *Historical and descriptive narrative of twenty years residence in South America*, London, 1825.
Stewart, J., *Bogotá in 1836-7; being a narrative of an expedition to the capital of New Granada, and a residence there of eleven months*, New York, 1838.
Sutcliffe, Thomas, *Sixteen years in Chile and Peru from 1822 to 1839 by the retired governor of Juan Fernandez*, London, 1841.
Temple, Edmund, *Travels in various parts of Peru; including a year's residence in Lima*, London, 1830.
Urdaneta, Rafael, *Memorias del general Rafael Urdaneta (general en jefe y encargado del gobierno de la gran Colombia)*, Madrid, 1916.
Van Rensselaer, Solomon, *A Narrative of the Affair of Queenstown in the War of 1812*, New York, 1836.
View of South America and Mexico by a citizen of the United States, 2 v., 1 port., New York, 1826.
Voto (el) de Venezuela o colección de actas y representaciones de la corporaciones civiles, militares y padres de familia de los departamentos de Venezuela, Maturín y Orinoco, Caracas, 1828.
Walford, Edith, *The Words of Wellington collected from his Despatches, Letters and Speeches*, London, 1875.
Walker, Alexander, *Colombia; being a geographical, statistical, agricultural, commercial and political account of that country, adapted for the general reader, the merchant and the colonist*, London, 1822.
Walton, William, *Present State of the Spanish Colonies; including a particular report of Hispaniola, or the Spanish part of Santo Domingo; with a general survey of the settlements on the south continent of America*, 2 v., London, 1810.
Wellington (Duke of), *Supplementary Despatches, Correspondence and Memoranda of Field Marshal, Arthur, Duke of Wellington, K. G.*, 15 vols., London, 1868-1882.
Weatherhead, W. Davidson, *An account of the late expedition against the isthmus of Darien under the command of Sir Gregor M'Gregor; together with the events subsequent to the recapture of Porto Bello, till the release of the prisoners from Panama; remarks on the present state of the patriot cause and on the climate and diseases of South America*, London, 1821.

3. PAMPHLETS

Documentos históricos de los hechos ocurridos en Pasto en la guerra de la independencia. Publicación oficial. República de Colombia. Departamento de Nariño, Pasto, 1912.

Hippisley, Gustavus, *Acts of Oppression committed under the Administration of M. de Villèle, Prime Minister of Charles X, in the years 1825-6, in a series of letters*, London, 1831.

Phillips's Speech on South American Liberty. The Speech of C. Phillips, Esq. as delivered at a splendid complimentary dinner given to Major General D'Evereux, on the cause of South American Freedom, at Morrison's Hotel, Dublin, August, 1819, London, 1819.

4. NEWSPAPERS AND PERIODICALS

Anglo-Colombiano (later *El Colombiano*), Bogotá, files of 1822-1825.
Annual Register, London, 1817-1826.
El Argos, Caracas, Sept. 6, 1825.
Bell's Weekly Messenger, London, files of 1817-1819.
British Monitor, London, files of 1818, 1819.
Cobbett's Weekly Political Register, London, files of 1818.
Correo del Orinoco, Angostura, files of 1820-22.
"Diario de operaciones de la División de Antioquía" in *Memorial del Estado Mayor del ejército de Colombia*, XI, No. 103, pp. 27-30, Bogotá.
"Documentos históricos" in *Memorial de Estado Mayor del ejército de Colombia*, No. 36, Bogotá.
Gaceta de Colombia, Caracas, files of 1822-1824.
La Gaceta de Curazao, April 22, 1820.
García, Gen. Andrés, of the Spanish army, report of the battle of Junín in *Repertorio Boyacense*, Tunja, Sept., 1924.
The Gentleman's Magazine and Historical Chronicle, XCI, Jan.-June, 1821, London.

Iris de Venezuela, Caracas, files of 1822.
Journal des Voyages, découvertes et navigations modernes, ou Archives Géographiques et Statistiques du XIXᵉ siècle, Paris, 1821-1829.
Lecuna, Vicente, "Relaciones fundamentales de la batalla de Carabobo" in *Boletín de la Academia Nacional de Historia*, IV, No. 16, Caracas, 1921.
London Champion and Sunday Review, London, files of 1817.
London Chronicle, London, files of 1816-1823.
Morning Chronical, London, files of 1816-1819.
The News, London, files of 1818.
Niles Weekly Register, Baltimore, 1817.
O'Leary, S. B., "Bolívar en el Perú" in *Repertorio Caraqueño*, I, Caracas, Oct. 28, 1879.
Prieto Villate, Elías, "Apuntamientos sobre la campaña de 1819" in *Repertorio Boyacense*, series V, No. 43, Tunja, July, 1917.
The Times, London, files of 1816-1825.

Vivanco, Carlos A., "Documentos históricos; oficio del Libertador al
Señor Luís López Méndez," in *Boletín de la Académia Nacional de
Historia*, VI, 279-288, Quito, 1921.

II. Secondary Works

I. BOOKS

Altamira y Crevea, Rafael, *Resumen histórico de la independencia de la
América española*, Buenos Aires, 1910.

Amunátegui, Miguel Luís, *Vida de Don Andrés Bello*, Santiago de Chile,
1882.

Andrade, Manuel de Jesús, *Ecuador. Próceres de la independencia;
índice alfabético de sus nombres con algunos bocetos biográficos*,
Quito, 1909.

*Apoteósis de Bolívar; ofrenda del estado Bermúdez en el primer cen-
tenario del libertador*, Caracas, 1883.

Azpúrua, Ramón, *Biografías de hombres notables de Hispano América*,
4 vols. in 2, Caracas, 1877.

Baralt, Rafael María y Diaz, Ramón, *Resumen de la história de Venezuela, desde el ano de 1797 hasta el de 1850*, 2 v., Paris, 1841.

Baraya, José Maria, *Biografías militares; o Historia Militar del país
en medio siglo*, Bogotá, 1874.

Becker, Jerónimo, *La independencia de América; Su Reconocimiento por
España*, Madrid, 1908.

Benedetti, Carlos, *Historia de Colombia*, Lima, 1887.

*Simón Bolívar. Libertador de la America del Sur por los más grandes
escritores americanos, Montalvo, Marti, Rodo, Blanco Fombona,
García Calderón, Alberdi*, Madrid, 1914.

Briceño, Mariano de, *Historia de la isla de Margarita (hoy Nueva
Esparta)* ; *Biografías del general Juan B. Arismendi y de la Señora
Luisa Cáceres de Arismendi*, Caracas, 1885.

Bulnes, Gonzalo, *Bolívar en Peru; últimas campañas de la independencia
del Perú*, Madrid, 1919.

Cartanos y Montijano, Manuel, *Páginas olvidadas de la historia militar
de España; sucinta narración de algunos hechos de armas de la guerra
separatista de América*, Toledo, 1892.

El Centenario de Simón Bolívar en la República Argentina, Buenos Aires,
1883.

Cevallos, Pedro Fermín, *Resumen de la historia del Ecuador desde su
origen hasta, 1845*, 6 v., Guayaquil, 1886.

Cortés, José Domingo, *Galería de hombres célebres de Bolivia*, Santiago,
1869.

Cortés Vargas, Col. Carlos, *Participación de Colombia en la libertad del
Perú*, 3 vols., Bogotá, 1924.

Crichfield, George W., *American Supremacy; the rise and progress of the Latin American republics and their relations to the United States and the Monroe Doctrine*, New York, Brentano, 1908.

Dávila, Vicente, *Diccionario biográfico de ilustres próceres de la Independencia Suramericana*, 2 vols., Caracas, vol. i, 1924, ii, 1926.

——, *Investigaciones históricas*, Caracas, 1923.

Destruge, Camilo, *Album Biográfico Ecuatoriano*, 5 vols., Guayaquil, 1903.

——, *Biografía del General Don Juan Illingworth*, Guayaquil, 1913.

Dictionary of National Biography (ed. Sidney Lee), 63 vols. and 8 supplementary vols., London, 1893.

Dufey, Pierre Joseph Speridion, *Abrégé de l'histoire des révolutions de l'Amérique méridionale, depuis les premières découvertes par les Européens jusqu'à nos jours*, Paris, 1827.

Florez Álvarez, Leonidas, *Campaña Libertadora de 1821; Contribución del ejército de Colombia a la celebración del primer centenario de la batalla de Carabobo*, Bogotá, 1921.

García Calderón, Francisco, *Latin America; its rise and progress*, London, 1913.

Gil Fortoul, José, *Historia constitucional de Venezuela*, 2 vols., Berlin, 1907.

González Chávez, Nicolás, *Cuadros sinópticos de la guerra de la independencia de los Estados Unidos de Colombia*, Paris, 1880.

Groot, José Manuel, *Historia eclesiástica y civil de Nueva Granada; escrita sobre documentos auténticos*, Bogotá, 1870.

Ibañez, Pedro M., *Las crónicas de Bogotá y sus immediaciones*, Bogotá, 1913-1917.

Koebel, William Henry, *British Exploits in South America; a history of British activities in exploration, military adventure, diplomacy, science and trade in Latin America*, New York, 1917.

Larrazábal, Felipe, *Vida del Libertador Simón Bolívar*, 2 v., Madrid, 1918.

Level, Lino Duarte, *Cuadros de la historia militar y civil de Venezuela desde el descubrimiento y conquista de Guayana hasta la batalla de Carabobo*, Madrid, 1917.

López Contreras, Eleazar, *El Callao histórico*, Caracas, 1926.

Lorente, Sebastián, *Historia del Perú desde la proclamación de la independencia*, Lima, 1876.

Machado, José E., *Cantón Lírico*, Caracas, 1920.

Mitre, Bartolomé, *The Emancipation of South America; being a condensed translation by William Pilling of the History of San Martín*, London, 1893.

Moncayo, Pedro, *El Ecuador de 1825 a 1875; sus hombres, sus instituciones y sus leyes*, Quito, 1907.

Monsalve, José D., *El ideal político del libertador, Simón Bolívar*, Bogotá, 1916.

Montenegro, *Geografía general para el uso de la juventud de Venezuela,* vol. iv, *Historia,* Caracas, 1837.

Mosquera, J. T., *Colombia,* London, 1822.

Mosquera, Tomás C. de., *Compendio de Geografía general política, física y especial de los Estados Unidos de Colombia,* London, 1866.

Mulhall, Michael George, *The English in South America,* London and Buenos Aires, 1878.

Navarro y Lamarca, Carlos, *Compendio de la Historia general de América,* 2 vols., Buenos Aires, 1913.

Negret, Rafael, *La Campaña del Sur, y especialmente la Batalla de Bombóná,* Bogotá, 1921.

Omiste, Modesto, *Historia de Bolivia,* Potosí, 1904.

Paris, R., Manuel, *Campaña del ejército libertador Colombiano en 1819,* Bogotá, 1919.

Paxson, Frederick Logan, *The independence of the South American Republics; a study in recognition and foreign policy,* Philadelphia, 1916.

Peñuela, Cayo Leonidas, *Album de Boyacá,* vol. i, *La campaña de 1819,* Bogotá, 1919.

Perkins, James Breck, *France in the American Revolution,* Boston and New York, 1911.

Petre, Francis Loraine, *Simón Bolívar, el Libertador; a life of the chief leader in the revolt against Spain in Venezuela, New Granada and Peru,* London and New York, 1919.

Posada, Eduardo, *Apostillas a la historia colombiana,* Madrid, 1918.

Restrepo, José Manuel, *Historia de la revolución de la República de Colombia en la América Meridional,* Besanzon, 1858.

Rivas, José M., *Biagrafía del ilustre prócer General Rafael Urdaneta,* Maracaibo, 1888.

Robertson, William Spence, *Francisco de Miranda and the Revolutionizing of Spanish America,* Washington, 1909.

——, *History of the Latin-American Nations,* New York and London, 1922.

Rodó, José Enrique, *Cinco ensayos,* Madrid, 1915.

Rojas, Marques de, *Simón Bolívar,* Paris, 1883.

Roosevelt, Theodore, *The Winning of the West,* 6 vols. in 3, New York and London, Putnam's New Library edition (no date).

Sánchez, Manuel Segundo, *Bibliografía Venezolanista; contribución al conocimiento de los libros extrangeros relativos a Venezuela y sus grandes hombres, publicados o impresos desde el siglo XIX,* Caracas, 1914.

Santana, Coronel Arturo, *La Campaña de Carabobo, 1821. Relación histórica militar,* Caracas, 1921.

Scarpetta, M. Leonidas y Vergara, Saturnino, *Diccionario Biográfico de los campeones de la Libertad de Nueva Granada, Venezuela, Ecuador, i, Perú; que comprende sus servicios, hazañas i virtudes,* Bogotá, 1879.

Schryver, Simon de, *Esquisse de la vie de Bolívar*, Bruxelles, 1899.

Shumacher, Herman Albert, *Biografía del Géneral Agustin Codazzi, traducido por Francisco Manrique*, San Fernando de Apure, 1916.

Steele, Matthew Forney, *American Campaigns*, 2 vols., Washington, 1909.

Temperley, H. W. V., *Life of Canning*, London, 1905.

Torrente, Mariano, *Historia de la revolución hispano-americana*, 3 v., Madrid, 1829-30.

Upton, Emory, *The Military Policy of the United States*, Washington, 1916.

Vallenilla Lanz, Laureano, *Críticas de sinceridad y exactitud*, Caracas, 1921.

Vicuña Mackenna, Benjamín, *El Wáshington del Sur; Cuadros de la vida del Mariscal Antonio José de Sucre*, Santiago de Chile, 1893.

Villanueva, Carlos A., *Fernando VII y los nuevos estados*, Paris, 1912.

Winsor, Justin, *Narrative and Critical History of America*, 8 vols., Boston and New York, 1884-1889.

2. PAMPHLETS

Andrade, Roberto, *Campaña de 20 días*, Quito, 1908.

Centenario de Boyacá, editado de orden de la junta de festejos del centenario por Raymundo Rivas, José Joaquín Guerra y Roberto Cortazar, individuos de número de la Academia Nacional de Historia, Bogatá, 1920.

Galán, Angel María, *Las legiones britanica e irlandesa*, Bogotá, 1919.

Lecuna, Vicente, " Capaña de Bombaná," extracto del No. 37 de *Cultura Venezolana*, Caracas, 1922.

Un Rasgo de Bolívar en campaña, New York, 1835.

Sola, Henry de, *Biografía del Almirante Brión*, Caracas, 1921.

Yañez, German G., *Junín y Ayacucho*, Lima, 1924.

3. PERIODICALS

Acevedo, T. Luís, "Batalla de Boyacá" in *Memorial del Estado Mayor del ejército de Colombia*, XIV, Nos. 145-146, Bogotá, 1924.

"Carabobo" in *All the Year Round*, XIX, No. 465, pp. 367-371, London, March 28, 1868.

Cortés Vargas, Col. Carlos, "De Arauca a Nuncia" in *Memorial del Estado Mayor del ejército de Colombia*, No. 89, Bogotá, Sept., 1919.

——, "Pántano de Vargas" in *ibid.*, XIV, Nos. 145-146.

Crockett, Cary I., "Carabobo" in *U. S. Infantry Journal*, XXV, pp. 373-383, Washington, 1924.

Florez Álvarez, L., "Acción de la marina colombiana en la guerra de independencia" in *Memorial del Estado Mayor del ejército de Colombia*, No. 89, Bogotá.

Kirkpatrick, Frederick Alexander, "Englishmen in South America; Bolívar's British Legion," The *Times South American Supplement*, London, May 30, 1912.

Lecuna, Vicente, "La campaña de Carabobo y la diversión de Bermúdez" in *Hispania*, II, 859-864; III, 906-910, London, Dec. 1, 1913 and Jan. 1, 1914.

El Luchador, Valencia, May 10, 1912 reprints a translation of an article on the Germans in the war of South American independence from *Sud-u-mittel Amerika*, Berlin, Jan. 17, 1912.

Maldonado, C. Rodríguez, "Sir Gregor McGregor" in *Boletín de Historia y Antigüedades*, V, No. 53, pp. 264-269, Bogotá, Feb., 1908.

Martínez L., Jorge, "Pántano de Vargas" in *Memorial del Estado Mayor del ejército de Colombia*, VI, Nos. 43-44, pp. 8-11, Bogotá, 1916.

Memorial del Estado Mayor del ejército de Colombia, No. 122, article on Carolina O'Leary Soublette de Portocarrero.

La Nación, Caracas, Oct. 26, Nov. 23, 25, 30, Dec. 8, 9, 10, 1910.

Negret, Gen. Rafael, "Batalla de Yaguachi," in *Memorial del Estado Mayor del ejército de Colombia*, XI, No. 110, pp. 337-341, Bogotá, 1921.

——, "Junín" in *ibid.*, nos. 145-146, pp. 310-311.

Parra Pérez, C., "Bolívar y sus amigos del extranjero" in *Cultura Venezolana*, III, pp. 303-312, Caracas, Dec., 1919.

Peñuela, Cayo Leonidas, "Coronel Jaime Rooke" in *Repertorio Boyacense*, series VI, No. 64, Tunja, February, 1923.

Pérez Díaz, Lucila L. de, "La batalla de Boyacá, su importancia militar y política" in *Cultura Venezolana*, III, 313-331, Caracas, 1919.

Posada, Eduardo, "Ruperto Hand" in *Boletín de Historia y Antigüedades*, VI, No. 662, pp. 97-105, Bogotá.

——, "Luís Aury" in *ibid.*, VII, No. 78, pp. 337-367, Bogotá, Nov., 1911.

Santana, Col. Arturo, "La batalla de Boyacá" in *Memorial del Estado Mayor del ejército de Colombia*, II, No. 6, pp. 375-389, Bogotá, Jan. 1, 1913.

Schoffer, Carlos, translation in *El Universal*, Caracas, June 12, 1911 from "Germans in Venezuela; conquerors and warriors" in Sud-u-Mittel Amerika, Berlin (no date).

Tovar y R., Enrique D., "Bolívar en Carás" in *Cultura Venezolana*, III, 158-194, Caracas, 1919.

Vallenilla Lanz, Laureano, "Centenario de Boyaca" in *Cultura Venezolana*, III, 137-157, Caracas, 1919.

Vivanco, Carlos A., "The Ecuadorian Campaign 1821-1822" in *Inter-America* (English edition), V, 219-231, 312-329, New York, 1922.

Zornosa, Mayor Jorge, "Los Batallones Libertadores" in *Memorial del Estado Mayor del ejército de Colombia*, No. 15, pp. 13-17, Bogotá, 1925.

INDEX

Achaguas, British Legion at, 134, 227, 230

"Active," frigate, 109

Acton, Capt., 149

Adlercreutz, Count Friedrich de, mounts gun on top of La Popa, 250; recommended by Montilla, 251; inspects arms furnished by Robinson, 350; career of, 359-360; engineering knowledge of, valuable to patriots, 372; on Montilla's staff, 250, n. 2; testing ordnance, 256, n.3; at Puerto Cabello, 284, n. 1

Agua Santa, Fort, key to Cumaná, 124; attack on, 125-128; British intrepidity at, 394

Aicken, Private Stephen, 241, n.

Albion Battalion, in invasion of New Granada, 135, 192; at battle of Boyaca, 206, 207, 214, 215; formed from Second Rifles, 220; sent to Popayán, 220; Englishmen in, to receive full pay, 221; in campaign of the south, 227; men of, apply for passports, 249, 250; in skirmish at La Plata, 263; at Pitayó, 264; crosses the Juanambú, 265; marches to Esmeraldas, 267; sails to Guayaquil, 267; desertions in, 267; recaptures lighters at Guayaquil, 268; at Yaguachi, 268; at Pichincha, 272, 386; at Quito, 279; sent to Bogotá, 281; disbandment of, 282; name borne by foreign contingent, 341; von Clauditz promoted in, 353; Mackintosh the last leader of, 372; service of, classified, 373; acquires esprit de corps under Mackintosh, 384; members of, return home, 393; greeted by Indians, 399; payments to, 379, n. 3.

"Alejandro," corvette, carried off by mutineers, 267; furnished by Robert Bell, 303, n. 2

"Alerta," ship, 151

Althaus, Col. Clement, chief of engineers in army of Peru, 357; tragic death of, 357; on the staff at Ayacucho, 312, n. 2

Amar, Antonio, learns of conspiracy, 342; relieved as viceroy, 343

"Amelia," sailing of, from England, reported, 107; sent to McGregor, 151; sails for Rio Hacha, 151

Amelia Island, captured by McGregor, 141, 142; turned over to Commodore Aury, 142, 344, n. 3; collapse of McGregor's scheme at, 154; and Angostura, 158, 159

Americans, first to come to Venezuela, 341; as officers in republican navies, 347, 373; aid furnished by merchants, 350

"Ana," transports Albion Battalion, 267, 281; seized by mutineers, 267; leased as transport, 303, n. 2

Angostura, besieged by Piar, 26; established as capital, 27; arrival of first contingents at, 69-72; description of, 71; British brigade formed at, 72; arrival of Elsom's recruits at, 83, 84; discontent of foreigners in, 88-91; banquet to Col. Hippisley at, 90; complaints of foreigners in, 90-92, 94-97; hardships suffered at, 91-96; arrival of Beamish's battalion at, 114; and Amelia Island, 158, 159; McDonald sails for, 163; Great Colombia organized by congress at, 219; treasury at, replenished, 379; not a safe capital, 385; weakness of Battalion of, 387

Antwerp, 145

Antioquía, controlled by royalists, 217; Rifles sent toward, 222; captured by Córdoba, 222; Battalion of, in campaign of Magdalena, 223, 223, n. 2; gold mines in, 399, n.

449

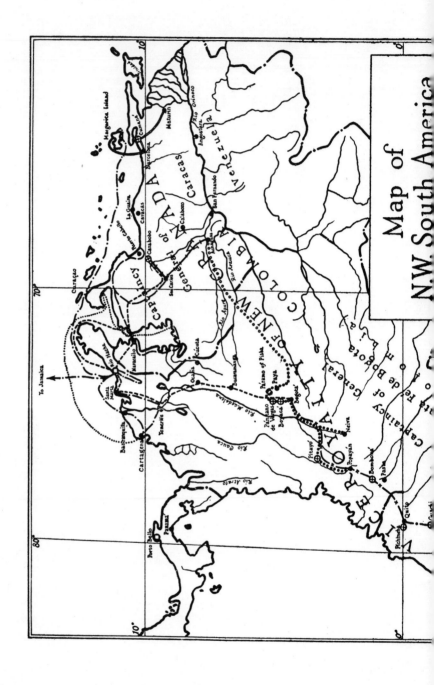

Map of
N.W. South America

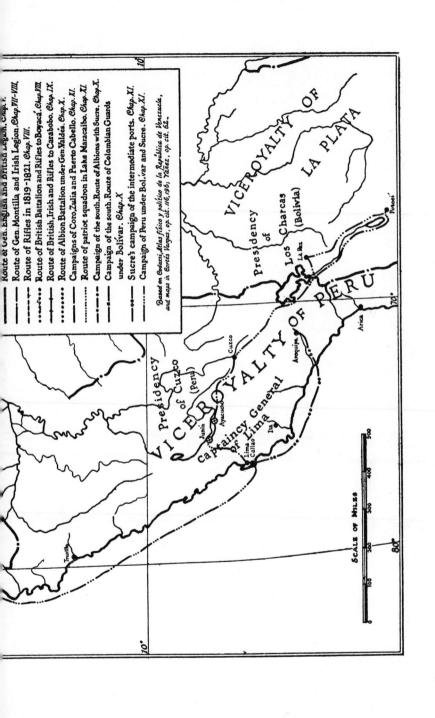

Route of Gen. English and British Legion. *Chap. V.*

Route of Gen. Montilla and Irish Legion. *Chap. VII.-VIII.*

Route of Rifles in 1819-1821. *Chap. VIII.*

Route of British Battalion and Rifles to Boyacá. *Chap. VIII.*

Route of British, Irish and Rifles to Carabobo. *Chap. IX.*

Route of Albion Battalion under Gen. Waldés. *Chap. X.*

Campaigns of Coro, Zulia and Puerto Cabello. *Chap. XI.*

Route of patriot squadron in Lake Maracaibo. *Chap. XI.*

Campaign of the south. Route of Albions with Sucre. *Chap. X.*

Campaign of the south. Route of Colombian Guards under Bolívar. *Chap. X*

Sucre's campaign of the intermediate ports. *Chap. XI.*

Campaign of Peru under Bolívar and Sucre. *Chap. XI.*

Based on Codazzi, Atlas físico y político de la República de Venezuela, and maps in Cortés Vargas, op. cit. 116, 196; Yáñez, op. cit. 62.

VICEROYALTY OF LA PLATA

Presidency of Los Charcas (Bolivia)

La Paz

VICEROYALTY OF PERU

Presidency of Cuzco (Peru)

Cuzco

Arica

Anquipa

VICEROYALTY OF PERU

Captaincy General of Lima

Junin

Ayacucho

Lima
Callao

Iu

Trujillo

Potosi

SCALE OF MILES

100 200 300 400 500

10°

70°

80°

10°